The Art of Resistance

AUSTRIAN AND HABSBURG STUDIES
General Editor: Howard Louthan, Center for Austrian Studies, University of Minnesota

Volume 1
Austrian Women in the Nineteenth and Twentieth Centuries: Cross-Disciplinary Perspectives
Edited by David F. Good, Margarete Grandner, and Mary Jo Maynes

Volume 2
From World War to Waldheim: Culture and Politics in Austria and the United States
Edited by David F. Good and Ruth Wodak

Volume 3
Rethinking Vienna 1900
Edited by Steven Beller

Volume 4
The Great Tradition and Its Legacy: The Evolution of Dramatic and Musical Theater in Austria and Central Europe
Edited by Michael Cherlin, Halina Filipowicz, and Richard L. Rudolph

Volume 5
Creating the Other: Ethnic Conflict and Nationalism in Habsburg Central Europe
Edited by Nancy M. Wingfield

Volume 6
Constructing Nationalities in East Central Europe
Edited by Pieter M. Judson and Marsha L. Rozenblit

Volume 7
The Environment and Sustainable Development in the New Central Europe
Edited by Zbigniew Bochniarz and Gary B. Cohen

Volume 8
Crime, Jews and News: Vienna 1890–1914
Edited by Daniel Mark Vyletta

Volume 9
The Limits of Loyalty: Imperial Symbolism, Popular Allegiances, and State Patriotism in the Late Habsburg Monarchy
Edited by Laurence Cole and Daniel L. Unowsky

Volume 10
Embodiments of Power: Building Baroque Cities in Europe
Edited by Gary B. Cohen and Franz A. J. Szabo

Volume 11
Diversity and Dissent: Negotiating Religious Differences in Central Europe, 1500–1800
Edited by Howard Louthan, Gary B. Cohen, and Franz A. J. Szabo

Volume 12
"Vienna Is Different": Jewish Writers in Austria from the Fin de Siècle to the Present
Hillary Hope Herzog

Volume 13
Sexual Knowledge: Feeling, Fact and Social Reform in Vienna, 1900–1934
Britta McEwen

Volume 14
Journeys Into Madness: Mapping Mental Illness in the Austro-Hungarian Empire
Edited by Gemma Blackshaw and Sabine Wieber

Volume 15
Territorial Revisionism and the Allies of Germany in the Second World War: Goals, Expectations, Practices
Edited by Marina Cattaruzza, Stefan Dyroff, and Dieter Langewiesche

Volume 16
The Viennese Café and Fin-de-Siècle Culture
Edited by Charlotte Ashby, Tag Gronberg, and Simon Shaw-Miller

Volume 17
Understanding Multiculturalism: The Habsburg Central European Experience
Edited by Johannes Feichtinger and Gary B. Cohen

Volume 18
Sacrifice and Rebirth: The Legacy of the Last Habsburg War
Edited by Mark Cornwall and John Paul Newman

Volume 19
Tropics of Vienna: Colonial Utopias of the Habsburg Empire
Ulrich E. Bach

Volume 20
The Monumental Nation: Magyar Nationalism and Symbolic Politics in Fin-de-siècle Hungary
Bálint Varga

Volume 21
The Art of Resistance: Cultural Protest against the Austrian Far Right in the Early Twenty-First Century
Allyson Fiddler

THE ART OF RESISTANCE

Cultural Protest against the Austrian Far Right in the Early Twenty-First Century

Allyson Fiddler

berghahn
NEW YORK · OXFORD
www.berghahnbooks.com

First published in 2019 by
Berghahn Books
www.berghahnbooks.com

© 2019, 2025 Allyson Fiddler
First paperback edition published in 2025

All rights reserved. Except for the quotation of short passages
for the purposes of criticism and review, no part of this book
may be reproduced in any form or by any means, electronic or
mechanical, including photocopying, recording, or any information
storage and retrieval system now known or to be invented,
without written permission of the publisher.

Library of Congress Cataloging-in-Publication Data
Names: Fiddler, Allyson, author.
Title: The art of resistance : cultural protest against the Austrian far
right in the early twenty-first century / Allyson Fiddler.
Description: New York : Berghahn Books, 2019. | Series: Austrian and Habsburg
studies ; volume 21 | Includes bibliographical references and index.
Identifiers: LCCN 2018018982 (print) | LCCN 2018041073 (ebook) | ISBN
9781789200478 (ebook) | ISBN 9781789200461 (hardback :alk. paper)
Subjects: LCSH: Austria--Politics and government--21st century. | Protest
movements--Austria. | Right-wing extremists--Austria. | Right and left
(Political science)--Austria. | Political parties--Austria.
Classification: LCC DB99.2 (ebook) | LCC DB99.2 .F53 2019 (print) | DDC
322.409436--dc23
LC record available at https://lccn.loc.gov/2018018982

British Library Cataloguing in Publication Data
A catalogue record for this book is available from the British Library

EU GPSR Authorized Representative
LOGOS EUROPE, 9 rue Nicolas Poussin, 17000, LA ROCHELLE, France
Email: Contact@logoseurope.eu

ISBN 978-1-78920-046-1 hardback
ISBN 978-1-83695-072-1 paperback
ISBN 978-1-83695-207-7 epub
ISBN 978-1-78920-047-8 web pdf

https://doi.org/10.3167/9781789200461

To Kirsty, Alistair and Mark, beloved partners in *Schnitzeldom*

Contents

Acknowledgements	viii
Introduction	1
1. Austria Gets the 'Blues': Setting the Scene for Protest	11
2. Performing Politics: On the Sounds, Symbols and Sites of Resistance	29
3. Novel Responses: Protest in Prose	65
4. Projecting Protest: Resistance on Screen	109
5. Staging Resistance: Dramatic Themes and Interventions	142
Conclusion. The Colours of 2016 and 2017: Green, Blue … Turquoise	184
References	193
Index	207

Acknowledgements

I did not write this book as a participant observer of the demonstrations and protests against the millennial turn in Austrian politics but as an academic who is both fascinated by the cultural life of contemporary Austria and aghast at the inroads that are still being made by far-right politics in Austria and in many other countries besides. *The Art of Resistance* covers materials that are self-evidently protest works, but it also chooses to read materials for the ways in which they might be said to voice resistance to political developments in Austria. These works can also be interpreted in other ways.

My readings of cultural phenomena are inspired by and indebted to numerous artists, writers, friends and academics with whom I have enjoyed discussions and email exchanges over the years. It is not possible to detail the quantity and nature of each piece of assistance or inspiration in the jigsaw of research that constitutes this book or to mention everyone by name. The help has ranged from discussion and debate, a friendly ear, accommodation and welcome distraction in Austria, to the provision of material (films, music tracks, theatre programmes and books) that would otherwise have been difficult to obtain. I must therefore satisfy myself here with a mere alphabetical list. Some of these helpers will possibly not remember our contact, either because the book has taken a while in its path towards publication or because our dealings were very brief. Others will be well aware of our interactions and may agree or disagree with my analyses here. I take full responsibility for the interpretations offered, but I am grateful to you all: El Awadalla, Fred Baker, Franz and Andrea Brandstetter, Eva Brunner-Szabo, Harald Friedl, Brigid Haines, Martin Iddon, Maria-Regina Kecht, Anthony Murphy, Martin Reinhart, Jay Rosellini, Thomas Stuck, the Thomaneks, Walter Wippersberg (posthumously), Ruth Wodak, Julia Starsky and Martin Zellhofer. Luca Faccio graciously provided the book's cover image.

The research for this book would not have been possible without the fillip of Arts and Humanities Research Council (AHRC) matched leave funding. Travel grants also made it possible for me to disseminate some of my early findings at important conferences abroad. Permissions have been obtained to incorporate some previously published work into the present study, and acknowledgements are made throughout where earlier versions of my work have been included. Unless otherwise indicated, all translations are my own. I would like to acknowledge the valuable assistance of the AHRC along with that of my home institution, Lancaster University, the Faculty of Arts and Social Sciences and the Department of Languages and Cultures. Berghahn Books are owed special thanks for their patience and valuable assistance. I should like to express my gratitude to the anonymous peer reviewers too, whose perceptive comments were particularly helpful. Last but not least, my appreciation is extended to the community of Austrian Studies scholars across the globe and to countless university students over the years with whom I have enjoyed many fascinating discussions on the culture and history of the Austrian Second Republic.

INTRODUCTION

In February 2000, the far-right Freedom Party of Austria was sworn into government in coalition with the Austrian People's Party. This single event is at the heart of the cultural phenomena discussed in the present volume. The electoral success of the Freiheitliche Partei Österreichs (FPÖ) a few months earlier prompted shocked reactions around the world and spawned immediate protest in the streets of Vienna. The primary reason for the international anxiety was the increasing reputation of the FPÖ as an extreme-right organization whose charismatic leader Jörg Haider was well known for making statements that appeared to endorse Nazi era policies. The United Kingdom's left-liberal *Guardian* newspaper pinpointed Haider's ambitions on the morning after the election: 'Hitler admirer scents power after election blow for ruling coalition'.[1] The millennial *Wende* (or turn), as this endorsement of the right was dubbed, marked only the second time in the history of postwar Austria that the FPÖ had played a role in government. In 1983, it had been as a very minor party (5 per cent of the vote) and for a period of only three years in partnership with the socialist party, the Sozialistische Partei Österreichs. For most of the political history of postwar Austria there have been grand coalitions between the 'black' ÖVP and the 'red', Sozialdemokratische Partei Österreichs (Social Democrat party, to which the SPÖ changed its name in 1991).

The Art of Resistance illuminates the cultural responses to the politics of turn-of-the-millennium Austria and provides contextual background to help take stock of a seismic wave of artistic and everyday protest. The questions that inform my analysis include establishing how widespread cultural protest was, what themes recurred and which aesthetic strategies are deployed. The corpus of materials I consider here cannot lay claim to comprehensiveness but I have been able to identify and discuss a wide variety of genres and styles. In addition to the performance of everyday protest and the cultural enactment of resistance on the street through demonstrations, speeches, dances, graffiti and so on, I analyse examples of music, novels and short stories, films and dramas. The works are concentrated around the early years of the coalition government of the FPÖ and the ÖVP, that is to say 2000 to 2002, but the timespan includes at the earliest point

Elfriede Jelinek's *Ein Sportstück* (1998) and Walter Wippersberg's *Die Irren und die Mörder* (1998). These instances represent the way in which artists have been sensitive to social and political trends and have functioned as cultural warning signals in flagging up extreme-right thinking in society. Robert Menasse's *Das Paradies der Ungeliebten* (2006) and Marlene Streeruwitz's election novels *So ist das Leben* (2006) and *Das Leben geht weiter* (2008) are the latest works that feature. The start and end points to the analysis here are primarily delineated by the elections of 1999 and 2006 but with some licence to look at relevant works in the immediate run-up to the *Wende*. This terminology is widely used in scholarship about the period, even if the concept of a turn in Austrian politics is itself disputed (see Chapter 1).

The term 'resistance' is not unproblematic either (see Chapter 2), but it was used extensively by demonstrators and artists alike, and this study aligns itself with the near synonymous deployment of the word for protest. It does not seek to establish resistance as a more active, more 'committed' manifestation of protest.[2] There was a very real sense that artists, thinkers and public protesters were indeed trying to offer resistance to the encroaching normalization of far-right thinking and protective, nationalist politics. Some effected their protest overtly and actively whilst others voiced their ideological resistance in the words of their songs, the plots of their novels, or in the scenarios of their films. One further terminological knot must be acknowledged here since it is not one that is unpicked in this study. Artists and protestors do not often differentiate between the vocabulary of 'far right', 'extreme right', 'populist', 'nationalist' and so on. I have used the terminology in an equally catholic manner. There is recent, prize-winning scholarship investigating which tenets of FPÖ thinking and which guiding principles of the far-right *Burschenschaften* – or fraternities, to which most male FPÖ politicians belong – can even be described as 'neo-Nazi' and not just 'far right'.[3]

Periods of history continue to feature in artistic works for many decades or even centuries afterwards and the present work does not seek to interpret those that have been published or released in the mere dozen years that have followed the catalyst era of 2000 to 2006. *The Art of Resistance* captures and analyses the art of those coalition years.[4] Equally, political fiction or political art is a frequent topic of study in many countries and of many eras. The texts considered here might very well have found themselves discussed in a general volume on political art in Austria or in a study without the specific focus of resistance I have established here. This would have been to lose the distinct thread that connects them and to render the body of materials collected and critiqued here simply a sizeable body of novels, dramas, films, songs and art events that have a political theme or setting. I argue that what gives the works here their raison d'être and their artistic power is indeed their status as art that promotes or bears the traces of reaction and resistance to the politics of the FPÖ or to the political direction presented by the combined forces of the conservative right and the populist far right. I have not aimed to provide a balance by profiling and interpreting literature and art that is pro-far right, even if I had been able to find many such examples. Sometimes the links between the artistic product and real-life politics are obvious, as in the satirical graphic novel *Jörgi, der Drachentöter* (2000) by Gerhard Haderer and Leo Lukas. In other cases, I demonstrate that the works can be read as voicing protest and exposing far-right politics or mercenary, pro-nationalist politicians of all political colours. Wippersberg's trilogy of novels *Die Irren und die Mörder* (1998), *Ein nützlicher Idiot* (1999) and *Die Geschichte eines lächerlichen Mannes* (2000) spans both of these approaches.

The culture discussed here is predicated on political history, and it is for this reason that the background to the increase in popularity of the Austrian Freedom Party is the subject of my first chapter. Chapter 1 ranges over the last decades of the twentieth century, with particular emphasis on a number of key moments and concepts in postwar Austrian history (the victimization myth, the Waldheim affair and the ascendancy of the FPÖ under Jörg Haider are major themes here). If the politics of the millennium have generated so much cultural protest, then it is not simply due to the symbolism of the election itself, but to strategies or policies that have been espoused by the coalition and that spark indignation or protest. One of the guiding questions in my research has been to identify the cause for protest. This might include reactions to cuts in welfare provision (see El Awadalla's short story '18. bezirk: gretl', for example) or objections to the insistence on 'traditional' family values and the desire to see a higher birth rate for 'native' Austrians (whether in a song by Conny Chaos und die Retortenkinder entitled 'Lisi Gehrer' or as implied in Jelinek's short drama *Das Lebewohl (Les Adieux)*). The protests most certainly provide responses to the Austrian government's policies on immigration and to public antipathy towards migrants and the place they occupy in Austrian society. Examples of art that fights back against xenophobia are to be found in all the cultural forms discussed here and range from the high-profile installation event of the Vienna Festival of 2000 'Bitte liebt Österreich' ('Please Love Austria') initiated by German performance artist Christoph Schlingensief to countless other examples where racist attitudes or policies are protested or pilloried. Racist characters are held up for derision in plays such as Franzobel's *Olympia* (2000) and Marlene Streeruwitz's *Sapporo.* (premièred in 2000). Racist attitudes expose themselves with great irony in the documentary portmanteau film *Zur Lage* (Barbara Albert, Michael Glawogger, Ulrich Seidl and Michael Sturminger, 2002) and were a target of demonstrators' anger throughout the anti-coalition demonstrations and rallies. When the theme of racism comes to the fore, the topic of historical racism, of coming to terms with the Nazi past or, indeed, of the persistence of anti-Semitism and xenophobia into the present day are never far away. Wippersberg's *Die Wahrheit über Österreich: oder Wie man uns belogen hat* (2000) takes the mockumentary approach to Austrian history, whereas Ruth Beckermann's *Homemad(e)* documentary of

2001 is both a geographical portrait of the present and a sensitive journey into the remembered past for the residents (some of whom are Jews) of a particular Viennese district.

I do not claim here any special entitlement or capacity for the Austrian people as civic protesters or indeed for Austrian artists as generators of cultural protest. In the context of cultural expressions against far-right politics and politicians, there are contemporaneous examples from other countries that adopt similar aesthetic strategies to those in my findings here. The films *Il caimano* (dir. Nanni Moretti, 2006) and *Bye Bye Berlusconi* (a German-Italian production by Jan Henrik Stahlberg, 2006) approach the subject of populist political leader Silvio Berlusconi with black humour, but also with ambiguous, thought-provoking endings. They play self-referentially with the problems of media representation and are in essence films about making films about Berlusconi and his financial and personal malpractices. In France, the former leader of the ultra-nationalist, right-wing Front National, Jean-Marie Le Pen, was clearly the subject of pillory in Mathieu Lindon's current affairs-based novel of 1998, *Le Procès de Jean-Marie le Pen*, featuring the trial of a Front National supporter for the violent, unprovoked murder of a French-Algerian immigrant. Found guilty in France on several counts of libel, the author was subsequently taken to the European Court of Human Rights, where most counts against him were indeed upheld. Many high-profile French writers backed Lindon's case in the media, including Marie Darrieussecq, whose hugely popular but highly disturbing first novel, *Truismes,* of 1996 can be read amongst other things as a bizarre satire of the rise of proto-fascist politics in contemporary France. Perhaps Lindon's *à clef* characterization was more obvious than some of the Austrian writing I look at (for example, Erika Pluhar's novel *Die Wahl* (2003)). Allegorical techniques have been used in France, too, to depict society's degeneration, for example in Darrieussecqu's political allegory on the increasing bestiality of contemporary 'civilization'. The slim publication of a dozen or so pages entitled *Matin brun* by Franck Pavloff is another example of French literary reactions to the extreme right. Pavloff's 1998 children's story became an international bestseller in 2002 after Jean-Marie Le Pen beat Lionel Jospin in the first round of the presidential elections. It is a simple tale of two young men's acceptance of the regime's increasingly invasive discrimination, as first of all only brown dogs are allowed in society and all others are exterminated, then subsequently nonbrown cats are eliminated too. Pavloff writes a punchy, highly convincing short story that invites its readers to question just how far tacit acceptance of xenophobia can progress before people take action. Allegory and dystopia feature in the novel by Ernst Molden, *Doktor Paranoiski* (2001), in many of the short stories, and in Peter Kern's film *1. April 2021 – Haider lebt* (2002).

Can we derive an expressly Austrian typology of the materials covered in this study? In light of these brief international comparisons, there is no doubt that this is not possible. It is not my intention to pursue here a scholarly competition with other nations whose artists and populations are seeking to process sociopolitical change in their own countries and perhaps also produce aesthetic resistance to political developments. Scholars of Austrian Studies are often asked how Austria's art or artistic approaches and themes differ with regard, most predominantly, to those of Germany. Enquiries centre on whether Austria's art, literature, drama or filmmaking is a replica of Germany's or what the differences might be beyond merely lexical or dialectal differences reflecting Austrian linguistic specificities. (There are, indeed, plenty of works studied here that avail themselves of dialect in their writings, song texts or screenplays.) But this is not a defensive study that is bent on arguing for Austrian aesthetic particularities. It does not ask, for example, whether the protest art charted here is somehow a reflection or extension of the much-vaunted linguistically sceptical experimentalism of twentieth-century Austrian writing, in particular. The research for this volume is not carried by a quest to confirm that culture from Austria is more humorous in style and less serious – or political – in intent than its German counterpart. Such enquiries are relics of debates on the cultural politics of postwar Austria with regard to the 1950s, 1960s and early 1970s in particular.[5]

There is equally no wish to make the works studied here become markers of Austrian art and literature *tout court* and have them stand as the only emblems of a 'period' in Austrian art.[6] Indeed, the strategies that have been adopted in the art discussed here are common to critical and political art of different language communities, countries and eras. In addition to the common adoption of satirical or other humour-based approaches and of dystopian scenarios, many artists use the popularity of their medium to make their criticism heard or to underline it through the genre of its execution. The music I consider in Chapter 2 is a prime example of how popular dissemination seeks to reach mass audiences with, in most if not all cases, a younger audience target in mind. Kern's mockumentary film aesthetic in *1. April 2021* is an instance where the playful undermining of the TV documentary produces a sometimes subtle and sometimes jarringly obvious mismatch of deadpan delivery and comically fictive content. Other artists essay a more reflective analysis, based on documentary techniques or authentic, personal stories, as does Ruth Beckermann, for instance, in *Homemad(e)* or Frederick Baker with his demonstration recording and projectionist experiments in *Erosion und Wi(e)derstand* (2003). Feminist and gender-related readings of Austrian politics represent another critical approach that recurs across the genres of our study. They feature in the novels of Marlene Streeruwitz, for example, in short stories by various authors and in activism and cultural interventions. Feminist organizations as well as lesbian and gay rights groups were well represented at the demonstrations.

The symbolism, political targets and personalities are, of course, specific to Austria, and the study is sensitive to the need to explain these at relevant points without impeding the textual or cultural readings. In Chapter 1, I introduce some of the precursors to turn-of-the-millennium protest, particularly in the form of resistance in the Waldheim era when the election campaign and subsequent success of Kurt Waldheim's presidential bid polarized Austrian society and gave rise to a rich vein of cultural protest and to mass demonstrations on the streets. The study does not seek to use the 1980s as a benchmark for evaluating the millennial protests even whilst recognizing that the Waldheim affair and its aftermath represent a turning point in the Second Republic's political and cultural history. It has been suggested that the cultural exchanges between writers and politicians (or the allusions by each to the other) of the 1980s and 1990s (Jelinek and Haider are the most cited pairing) may be seen as 'one inevitable but in the end unproductive aspect of the postwar scene', but further that 'this did not prevent . . . writers from exposing what they saw as the malaise of Austrian society'. Anthony Bushell notes correctly that this is part of a long tradition in German-speaking literature for creative writers to pursue a 'didactic, even moral role'.[7] The impetus to the cultural analysis here is not to try to detect a causal impact of the critical art on the political developments in Austria after the Wende or even to suggest that this is possible or measurable. The millennial protests and manifestations of resistance stand in their own right and are copious and wide-ranging. If the works, publications, performances and actions have had an impact on society, then it has been in resisting far-right thinking on their pages and stages, in their songs, on the film screens and in public places. Their impact must surely also have been in providing a voice for many and a means for protesting that was creative, visible or audible and that could help to educate, to resist or just to bring people together in solidarity.

After the first chapter explaining the rise of 'blue' Freedom Party politics in Austria, each of the subsequent chapters covers a different genre or locus of protest. In Chapter 2, 'Performing Politics: On the Sounds, Symbols and Sites of Resistance', I first consider how protest activities interacted with the public space of protest and explain some of the insignia and symbolism of protest. I cover the enacting of everyday cultural resistance in Austria's capital city, Vienna, during and accompanying the demonstrations, reading the acts, accessories and symbols of protest as well as the widely known, organized performance of Schlingensief's *Big Brother*-style event, 'Bitte liebt Österreich'. The chapter characterizes the sites and spaces of popular resistance and cultural protest activities. It also addresses the soundscape of the city and of protest music. Some of the musical items were performed during the protests, while some were broadcast in anti-coalition radio programmes. The chapter deconstructs the protest marches or 'hikes' to show how the act of walking was performed in a resistant manner. Here, as in all subsequent chapters, I have included artistic responses by domestically well-known and internationally acclaimed artists as well as by lesser-known performers, writers and filmmakers. Background information is provided for most of the artists who feature here, but ultimately the texts and artefacts must speak for themselves. Some of the examples of resistance are by lay members of the public, illustrating the fact that political resistance can be a creative force for all and that nonprofessionals also have important and interesting things to say. Nearly all of the artists featured in this volume are Austrian, although international support is also highlighted.

I felt it was important to select materials that had something distinct and stimulating to offer rather than seeking to expand the scholarly literature on a select few, even whilst recognizing that there are flagship authors (filmmakers, artists and playwrights) who must feature in the study. The 'Novel Responses' of Chapter 3 include examples of prose writings of very different lengths. There are novels by Ernst Molden, Erika Pluhar, Marlene Streeruwitz and Walter Wippersberg. Numerous short stories are also explored here for their resistance against the black-and-blue regime. There are illustrative examples by Paulus Hochgatterer, Eva Jancak, Dieter Schrage, El Awadalla, Luca Kilian Kräuter, Hoppelmann Karottnig, protest artists 'United Aliens', Richard Weihs, Brigitte Tauer, Ludwig Roman Fleischer, Sylvia Treudl and Monika Vasik. The chapter concludes by discussing the graphic novel *Jörgi, der Drachentöter* (2000) by cartoonist and writer Gerhard Haderer and writer and cabarettist Leo Lukas. The literary text is the basis for my readings. I explore the themes at play and the techniques employed by the authors. The styles include dystopian adventure, feminist analysis, the topos of tourism, autobiographical moments of personal politicization and the perspectives of childhood, of older age and of fantasy.

Chapter 4, 'Projecting Protest: Resistance on Screen', also draws on examples of widely different lengths. Shorter films from the series 'Die Kunst der Stunde ist Widerstand' ('Resistance is the Art of the Moment') are scrutinized for their various styles and approaches. For example, films by the Schnittpunkt production team and by a collective made up of the Volxtheater Favoriten/Videogruppe, Rosa Antifa Wien and Martin Gössler capture demonstration activities and cultural interventions. Dieter Auracher edits news footage to undermine Chancellor Wolfgang Schüssel's anti-demonstration philosophy, while Ewa Einhorn and Misha Stroj also use interview footage to allow political rhetoric to expose its own falsehoods. Thomas Horvath and Niki Griedl deploy the perspectives of childhood to suggest racist attitudes in Austria and to support Austria's repudiation by the European Union. Martin Reinhart's *Pinocchio* plays on the well-known children's story and uses graffitied posters of Jörg Haider to deconstruct an FPÖ campaign slogan. Bernadette Huber's is a more provocative, experimental style, forcing the viewer to think about whether far-right thinking might be innate in Austrians. Hubsi Kramar, the cabarettist and Hitler impersonator, features in a film by Franz Novotny, and humorous films by Studio West and the now highly famous Maschek cabaret duo complete the analysis of the very short form.

The work of Austro-British filmmaker Frederick Baker captures demonstration footage and uses the techniques of projectionism in a style that suggests a reverse archaeology – adding memory layers and symbolism back on rather than removing them. At 20 minutes in length, Baker's film is still in short-length format, as are the various contributions by Albert, Glawogger, Seidl and Sturminger that combine to make up the film *Zur Lage*. Feature-length documentary is represented by the film-essay style of Beckermann, and Wipperberg plays with the conventions of television histories and with documentary tropes. Kern's style is that of outright satire and metareferential playfulness as a fictive investigative journalist sets out on a quest to locate missing, ousted politicians Jörg Haider and Wolfgang Schüssel. The plethora of different styles evinces a great richness in the filmic protest examples.

The final genre from which I draw is the drama, and in 'Staging Resistance', Chapter 5 first examines short works by Antonio Fian and Elfriede Jelinek that feature politicians as characters. The second part of the chapter takes a thematic approach to measure the political temperature. Sport often plays an important role in the forging of national consciousness, and I consider here the implications of this idea for Austrian identity in the postcoalition period. Not only was there a heightened use of sporting imagery in political rhetoric, but essayists and writers also chose to use sport as a thematic lens or starting point for advancing their own cultural-political critique of contemporary Austrian politics. Jelinek's *Ein Sportstück* (1998), Franzobel's *Olympia* (2000), Streeruwitz's *Sapporo.* (2002) and Robert Menasse's *Das Paradies der Ungeliebten* (2006) all challenge the political climate of contemporary Austria in this way. The chapter concludes by enquiring about the contribution made by the theatre as an institution and investigates how drama took to the streets to make itself heard and seen.

My Conclusion returns to the political situation of the present from the standpoint of early 2018. On 18 December 2017, the Austrian President, Alexander Van der Bellen, presided over the inauguration ceremony for his country's new government – a further coalition of the Austrian People's Party (ÖVP) and the Freedom Party of Austria (FPÖ). This time, there was no international hue and cry. The political landscape has changed immeasurably since the elections and inauguration that prompted this book (in October 1999 and February 2000 respectively). I reflect on the political situation today and ask what might be the direction and form of new political protest art. That the FPÖ would be admitted to political partnership once again was hardly foreseeable in 2006 at the end of the millennial coalitions with the far right. The fact that just a decade later this has indeed happened makes it highly timely that we take stock of the wave of cultural protest against the politics of early twenty-first-century Austria and advance a reading of these works here. Whether there will be such a body of protest and cultural resistance to the government of Chancellor Sebastian Kurz (ÖVP) and Vice-Chancellor Heinz Christian Strache (FPÖ) and to the politics of the late

2010s remains to be seen. Austria's political developments have doubtless been influenced by events beyond its borders, and with many countries of Western Europe experiencing electoral gains for far-right parties, Austria's own renewed coalition with the FPÖ has prompted little reaction internationally. Political events such as the United Kingdom's decision to leave the European Union ('Brexit') and the political direction of the USA under President Trump have given artists and protesters in those countries and beyond heightened grounds for civil and artistic protest. The final chapter of this book identifies some of the burgeoning protest on Austria's streets and in its works of art but stresses once again that the reasons for protesting are often multiple. Elections might form the catalyst, but it is the policy-making and enforcement that produce physical and cultural resistance. I draw attention to examples of new political writing and filmmaking in contemporary Austria and trust that the pages of this book will stand as testimony to the creativity of cultural resistance and to its potentially galvanizing effect.

Notes

1. Kate Connolly, 'Big Vote for Right in Austria', *The Guardian*, 4 October 1999, retrieved 8 April 2018 from https://www.theguardian.com/world/1999/oct/04/austria.kateconnolly.
2. For a highly nuanced typology of resistance, see Jocelyn Hollander and Rachel Einwohner, 'Conceptualizing Resistance', *Sociological Forum* 19(4) (2004), 533–54.
3. See Hans-Henning Scharsach, *Stille Machtergreifung: Hofer, Strache und die Burschenschaften* (Vienna: Kreymayr and Scheriau, 2017). Scharsach's book received the Bruno Kreisky prize for the best political book of 2017.
4. Thomas Stangl's *Regeln des Tanzes* (Graz: Droschl, 2013), for example, is a novel that is partly set against the backdrop of the 2000 protests. One of the main characters experiences a new sense of meaning in her life as a result of her participation in political resistance.
5. I rehearse some of these in Allyson Fiddler, *Rewriting Reality: An Introduction to Elfriede Jelinek* (Oxford: Berg, 1994), especially 'The Austrian Literary Context', 17–26.
6. There are differentiated studies of the variety of art and literature of the first decade of the twenty-first century. See, for example, Michael Boehringer and Susanne Hochreiter (eds), *Zeitenwende: Österreichische Literatur seit dem Millennium: 2000–2010* (Vienna: Praesens, 2011); or Allyson Fiddler, Jon Hughes and Florian Krobb (eds), *The Austrian Noughties: Texts, Films, Debates*, special issue, *Austrian Studies* 19 (2011).
7. Anthony Bushell, *Polemical Austria: The Rhetorics of National Identity: From Empire to the Second Republic* (Cardiff: University of Wales Press, 2013), 246.

Chapter 1

AUSTRIA GETS THE 'BLUES'
Setting the Scene for Protest

The Millennial Wende

The application of the word Wende to the political events of turn-of-the-millennium Austria merits a little elaboration. Austria has had its Wende, or 'change of direction', too. The connotations are significantly different from the more commonly associated German events of 1989–90 when the Berlin Wall fell and Germany became reunified. By and large, apart from prompting some infrequently voiced regret about post-Wall Germany's complete erasure of a number of positive aspects of its former socialist sister state, the German Democratic Republic, 'die Wende' is a term that suggests almost universally positive associations. This is not the case for Austria at the threshold of the twenty-first century. Here, the term denotes a kind of shorthand for the country's 'turn' to the much farther right. The year 1999 was when the populist, right-wing Freiheitliche Partei Österreichs (FPÖ) – whose party colour is blue – obtained its largest electoral share in the general election (26.9 per cent), very narrowly pipping the 'black' Österreichische Volkspartei (ÖVP) into second place. The party in top position, with 33.2 per cent, the red-coded Sozialdemokratische Partei Österreichs (SPÖ), did not have enough votes to rule on its own and would have needed to form a coalition to do so. Despite pre-election undertakings from the ÖVP that it would go into opposition if it did not achieve second position in the polls, the final result of months of negotiations was, indeed, that Wolfgang Schüssel, the leader of the third-placed ÖVP, took office as Chancellor, with the new head of the FPÖ, Susanne Riess-Passer, as his deputy. Thus, Austria got its political 'blues' or, more correctly, its 'black-and-blues'.[1]

The significant electoral success of the FPÖ was the subject of heated discussion and debate at the time both in Austria and abroad. Political scientists and election commentators proposed a variety of reasons for it. A common theory was that there had been a significant protest vote by the general electorate, who were tired of the dominance of the two major parties, the ÖVP and the SPÖ, and were voting FPÖ in an attempt to stir up the electoral landscape and upset the political status quo. Although the FPÖ's share of the vote diminished significantly to just 10 per cent in 2002, subsequent elections have not borne out the protest vote theory. National elections in 2006 and 2008 saw the combined results of the FPÖ and its breakaway party, the Bündnis Zukunft Österreich (BZÖ), at 15.1 per cent and 28.2 per cent respectively.[2] The elections of 2013 returned 20.5 per cent for the FPÖ alone. Other new right-wing or neocorporatist parties that have emerged since 2000 also gained seats in government, such as Team Stronach with its first national election participation at 5.7 per cent (the party was dissolved in 2017) and the Neos (Neues Österreich at 5.0 per cent), but the BZÖ achieved only 3.5 per cent and thus no seats in Austria's parliament. Looking ahead to the present day, the FPÖ is very far from being a spent force, as the Conclusion to this book underlines. October 2017 saw the FPÖ repeating its 1999 success with nearly 26 per cent of the vote, this time only just coming third to the SPÖ's 27 per cent and with the ÖVP under its new leader Sebastian Kurz (and new colour of turquoise) garnering the leading share of 31.5 per cent. If Schüssel was dubbed the 'Wendekanzler' (the Chancellor of the political turn),[3] Kurz was flagged on the day of the 2017 elections as 'der neue Wende-Kanzler'.[4]

The idea of a turn to the right in Austrian politics would seem a rather pervasive concept, given that a little over a decade after the far right ceased political power-sharing in 2006, there is renewed talk of Austria's 'turn' to the right.[5] Perhaps, as many were already arguing in the immediate aftermath of the controversial 1999 elections, the supposed millennial turn to the right was merely an electoral manifestation of a political trajectory that saw Austria – and many other countries besides – becoming ever more populist and neoliberal. In the words of activist and academic Gini Müller, 'in Österreich hat sich mit *den Wahlen 1999 die Normalität nur ein Stück weiter nach rechts verschoben*' (*the Austrian elections of 1999 just shifted normality a bit further to the right*).[6] The FPÖ's success of 1999 was seen by some merely as the culmination of two and a half decades of steeply rising election results, brought in primarily by the party's highly charismatic and telegenic leader, Jörg Haider, who took over the leadership of the FPÖ in 1986. The coalition government of ÖVP-FPÖ inaugurated in February 2000 was not, as is sometimes reported, the first taste of national governance for the FPÖ. The 1983 elections saw the SPÖ (47.6 per cent) lose its absolute majority but stay in government by going into coalition with the FPÖ under Norbert Steger. Ironically, 1983 brought the FPÖ only 5.0 per cent, its lowest ever yield since its foundation in 1949 as the Verband der Unabhängigen

(VdU; the party was renamed the FPÖ in 1956). The shock wave produced at the turn of the millennium was triggered by the election result of October 1999, but turned into a significant event provoking reaction when the party assumed its share of power in February 2000.

Political historians have traced how the FPÖ's ascendancy under Haider is matched by its increasing distance from 'liberal' politics per se and its espousal of nationalist, anti-immigrationist policies. In 1993, a breakaway group of liberals under Heide Schmidt left the party to form the Liberales Forum, in protest against the nationalist policies being advanced by Haider and his allies. The 'Österreich zuerst' (Austria First) referendum of 1992 asked for popular approval to 'shore up' Austria against immigration, to reject bilingualism in schools and to increase domestic policing (particularly against asylum seekers). As Ruth Wodak and Anton Pelinka note, 'by 1993, the FPÖ's party policy and platform had become anti-foreigner, anti-European Union, and widely populist, very similar to Le Pen's party in France'.[7] Nevertheless, the referendum was far from successful. The pressure group SOS Mitmensch was established in 1992 precisely to counter the anti-foreigner referendum and attracted 300,000 people to its 'Lichtermeer', candle-lit protest of 23 January 1993.[8] Around this time, and with Austria joining the EU in 1995, Haider's FPÖ changed its formerly pan-Germanist approach to Austrian national identity in favour of acknowledging Austria's independent – but still Germanic – character and status. Many of the other political parties adopted anti-immigrationist stances, as the fall of the Berlin Wall saw migration from former Eastern Bloc countries, and many agreed with the argument that the EU should not see further expansion 'to the east' ('Osterweiterung'). In the 1999 campaign, other parties were campaigning along similar lines, but none of the slogans used was 'as explicit as those used by the FPÖ in the 1999 election campaign, when the most prominent FPÖ campaign poster read "Stop der Überfremdung" ("Stop foreign infiltration"), a term coined by the Nazis and used by Goebbels in 1933'.[9] This slogan and many other similar ones give a sense of why in 1999/2000 the advent of political power-sharing by the FPÖ was the cause for international condemnation as well as domestic disbelief amongst the vast majority of the population. In 1983, by contrast, the FPÖ's slim vote and minor coalition participation was not deemed dangerous or indicative of a xenophobic development in Austrian politics.

In 2000, the United States temporarily recalled its ambassador for talks, and Israel withdrew its ambassador between February 2000 and February 2004. Austria took the decision to close its Cultural Institute in Paris in 2000 in response to French protests.[10] The EU put in place superficial diplomatic measures against Austria on 4 February 2000, pending an official report commissioned by the fourteen Member States from the President of the European Court of Human Rights, Luzius Wildhaber. The three investigators appointed by the European Court, Martti Ahtisaari, Jochen Frowein and Marcelino Oreja, became, in common parlance, 'die drei Weisen' ('the Three Wise Men') and the report they published in September 2000 became known as the 'Weisenbericht'. The authors explained their remit to have been 'to prepare a report based on thorough investigation of: the Austrian Government's attitude to common European values, in particular regarding the rights of minorities, refugees and immigrants' and 'the development and political nature of the FPÖ'.[11] However, the 'wise men' had not been given the task of formulating any policy proposals. The report came to the conclusion that Austria was abiding by common European Union (EU) principles and that its asylum and immigration policies did not show any grounds for serious concern.[12] Nevertheless, the FPÖ was criticized on a number of counts, not least for its attempts to silence its opponents, particularly through frequent use of libel cases (paragraph 93), for its 'ambiguous language', including 'statements that can be interpreted as xenophobic or even racist' (paragraph 88), and for not taking action against members who use such language in public (paragraph 89). In his evaluation of the EU intervention, international law specialist Waldemar Hummer concludes that 'in this way, the Fourteen, after a total of seven-and-a-half months (!) [sic], lifted the sanctions against the Austrian Government but simultaneously reached agreement to jointly exercise special vigilance in regard to the FPÖ'.[13]

These so-called 'sanctions' amounted to little more than refusing to support Austrian candidates for higher office in international organizations and discontinuing bilateral contacts between individual governments and Austria. The terminology used by the EU was that of 'measures' being taken against Austria. However, to this day, the Austrian government and common media coverage still talk of 'sanctions' against Austria.[14] It has been argued that in deploying the term 'sanctions', the Austrian government was able to turn the EU's investigation into possible extreme-right elements of its government into an attack on Austria and the Austrians.[15] The resultant closing of ranks, or 'Schulterschluss', is reminiscent of the other major political scandal in postwar Austria, the Waldheim affair of the mid 1980s (see below). However, the scale of international interest in Austria generated by the millennial elections – and, as this book attests, the extent of the cultural protest it engendered – far exceeded the diplomatic ramifications and expressions of artistic resistance of the 1980s. My chapter heading is somewhat ironic, of course. Austria might have seen a rise in the 'blue' party, but the reaction was not simply sadness, depression or lamentation. The major emotions would appear to have been anger and disbelief.

In 2005, more internal strife erupted in the FPÖ, this time between its leaders and a group including Andreas Mölzer, Haider's former cultural advisor, and Heinz-Christian Strache, the current leader of the FPÖ. The result was the birth of the new 'orange' party, the Bündnis Zukunft Österreich (BZÖ), with Haider initially at its helm and certainly still very much calling the shots, even when his friend Peter Westenthaler took on the leadership from 2006 to 2008. All of the FPÖ politicians with a government mandate defected to the BZÖ in 2005. Wolfgang Schüssel simply carried on with the government until new elections in 2006, meaning that the 'black-blue' coalition became a 'black-orange' one. Haider's popularity was undoubtedly a major reason for the party's success in 2008, when it achieved 10.7 per cent of the vote. Haider had taken on the leadership from Westenthaler, who had just been issued a prison sentence for giving a false statement under oath at a trial involving his personal bodyguard.

Haider's death, following a high-speed car crash in the early hours of 11 October 2008, just two weeks after his party's election success, produced a massive outpouring of grief, particularly in his adopted homeland of Carinthia, where he served for many years as governor or *Landeshauptmann*. Conspiracy theories abounded, but the subsequent inquest concluded without any doubt that Haider's vehicle was in sound working order. However, he had been driving it at 142 km per hour and with three times the permitted blood alcohol limit in his body. In addition, there were rumours of Haider's secret homosexuality that were fuelled by his deputy, Stefan Petzner, announcing afterwards that the leader had been his 'Lebensmensch' (most important person in his life), much more than just a 'friend'. Petzner later regretted his emotional interviews and the questions that they invited. Haider's widow successfully prosecuted newspapers who alleged that her husband had been homosexual. Even after his death, the media could be charged for bringing Haider's name into disrepute if they made such assertions.[16] Haider's name, however, has been associated with much bigger, genuine scandals following his death, as the financial mismanagement of the later nationalized Hypo Adria Bank has come to light as well as Haider's personal exploitation of the bank for his own political ends. As the *New York Times* commented: 'Mr. Haider, who once inspired fears of an extreme-right resurgence in Europe, is now posthumously a central character in a scandal involving Hypo Group Alpe Adria, a bank formerly owned by the state government. Authorities are investigating well over 40 people on suspicion of fraud, bribery and other charges.'[17]

This is not to imply that there had not been huge criticism of Jörg Haider during his lifetime. Many of the artists and intellectuals discussed in this volume are, in fact, seasoned 'Haider watchers' and have repeatedly warned against what they have seen as the increasingly tolerant attitude to racism in Austrian society, and against the ways in which public figures have downplayed Austria's war crimes. The Waldheim affair of 1986 can be seen as a vital moment of crystallization, both in the process of Austria's examination of its Nazi past and in terms of the birth of a civil society and of dynamic social protest movements in Austria.

The Waldheim Affair: A Previous Wende

The ÖVP's choice for the Austrian presidential elections of 1986 was not a controversial candidate from the outset. Kurt Waldheim had served two terms of office as the Secretary General to the United Nations and was a diplomat of considerable international standing. His casually delivered story to an Austrian radio interview in 1985 that he had not been in the army for long and had 'not seen a single SS person during the whole war' was patently very far from the truth and unravelled to explosive effect.[18] A number of media investigations (by, amongst others, the German magazin *Stern* and the Austrian *Profil*) were able to unearth the facts that not only had Waldheim's unit, the 'Heeresgruppe Mitte', been involved in wartime atrocities in Yugoslavia and Greece, but also that Waldheim must have had knowledge of these. The World Jewish Congress (WJC) published successive documents and issued relentless calls for Waldheim to withdraw his candidacy, but the effect of increasing international pressure was merely to produce more solidarity amongst Austrian voters who saw not just Waldheim but the whole of Austria as being under attack. Waldheim repeatedly insisted that what he had done in the war was the same as hundreds of thousands of other Austrians had done, that is to say, quite simply his duty as a soldier. He thus cleverly appealed to a broad electorate, who saw his message as exonerating them and justifying any part they had played in the Nazi years.[19]

Fears that the interventions of the WJC would provoke increased anti-Semitism seemed to be confirmed. A mere indication of this can be given here to substantiate this claim. Insights include the utterance by Michael Graff, who was then dismissed from his post as General Secretary of the ÖVP, that 'so long as it's not proven that he [Waldheim] strangled six Jews with his own hands, there's no problem'.[20] Documentary filmmaker Ruth Beckermann's *Die papierne Brücke* (1987) captures the moment when her father is subjected to anti-Semitic verbal abuse during an anti-Waldheim demonstration following the President's inauguration. Beckermann uses her own archival footage of the Waldheim protests in the 2018 release *Waldheims Walzer*. In this context, the term 'Wende' denotes a positive step in delivering the moment in Austrian history that put paid to the lie of Austrian victimization and galvanized civic protest.[21] Austrian-born journalist Hella Pick sums up the results of the pressure placed on Austria as follows: 'Whatever one may think of the WJC's tactics . . . there can be no doubt that the exposure of Waldheim's lies led directly to a crucial turning point in Austrian thinking. It propelled Vranitzky [later SPÖ Chancellor of Austria] in 1991 to deliver his formal admission that many Austrians had backed Hitler's Third Reich and had been instrumental in its crimes.'[22]

The Waldheim 'affair', 'saga' or 'scandal', as it is variously dubbed, marks the period in which Austria's Second Republic finally began to explore the darker sides to the country's recent history. Writer Robert Schindel posits it as Austria's equivalent of Germany's 1968:

> In Germany the Waldheim affair began in 1968. For whatever reason the question, 'Father, what did you do in the war?' cropped up in 1968, and then the business of critically examining the parental generation's wartime past got underway – with full force, if with numerous wrong turns. In Austria, this was delayed by the 'victimization thesis', which was cultivated by every single administration of the Second Republic.[23]

The victimization myth or thesis has its origins in the Moscow Declaration of 1 November 1943. The statement by the Allied powers began to plan for the restoration of Austria after the war, but also contained caveats. Although Austria was indeed dubbed the first victim of Hitlerite aggression, the country was also warned that it 'bears responsibility for taking part in the war on the side of Hitler Germany … and that its own contribution to its liberation unavoidably be taken in consideration in the final settlement'.[24] This important qualification of Austria's responsibility did not play a major part in postwar identity-building. In fact, Austria's relationship with its own past and its war guilt has been subject to an incremental ebb and flow of partial avowal of guilt followed by renewed assertion of the country's status as the 'first victim' of Nazism.[25] Kurt Waldheim's election campaign and his subsequent success stirred Austrians to probe such questions, but the net result was not to kickstart a trajectory of increasing atonement. 'The "liar" Waldheim was elected for a six-year term as Austria's President', Hella Pick summarizes. Moreover, 'the WJC did provoke antisemitism: the Freedom Party, shifting to a right-wing xenophobic platform after Haider replaced Norbert Steger, made important electoral gains'.[26]

The mid 1980s sealed the end of a period that often bears Pope Paul VI's 1971 description of Austria as an 'island of the blessed'. A model of social partnership, the Austrian Second Republic was founded on the principles of military neutrality, consensus politics and proportional power-sharing or 'Proporz'. Historian Steven Beller explains why the Pope's praise for Austria is understandable, since 'Austrian society was still relatively conservative, the Church still a weighty factor in national life. The neo-corporatist social partnership exemplified Catholic teachings on economic organization, and had produced an enviable degree of social peace'.[27] When the peace was broken in the course of the Waldheim affair and beyond, protest and criticism made itself heard in political and diplomatic circles, as we have heard, but also at the grassroots level, as ordinary people protested on the streets, and intellectuals and artists used their skills to express their outrage and their desire to see Austrian society develop differently.

Resistance Preliminaries: Protesting against Waldheim

Robert Foltin's history of social protest in Austria notes that 'Waldheim's inauguration sees the beginning of years of protest activities against the Austrian President'.[28] Whilst these were not weekly events like those that were to mark the anti-Haider or anti-coalition protests of the early 2000s, they nevertheless attracted thousands of participants, for example, at demonstrations around the time of Waldheim's inauguration, or to protest against his visit to the Vatican in 1991 or, most notably, to express counternarratives during the events to mark the fiftieth anniversary of the Anschluss in 1988. The most well-known example of artistic intervention is Thomas Bernhard's play *Heldenplatz* (1988), commissioned by the German director of Vienna's Burgtheater, Claus Peymann. The scandal surrounding Bernhard's work was far-reaching. A play that paints a picture implying that anti-Semitism was still rife in 1980s Austria was more than many ordinary Austrians could bear. The scandal was fuelled by the Austrian media, such that the shock impact was assured, even before the play was staged.

The term 'resistance', which certainly became a catchword in the anti-coalition protests of 1999/2000 (see Chapter 2), was being used in the 1980s to mark the efforts being made to counter the apparent amnesia and indifference that Waldheim's attitude signified. Many Austrians wanted to forget the country's Nazi past, but a vocal minority were intent on preserving the memory of Austria's war years and its homegrown 1930s' variant of fascism, Austrofascism. They wanted to honour the lives that had been lost and guard against the return of extreme right-wing nationalist politics. The Republikanischer Club – Neues Österreich was founded in the midst of the Waldheim affair with the express intention of casting light on Austria's recent past. However, Doron Rabinovici, one of the founder members, makes it clear that Waldheim as such was not so much the root cause of Austria's willed ignorance and avoidance of its past, or the only reason for solidarity amongst artists and intellectuals; rather, he was merely an unsavoury symptom of Austria's broader problems.[29]

As happened once again at the time of the Schüssel-led coalition in the 2000s, conservative public voices in the 1980s recommended emigration to artists and intellectuals who criticized their own country. In a collection of responses to the 'democratic fascism' of the Waldheim era, the writer Michael Scharang quotes Erhard Busek, the ÖVP politician who was deputy mayor of Vienna in the late 1980s, sarcastically challenging intellectuals to 'go abroad and explain to people why Austria is so good that they choose to live here'.[30] Elfriede Jelinek picks this statement up in her acceptance speech on receiving the Heinrich Böll Prize in 1986. She makes links between the 1980s and the 1960s, and, more pointedly, to the policies of the 1930s and 1940s:

> In Austria, we don't just recommend emigration to our critical artists, we actually drive them out. We're quite thorough about these things. I'll just mention Rühm, Wiener, Brus, who left the country in the sixties. I'll not mention Jura Soyfer, who was murdered in a concentration camp, because that's too long ago and long since forgotten and, above all, forgiven. People forgive us for absolutely everything, you see.[31]

Jelinek used this opportunity to flag up her dissent from the political climate of mid 1980s Austria. The titular word play, 'In den Waldheimen und auf den Haidern' ('In the forested homelands and on the heaths'), deconstructs the normal expectations of rural idyll. Jelinek warns her listeners that all is not what it seems in Austria. This is not the land of innocence as suggested by beautiful classical music and the white Lippizaner horses of the Spanish riding school in Vienna. The latter are 'weiß wie unsere Westen', Jelinek comments, punning on the saying 'weiße Weste haben' (to be innocent/to have a clean slate). She continues: 'And the traditional suit worn by many Carinthians is brown, and it has large pockets that you can shove a lot into.'[32] In suggesting that many Austrians wear brown, the colour associated with the SA (the 'Brownshirts') and thus, *pars pro toto*, with Nazism, Jelinek's implied accusation of neofascist behaviour is hard-hitting and unambiguous. Her short drama *Präsident Abendwind* of the same year features a politician campaigning for the presidency as its protagonist.[33] The idea of repressing the past or of claiming to have forgotten past events is an important theme in this commissioned response to Nestroy's *Häuptling Abendwind oder Das greuliche Festmahl* (1862). In Jelinek's updated version of the satire, Abendwind describes himself as 'der Vorsitzende von dem Rat von die Vereinigten Pfitschiinseln [sic]' ('Head of the Council of the United Tiddly-Islands'), in a clear parody of Kurt Waldheim's General Secretaryship of the United Nations. Jelinek satirizes Waldheim's election campaign and, above all, his apparent amnesia about the war years he spent as a Wehrmacht officer. The cannibalism in Jelinek's version is a metaphorical reference not only to the 'swallowing up' of people by the Nazi state, but also to contemporary xenophobic attitudes and to the call by many in Austria to ignore or to counter foreign condemnation of Waldheim's candidature.

There are countless examples of artistic works, be they songs, novels, plays or films, that allude to Waldheim in some manner. Clearly, in the case of artists producing their work during Waldheim's campaign or presidency, it is an obvious line of enquiry to interrogate their writing or art for the protest it voices rather than just seeing it as referencing a political era or providing local colour. The present study of 'anti-Haiderization' or anti-far-right protest occasioned by the Austrian Wende is very conscious of the difficulty of distinguishing between artistic phenomena that merely use the political scene as a backdrop and those that seek to make a political point. However, in the present book, I probe how writers and artists use their distinctive voices to express dissension from the turn to the right as symbolized by the ÖVP-FPÖ coalition. In this sense, the coalition, too, must be seen as a symptom and not as the root cause of public and artistic disquiet. The examples of musical protests discussed in Chapter 2 also have their counterpart in the Waldheim era, for example, with Erste Allgemeine Verunsicherung's track 'Kurti' (also known as 'Wann man gehen muß' ('When You Have to Go')). The song thematizes the Waldheim affair and was initially the subject of legal proceedings by Kurt Waldheim (which were later withdrawn).[34] Domestic protesters were given prominent support by foreign artists in the 1980s too. A *Spiegel* cover story of 1988 featured the arc of 1938 to 1988 commemorations, with a picture of Waldheim and a piece entitled 'Waldheim: die Schlinge zieht sich zu' ('Waldheim: The Noose is Tightening'). *Spiegel* reports that Terence Trent D'Arby called off his 1987 sold-out concert in Vienna because he was not willing to have tax revenue flow to a country that had elected Waldheim as President.[35] Fellow American Lou Reed wrote a song entitled 'Good Evening Mr. Waldheim' (1989), in which the singer-songwriter's 'distaste for anti-Semitism can be heard'.[36]

The period that gave rise to a burgeoning social movement in Austria is mirrored in later works reflecting back on the Waldheim era. They do so with renewed insight, distance or perhaps to suggest an analogy with the present era. Robert Schindel's 2013 novel *Der Kalte* fictionalizes the era and depicts Waldheim in the character 'Wais', as Katya Krylova has demonstrated.[37] In English-language fiction, too, Waldheim's name and background are fictionalized, for example, as 'gray, astringent Kurt Haldweim' in Harry Turtledove's alternative history, which posits Germany as having won World War II.[38] The character's name is even more obviously a referent to its real-life counterpart than those in the *romans à clef* examined in Chapter 3 of this volume. Waldheim's biography continues to inspire literary adaptations and artistic allusions even after his death in 2007.[39] Srikanth Reddy's 2011 book-length poem, *Voyager*, has been called a 'poem by erasure'.[40] His fascination with the space probe Voyager and his reading of the English translation of Waldheim's autobiographical account *In the Eye of the Storm* combine to produce a highly political poem. In the words of fellow poet and critic Marjorie Perloff, Reddy's poem 'exposes "Waldheim's Disease" as much more than one individual's particular mendacity'.[41] Reddy reproduces extracts from Waldheim's writing in different versions. In the 'Epilogues', the same text is reproduced three times, each with most of the text simply crossed through, but leaving certain words visible and thus producing new meanings as these sparse words are put together by the reader. The poet uses Waldheim's practice of striking through the past, or selecting from it, as a literal device in his own writing.

A piece of portable sculpture came to symbolize the anti-Waldheim campaign more than any other work of cultural protest in Austria. When requests for parliamentary debate on Waldheim's background were declined, Chancellor

Fred Sinowatz remarked dryly that it would naturally be taken into account that Waldheim's horse had been a member of the SA and not Waldheim himself.[42] The plan was born to construct a six-metre-high wooden horse using a design sketch by sculptor Alfred Hrdlicka and to take it along to the anti-Waldheim protests.[43] The 'Holzpferd' was adorned with the cap of an SA officer drawn by cartoonist Manfred Deix. In the manner of a Trojan horse parody, the sculpture would appear – to the annoyance of the President – at various protests over the years, including those in Rome when Waldheim visited the Pope.[44] The wooden horse became the logo or symbol of its creators, the Republikanischer Club, and is still used on its webpage.[45] In the anti-coalition protests of 1999/2000 onwards, the horse would mutate into a donkey, although his creator, Manochehr Shahabi, a refugee student, only arrived in Austria in 1987 and was not aware of its predecessor. Shahabi describes wanting to mock the government in order to mirror the way the people were feeling mocked by their politicians. The 'Trojan donkey' first wore the signature bow tie of Wolfgang Schüssel and later a black-and-blue tie.[46]

Austria in the 1990s: From Culture Wars to Cultural Protests

The dozen or so years between the two major political flashpoints in postwar Austrian history – Waldheim's election in 1986 and the FPÖ's election to coalition in 1999 – were not free from controversy, either in political or in cultural terms. Jay Rosellini calls the 1990s the period in which the Austrian culture wars began 'in earnest'.[47] Rosellini marks Josef Haslinger's position as one of the poles in the contradictory positions of the time.[48] Haslinger saw the progress that had been made in Austria and did not succumb to 'despair and cultural pessimism':

> [Haslinger] praised Chancellor Vranitzky's 1993 speech in Israel (which Jelinek has dismissed as too little, too late), the ongoing revision of history textbooks, the dedication of memorials at the former Nazi concentration camps in Austria, the increase in pensions for those persecuted by the Nazis, and the recognition of the Sinti and Roma as a national minority.[49]

On the other hand, the cultural pessimist's line– and Jelinek is a prime example – would be to see the burgeoning anti-immigrationist, racist views that were becoming more vocal once again as a mere continuation of Austria's fascist past and to largely ignore the progress that had been made.

There can be no doubt that leftist intellectuals and artists who were highly critical of Austria and of high-profile politicians such as Jörg Haider and Kurt Waldheim were also a target for declarations by politicians and political parties on the state of contemporary Austrian culture. One of the low points in the smear campaign conducted by the FPÖ was undoubtedly its local election campaign of 1995, which featured a poster asking potential electors whether they liked a string of socialist artists and politicians, 'Scholten, Jelinek, Häupl, Peymann, Pasterk' or rather 'Kunst und Kultur?' (art and culture). The strapline featured underneath suggested that the FPÖ's preferred position was 'Freiheit der Kunst statt sozialistischer Staatskünstler' (freedom for art, not socialist, state-sponsored artists).[50] The populist right was taking a swipe at Jelinek and others for being sponsored by the state (meaning in Jelinek's case merely being staged at the Burgtheater) in order to suggest that certain kinds of art were receiving subsidies at the expense of a more traditional, less elitist kind of art. Art deemed to be avant garde or critical in whatever form was contrary to the FPÖ's assertions that culture should not be 'political' in nature. The criticism was disingenuous, of course, since art that professed traditional, 'liberal' views would not be called political by the FPÖ. Moreover, right-wing ideologues argued that there was too high a concentration of culture and arts funding for Vienna, and that this should be redirected more to the Länder and, by implication, to the traditional Austrian forms of culture. It was, however, Social Democrat Chancellor Viktor Klima who subsumed culture under the Ministry for Education, Science and Culture in 1997. But Jörg Haider viewed culture to be such an important strand of (FPÖ) politics that he wished it to be 'Chefsache', a matter for the top, and thus he dispensed with a party office for culture and chose to oversee it personally, with the assistance of personal friend and adviser, Andreas Mölzer.[51]

The case of artist Cornelius Kolig was one in which Haider took a personal interest back in his political homeland of Carinthia. The paintings of Kolig's grandfather Anton Kolig had adorned the local parliament building, but were removed in 1938 by the Nazis, who deemed his work degenerate. A similar scandal surrounded the plan to commission Cornelius Kolig for replacement art work. An international art market website reported in 2000 that 'Haider has been *waging a war* against a proposed fresco for the Carinthian parliament by Cornelius Kolig'.[52] Colig had experimented with the use of faeces in previous artistic works and this provided his opponents with what they felt was ample reason for barring his work as immoral. Artnet further informed its readers that: 'Haider also revoked the decision to buy a piece by avant-garde artist Meina Schellander, a move the artist believes is due to her work being "too modern", and the musical theater group Arbos has lost its subsidy in favor of projects focusing on folk music.'[53]

What becomes clear in these investigations of the realm of culture is that it is not a tangent to political debate or political events, but very much a domain in which politics itself is 'fought', as talk of culture 'wars' indeed suggests. As one scholar notes: 'It is quite obvious – and not even the FPÖ denies this – that the Kolig-debate was fought and kept alive as part of the regional election campaign, rather than because of conflicting conceptions about taste and justice.'[54] The present book does not seek to analyse further party-political views or to chart how political parties have sought to deploy culture as a kind of pawn. It is also not interested in providing a platform to present what might be considered to be pro-FPÖ art or culture that was in favour of the 2000 coalition formation in Austria. Instead, what the following chapters do is provide a space for the collection and analysis of cultural phenomena and artefacts themselves. Thus, the book constitutes the first large-scale study of the creative work of protest against the ÖVP-FPÖ coalition.

Individual arguments and views have been expressed in a considerable body of essay publications and full-length books produced both by creative artists themselves and by public intellectuals and artists on the subject of the Austrian Wende. Scrutinizing these as a separate genre is beyond the confines of the present volume and would take our focus away from the art and culture itself.[55] Key examples are, for example, the publications of *Falter* editor Armin Thurnher. Alongside his *Das Trauma, ein Leben: Österreichische Einzelheiten* (1999) and *Heimniederlage: Nachrichten aus dem neuen Österreich* (2000), there are many insightful anthologies, such as Isolde Charim and Doron Rabinovici's collection *Österreich: Berichte aus Quarantanien* (2000), which includes essays by Menasse, Jelinek, Schindel and many more. Robert Misik and Doron Rabinovici also brought out an anthology with the campaigning title *Republik der Courage: Wider die Verhaiderung* (2000). Their preface summarizes the atmosphere and beginnings of the protest movements, but suggests that it was too early to know whether the *Süddeutsche Zeitung* was right in calling this the 'Geburtsstunde der österreichischen Zivilgesellschaft' (the moment when civil society was born in Austria).[56] They record the very beginnings, starting with the initial call for signatories to oppose the coalition and its policies one week after the election in 1999, and how teams of people from various organizations such as SOS Mitmensch and the Republikanischer Club put their backs into organizing initial rallies of protest. There was a sense in Austria that at the very least, Austrian society was becoming repoliticized.[57] Awoken from the decades-long stasis of two-party consensus government, the Austrian population could now itself make a contribution to politics. Austrians certainly perceived that this was the time to make their voices heard.

Notes

1. The image of a change of colours is used in some publications examining Austria's political turn. See Gerfried Sperl, *Die umgefärbte Republik: Anmerkungen zu Österreich* (Vienna: Paul Zsolnay Verlag, 2003). However, the idea of a Wende or turn has endured in both German- and English-language publications: Reinhard Heinisch, *Populism, Proporz, Pariah: Austria Turns Right* (New York: Nova Science, 2002); Robert Kriechbaumer and Franz Schausberger, *Die umstrittene Wende: Österreich 2000–2006* (Vienna: Böhlau, 2012).

2. The Austrian Home Office provides information on all elections online. See http://www.bmi.gv.at/412/Nationalratswahlen/Nationalratswahl_2002/start.aspx. Originally, Bündnis *für die* Zukunft *Österreichs*, the party became known simply as Bündnis Zukunft Österreich.
3. See the title of a 2000 study by Joachim Riedl, *Der Wende-Kanzler: Die unerschütterliche Beharrlichkeit des Wolfgang Schüssel* (Vienna: Czernin, 2000). On the occasion of Schüssel's seventieth birthday in 2015, a *Kurier* newspaper headline asked its readers whether they could still remember the Wendekanzler: Bernhard Gaul, 'Erinnern Sie sich an den Wendekanzler', *Kurier*, 2 June 2015, retrieved 8 April 2018 from https://kurier.at/politik/inland/schuessel-wird-70-erinnern-sie-sich-an-den-wendekanzler/134.004.974.
4. 'Sebastian Kurz: Der neue Wende-Kanzler, oder kommt doch Rot-Blau?, *Kurier*, 15 October 2017, retrieved 8 April 2018 from https://kurier.at/politik/inland/wahl/sebastian-kurz-der-neue-wende-kanzler/292.279.028.
5. The English-speaking press also uses the image of Austria turning to the right. This applies to the general election of 2017 and throughout the protracted presidential elections of 2016, when the FPÖ's Norbert Hofer was a strong rival to the eventually triumphant Alexander Van der Bellen, a former Green Party leader.
6. Gini Müller, *Possen des Performativen: Theater, Aktivismus und queere Politiken* (Vienna: Verlag Turia und Kant, 2008), 86 (emphasis in original). Anthony Murphy argues that 'it is not enough to simply state that Haider's FPÖ was part of a "normalization" or "modernization" of the Austrian political system – if anything the old system is pretty much intact with a new type of conservative hegemonic control'. Anthony Murphy, 'The Rise of the Austrian Freedom Party in the 1990s: A Culturalist Approach', *Zeitschrift für Politikwissenschaft* 33(3) (2004), 297–307, at 306.
7. Ruth Wodak and Anton Pelinka, *The Haider Phenomenon in Austria* (New Brunswick, NJ: Transaction, 2002), xiii–xiv.
8. 'Lichtermeer', in Oswald Panagl and Peter Gerlich et al. (eds), *Wörterbuch der politischen Sprache in Österreich* (Vienna: Öbv, 2007), 251–52.
9. Wodak and Pelinka, *The Haider Phenomenon in Austria*, xv.
10. See Jacques Le Rider, 'The Austrian Crisis as Seen by a French Scholar of Germanic Culture', in Günter Bischof, Anton Pelinka and Michael Gehler (eds), *Austria in the European Union* (New Brunswick, NJ: Transaction, 2017), 56–66, at 63.
11. Martti Ahtisaari, Jochen Frowein and Marcelino Oreja, 'Report', adopted in Paris, 8 September 2000. Retrieved 8 April 2018 from http://www2.ohchr.org/english/bodies/hrc/docs/ngos/HOSI-1.pdf.
12. See 'Weisenbericht', in Panagl, Gerlich et al., *Wörterbuch der politischen Sprache in Österreich*, 470–71.
13. Waldemar Hummer, 'The End of EU Sanctions against Austria: A Precedent for New Sanctions Procedures?', *European Legal Forum* (2000/2001), 77–83, at 80. Retrieved 8 April 2018 from http://www.simons-law.com/library/nummerdetails.asp?Textnummer=12.
14. See the 'Chronologie der Beziehungen Österreich-EWG/EU'. Retrieved 8 April 2018 from http://www.parlament.gv.at/PERK/PE/EU/EUErweiterung/ChronologieBeziehungenAT-EU/index.shtml. I adopt the description of 'sanctions' in this book, too, as the term is widely accepted.
15. See Michael Frank, 'Raureif: Die Konfrontation der EU mit Österreichs Regierung im Jahr 2000 war ein bis heute verleugneter Erfolg', in Martin Strauß and Karl-Heinz Ströhle (eds), *Sanktionen: 10 Jahre danach: Die Maßnahmen der Länder der Europäischen*

Union gegen die österreichische Regierung im Jahr 2000 (Innsbruck: Studienverlag, 2010), 25–30, at 25.
16. 'Österreich: Toter Haider gewinnt Prozess zu seinem Sex-Leben', *Österreich*, November 2009. Retrieved 8 April 2018 from http://www.oe24.at/oesterreich/chronik/kaernten/Toter-Haider-gewinnt-Sex-Prozess/680657.
17. Jack Ewing, 'In Austria, Haider Haunts Investigation', *New York Times*, 20 October 2010. Retrieved 8 April 2018 from http://www.nytimes.com/2010/10/21/business/global/21iht-hypo.html?_r=0. The Austrian newspaper *Die Presse* also deploys the language of drama, talking not just of the 'characters', but of the whole scandal constituting 'a drama in five acts'. 'Milliardengrab Hypo: Ein Drama in fünf Akten'. Retrieved 8 April 2018 from http://diepresse.com/layout/diepresse/files/dossiers/hypo.
18. Quoted in Hella Pick, *Guilty Victim: Austria from the Holocaust to Haider* (London: I.B. Tauris, 2000). See especially 'Austria in the Dock: The Waldheim Saga', 149–69, at 159.
19. For an analysis of the infamous phrase 'Ich habe damals nichts anderes getan als Hunderttausende andere Österreicher auch, nämlich meine Pflicht als Soldat erfüllt' (I did nothing more than hundreds of thousands of other Austrians at the time: I carried out my duty as a soldier) and of how a number of Austrian authors have interacted with it, see Matthias Beilein, *86 und die Folgen: Robert Schindel, Robert Menasse und Doron Rabinovici im Literarischen Feld Österreichs* (Berlin: Erich Schmidt, 2008), 210–11.
20. 'Solange nicht bewiesen ist, daß er [Waldheim] eigenhändig sechs Juden erwürgt hat, gibt es kein Problem.' Michael Graff, quoted in Katya Krylova, 'Disturbing the Past: The Representation of the Waldheim Affair in Robert Schindel's *Der Kalte*', in Stephanie Bird et al. (eds), *Reverberations of Nazi Violence in Germany and Beyond: Disturbing Pasts* (London: Bloomsbury Academic, 2016), 107–24, at 109 (translation by Krylova).
21. Christiane Peitz, interview with Ruth Beckermann, 'Das war die Wende für Österreich', *Der Tagesspiegel*, 14 February 2018. Retrieved 8 April 2018 from https://www.tagesspiegel.de/kultur/regisseurin-ruth-beckermann-zur-waldheim-affaere-das-war-die-wende-fuer-oesterreich/20960474.html. During its development stage, the film had the subtitle 'The Art of Forgetting'.
22. Pick, *Guilty Victim*, 163.
23. 'In Deutschland hat die Waldheim-Affäre 1968 begonnen. Aus irgendwelchen Gründen gab es 1968 die Frage "Vater, was hast du im Krieg gemacht?", und mit voller Wucht, wenn auch mit vielen Fehlentwicklungen, setzte die Auseinandersetzung um die Kriegsvergangenheit der Elterngeneration ein. In Österreich war sie durch die "Opferthese", die von allen Regierungen der Zweiten Republik gehegt und gepflegt wurde, etwas verschoben.' Schindel, quoted and compared to the perspective on Waldheim of fellow writers Robert Menasse and Doron Rabinovici, in Beilein, *86 und die Folgen*, 83–84.
24. Quoted in Brigitte Bailer, 'They were All Victims: The Selective Treatment of the Consequences of National Socialism', in Günther Bischof and Anton Pelinka (eds), *Austrian Historical Memory and National Identity* (New Brunswick, NJ: Transaction, 1997), 103–15, at 103.
25. On the postwar legacy of the Moscow Treaty's 1943 designation of Austria as the first victim of Hitlerite aggression, see Heidemarie Uhl, 'Das "erste Opfer": der österreichische Opfermythos und seine Transformationen in der Zweiten Republik', *Österreichische Zeitschrift für Politikwissenschaft* 1 (2001), 19–34.
26. Pick, *Guilty Victim*, 163.

27. Steven Beller, *A Concise History of Austria* (Cambridge: Cambridge University Press, 2006), 272.
28. '[M]it der Angelobung Waldheims beginnen jahrelange Protestaktionen gegen den Bundespräsidenten.' Robert Foltin, *Und wir bewegen uns doch: soziale Bewegungen in Österreich* (Vienna: Edition Grundrisse, 2004), 301.
29. Doron Rabinovici, 'Nestbeschmutzer? Protest, Konfrontation und Institution: ein Blick zurück nach vorn', 1990. Retrieved 8 April 2018 from http://www.repclub.at/geschichte/.
30. '... ins Ausland fahren und erklären, warum Österreich doch so gut ist, daß sie hier leben.' Quoted in Michael Scharang, 'Diesen Staat kann kein Skandal erschüttern, denn er ist selbst ein Skandal', *Der Streit* 32 (1987), 4–6, at 4.
31. 'In Österreich wird kritischen Künstlern die Emigration nicht nur empfohlen, sie werden auch tatsächlich vertrieben, da sind wir gründlich. Ich erwähne nur Rühm, Wiener, Brus, die in den sechziger Jahren das Land verlassen haben. Ich erwähne nicht Jura Soyfer, der im KZ ermordet worden ist, denn das ist zu lang vergangen und daher zu lang schon vergessen und, vor allem, vergeben, denn uns verzeiht man einfach alles.' Elfriede Jelinek, 'In den Waldheimen und auf den Haidern'. Rede zur Verleihung des Heinrich-Böll-Preises in Köln am 2. Dezember 1986, *Der Streit* 32 (1987), 36. The full speech is published in Barbara Alms (ed.), *Blauer Streusand* (Frankfurt am Main: Suhrkamp, 1987), 42–44. Gerhard Rühm and Oswald Wiener were both members of the group of avant-garde writers known as the 'Wiener Gruppe', which was active in the 1950s and 1960s. Günter Brus is a writer and performance artist and is known mostly for his performances as a 'Wiener Aktionist' in the 1960s.
32. 'Und die Kärntneranzüge zahlreicher Bewohner sind braun und haben große Taschen, in die man einiges hineinstecken kann.' Jelinek, 'In den Waldheimen und auf den Haidern' clearly plays on the politicians' names and their proximity to geographical terms. See also Allyson Fiddler, *Rewriting Reality: An Introduction to Elfriede Jelinek* (Oxford: Berg, 1994), Chapter 4, 'Nature and "Heimat": Demystification of the "Alpenrepublik"', 99–125, at 101.
33. Elfriede Jelinek, 'Präsident Abendwind', in H. Wiesner (ed.), *Anthropophagen im Abendwind* (Berlin: Literaturhaus Berlin, 1988), 19–36.
34. Erste Allgemeine Verunsicherung, 'Kurti', B side, *Burli/Kurti*, Austria: EMI Austria, 1988.
35. Siegfried Kogelfranz, 'Waldheim: die Schlinge zieht sich zu', *Der Spiegel*, 25 January 1988, retrieved 8 April 2018 from http://www.spiegel.de/spiegel/print/d-13528122.html.
36. Tom Gross, 'Lou Reed's Stand for Israel and against Anti-Semitism', *National Review*, 28 October 2013. Retrieved 8 April 2018 from http://www.nationalreview.com/corner/362344/lou-reeds-stand-israel-and-against-anti-semitism-tom-gross. The song features on Lou Reed's album *New York*, CD. United States: Warner, 1989.
37. On Schindel's novel, see Krylova, 'Disturbing the Past'.
38. Harry Turtledove, *In the Presence of Mine Enemies* (New York: ROC, 2003), 252.
39. The English-language Wikipedia entry 'Kurt Waldheim' contains a long list of 'Media References', including filmic, graphic novel and music references: https://en.wikipedia.org/wiki/Kurt_Waldheim. The German-language entry 'Waldheim-Affäre' also includes a substantial section on 'Kunst'. The authors rightly observe: 'Die Waldheimaffäre inspirierte manche Künstler zu Werken und Stellungnahmen und beeinflusste den Umgang

40. Brian M. Reed, 'In Other Words: Postmillennial Poetry and Redirected Language', *Contemporary Literature* 52(4) (2011), 756–90, at 775.
41. Marjorie Perloff, quoted on the dust cover of Srikanth Reddy, *Voyager* (Berkeley: University of California Press, 2011).
42. The editors, 'Bedenkjahr, Holzpferd, Sinowatz: Das Lexikon der Waldheim-Jahre', *Der Standard*, 16 June 2007. The website version of this article on Waldheim's passing notes that the comments feature had to be disabled due to the irreverence of some of the postings: retrieved 8 April 2018 from http://derstandard.at/2921054/Bedenkjahr-Holzpferd-Sinowatz-Das-Lexikon-der-Waldheim-Jahre.
43. A photo from the Austrian National library's picture collection features the wooden horse and a placard with the equation 'Doing one's duty under National Socialism = Mass murder'. Retrieved 8 April 2018 from http://www.bildarchivaustria.at/Preview/1357708.jpg.
44. See Georg Hoffmann-Ostenhof, 'Das Holzpferd', in Milo Dor (ed.), *Die Leiche im Keller: Dokumente des Widerstands gegen Dr. Kurt Waldheim* (Vienna: Picus, 1988), 14.
45. See Kuno Knöbl, 'Die Geschichte des Waldheim-Holzpferdes' for the background to the horse's origins. Retrieved 8 April 2018 from http://www.repclub.at/geschichte.
46. Manocher Shahabi, 'Der trojanische Esel', in Frederick Baker and Elisabeth Boyer, *Wiener Wandertage: eine Dokumentation* (Klagenfurt: Wieser, 2002), 311–13.
47. Jay Rosellini, *Haider, Jelinek, and the Austrian Culture Wars* (Createspace Independent Publishing, 2009), 138. My discussions here are indebted to Rosellini's perceptive analysis of the 1990s.
48. Josef Haslinger's *Politik der Gefühle: ein Essay über Österreich* (Darmstadt: Luchterhand, 1987) is one of the important contributions in the long list of studies of Austrian politics and Austrian mentality.
49. Rosellini, *Haider, Jelinek, and the Austrian Culture Wars*, 139–40.
50. The poster can be viewed at http://www.demokratiezentrum.org/wissen/bilder.html?index=562. Rudolf Scholten, Michael Häupl and Ursula Pasterk (all SPÖ) held influential positions in the 1990s, Häupl as Mayor of Vienna and Scholten as Minister for Culture.
51. Andreas Mölzer, *Zur Identität Österreichs: Gedanken zum Millennium 1996* (Vienna: Österreichische Landsmannschaft, 1996).
52. Emphasis added. See Artnet, 'Haider's Cultural Scene in Carinthia', 3 September 2000, retrieved 8 April 2018 from http://www.artnet.com/magazine/news/artnetnews/artnetnews3-9-00.asp.
53. Artnet, 'Haider's Cultural Scene in Carinthia'.
54. Bernhard Hadolt, 'Shit and Politics: The Case of the Kolig Debate in Austria', *Iš: Medische Antropologie* 11(1) (1999), 179–98, at 180.
55. Other scholars have investigated some of these highly important essays. See, for example, Geoff Howes, 'The Politics of Rhetoric in Some Recent Austrian Essays', *New German Critique* 93 (2004), 43–53; and Dagmar Lorenz, 'The Struggle for a Civil Society and Beyond: Austrian Writers and Intellectuals Confronting the Political Right', *New German Critique* 93 (2004), 19–41.

56. Robert Misik and Doron Rabinovici, 'Vorwort: Aufbruch der Zivilgesellschaft', in Robert Misik and Doron Rabinovici (eds), *Republik der Courage Wider die Verhaiderung* (Berlin: Aufbau, 2000), 9–14, at 10.
57. For analysis of this period of intense debate, see Janet Stewart, ' "Nicht die Kunst darf sich vereinnahmen lassen": Franzobel, Literature and Politics in the "New Austria"', *German Life and Letters* 55(2) (2002), 219–33.

Chapter 2

PERFORMING POLITICS
On the Sounds, Symbols and Sites of Resistance

Tu Felix Austria, Protest!

Austria, a small European country of just under nine million inhabitants, has but a slim track record in protest movements or civic unrest.[1] This might suggest that the art associated with protest might also be rather slight, but this is indubitably not the case, as the present volume demonstrates. Political engagement and protest are, of course, not always born out of specifically 'political' events, and the performances of the avant-garde Wiener Gruppe or Wiener Aktionisten artists are just one case in point. Equally, there have been only rare moments in postwar history when Austria's political leaders or specific political events have attracted international attention. Chapter 1 has signalled the importance of one such occasion, namely the Waldheim affair of the 1980s, both in terms of how it galvanized public protest and in terms of how the foundations were laid for future social movements to prosper via an organization such as the Republikanischer Club, for example, and via popular consensus around the need to face up to Austria's fascist past. The 1980s saw a new stage in Austria's changing self-understanding as a nation. It is precisely because of the infrequency of civil protest in Austria and the relative scale of the millennial protests for such a small country that this particular wave of anti-government opposition attracted such attention and is so significant in the history of the Second Republic. As we will see in the following discussion, the cultural phenomena associated with the anti-coalition protests are extensive and highly creative. This chapter seeks to capture some of these contributions in the context of an analysis of the phenomenon of cultural resistance as an everyday practice and as a mode of political response.

When *Time* magazine elected as its 'person of the year' in 2011 'the protester', it was obviously not the peaceful protests of the alpine republic that influenced how it viewed the generic protester. The journalist qualified that 'the stakes are very different in different places. In North America and most of Europe, there are no dictators, and dissidents don't get tortured. Any day that Tunisians, Egyptians or Syrians occupy streets and squares, they know that some of them might be beaten or shot'.[2] Social wellbeing is enjoyed by the vast majority of the Austrian population. It is a rich European nation by every index for measuring the welfare, health and progress of a nation. Additionally, Austrians do not need to fight for political empowerment; rather, it is the intact, legitimate system of democratic election that brought about the result against which so many thousands of Austrians protested and that caused the EU Member States to levy sanctions against Austria in 2000. Austria is not known as a country of protest or strife. Whilst the motto of centuries-long Habsburg foreign policy strategy, 'Bella gerant alii, tu felix Austria nube' (Let others wage war: thou, happy Austria, marry), as well as the pope's acclamation of peaceable, democratic 1970s Austria as an island of the blessed,[3] are doubtless somewhat mythologized descriptions of Austria, the general characterization of its postwar determination to seek consensus and peaceable solutions has a strong basis in its system of political governance.

With the inauguration of the ÖVP-FPÖ coalition government in February 2000, mass anti-government demonstrations known as the 'Donnerstagsdemonstrationen' (Thursday Demonstrations) became a regular feature of Viennese and Austrian everyday life, showing that the Austrian people were, indeed, capable of large-scale public protest. Of course, political dissent and debate take place in private spaces too, as well as in the social, public spaces of the bar, restaurant and café. But it is in the more visible public spaces that effective protest generally finds expression, whether as the collective, organized act of demonstrating along with all its attendant visible and audible manifestations or in more clandestine, smaller group or individual acts of protest such as graffitiing and sticker-posting.

This chapter sets out to explore some of the immediate appropriations of public space for the manifestation of protest in everyday culture. In discussing the cultural manifestations of protest, I do not focus on the cultural policies, or 'Kulturpolitik' of political parties, or specifically on the ways in which politics more broadly is conducted – that is, how the 'culture' of political work has developed or changed.[4] Instead, in the chapters of this book I address a wide selection of cultural outpourings mostly in the form of films, novels and plays that express opposition or criticize the ideas of the 'new' Austria. I probe the contribution made by these works of art and the aesthetic approaches they employ. The present chapter, on the other hand, concerns itself less with published cultural artefacts and more with the everyday performance of cultural resistance in Austria's capital city, Vienna. This is not to claim that cultural protest only happened in the country's capital, but Vienna was the location of the largest Thursday mass protests and provides a concentrated locus for my analysis. Thus, some of the sites of popular resistance, the graffiti, the literary readings, protest activities, accessories and insignia will be discussed alongside the better-known, organized performance of Christoph Schlingensief's *Big Brother*-style event, 'Bitte liebt Österreich' (2000; 'Please Love Austria'). At a time when politics itself seems to hinge on the effective public performance of politicians (see Chapter 5) and on the appropriation of public media for the broadcasting of political messages, it can hardly be surprising that new forms of interactive cultural protest are forged and that activist cultural practitioners choose to adopt hybrid media forms to unsettle, ironize and recolonize public spaces. This is precisely what happened in Vienna around the turn of the millennium.

The composition of the weekly demonstration walks and the many other protest actions is not characterized by a uniform body of protagonists. There is no signal prototype or iconic protester who represents the Austrian demonstrations or who has been idealized by media representations as a catalyst to the protest events in the way of, for example, the Tunisian fruit seller who set himself on fire in 2011.[5] The Austrian protesters of 1999/2000 onwards came from all 'walks' of society and from a variety of different party-political and politicocultural positions. Political groups and organizations had many different motivations for objecting to what was talked about at the time as the political turn in Austria. As one might expect, the left wing represented a large proportion of the protesters and encompassed a broad range of different groupings, not just the SPÖ. But there were many ÖVP voters too. The latter felt aggrieved that their party had reneged on its pre-election reassurance that it would not be negotiating a coalition with the FPÖ. Anglo-Austrian filmmaker, activist and academic Frederick Baker maintains that all of the different groupings were united by their common ground of expressing resistance to the coalition government:

> The word 'resistance' was reborn on 2 February 2000. I remember the peculiar calm at the start of the first demonstration. Those taking part were so diverse and the situation so complex. The simple word 'resistance' united Greens, Social Democrats, Communists, disillusioned ÖVP-voters, and floating voters alike.[6]

Adopting the terminology of resistance was itself not without controversy. Hitherto associated mostly with resistance against fascism (historical fascism, or policies and people seen as neofascist), the term 'Widerstand' was explored very thoroughly by Doron Rabinovici, himself a major voice in the anti-*schwarzblau* protests. Rabinovici and others feel that to use the term 'Widerstand' in this new and multiple other contexts is to devalue those who have resisted dictators and oppressive regimes, often suffering atrocious personal consequences.[7] Nevertheless, the term gained purchase, not least because it stands as a common denominator shared by the many different political positions and causes that were unified in the movement of people against the coalition government. One-word slogans are also easy to say in chorus by masses of people, although the protests spawned a long list of other slogans, either shouted by the protesters or on banners and placards.[8]

The demographic and political mix was evident at the anti-coalition protests, with film documentations released at the time (see Chapter 4) providing an insight into the breadth of the protest movement and activities. The collections of photographers also attest to the demonstrations having drawn attendance from far afield.[9] There were anti-fascist groupings, lesbian and gay rights groups (such as RAW, 'Rosa Antifa Wien'), or women's groups, such as 'Ceiberweiber', whose objections of course encompassed the new government's decision to abolish the Frauenministerium[10] as well as the traditionalist gender views and family policies of the consolidated right wing. The placards and banners are testimony to the many positions and individual platforms from which protesters came and to the complex and multiple grounds participants had for expressing themselves. Two pensioners, Romana Müllner and Anneliese Gesswein, could be seen with their placard demanding solidarity with the Sinti and Roma people of Austria, for example.[11] Generally demonstrating as a group of three elderly friends, the group were dubbed 'Die drei Weisinnen' ('the Three Wise Women') to echo the nickname of the EU sanctions report by the 'Three Wise Men' (see Chapter 1). Whether ordinary folk like Müllner or famous cabarettists like Alfred Dorfer, protesters refuted in their speeches and writings the allegation that the demonstrations were populated, as politicians such as Wolfgang Schüssel had maintained, by 'lefties' and by the 'internet generation', a bunch of anarchists, terrorists, social outcasts and spongers.[12] Müllner and friends generally walked at the back of the demo, attending every week bar one for two years. They were in an excellent position to be able to see the supposedly countless wanton acts of violence and damage carried out by the protesters. Müllner confirms, to the contrary, that the demonstrations were peaceable but loud; she thanked the many spectators who had waved or signalled their support from their apartment windows or beeped their car horns in solidarity.[13]

When contemplating this 'local' protest and any potential overlaps with a wider network of social movements and protest issues, a glance at the programme agenda of the FPÖ and, indeed, of the coalition between the two parties, the People's Party and the Freedom Party, suggests that the economic agenda of further privatization, cuts in health, education and welfare spending, and greater spending on defence and on law and order are very much in line with neoliberalist manifestoes in many countries, certainly in Europe and North America. Rick Kuhn provides a summary from an international, socialist perspective, indicating that the government's objectives included 'cutting immigration quotas ... targeting illegal immigrants, discrimination in schools against children who do not speak German . . . as well as standard conservative measures like further privatisations, cuts in health, education and welfare spending, greater outlays on defense, law and order' that are not specific to Austria.[14] It was the expression of anti-immigrationist views in their much more provocatively racist form that was the most obvious cause of the EU's sanctions against Austrian in 2000 pending an investigation into whether or not the country's political parties and by implication its inaugurated government was guilty of xenophobic practices. I maintain, then, that although in turn-of-the-millennium Austria the protests look very local, they can be seen as a microcosm of more globalized protests.

Austria was dubbed by many at the time as a kind of exemplification of, or even catalyst for, a spread of legitimization of extreme-right-wing political parties. Where journalist Sigrid Löffler spoke in the 1990s about the 'Verhaiderung' or Haiderization of Austria, at the turn of the millennium, philosopher and social scientist Oliver Marchart was heralding the process of 'Austrifying' Europe: 'the Austrian events in fact announced a movement towards what I would call the 'fourth' way of the ultra-right . . . conservative parties all over Europe – with the notable exception of France – started to form coalitions with the extreme xenophobic right wherever they could. So, it did not come as a surprise that the EU would not react anymore'.[15] Marchart would seem to have been remarkably prescient. With Austria inaugurating an ÖVP-FPÖ coalition once again in the final days of December 2017, there has been no international outcry from the EU or indeed much response at all to Austria's renewed acceptance of the far right into its national council.

Wandering Thoughts

The two modes of protest I have elected to discuss here are chosen for their apparently contrasting nature. They are, however, both prime examples of the ways in which artistic productions can probe or provoke new models of civic participation and problematize too easy categorizations such as 'art' or 'politics'. In particular, I will examine more closely two modes of street protest: first, the protest 'marches' themselves (the above-mentioned 'Donnerstagsdemonstrationen') and their artistic correlatives; and, second, a performance installation by German artist Christoph Schlingensief, entitled 'Bitte liebt Österreich'. Observations about the imaginary associative 'soundscape' of these two urban activities will allow us to consider the ways in which these actions or activities imagine a different kind of Austrian cityscape and governance. The chapter then homes in on the actual musical protest generated in response to the black-blue protests and analyses some of their identifying features. However, also of importance in this chapter are the markers of everyday protest exhibited, performed and disseminated by the protesters, that is, the insignia, 'accessories', graffiti, chants and slogans.

It can be argued that the weekly Thursday protest marches occupy a similar hybrid artistic function to Christoph Schlingensief's art installation. The walks are also shot through with acoustic resonances, both 'diegetic' in the physical narrative or action space of the marches themselves (the sounds, songs, chants and traffic of the demo) and also 'imaginary' in the interpretative provocations triggered by this protest phenomenon (for example, the allusions made in popular protest music). There is nothing new at all about protest marches or, indeed, about them being accompanied by music, either as prearranged instrumental accompaniment or as spontaneous protester-generated noise. Theorists tell us that:

> walking can represent an act of spatial transformation (displacing cars with politicized pedestrians, obstructing sidewalks with striking workers, and filling otherwise empty public squares with political demonstrators) ... forms of collective walking represent important moments of political praxis and subject formation. By literally falling in step with the crowd, individuals experience a sense of social solidarity and 'collective effervescence' (Durkheim 1965) that can transform social consciousness.[16]

In Vienna, the objective of the protest marches and the reasons for this mass 'social solidarity' were not primarily to do with any notion of conquering a particular public space in the sense of 'Reclaim the Streets'-style protests, nor were they about making environmental protests about the streets. The routes taken by the demonstrators were different every week, sometimes being kept secret until the last moment to avoid the possibility of being obstructed by the police. The precise routes, duration and associated events of individual demos are not easily established, nor is it necessary in order for us to see artistic and political meanings. Partial chronologies and accounts are still available for consultation in print and on the internet.[17]

The protest walks that sprang up in Austria's capital city continued weekly every Thursday for two years and then just sporadically after that time. Following a first mass rally on 19 February 2000, the subsequent weekly gatherings became known as the 'Donnerstagsdemonstrationen', a term that has become anchored in the political memory of contemporary Austria and is redolent of the famous 'Montagsdemonstrationen' (Monday demonstrations) in the months before the fall of the Berlin Wall and the – better-known – political Wende of 1989. The events were also quickly known as the 'Wiener Wandertage' or Viennese hiking days, with even Vienna's chief of police, Peter Stiedl, talking about individual events as a 'long night of hiking' (lange Wandernacht).[18] Some see in the hiking terminology an allusion to the predominantly (though, as attested above, not exclusively) young demographic of the walks and feel that the term is suggestive of a kind of school outing or 'Klassenausflug'.[19] A stronger argument for the terminology is in the demonstrators' insistence that their protests be peaceable and consensual. No one was forced to join and the procession encompassed many different perspectives. The writer Marlene Streeruwitz elaborates on the poetics of walking in her thoughts on the protest movement. It is important to stress the very mode of *walking* as opposed to *marching*, she insists: 'What we do is hiking. Not marching. That's a first step.'[20] The puns are almost impossible to avoid, but as well as this being 'a first step' in what Streeruwitz and many others saw as a different kind of political project, it is also a different way of elaborating or amplifying a kind of protest that does not simply counter violent discourse and action with more of the same: 'the Thursday hikes are a statement. Against racism. Going along means making this statement. Every man and woman stomps out their own statement against racism'.[21] The point of the protest walks is summed up in one of the preferred slogans of the protesters, 'Wir gehen solange bis Ihr geht' ('we'll be walking until you take a hike'). Movement or motion is designed to cause more movement – that of the coalition government out of office.[22] One group of protesters donned long trench coats and dark glasses, calling themselves the 'GehSTAPO'. Their word play suggests not that the state machinery's controlling ways were 'geheim' (secret), as in the implied national socialist precursor, the Gestapo, but that an extreme-right government should just *go* ('geh').

The role of hiking in Austria's domestic and foreign tourist and leisure industry is significant, but is not my focus here; it is a trope that emerges in some of the examples discussed in later chapters too. What is of significance here is that the protest movement colonizes a rurally connoted term for its – urban – protest activities. 'Wandern' is not really something one does in the city, but a new kind of wanderlust certainly burgeoned as the protests tapped into different participant groups and their motivations.[23] Rebecca Solnit underscores the hybridity of this protest form: 'Public marches mingle the language of the pilgrimage, in which one walks to demonstrate one's commitment, with the strike's picket line, in which one demonstrates the strength of one's group . . . and the festival, in which the boundaries between strangers recede.'[24] The Viennese walks themselves took multiple different routes through the city and were not ostensibly planned by any individuals or organizers. 'There is no organizer, the demo organizes itself', Baker and Boyer maintain, and the textbook entry in a lexicon of Austrian political terminology published seven years later talks of the phenomenon as being 'von einer relativ inhomogenen Personengruppe wie der "Plattform Demokratische Offensive" getragen' (carried by a relatively diverse group of people, like the Democratic Offensive Platform).[25] The walks spawned a wide range of art forms either as accompaniments to the protests (dances, slogans on banners, songs being sung, poetry being performed) or as later accounts of or reflections on the protest walks (short stories, poems, films, photography and so on). There were several collections of many of these artistic outpourings published during the times of the first coalition itself. They include a collection of the resistance readings that took place weekly near the alternative 'Embassy of Concerned Men and

Women Citizens' (Botschaft besorgter Bürger und Bürgerinnen), a self-styled *Führer* or old-fashioned 'Guidebook', and an anthology of pieces by women against right-wing politics.[26]

With both the Schlingensief installation event and the Viennese hiking days, it is possible to see how the activities engage with their local space, how they interact with the already imbued significance of those spaces and the practices associated with them, and how they come to inscribe new meanings onto those urban spaces. (Some protesters literally inscribe meanings in the form of graffiti, but this sense is addressed below.) The terminology 'Wiener Wandertage' almost symbiotically invokes the Vienna Woods, the extensive woodland and meadows flanking Vienna's northwest boundary, much extolled in painting, for example by the Biedermeier artist Ferdinand Georg Waldmüller, and in music many times over. Society balls to this day have their guests waltzing to Johann Strauss' 'Tales from the Vienna Woods' (1868). These, then, are the romantic associations of peaceable, carefree Viennese walks in the city and its environs that the protesters wished to debunk. However, the demos were not 'eco'-protests and did not have the *Wienerwald* (Vienna Woods) as their destination. The walks would generally incorporate some of Vienna's grand, inner circular avenue, the 'Ringstraße' and would certainly focus on the inner districts of the city. The main site for the protesters' rallies – and, indeed, for most large-scale public commemorations in Vienna, such as those for the Austrian Nationalfeiertag on 26 October – was the Heldenplatz or Heroes' Square, in front of the Imperial palace, the Hofburg, that now houses a museum and the national library. The protest movement could be said to be offering a different mobile performance or 'reading' of Vienna's urban spaces. They take an ironic approach to the normal walker's interaction with the city space. In a sense, they usurp the leisurely pace of the touristic gazer in city-sightseeing and project different readings onto the touristic sites of Vienna – the parliament building, the state theatre and the Viennese opera house. A photo of one of the demos is made to look like a picture postcard and is marked 'Best wishes from the Heldenplatz' in the manner in which tourists normally sign off their greetings home. This time, however, it is not the normal, sanitized and nostalgic view of Habsburg Austria and the splendour of its imperial architecture that is on display, but the sea of people with their banners aloft, assembled in front of the Hofburg to protest against the inauguration of the coalition government.[27]

As with Schlingensief's 'Bilderzerstörungsmaschine' (image destruction machine), protesting members of the public and artist-protesters alike are engaged in destroying images and in working, often unconsciously, against what has been called the 'postcarding of the past'. Richard Price coins this term to talk about the way in which a location can be stripped of its problematic past and used to express the sanitized or commodified meaning that suits the message or regime of the present day.[28] As a 'lieu de mémoire', or memory space,[29] the Heldenplatz has become strongly associated with a particular twentieth-century colonization of its space: it was from the balcony of the Hofburg palace that Adolf Hitler proclaimed his homeland's entry into the Third Reich.[30] For this reason, Streeruwitz feels that it was important to have five or six Jewish civil servants addressing the rally she documents on 20 February 2000: 'it was particularly important on this, the Heroes' Square. 300,000 people applauded enthusiastically. Showed solidarity. It was a strong pledge to change the culture of this country'.[31] Events like this, then, work at imbuing the space – here of the Heldenplatz – with different meanings, in the manner of the Heldenplatz 'postcard' described above.

Inscribing, Projecting and Embodying Resistance

Graffiti is not always intended to interact with the specific surface that has been chosen for its inscription and thus might not directly use the specific location for its impact. After all, toilet doors, school desks, trees and many other objects have had to bear their inscribers' thoughts, protests or love declarations throughout the centuries. With regard to politically motivated graffiti that appeared around the time of the anti-coalition protests, it is not possible to gain a general overview of publicly committed graffiti, but through photographs or films, we can see some of the protests that were scrawled, sprayed or stuck on surfaces around this time. A simple road sign for 'No Entry' is inscribed with 'No Jörg', for example, changing the traffic sign into a political statement. The 'No Entry' sign is, we note, a circle of red, white (a horizontal strip) and red. The Austrian flag's colours combine with an internationally accessible message to suggest that Austria does not want Jörg Haider. Walls are sprayed with 'Widerstand' or with 'O 5', a re-adoption of the anti-Nazi resistance symbol during Austria's years of annexation (see Chapter 4).

These and other examples feature in Anglo-Austrian filmmaker Frederick Baker's work. Baker performs a kind of *mise-en-abyme*, just like Schlingensief does in his installation. Schlingensief has a play within a play as asylum seekers, supposedly taken from their 'real' containers or camps, are put into an artistic container in the middle of Vienna. Elfriede Jelinek also attended the installation to create with the inmates a little puppet theatre play, which the container inmates then performed. For his film *Erosion und Wi(e)derstand* (2003), Baker takes images of graffiti from the Thursday demos of 2000 and reprojects them onto the walls of Vienna in 2001 and 2002.[32] 'Widerstand' is re-inscribed onto the walls of the Café Ritter. In the second part of the film, shot in 2002, the filmmaker takes his film-projector to a protest walk and beams footage of previous marches onto the bodies of those at the current one, including onto the bodies of policemen at the event. The body of the state, in the form of the policeman, is co-opted as a strategy of resistance. Aesthetically, Baker contains the images of the Thursday demos by capturing them on film, but with the intention of allowing them to continue to flow, by casting them out onto different screens as a live action or, indeed, by keeping them on film to be rescreened at a later date. The filmmaker keeps the images recirculating.

Julia Zdarsky is another artist whose projection interventions featured at protest rallies. Her chosen surfaces were the buildings of power, for example, the Austrian chancellery, the Prime Minister's offices on the Ballhausplatz, at the other end of the Heldenplatz to the Hofburg. According to fellow projectionist, Baker, Zdarsky – or Starsky as her pseudonym became – projected from the top of a double-decker bus during a two-month period of the protests. 'In the cold Viennese winter of 2000 the projector became a tool in the democratic process', Baker observes.[33] As with Baker's reprojection of the word 'Widerstand', Starsky's installations are also a kind of projection graffiti, albeit only temporary in nature. Her Vienna 2000 project was termed 'Zufallsindoktrinator' ('the accidental indoctrinator'), the aim being to produce 'plötzliche erleuchtungen von kurzer dauer [*sic*]' ('sudden, transient realizations').[34] On her webpage description of the project, the artist declares her intention to counter the phraseology of power and politics. By playing with the politicians' catchphrases or simply beaming them back in slightly modified form, she highlights their absurdity and gives the spectator a new context and time to reflect on what might be the essence of some of the policy-making. The simple 'jeda is a minderheit' ('everyone's a minority'), for example, with its lower-case lettering, its dialect-sounding, gender-neutral modification of the masculine pronoun 'jeder' (or the feminine form 'jede') to the coinage 'jeda' sends back a message to the Kanzler that the rights of so-called minorities should not be disregarded.[35] To an extent, then, the artistic work of Starsky is site-specific. She glosses her work, noting that 'the accidental indoctrinator's interventions into public spaces open up an understanding of the contingency of thought and behaviour patterns'. They promote an understanding of what is possible in public space, she states, 'and how the public can render this space public in a very different way'.[36] The public is key to her endeavour and is needed to help read the space differently.

Public architecture is often a focus for 'occupation' activities or graffiti actions. In Vienna, one of the obvious choices is the parliament building with its Pallas Athene fountain, statue and grand entrance crescent. Situated on the Ringstraße not far from the Hofburg, the Pallas Athene structure symbolizes both democracy (the parliament) and justice and wisdom (the Justizpalast is nearby). A number of demo activities utilized this location, but the most controversial occasion was on 28 May 2001, when a group of Performing Resistance activists (including Hubsi Kramar) climbed up and chained themselves onto the fountain, unfurling an enormous banner with the slogan in red letters: 'Widerstand'. A full chronology of the events can still be read.[37] Parliamentary responses to enquiries submitted by then FPÖ politician Helene Partik-Pablé are also available to read and to answer questions about how much damage had been caused by the Thursday demos, how many people were involved, whether the identities of people involved in a university sit-in had been established and so on and so forth. The extent of the damage was not significant.[38]

Whereas Christoph Schlingensief's 'contained' art spilled further and further out into political meanings, the fluid action of the Thursday protest walks is, by definition, not contained. The police and political parties did try to contain the walks (unsuccessfully) by pursuing individuals they deemed to be the organizers and demanding that the events be registered in advance. The walks became art, too, as we see here. There is, no doubt, a certain dramaturgy of events to any protest rally – with prominent public intellectuals and supporters invited to appear and address participants. Then there is the performance 'costume' of protesters that ranged from the simple placard as stage 'prop' to the more elaborate outfit normally involving the protest colour of orange (later, ironically, the colour to be adopted by Haider's new political party, the Bündnis Zukunft Österreich, in 2005), but also frequently with symbolic use of the blue party colour of the FPÖ and the black of the ÖVP.

'Containing' the Protest: Thinking outside the Box

It is difficult to categorize Christoph Schlingensief's contribution to the post-Wende protests. On the face of it, his commissioned piece for the Vienna summer festival of 2000 ('Wiener Festwochen') can readily be identified as art. Schlingensief had been asked by festival director Luc Bondy to create a piece for the festival and it is fair to say that an expression of protest against Austria's coalition government was part of the design specification. The artwork or site-specific installation is internationally known and has generated a sizeable secondary literature.[39] The installation, its conception and construction, the progression of the six-day duration of the artwork, together with interviews with Schlingensief and contemporaneous reactions from many different commentators (artists, philosophers and collaborators, as well as television news contributors), have all been captured on Viennese filmmaker Paul Poet's 2002 documentary of the event, *Ausländer raus! Schlingensiefs Container* (*Foreigners out! Schlingensief's Container*).[40] Clearly, my discussion of the work of art here is both made possible by the DVD release as well as mediated through the film, together with its paratextual framework of materials (commentaries, interviews and so on). However, this applies to all of the cultural events and artefacts discussed in this chapter. The author of the present study was not a participant observer.

'Bitte liebt Österreich' was conceived along the lines of the immensely popular international reality TV franchise *Big Brother*. Essentially, it involved the short-term enclosure in a temporary, building container 'house' of a group of asylum-seeking participants. Those living in the container were to have their activities observed on a web TV platform (emulating the *Big Brother* formula) and each evening would see the announcement of the vote as to which inmate would be evicted from the house and then, purportedly, driven to the Austrian border to be expelled from the 'house' of Austria. At the event's inauguration, the container guests were announced and taken off their bus into the makeshift house to the sounds of 'welcoming' brass band music. Christoph Schlingensief encouraged the tourists who might be present – from Japan, Belgium and France, for example, and anyone who might be passing by – to take photographs and show them to people at home with the message that what they were witnessing was Austria and the future of Europe.

Schlingensief's artistic ruse invites multiple levels of meaning and has a strong dialectical force. It is not an easy piece for its ambulatory audience to read (or, indeed, for those who followed the web TV coverage at the time).[41] Those who stopped to engage with the installation could become spectators, or voyeurs, and thus silent collaborators in the process of evicting the foreigners. Many became vocal, and fierce arguments ensued between individual members of the public and between the public and Schlingensief himself. Schlingensief utilized a number of opinionated visitors (a veteran wearing his uniform jacket, cap and medals; a frenzied, middle-aged woman), sometimes giving them his loudhailer to spout their pro-eviction, anti-foreigner message and unwittingly become artistic *agents provocateur*. Pursuing the projectionist strategies discussed above, Tara Forrest underlines how Schlingensief's installation can also be said to function in terms of a kind of projection, albeit in a metaphorical sense: 'In a statement that recalls [Alexander] Kluge's analysis of both the "film in the spectator's head" and the symbiotic relationship between an active, reflective mode of engagement and a dynamic public sphere, Schlingensief describes the container compound as "an empty surface" upon which the audience was able to "project" their own film.'[42]

The hybridity and paradigm-shifting force of the 'Bitte liebt Österreich' installation can be seen in conjunction with aesthetic theories and performance practices of participation. We could see Schlingensief's installation along Nicolas Bourriaud's lines of the artwork as 'social interstice', whereby art 'take[s] as its theoretical horizon the realm of human interactions and its social context, rather than the assertion of an independent and *private* symbolic space'.[43] Bourriaud's idea of 'relational aesthetics' sees meaning as something that is collectively or socially produced and interpreted. It is about 'judging artworks on the basis of the inter-human relations which they represent, produce or prompt'.[44] Schlingensief himself advocated Joseph Beuys' idea of 'the "social sculpture", "a social organism as a work of art" that would help mould and shape life'.[45] As the week of the installation drew on and the debates picked up on the street and in the newspapers and bulletins, tension mounted and the work of 'art' spilled out and became a work of politics. The festival organizers even distributed flyers explaining that this was a work of art – which Schlingensief purportedly endeavoured to retrieve and destroy. A lorry was parked in the vicinity denouncing the installation as a dangerous game that played on people's emotions and inviting objectors to complain to the city's mayor. Questions were raised as to the misuse of public funding and pressure was put on the organizers.[46]

Timon Beyes sees Schlingensief's container action[47] as functioning in the manner of Jacques Rancière's ideas of 'intervention'. For Rancière, 'politics is first and foremost an intervention upon the visible and the sayable'.[48] Schlingensief follows Rancière's idea that disagreement is a key political tool. Both philosopher and artist recognize the constructive power of creating and tapping into a field of tensions. This, commentators note, is what Schlingensief does by not making it clear what is art and what is politics, by blurring boundaries and not making it easy for viewers to know how to react. By repeating anti-foreigner slogans from Jörg Haider's speeches and by having a huge banner saying 'Foreigners out' on the top of the *Big Brother* container, Schlingensief forces a kind of 'double bind': 'Those who oppose the removal of the "Foreigners out" sign are put in an awkward position due to its content; those who want it removed find themselves advocating censorship of art.'[49] Apart from this abstract theorization of the internal contradictions, the event itself was not easily understood by the Thursday demonstrators, whose protest walk even attempted to shut down the installation. Political affiliation or voting preference was not the only credential for understanding or navigating the difficult dynamics of Schlingensief's artwork.

Schlingensief described his enterprise as a mechanism endeavouring to destroy the image of things,[50] an objective he surely achieved. As site-specific art, his installation obviously impacted on the cityscape and city practices of Vienna. Its specific location outside the Viennese opera house at the foot of one of the city's most prestigious shopping avenues meant that it disrupted the foot-flow of shoppers, employees and tourists from home and abroad. In short, the location of the action might have been spatially 'contained' as art, but the effects of the action exploded out into many discussion spaces (domestic, journalistic, political and medial). The installation space does not use the Heldenplatz, or the Ballhausplatz, the location of Austria's Chancellery, at the epicentre of meeting and rally in Vienna, as discussed above. The choice of location departs from the normal political logic, once again preventing easy categorization. However, the opera house location nearly did not happen, as the artist recounts in an interview. Opera house staff claimed that the action 'is a strain on our singing business, the practice rooms would then be out of use, the singers cannot practise, the voices will lose clarity, we must object'.[51] Other spaces were offered by the city government, their preference being the car park at the back of Vienna's Jugendstil Secession art museum, a distance away from the central pedestrian zone. In the end, the opera house staff expressed their satisfaction with a location outside their building further forward than the one that had been suggested. It seems likely that the Vienna opera house feared reputational damage and tourist repulsion. The spokesperson's stated objection to how the installation would impact on 'clarity of voice' is, in fact, one of the intentional outcomes of Schlingensief's piece. Into the soundscape of the Herbert-von-Karajan Square were injected – the 'found' or documented sound of Haider's speeches, Schlingensief's provocative, apparently pro-FPÖ loudhailer announcements, the arguments of passers-by and the mock-celebratory 'oompah' music of the brass band next to the container site. The 'imaginary' sound of opera music plays along silently only in the viewer/participant's head. Poet's film deploys a similar estranging technique by using incidental, nondiegetic music from the *fin-de-siècle* Wiener *Lied*, 'So a Kongoneger hat's halt guat' ('It's a Fine Life for the Congo Negro'). Superficially, the lyric would appear to flatter the appearance of the black Congolese, but the text is really full of discriminatory clichés and belies the colonialist politics of its origins.[52] I have begun to discuss here not just physical cityscapes but also the soundscape of Vienna's protests. In the following section, I consider more closely the plethora of musical and sound interventions into the politics of the FPÖ-ÖVP coalition.

Political Soundings

The following discussion seeks to capture and analyse a moment in music-making in Austria when musicians from a wide range of backgrounds (albeit mostly popular musical) used their art to try to cut across state politics by countering this with different melodies, different rhythms and different messages of what it means to be Austrian.[53] Music is a tool that is occasionally used by politicians too, but it is not within my remit here to examine, for example, either the Carinthian folk-song singing appearances of Jörg Haider or the much more prolific 'rapping' of H.C. Strache, his successor as FPÖ leader.[54] Rather, the endeavour here is to demonstrate the wide-ranging contribution made by musician-protesters and to undertake an analysis of their thematic and aesthetic practices. I hope to draw attention to a genre of protest that ought to have a wider impact and thus to augment music history and scholarship, which in the case of Austria is ordinarily more interested in the dominant idiom of mainstream, classical music. Whereas Barbara Lebrun can attest, for example, to the 'Frenchness' of protest and demonstrate the long heritage of musical protest forms in France, similar claims are difficult to make for Austria.[55]

One might expect official, state-associated music to be used by protest movements in political parody, but the Austrian national anthem, for example, does not feature in my corpus. The national anthem was used in this way during the demos and is an element in a few of the short protest films that were made around the time of, and in reaction to, the FPÖ-ÖVP coalition government. Film music is not a category considered here as I concentrate on music as a separate genre and not in combination with visual material. However, one example can attest to the explosively political possibilities of combining music and visuals. The music in Bernadette Huber's short film *Wie böse ist Österreich?* (1999; *How Evil is Austria?*) could itself have been deployed for shock value by changing its musical style or its lyrics; yet this is not the strategy chosen (see also Chapter 4).[56] Instead, to an orchestral rendering of the Austrian anthem 'Land der Berge' (1947), Huber's close-up visuals show a miniature national flag being born out of a woman's vulva and the expected colours of red-white-red turning to blue-white-blue (blue being the colour of the Freedom Party).

A national anthem is an exceptional category of music and does not sit easily with musicologist Philip Tagg's proposition that 'it's almost as if not seeing the music prevents us from consciously acknowledging its existence as music'.[57] Anthems tend to have a performative function – as part of the ceremonial process in awarding Olympic medals or in concluding university degree-awarding ceremonies. If Tagg talks of our 'scopocentric need for visual concretion of what we hear in order to consciously register its existence and, consequently, its potential effects'[58] and intends this to refer to visuals that show music being physically made, then Huber's visuals in fact do something similar. They do not necessarily invite the listener-viewer to muse over the chord progressions, cadences or dynamics of Austria's hymn, but they certainly ask the audience to register how Austria performs itself (not just literally through music) and to consider the potential effects of its national executive's actions.

Connoisseurs of Austrian popular music might expect the nationality-referencing genre of 'Austropop' to have steered clear of political intervention. Sometimes deemed to be a pejorative marker for a particular kind of engineered sound and trite lyric, frequently with dialect lyrics or flavour,[59] Austropop is not as uniformly anodyne as assumed. Christian Karner points out that Austropop has functioned as a 'site of political resistance and medium of cultural critique' through the decades.[60] Edward Larkey draws our attention, for example, to the hugely popular singer Hubert von Goisern's reworking of the Haydn-composed 'Gott erhalte Franz den Kaiser' hymn for the Habsburg Emperor Francis II and locates Goisern's reworking ('Gott erhalts', 1994) as, in part, a protest against the anti-foreigner campaign of Jörg Haider's FPÖ in the run-up to the referendum on accession to the EU in the early 1990s.[61]

The corpus under discussion here is an eclectic range of music that the author has assembled and sees as having common cause. It does not seek to be inclusive, nor is it possible to quote from all of the materials listed here. The music referenced dates from on or around the time of the first FPÖ-ÖVP coalition of 2000–2003 or from the early period of the second FPÖ-ÖVP coalition (2003–2007). The better-known, longstanding, rock and pop bands are represented, ranging from the heavy-metal style of Drahdiwaberl, the melodic, narrative-style Austropop of the legendary Wolfgang Ambros, Rainhard Fendrich and Georg Danzer, known collectively as Austria 3, and indeed the celebrated, satirical pop of the commercially highly successful, Erste Allgemeine Verunsicherung. Independent Austrian punk, rock and hip-hop artists mentioned include Brambilla, Conny Chaos und die Retortenkinder, and the Kaputtnicks, as well as a piece by the German punk band Die Ärzte. A rerelease by left-wing British protest folk and rock group Chumbawumba also lends the Austrian protesters 'prominente internationale Schützenhilfe' (prominent international support).[62] Some of the music discussed here was collected and aired as a retrospective by the radio station Radio Orange in 2004, coincidentally the first year of Austria's now annual Protest Songcontest event, which was inaugurated amongst the burgeoning of Austrian protest music in the early twenty-first century. The popular music corpus is augmented here by some additional reference to mock-choral work by a collective called Performing Resistance, a choral piece entitled 'Hohes Haus Musik: Kantate in F-Dur' by Gegenstimmen, electronic music by British-Austrian collaboration FURT and experimental, microtonal work by Austrian composer Georg Friedrich Haas from 2004.

It is not possible, nor would it yield much to establish the sales figures of these songs and use them as some kind of proof of the endorsement they have received or influence they have exerted. Listeners and fans buy music for all sorts of reasons and not just as signs of political allegiance. Moreover, many of the protest songs were given away or were downloadable for free after their public airing at concerts or demos. Analysis of the music played and the frequency and medium of broadcast would, of course, be interesting to ascertain, but must remain a project for musicological researchers. Instead, the tracks and compositions are interrogated for the various ways in which they express their counterhegemonic messages and give musical form to political criticism of Austria around the turn of the millennium.

I set aside the pessimistic view associated with Theodor W. Adorno that 'far from challenging the system, most music is part of the system'.[63] Instead, with Oliver Marchart it is possible to regard the musical protest practices as examples of burgeoning 'Soundpolitisierung' (sound politicization). Marchart asserts that it is not the type of sound itself that is to be identified as subversive, but that sound or music functions as a medium through which a community can grow and express its sense of political awareness:

> The political is now no longer sought in the sound itself, in the materiality (for example, its digital form) or indeed in its supposedly democratic means of production. The premise is no longer one that assumes electronic music to be inherently subversive or progressive or liberating ... Rather, it's a matter of a specific scene or community publicly opposing a government and demonstrating this with the means at their disposal. This is what constitutes its politicization.[64]

Furthermore, Marchart maintains that at that juncture at least (that is, in 1999/2000 shortly after the election shock), it was not a coherent set of political demands or position statements that was needed, but rather just one demand and that this boiled down to: 'Keine Koalition mit dem Rassismus. Oder noch kürzer: Weg mit der Regierung' (no coalition with racism. Or, more succinctly: down with the government).

As might be expected with a body of music that has been inspired by the same cause, it is possible to make some generalizations about the lyrics in this corpus. First and foremost, many of the songs contain statements that denounce the new government's policies and bear testament to the effect that the songwriter or singer did not vote for the FPÖ and does not hold with what the ÖVP-FPÖ coalition is deemed to stand for. The perceived xenophobia and anti-immigration stance of the FPÖ comes in for criticism, as do the planned reductions in welfare, cuts to the arts, and the proscriptive measures of the public media. Second, the broad sentiments or indeed the verbatim statements made by politicians (of either coalition party) also feature in many of the tracks analysed here. In 2000, hip-hop band Kaputtnicks rapped their own 'Brief an den Kanzler':

> Just think of 'free hormone treatment' or 'stop foreigners flooding in'
> After the event, we've no use for your apologisin'
> Stuff like 'naturally aggressive people whose skin is black',
> It should be the state to take action and fight back!
> Seems like 60 years isn't quite enough repression
> The new Right has arrived and is seeking acclamation.[65]

Austrians and Austria-watchers will recognize the FPÖ slogan 'Stop der Überfremdung' from the FPÖ campaign of 1999 (it also formed part of the 'stage' décor at Schlingensief's installation) and the controversial campaign by the then deputy leader of the FPÖ, Thomas Prinzhorn, who complained in 1999 that fertility treatment for immigrants was being funded by the Austrian state.[66]

Furthermore, as in other forms of artistic protest against the Austrian coalition government of 2000, there are direct criticisms of the then party leaders, Jörg Haider and Wolfgang Schüssel. Other politicians also attracted the opprobrium of the music scene. Foreign Secretary Benita Ferrero-Waldner (ÖVP) or Finance Minister Karl-Heinz Grasser (FPÖ) are two further examples. In the number 'B.E.N.I.T.A' by punk band Brambilla, the Foreign Secretary's smile functions like the Cheshire cat's, ubiquitous and immutable. Metonymically, the smile stands for the politician, but also suggests that the Austrian government's approach is one of smugness and superficiality. Ferrero-Waldner was alleged to have misled the media and the Genoese police, and to have made little diplomatic effort to secure the release of seventeen Austrian protesters against the G8 whose guilt she implied, claiming that they were already known to Austrian police, or 'amtsbekannt':[67] 'Can we really be surprised? / The killer argument "already known to the authorities" / And in the gaps between interviews / Can that smile really be sincere?'[68] The punk band Conny Chaos und die Retortenkinder pillory two other politicians by implication if not by explicit name in the number 'KHG' (probably named after Karl-Heinz Grasser, the FPÖ Minister of Finance from 2000 to 2004) and satirize the 'tax amnesty' that he wanted to introduce to allow tax defaulters to pay missing taxes anonymously. Meanwhile, in the track 'Lisi Gehrer', the eponymous ÖVP politician Elisabeth Gehrer's 2003 criticism of young Austrians too busy partying to settle and have children forms the background to the singer's heavily ironic narrative about refusing the advances of a joint-smoking 'Lisi Gehrer' at a party.[69]

Much as in a *roman à clef*, a fourth aspect in this musical typology includes songs where the intended object of attack or satire is very easily decodable, even if names are not mentioned directly. When German punk band Die Ärzte sing in 'Halsabschneider' from the perspective of God looking down on the world and musing that he hasn't done a bad job, the 'Arschloch' ('Arsehole') whose existence he bemoans in Austria, and rhymes with 'immer noch' ('still'), is not expressly named as Jörg Haider. This is, nevertheless, the equation the listener is invited to make. At 1 minute and 29 seconds, the track is very short. Together with its simple, clearly audible lyrics, melodic guitar line and occasional 'ah-ing' backing vocals, the laconic message 'aber leider gibt's in Österreich ein Arschloch/Immer noch' ('in Austria, alas, there's an arse/it's still a farce') is in sharp contrast to the angry musical style of the Kaputtnicks (above), but is nonetheless emphatic in suggesting the reprehensibility of the 'arsehole' it lampoons.[70]

Sampling and Plundering

One of the common aesthetic devices in this corpus right across the spectrum of musical genres is the use of what we could term textual leitmotifs or recurring themes. In the song-texts, as indeed in the literary materials of Austrian turn-of-the-millennium protest (in dramas by Elfriede Jelinek and Antonio Fian or in films by Walter Wippersberg and others), well-known public remarks by politicians are embedded into the texture of the artistic work. Stefan Weber, lead singer of the heavy-metal band Drahdiwaberl, uses the first-person plural to denote himself and fellow band members with humorous intent as all those forces that Chancellor Wolfgang Schüssel, his government and the pro-coalition media have decried as being behind the democratic protests against the new coalition government, that is, 'Anarcho-chaoten' ('rowdy anarchists'), 'Stalinisten' and 'die Internetgeneration'. The backing singers' lyrics in the protest song 'Torte statt Worte' ('Cream Pies, Not Words')[71] acknowledge the irony that Drahdiwaberl's 'best lines' are attributable to Wolf Martin and the pseudonymous Staberl. Martin wrote a daily poem for the arch-right-wing tabloid *Die Krone* until shortly before his death in 2012.

The text of the cantata in F major, 'Hohes Haus Musik', incorporates a line or two from Wolf Martin's provocative verses as well as excerpts from Wolfgang Schüssel's opening legislative speech. As well as this 'Regierungserklärung', Erke Duit also set to music text excerpts by critical writers such as Elfriede Jelinek, Margaret Kreidl, the dialect poet 'Hömal' and others. The performers are 'Gegenstimmen', a democratic, left-wing protest choir, a group that formed in 1989 to offer regular musical opposition to violence, war, fascism and inequality. With this piece (performed in several different venues in the summer of 2002), the intention was to express common cause with critical writers and to use their combined voices to express criticism rather than to wallow in suffering.[72] A published programme prints the texts but only supplies one page of the four-part vocal score, an excerpt taken from the opening chorus 'Das Leiden' ('The Suffering').[73]

At the other end of the spectrum is the very well-known band Erste Allgemeine Verunsicherung (EAV, formed in 1977 and regularly charting successfully in Austria), which has for four decades made a living out of comic-satirical song-writing. The band has enjoyed thirteen Top Ten singles, with its most successful track staying in the charts for twenty-two weeks. The track 'Valerie, Valera: Haiders Sprung in seiner Schüssel' uses spoken inserts between the sung verses and choruses. In a reasonably good imitation of Haider's regionally inflected German, a voice quotes verbatim the infamous and begrudging elucidation Haider offered to a journalist who probed his use of euphemistic terms to describe Nazi atrocities: 'In the Third Reich there were incidents that were not excusable. If you want, then yes, it was mass murder.'[74] There is also an element of musical allusion or intertextuality in EAV's piece. The song obviously references 'The Happy Wanderer' (Friedrich-Wilhelm Möller, 1953) in the hikers' refrain of 'Falderie/Faldera' and further attests to the richness of the walking or 'wandering' theme (see above). EAV's song also nods to the 'music' of Austria's football terraces with the insertion of 'immer wieder, immer wieder, immer wieder Austria' ('Austria, again and again and again').

The item that best exemplifies the use of musical intertexts is the composition 'Volksmusik' by Richard Barrett and Paul Obermayer. The two artists are the basis of a collaboration called 'FURT', which mostly performs semi-improvised electronic music.[75] Barrett and Obermayer contemplated declining an invitation to appear in Vienna during 2000 (as many artists and organizations did at the time), but instead offered this prerecorded piece 'created specifically for this concert, in solidarity with the resistance against Austrian neofascism'[76] to a festival at the Sammlung Essl near Vienna. 'Volksmusik' is a fifteen-minute-long composition, which adopts different techniques to the duo's live performances, with the use of what they have called 'plunderphonics', following John Oswald's term:[77]

The point of 'plunderphonics' seems to be that the found sounds are placed in quotation marks, so that the listener is supposed to recognize, if not their exact origin, then a sense of their cultural embeddedness, and thus their 'difference' from the aesthetic intent of the music of which they form part and which is intended to be understood as 'subverting' them, by removing them from their original context and placing them in one which contradicts their original (most often commercial) function. This isn't what FURT is trying to do, although we have made excursions in that direction (most obviously in Volksmusik, on the *Defekt* CD), and of course we are aware that sound-materials do have a 'double life' (as 'pure' sonic events but also as connotation).[78]

FURT do not list their sampled sources. Hannah Skrinar, however, detects 'shades of Wagner or Strauss; hard to tell which exactly'.[79] The recording suggests Austrian musical samples in the form of highly slowed-down Bruckner and certainly a rendition of Lehár's 'Dein ist mein ganzes Herz' (at 1:53). Charlie Chaplin is also excerpted from the film *The Great Dictator* (dir. Charles Chaplin, 1940). Chaplin's nonsense German words are fragmented, sampled and regularly repeated ('Hai – der – Hai – der – Hai – der'; at 4:21) in one particular section, with the effect that the repeated nonsense word sounds like it refers to the politician Jörg Haider. Here, FURT practises a kind of musical *mise-en-abyme* as it ironizes and samples Chaplin, who earlier parodied Hitler-noises. 'Volksmusik' finishes with the eerie, distorted tones of what sounds like an alpine horn (14:45) or possibly slowed-down yodelling (e.g. 10:29 or 13:27), just as it begins with a standard 2/4-time 'oompah' brass band music. The musical phrase is then interrupted and repeated over and over like a broken record or scratched CD to frustrate our sense of musical closure and to question the connotations of what might be read as 'volkstümlich', or popular idiom, in the case of the alpine horn/yodelling examples, or as military-style nationalist music in the case of the brass marching music. Philip Bohlman explains that 'nationalist music . . . frequently turns to folk music, laying claim to its authenticity',[80] and Austria is no exception in this regard.

With FURT's own manifesto in mind, the duo are clearly subverting the romantic idiom as well as the local Volksmusik genre. 'Volksmusik' thus functions very differently from most of the music discussed here. Music that has been played at protest concerts or danced to at demonstrations (see below) might well foster 'muscular' or indeed 'sonic' bonding following Thomas Turino's suggested coinage: 'William H. McNeill suggests the term "muscular bonding" for the sense of oneness derived from marching or dancing together in close synchrony; we might add the term "sonic bonding" when this occurs through music making.'[81] FURT's logic questions and frustrates easy bonding or identification by continually subverting musical idiom and by requiring an active listener to decode and decipher the music and its messages. FURT's 'Volksmusik' represents a somewhat paradoxical musical example, then. In musical terms, it does not promote the sense of 'wholeness' and 'integration' that, theorists argue, can be facilitated by artistic communication.[82] 'Volksmusik' cannot be easily identified with, hummed along to or otherwise participated in via dance, or by anticipation of its harmonic progression. Nevertheless, the intellectual challenge of the piece with its resistant music and political appeal does precisely call out for common identification, if not by listeners' common experience of being caught up in the music, then certainly through a process of allegiance-building or common cause with the political intent of the composition and its performance.

Do Actions Speak Louder Than (Song) Words?

'Pop-music', according to sociolinguist Peter Trudgill, 'is a field where language is especially socially symbolic, and typically low in communicative function, high on the phatic and self-expressive'.[83] The affective quality of popular music[84] means that lyrics do not generally function to command or indeed to initiate action and are not generally received by listeners in this way. This may be the reason why British band Chumbawamba did not attract legal claims of incitement for their memorable chant 'Give the fascist man a gunshot' in the track 'Enough is Enough (Kick it Over)' when the bullet's target is easily decodable – in their post-2000 iterations of the song – as Jörg Haider.[85] The single was remixed and rereleased as a CD single in 2000 and given away at concerts in Austria as 'a gesture of solidarity towards Austrian anti-fascists'.[86] The fact that the lyrics are in English, and thus are not so immediately comprehensible to a German-speaking audience, is not in itself grounds for the lack of litigious attention. German-speaking musicians quite commonly employ phrases in English. The Kaputtnicks' rap is predominantly in German, but they reserve a line or two of the choicest language to be rapped in English: 'yeah we live in Austria, but fuck this government'.

However, Austrian musicians were not entirely free from legal pressures. Some Austrian political leaders, the FPÖ and ÖVP politicians who were the target of song lyrics during this period, for example, sought to mete out punishment against compatriots who had offended them. In the present context, we can point to threatened legal action by the FPÖ that forced hard-rock band Drahdiwaberl to remove two planned tracks, 'Schulterschluss' and 'Stecker raus und Tschüsserl', from its *Torte statt Worte* CD.[87] Similarly, Klaus Eberhartinger of Erste Allgemeine Verunsicherung found that although Haider did not take legal action against him for 'Valerie, Valera', the public broadcasting service ORF (Österreichischer Rundfunk) would not play the track. This is tantamount to a kind of state-instigated censorship, with the national public radio station intervening and determining what the state's citizens should not hear.[88]

Drahdiwaberl's 'Torte statt Worte' is an ironic call to arms by wielding cakes, even if it otherwise tries to counter the idea of song-text as affective rather than instructive in nature. This number was dubbed the 'Urhymne aller Widerstandsnummer' (the prototype of all resistance tracks) by Radio Orange

DJs,[89] whose retrospective of millennial protest songs was aired on 13 December 2006. The DJs even passed comment on how the verb 'torten' (to throw a custard pie at somebody) had only recently been coined. The words of lead vocalist and founder member Stefan Weber can, then, be read as a kind of homage to those who do not just talk (or *sing* words, perhaps, like his band and others), but instead take action. Reputedly, the first pie-in-the-face of the resistance campaign, and the catalyst for this track, was in April 2000 and was directed at Hilmar Kabas, the leader of the Viennese branch of the FPÖ.[90]

The problem with throwing lyrics – as opposed to throwing pies (assuming that these hit their targets) – is that their intended meanings are subject to slippage or to misunderstanding. Simon Frith writes of the Republican Party's attempt to hijack Bruce Springsteen's 'Born in the USA' in 1984. He points out how the latter laid claim to a certain sort of veteran soldiers' experience and anti-Vietnam war stance, whereas the sheer impact of the music was very different. '"Born in the USA!"', he says, '[is] a musical phrase which is, in rock convention (its texture, its rhythmic relentlessness, its lift), not bitter but triumphant. In other words, for a rock listener what comes across from this song is not the intended irony of the chorus line, but its pride and assertiveness.'[91] Something similar could be said for the lyrical 'I am from Austria' (original title), rereleased in 2000 (originally Reinhard Fendrich, 1990, but reissued in 1998 by Austria 3, the collaboration of three big names in Austropop, namely Reinhard Fendrich, Wolfgang Ambros and Georg Danzer). Karner argues persuasively that the lyrics have been somewhat overlooked and that the song has been misunderstood as 'a concession to the narrow, ethnic nationalism usually associated with Haider'.[92] As with the Springsteen example, the lyricist's intention has not prevented the titular refrain being repeated or appropriated as a badge of national pride regardless of political persuasion. The song 'I bin aus Österreich' ('I'm from Austria') by STS, bearing an Austrian dialect title with the same meaning, must, on the other hand, be understood as a deliberate work of political resistance, with its inclusive lyrics and articulating, 'a counter-hegemonic discourse challenging the premises of an ethnic nationalism and replacing it with a more open, multicultural conception of Austrian society'.[93]

'Most people are happier to talk in public than to sing', Frith asserts and adduces various social reasons: 'the fact is that most of us experience singing (unlike speaking) as a *performance* . . . singing draws a different sort of attention to the words . . . and to the singer, hence the embarrassment. Singing seems to be self-revealing in a way that speaking is not'.[94] However, we should consider whether it is not, in fact, the reverse that holds true for crowd singing. Frith's argument might only apply to solo performance. My supposition is that most of us are more likely to join in singing (or chanting) resistant texts as a group than we are to solo-compose or to 'speak' resistant text on our own, to voice resistant contributions at a political meeting, say, or a rally.

Uses of Music in the 1999/2000 Protests

With regard to the performative uses of music and sound in the context of the anti-coalition demonstrations, a good example of demonstrators using art to effect protest is the group Performing Resistance, who sang or, perhaps better, 'intoned' their performance live as protest in the streets, often as part of the weekly Thursday demonstrations. The group describe one piece as a 'Chor der Nachbeter mit basso obstinato [sic]' (2000) and it, too, employs the device of verbatim replication of quotations by Jörg Haider and other political figures. Although the chorus provides a confirmatory echo of the prayer leader's incantations of objectionable FPÖ statements, the 'obstinate' bass expresses quizzical disbelief as first one voice then a cacophonous mélange of voices ask, rhetorically, 'Was hat er gesagt?' ('what did he say?') at different times and at different pitches. The result is that the seamless performance of the calls and responses is interrupted and called into doubt as the vehemence of the obstinate voices stops the procession of supplicants.[95] Thus, the performance of blind musical obedience (responding in unison to the call) is ruptured and the group thereby suggest or invoke a breaking-up of uniform, far-right thinking.

The first verse of the performance piece begins with the group's 'performance' of former Deputy Mayor of Klagenfurt Reinhard Gaugg's 1993 interview answer to the question 'Was sagt Ihnen das Wort "Nazi"?' ('what does the word "Nazi" mean to you?'). His answer was: 'neu, attraktiv, zielstrebig, ideenreich' ('new, attractive, determined, imaginative').[96] The musical genre is chosen deliberately. In deploying a choir, or chorus, the group ironically replicates the group of acolytes and obedient voices that surrounded Jörg Haider, but then breaks down that choric unison to destroy the conviction that such ideology can speak with one voice. The piece thus performs a kind of musical destruction of the FPÖ's 'liturgy'. There are similarities in this regard to the – spoken – chorus used by Elfriede Jelinek in her short drama *Das Lebewohl*, a piece that was also performed in the Wiener Festwochen as a contribution by the playwright to the protests.

Thomas Turino draws our attention to the context in which art is performed and builds on the notion that 'the arts are founded on the interplay of the Possible and the Actual and can awaken us from habit. The arts – music, dance, rituals, plays, movies, paintings, poems, stories – are a type of framed activity where it is expected that the imagination and new possibilities will be given special license'.[97] The interesting thing about some protest art and music (and some kinds of performance art and installation) is that it breaks the expected or normally required frames or appropriates the 'wrong' frame, just like the above parodic chorus example flouts the expected call and response normally contained within the church. The frame is different for the texts of projectionist-artist Julia Zdarsky, who beamed her texts onto the wall of the Kanzleramt, or for filmmaker

Frederick Baker, who projected images onto the backs of policemen during the Thursday demonstrations. It is different, too, for the 'Volkstänzer', who brought dance out into the streets during the Thursday demos. In Western Europe, dance is most often an indoor and usually a fixed-location activity, sometimes for participation and sometimes for show.

Admittedly, there are dances such as the toyi-toyi in South Africa that are an integral part of political expression. They are not performed as an end in themselves, but rather as part of the means of effecting protest. The political act of the Viennese 'folk dancers' in 2000 and beyond was to make dance a political vehicle, just as the Thursday demonstrators made their weekly walks a subversive act and not just a keep-fit exercise or a mode of self-transportation. Whereas one might normally understand a folk dance to be part of a folkloristic ritual or traditional cultural practice, the group of people who gathered in public locations such as in front of the opera house[98] met in order to make a noise and to dance the people's dance of protest, and precisely not a twee rendition of something involving Lederhosen and Dirndl. Thus, there is no specific protest music or dance type associated with this instance of protest (though the folk dance genre is implicitly denigrated by the group's ironic name). As a protest activity symbiotically linked to music, the Volkstanz invitation or 'call to dance' saw a proliferation of different DJs, bands, hip-hop artists, orchestras and groups leaving the usual urban club scene and take to the streets under the banner of dancing for dissolution (of the government), or 'Abtanzen für Abdanken'.[99]

'Key' Change and Iconic Steps

Ballroom dancing – waltzing in particular – is the symbolic dance of social power in Austria, due to its ready association with the social occasions of high society. Performing Resistance (together with Volkstanz and Tanz*Hotel) staged an action called the 'Rechtswalzer' (right-hand waltz), mobilizing the name of the type of Viennese waltz that starts with the lady moving to the right, to perform instead an inelegant 'dance' of huge, inflatable black tyres with blue lettering on them with the elided party acronyms 'FPÖVP'.[100] The protesters were symbolizing the way in which the people of Austria had been 'rolled over' by their politicians moving clumsily to the far right. The accompanying song was a parody of the national anthem that plays on a political scandal of early 2000 and began 'Land der Humpe, Land der Dumpe'. The leader of the Viennese FPÖ was heard to have called the Austrian President, Thomas Klestil, a 'Lump', but then denied this, saying that he could not remember exactly what word he had used, but that it was actually 'Hump' or 'Dump' (thus hiding behind euphemistic, infantile coinages).[101]

The annual Wiener Staatsopernball is the society event most readily associated with ballroom dancing and attended by celebrities and the upper echelons of society. Therefore, unsurprisingly it is also the locus for political and social protest groups. At the 2000 State Opera ball, actor, comedian and activist Hubsi Kramar arrived dressed as Adolf Hitler, entered the opera house foyer and then found himself being evicted and arrested by the police. Kramar reflects on the action in Frederick Baker's 2010 filmic commemoration of the protests, *Widerstand in Haiderland*.[102] Kramar's approach is to don the full Hitler costume and embody the person rather than simply adopting the metonymic moustache, a comic technique used the world over to decry someone as a 'Nazi'. Haider's photograph on the anti-European Union FPÖ campaign poster of 1994, 'Österreich zuerst', was graffitied with a Hitler moustache, for example.[103] Hackers were able to post a picture of Haider with a Hitler moustache on the Salzburg branch webpages of the FPÖ in 2001, and in 1999, a fake FPÖ homepage was set up, using a domain name that did not have the Umlaut (FPO) and thus still looked highly plausible. Meme warfare was certainly in its infancy as a resistance strategy in the early days of the new millennium. The new generation of interactivity and internet capability, known widely as 'Web 2.0', was not in general usage until around 2004, when much more user-generated internet content became possible. Equally, social media such as Facebook, Instagram, Twitter and so on did not yet exist. The mobilization of protest could be announced on the internet and via email and mobile phone, but the rapidity of social media communication and viral spread of images was not yet at the advanced state it is now towards the end of the second decade of the twenty-first century. That said, protester-gamers were quick off the mark to develop internet games. The stay-at-home protester did not need to walk anywhere to effect his or her protest, or could come back from a demo and play a kind of politicians' infamous quotation pelmanism game called 'Spielsalon 05', or indulge in some 'Haider-bashing' or some 'Mascherljagd im Bärental' ('bow tie hunting in the Bärental valley').[104]

When it came to finding a symbol with which to pillory the new Austrian Chancellor, Wolfgang Schüssel, the answer was self-evident. Schüssel always wore a bow tie (in Austrian German, a 'Mascherl') with his shirt and jacket, never a standard neck-tie, or at least not until June 2000 when he attended the EU summit in Feira, Portugal and seems to have changed his sartorial preferences.[105] One of the many stickers that featured in visual statements and actions of protest was a black bow tie with a blue centre and bearing a red cross through the whole tie. There were variations, such as a simple bow tie with the words 'No' written on it. Even EU ministers from other countries reportedly wore badges or signs of the rejected bow tie, signalling their support for the EU sanctions against Austria.[106] Many other physical objects and costumes formed part of the Thursday demos' *mise-en-scène* as well as becoming protest markers of ordinary citizens in their daily lives. People crafted their own earrings, T-shirts, umbrellas, ties, coats, bicycle paniers and so on.[107]

Chancellor Schüssel also unwittingly inspired one of the most voluble and ubiquitous ways in which sonic protest made itself heard in the early days of the protests, not in the form of fully fledged words or music, but in the iconic use of sound. Jacques Attali's 1970s' investigation of noise seems pertinent to the noises of protest too. He advises that 'we must learn to judge a society more by its sounds, by its art, and by its festivals, than by its statistics. By listening to noise, we can better understand where the folly of men and their calculations is leading us, and what hopes it is still possible to have'.[108] One of the loudest, 'unscored' noises during the Austrian protests was produced by the jangling of keys. In semiotic terms, this musical 'sign' takes on iconic significance. 'Iconic processes are fundamental to musical meaning in terms of style . . . recognition and are basic to our cultural classification of most things', Turino explains.[109] He then furnishes examples along the lines of how we might come to associate the sound of kettle drums with the roll of thunder or with cannons, according to a larger context, such as our geographical, historical or cultural origins. However, it is not the musical colour or timbre of key-shaking that is iconic or suggestive of the would-be Chancellor's character. Rather, the near-homonym of 'Schüssel' (the Chancellor's surname) and 'Schlüssel' (key or keys) meant that an obvious protest became the jangling of key fobs to indicate 'kein Schlüssel für Schüssel' as protesters demanded that his administration should not be let in, as it were, given the keys to the chancellery.[110] Since, as Turino suggests, 'most people the world over connect the majority of musical signs to their objects either through resemblances or through cooccurence',[111] the key jangling becomes an iconic sound during this period, the performance of which is instantly recognizable as a political demand. In the music of protest, the other meaning of 'Schüssel' (bowl) becomes useful to comic activists such as the band Erste Allgemeine Verunsicherung, who impugn the incoming Chancellor's sanity and imply that he has lost his marbles or, rather, in German, that he has a leak in his bowl, 'einen Sprung in der Schüssel'.[112]

Wolfgang Schüssel's chancellorship of Austria in fact continued until 2007, with the Chancellor holding on to his keys over a further national election in November 2002 and remaining in coalition with the FPÖ. Given the longevity of the coalitions of the centre right and populist right in twenty-first-century Austria and the electoral share garnered by parties of the far right in various elections since, observers might find themselves asking whether all of this singing and dancing was not a waste of time and effort, all 'in vain', as the 2000 composition by microtonal Austrian composer Georg Friedrich Haas called his 63-minute piece.[113] Haas is on record as having 'channeled his frustration and anger into the composition of that turbulent piece, after his nation voted a far-right government into power in 2000'.[114]

Conclusion: Personal Tastes, Personal Decisions

The musical samples above give an indication of how vastly different aesthetic ideas can be mobilized to express protest or 'resistance' within one particular art form. Protest-minded radio listeners and song-singing demonstrators do not have to agree on matters of musical taste. There is a track, it would seem, for everybody, even if microtonal or electronic music does not lend itself very obviously to acting as a rousing protest accompaniment. The taste buds were catered for very well in literal terms during the anti-black-and-blue protests. A resistance bakery 'Widerstandsbäckerei' featured regularly with its trolley of wares including blue-and-black 'Kekse gegen SchwarzBlau [*sic*]' ('biscuits against Black/Blue') glazed with a red hand indicating 'stop'.[115] One commentator pointed up the rather 'stale'-sounding (*altbacken*) or contrived names given to the baked goods on offer, though the ingenuity of the word plays is occasionally entertaining. There were: 'Krisenkipferl', 'Putsch-Krapferl', 'Haider-geh-endlich-in-Oarsch-Golatschen', 'Antimascherl-Muffins', 'Westenthascherl' and 'Prinzhormonrollen' ('crisis croissants', 'putsch-doughnuts', 'sod-off-Haider pastries', 'anti-bow-tie muffins', 'Westenthal-turnovers' and 'Prinzhornmoan-rolls').[116] One of the more unusual slogans at the protests, then, was the cry of 'Backe(l)n statt Hackeln' ('get baking instead of slaving'), an ironic jibe at the pension reforms being proposed by the FPÖ during this era under the deliberately chosen working-class-evoking, dialect word for working very hard, 'hackeln'.[117]

The range of protest activities and the creative force behind them is fully evident both in the works of the professional artists discussed here as well as in the everyday acts and creations of normal citizen protesters. Some protests will have been less appealing to popular tastes or will have met with disapproval rather than support. Violent acts were certainly not justified by commentators or called for by the intellectual voices advocating resistance and protest in Austria's newspaper columns. On the other hand, 'Scrotum gegen Votum', a protest action involving the scanning and displaying of images of male genitalia, will have produced some reactions of disgust or laughter on either side of the protest debate. This is all part of the plan, one observer comments, and points out that the award-winning protest is as shocking and absurd as the racist arguments they are countering: 'Irritated? Shocked? Good! That's deliberate. This campaign is absurd. Racism is absurd. But they are using racism in their political campaigns once again. We can show resistance below the belt, too.'[118] This action was initiated by a group called Monochrom and was purportedly a *re*action to 'Titten gegen Rassismus' ('tits against racism'), a protest that has been seen as a precursor of the kinds of bare-breasted protests of the highly controversial international protest group Femen.[119] Activities of this kind are, doubtless, a matter of personal taste and interpretation, but they certainly draw media attention to the protests and, by association, to the cause that is being championed or protested against.

Personal stances were taken in considerably less sensational form by many well-known figures in Austrian society around the time of the October 1999 election, a number of whom announced their intention to leave Austria should the FPÖ form part of Austria's government. Singer-songwriter Reinhard Fendrich and playwright Elfriede Jelinek were two such voices, though both ended up staying, with Jelinek famously issuing a temporary ban on her plays being staged in Austrian state theatres. Her play *Das Lebewohl (Les Adieux)* was given its first performance as an open-air drama protest during the Viennese Festwochen with the German actor Martin Wuttke playing the monologuing 'Haider-Figur'. The play is discussed in Chapter 5, but could equally feature in the present chapter's discussions: the staging was a phenomenon of the streets, a part of the demo culture and, indeed, pivots around the decision taken by Jörg Haider to leave Vienna (and his role as FPÖ party leader) for his political homeland of Carinthia. The theme of 'staying versus leaving', then, mutates in Jelinek's work, where the Freedom Party 'movement' is itself mocked. Decisions were being made by foreign nationals in Austria as well as by visitors planning to travel to Austria. Thus, Gerard Mortier announced that he would shorten his directorship of the Salzburger Festspiele and leave after the 2000 festival.[120] Members of the Internationale Vereinigung für Germanistik even deliberated whether the 2000 meeting, planned for Vienna, should take place or whether in travelling to the conference they would implicitly support the Austrian regime.[121]

This chapter has seen a plethora of different examples of the kinds of art forms spawned by the protest walks and by artists expressing their protest. It has highlighted a tension between movement and stasis, and between mobility and 'jamming' as an artistic and political strategy. Culture jamming, or 'hijacking the methods and means of commercial culture to communicate radical messages',[122] was a widely used tactic during the protests, but physical stoppage or blocking was a vital part of the resistance movement too. Even from the vantage point of the late 2010s, in the age of instant social media petitions, physical protest marches and rallies are still indispensable. Movement and nonmovement are both important modes, physical blockage still being one of most effective and most visible tools of any protest movement. By blocking streets and creating disruption, attention is drawn to the protesters and their demands. In stopping the march or walk to stand still and 'rally', speeches can be heard, views can be exchanged, information can be given and celebration can take place. The semantics of the call for resistance draw attention to this process, asking listeners to stand against something (*wider*stehen) or to make it stop. A particular sticker protest example will stand here as a concluding encapsulation of the tensions inherent in stopping and moving, in walking as a protest to demand that a government leaves office. Itself a device to allow pedestrians to stand still and yet still effectively 'walk' up or down, the escalator on Austrian public transport systems reminds the passenger to stand on the right-hand side ('Bitte rechts stehen'). Authentic-looking stickers were added below the official ones requesting that the reader think left-wing and not right-wing thoughts: 'Bitte links denken!' The following chapters ask how novelists, filmmakers and playwrights made their audiences and readers think about, or indeed also be entertained by, the political situation in Austria in the early years of the twenty-first century.

Notes

1. See Foltin, *Und wir bewegen uns doch*.
2. Kurt Andersen, 'The Protester', *Time*, 14 December 2011. Retrieved 1 May 2018 from http://content.time.com/time/specials/packages/article/0,28804,2101745_2102132_2 102373,00.htmln.
3. See Beller, *A Concise History of Austria*, 272.
4. For research that illuminates these angles, see the essays in Konrad Becker and Martin Wassermair (eds), *Kampfzonen in Kunst und Medien: Texte zur Zukunft der Kulturpolitik* (Vienna: Löcker, 2008) and in Emmerich Tálos (ed.), *Schwarz-Blau: eine Bilanz des 'Neu-Regierens'* (Vienna, Lit Verlag, 2006), especially, Michael Wimmer, 'Staatliche Kulturpolitik in Österreich seit 2000: Zur Radikalisierung eines politischen Konzeptes', at 248–63.
5. See Andersen, 'The Protester'.
6. 'Das Wort "Widerstand" wurde am 2. Februar 2000 . . . wiedergeboren. Ich erinnere mich an die eigenartige Stille am Beginn der ersten Demonstration. Die Teilnehmer waren so unterschiedlich und die Situation so komplex. Das simple Wort "Widerstand" einte Grüne, Sozialdemokraten, Kommunisten, enttäuschte ÖVP-Wähler und Wechselwähler.' Frederick Baker, 'Der 19. Februar 2000: Die Geburt eines Widerstand-Oratoriums', in Baker and Boyer, *Wiener Wandertage*, 171–77, at 171.
7. Doron Rabinovici, *Der ewige Widerstand: über einen strittigen Begriff* (Vienna: Styria, 2008).
8. See Baker and Boyer, *Wiener Wandertage* for lists of different slogans heard at various marches throughout the resistance campaign: e.g. 'Slogans 19. Februar 2000' (147–48), 'Slogans März-Juni 2000' (203–6) and 'Slogans Juli-September 2000' (259–63).
9. Retrieved 6 May 2018 from http://www.shifz.org/puzzle/austriap.html. See the unlabelled photograph in front of the Vienna Parliament building on the website of the Vienna-based art group Shifz, with anti-Nazi league members from the United Kingdom clearly having made the journey over to Vienna in solidarity. Luca Faccio photographed and exhibited on the Thursday demonstrations extensively, for example, 'Demoflexion: Portrait of a Protest, Vienna University of Technology, Academy of Fine Arts Vienna, Literaturhaus Wien and Arbeitermuseum Steyr, Videoinstallation MAK Night' (Museum of Applied Arts, Vienna). Retrieved 6 May 2018 from http://www.luca-faccio.com/cv.html.
10. The business undertaken by the Women's Ministry was absorbed under the Ministerium für Gesundheit und Soziales until 2003, when another new 'Ministerium für Gesundheit und Frauen' took over responsibility.

11. Image no. 64 (n.p.), in Baker and Boyer, *Wiener Wandertage*, illustrations between 336 and 337.
12. Dorfer, quoted in Baker, 'Der 19. Februar 2000', 175 and Romana Müllner, 'Wer sind die Demonstranten?', 266–69, both in Baker and Boyer, *Wiener Wandertage*. Dorfer's regular Thursday evening television programme *Dorfers Donnerstalk* later appeared on DVDs. Alas, there is not the space here to consider the many critical and comedic thematizations of contemporary politics on television and in the newspapers.
13. Müllner, 'Wer sind die Demonstranten?', 267.
14. Rick Kuhn, 'The Threat of Fascism in Austria', *Monthly Review* 52(2) (2000), 21–35. Retrieved 6 May 2018 from https://archive.monthlyreview.org/index.php/mr/article/view/MR-052-02-2000-06_3.
15. Oliver Marchart, 'Austrifying Europe: Ultraright Populism and the New Culture of Resistance', *Cultural Studies*, 16(6) (2002), 809–19, at 810.
16. Yarimar Bonilla, 'The Past is Made by Walking: Labor Activism and Historical Production in Postcolonial Gaudeloupe', *Cultural Anthropology* 26(3), 313–39, at 315. The Durkheim reference is to Emile Durkheim, *The Elementary Forms of Religious Life* (New York: Free Press, 1965).
17. See 'Chronologie der Ereignisse', in Baker and Boyer, *Wiener Wandertage*, 491–501; and the anarchist newsletter *Tatblatt*'s chronology, retrieved 6 May 2018 from http://www.tatblatt.net/132chronologie-maerz.htm.
18. 'Bunte und lautstarke Opernball-Demo', *Der Standard*, 3 March 2000. Retrieved 6 May 2018 from http://derstandard.at/178785/Bunte-und-lautstarke-Opernball-Demo.
19. Entry for 'Donnerstagsdemonstration' in Panagl, Gerlich et al., *Wörterbuch der politischen Sprache in Österreich*, 105–6.
20. 'Es wird gewandert. Und nicht marschiert. Das ist ein erster Schritt.' Marlene Streeruwitz, *Tagebuch der Gegenwart* (Vienna: Böhlau, 2002), 36. Several bicycling demonstrations were planned, but not many were carried out. Cycling would seem to inhibit the desired tempo of the demos and make the accompanying protest activities difficult to undertake.
21. 'Die Donnerstag Wandertage sind ein Statement. Gegen Rassismus. Mitgehen bedeutet, dieses Statement zu machen … Jeder und jede "ergeht" sich das eigene Statement Antirassismus.' Streeruwitz, *Tagebuch der Gegenwart*, 37.
22. The desired outcome is used as the title of an edited anthology. See El Awadalla and Traude Korosa (eds), *…Bis sie gehen: vier Jahre Widerstandslesungen* (Vienna: Sisyphus, 2004).
23. Walking in Vienna has a history of activist aesthetic protest. However, these mass protests are very different in style and message from the solo 'Wiener Spaziergang' (1965) of Viennese actionist Günter Brus.
24. Rebecca Solnit, *Wanderlust: A History of Walking* (London: Verso, 2001,) 216.
25. 'Es gibt keinen Veranstalter, die Demo organisiert sich selbst.' Baker and Boyer, 'Vorbemerkung', in Baker and Boyer, *Wiener Wandertage*, 7–8, at 7; and Panagl and Gerlich, 'Donnerstagsdemonstration', in Panagl, Gerlich et al., *Wörterbuch der politischen Sprache in Österreich*, 105–6, at 105. https://de.wikipedia.org/wiki/Kurto_Wendt cites Kurto Wendt as one of the organizers of the events. In Baker and Boyer's book, the biographical line for Kurt Wendt states that he is 'aktivist des aktionskommittees' (Baker and Boyer, *Wiener Wandertage*, 52).

26. Awadalla and Korosa, ...*Bis sie gehen*; Baker and Boyer, *Wiener Wandertage*; Milena Verlag (ed.), *Die Sprache des Widerstandes ist alt wie die Welt und ihr Wunsch: Frauen in Österreich schreiben gegen Rechts* (Vienna: Milena, 2000). The latter collection not only published contemporaneous pieces penned especially with the 1999/2000 Wende in mind, but also included a number of older, relevant items.
27. The image can be seen at http://www.shifz.org/puzzle/austria.html.
28. Richard Price, *The Convict and the Colonel: A Story of Colonialism and Resistance in the Caribbean* (Durham, NC: Duke University Press, 2006), 173.
29. I refer here to Pierre Nora's theories on the space as 'symbolic element of the memorial heritage of any community'. See Pierre Nora and Lawrence D. Kritzman, *Realms of Memory: Rethinking the French Past* (New York: Columbia University Press, 1996), xvii.
30. Ernst Hanisch, 'Wien Heldenplatz', *Transit. Europäische Revue* 15 (1998), 122–40. Retrieved 6 May 2018 from http://www.demokratiezentrum.org/fileadmin/media/pdf/hanisch.pdf.
31. 'Gerade auf diesem Platz war das wichtig. Und 300 000 Personen jubelten ihnen zu. Solidarisierten sich . . . Das war ein großes Versprechen auf eine Änderung der Kultur in diesem Land.' Streeruwitz, *Tagebuch der Gegenwart*, 20.
32. Frederick Baker, *Erosion und Wi(e)derstand*, Austria: Frederick Baker, 2003. The parenthetical 'e' makes the second word suggest both resistance and the return of uprising or resistance.
33. Frederick Baker, *The Art of Projectionism* (Vienna: Czernin, 2008), 53.
34. Julia Starsky, *Starsky: Gesamtkatalog* (Vienna: Starsky, 2014), 5.
35. Starsky, 'zufallsindoktrinator', in *Starsky: Gesamtkatalog*, 62–74, at 70. The artist's webpage features a short video which begins with this particular projection. Retrieved 6 May 2018 from http://starsky-projections.com/shame.
36. 'Die interventionen des zufallsindoktrinators im öffentlichen raum eröffnen ein begreifen der bedingtheit von denkstrukturen und verhaltensmustern.' 'Und wie die öffentlichkeit diesen raum plötzlich in anderer weise öffentlich macht.' Starsky, *Starsky: Gesamtkatalog*, 129.
37. 'Widerstandschronologie', *Tatblatt*, 1 May 2001. Retrieved 6 May 2018 from https://www.nadir.org/nadir/periodika/tatblatt/132chronologie-2001-05.htm.
38. See, 'Donnerstags-Demonstrationen (983/J)'. Retrieved 6 May 2018 from http://www.parlament.gv.at/PAKT/VHG/XXI/J/J_00983/index.shtml.
39. See the excellent collection by Matthias Lilienthal and Claus Philipp (eds), *Schlingensiefs Ausländer Raus: Bitte Liebt Österreich. Dokumentation* (Frankfurt am Main: Suhrkamp, 2000).
40. Paul Poet, *Ausländer raus! Schlingensiefs Container*. DVD, Austria: Bonus Film, 2005. When referring to the installation or artwork, I shall use Schlingensief's term 'Bitte liebt Österreich'. References to Poet's film will be to *Ausländer raus!*
41. Schlingensief had reckoned on about 50,000 'hits' per day, but the action attracted 80,000 hits an hour. See 'Freiheit für alles: Gespräch zwischen Alexander Kluge und Christoph Schlingensief', Part One, 136–49, at 148, in Lilienthal and Philipp, *Schlingensiefs Ausländer raus!* The tourist encouragement sequence is at 08:17.
42. Tara Forrest, 'A Realism of Protest: Christoph Schlingensief's Television Experiments', *Germanic Review: Literature, Culture, Theory* 87(4) (2012), 325–44.
43. Nicolas Bourriaud, *Relational Aesthetics*, trans. Simon Pleasance and Fronza Woods, with the participation of Mathieu Copeland (Dijon: Les Presses du réel, 2002), 14.

44. Bourriaud, *Relational Aesthetics*, 112.
45. Beuys, quoted in Timon Beyes, 'Uncontained: The Art and Politics of Reconfiguring Urban Space', *Culture and Organization* 16(3) (2010), 229–46, at 233.
46. Schlingensief's artistic methods of negative portrayal and irony show similarities to Jelinek's. Both run the risk of being seen as promoting precisely the sorts of things they are criticizing – in this case, racism. The email responses to Schlingensief's 'Bitte liebt Österreich' event can be read in *Profil* magazine's archives and testify to the outrage.
47. Beyes, 'Uncontained'.
48. Jacques Rancière, Davide Panagia and Rachel Bowlby, 'Ten Theses on Politics', *Theory and Event* 5(3) (2001). Retrieved 6 May 2018 from http://muse.jhu.edu/article/32639.
49. Beyes, 'Uncontained', 237.
50. Birgit Flos uses the term 'Bilderzerstörungsmaschine' (image destruction machine) in Birgit Flos, 'Eintritt ins gestörte Bild: Paul Poet dokumentiert Schlingensiefs *Ausländer raus*', DVD notes, in Paul Poet, *Ausländer raus! Schlingensiefs Container*. DVD, Austria: Bonus Film, 2005.
51. '... belastet unseren Sängerbetrieb, die Probenräume können dann nicht mehr genutzt werden, die Sänger können nicht mehr proben, die Stimmen werden dadurch unklar, wir lehnen das ab.' Lilienthal and Philipp, *Schlingensiefs Ausländer raus*, 42.
52. Words by Wilhelm Wiesberg, music by Johann Sioly. See Eva Maria Hois, 'Wienerliedtexte der Jahrhundertwende als Spiegel sozio-ökonomischer, technischer und politischer Entwicklungen', *Newsletter Moderne*, special issue 1, 'Moderne – Modernisierung – Globalisierung' (March 2001). Retrieved 6 May 2018 from http://www-gewi.kfunigraz.ac.at/moderne/dok.htm.
53. An earlier version of my analysis of Austrian protest music was originally published as Allyson Fiddler, 'Performing Austria: Protesting the Musical Mation', *IASPM@Journal* 4(1) (2014), 10.5429/2079-3871(2014)v4i1.2en and is used here with permission of the journal.
54. Haider's contribution to male voice choral singing appears on a charity DVD released the month after his death; Strache (or 'H.C.', to which his name is often abbreviated) has produced several raps as part of his political campaigning. On the subject, see Beret Norman, 'The Politics of Austrian Hip-Hop: HC Strache's Xenophobia Gets Dissed', *Colloquia Germanica* 39(2) (2006), 209–30.
55. Barbara Lebrun, *Protest Music in France: Production, Identity and Performance* (Farnham: Ashgate, 2009), 2.
56. Bernadette Huber, *Wie böse ist Österreich?*, 1999, Programme 3. Retrieved 6 May 2018 from http://www.medienwerkstatt-wien.at/files/titles/kunst-der-stunde.htm.
57. Philip Tagg, 'Caught on the Back Foot: Epistemic Inertia and Visible Music', *IASPM@Journal* 2(1–2) (2011), 12. Retrieved 6 May 2018 from http://dx.doi.org/10.5429/2079-3871(2011)v2i1-2.2en.
58. Tagg, 'Caught on the Back Foot'.
59. See Edward Larkey, 'Austropop: Popular Music and National Identity in Austria', *Popular Music* 11(2) (1992), 151–85.
60. Christian Karner, '"Austro-Pop" since the 1980s: Two Case Studies of Cultural Critique and Counter-Hegemonic Resistance', *Sociological Research Online* 6(4) (2002). Retrieved 6 May 2018 from http://dx.doi.org/10.5153/sro.654.

61. Edward Larkey, 'Americanization, Cultural Change, and Austrian Identity', in David F. Good and Ruth Wodak (eds), *From World War to Waldheim: Culture and Politics in Austria and the United States* (New York: Berghahn Books, 1999), 210-35, at 227.
62. M. Zellhofer, 'Steckt's den Kopf nicht in den Sand, das Zauberwort heißt Widerstand!', *Unique* (University of Vienna, Student Union magazine) 6 (2006).
63. Stephen Duncombe, Introduction to 'Adorno, On the Fetish-Character in Music and the Regression of Listening', in Stephen Duncombe (ed.), *Cultural Resistance Reader* (London, Verso: 2002), 275–303, at 276.
64. 'Das Politische [wird] nicht mehr im Sound selbst, im Material (z. B. der Digitalität) oder in ihren angeblich demokratischen Produktionsbedingungen gesucht ... Man geht nicht mehr davon aus, daß elektronische Musik an sich subversiv oder fortschrittlich oder befreiend sei. ... Vielmehr geht es darum, daß eine bestimmte Szene oder Community sich öffentlich der Opposition gegen eine Regierung anschließt und das mit den ihr zu Verfügung stehenden Mitteln demonstriert. Darin besteht ihr Politik-Werden.' Oliver Marchart, 'Was heißt Soundpolitisierung?', 2001, n.p. Retrieved 6 May 2018 from http://www.volkstanz.net/mind_nut/01.htm..
65. 'Ich sag nur "Gratishormone" oder "Stop der Überfremdung", / für nachträgliche Entschuldigungen keinerlei Verwendung / "von Natur aus aggressive Menschen schwarzer Hautfarbe" / gegen solche Sprüche vorzugehen ist sonst Staatsaufgabe / Doch 60 Jahre der Verdrängung reichen offenbar aus / die neue Rechte ist gekommen, und sie sehnt sich nach Applaus.' Kaputtnicks, 'Brief an den Kanzler'. Austria: Geco Tonwaren, 2000. Retrieved 6 May 2018 from https://www.youtube.com/watch?v=1tiZP5z99YI.
66. Mia Eidlhuber, 'Du sollst recherchieren! Die gängigen Vorwürfe an Haider und was Sie darüber wissen sollten', *Die Zeit*. 17 February 2001, 1–5, at 4. Retrieved 6 May 2018 from http://www.zeit.de/2000/08/200008.reden_tabelle_2_.xml/seite-4.
67. Foltin, *Und wir bewegen uns doch*, 264.
68. 'Da darf man sich nicht wundern / Das Totschlagargument "amtsbekannt" / Und in den Interviewpausen / Kann dieses Lächeln wirklich ehrlich sein?' Brambilla, 'B.E.N.I.T.A.', *Little Terror Creek* (CD). Austria: Lunadiscs/Knallcore and Bloodshed 666, 2002.
69. Conny Chaos und die Retortenkinder, 'KHG', *Retorte Rockt!* (4-track demo-CD). Austria: Broken Heart Records, 2004 and 'Lisi Gehrer'; Austria: Broken Heart Records, 2004. See also: https://retortenkinder.bandcamp.com/track/lisi-gehrer-psc-version-08.
70. Die Ärzte, 'Halsabschneider', B-side of *Wie es geht*. Single. Germany: Hot Action Records, 2000.
71. Drahdiwaberl, 'Torte statt Worte', *Torte statt Worte*. Austria: Drahdiwaberl Music, 2000.
72. See the announcements of the 'abendfuellendes Chorwerk' at http://akin.mediaweb.at/2002/18.02/18woche2.html and in 'Singen gegen Schwarz-Blau', *Der Standard*, 24 May 2002. Retrieved 6 May 2018 from https://derstandard.at/960913/Singen-gegen-Schwarz-Blau. The choir's webpages do not refer to the 'Hohes Haus Musik' cantata. Retrieved 6 May 2018 from http://www.gegenstimmen.org.
73. Chorvereinigung Gegenstimmen (eds), 'Hohes Haus Musik: Kantate in F Dur' (Vienna: Alwa & Deil, 2002), 1–24, at 10. The music is scored for soprano, alto, tenor and bass.
74. 'Im dritten Reich gab es Vorfälle, die nicht entschuldbar waren. Wenn Sie so wollen, dann war es halt Massenmord.' Erste Allgemeine Verunsicherung, 'Valerie, Valera:

Haiders Sprung in seiner Schüssel'. Promo Single CD. Germany: Blanko Musik, 2000. For the Haider quotation, see Hubertus Czernin (ed.), *Wofür ich mich meinetwegen entschuldige: Haider, beim Wort genommen* (Vienna: Czernin Verlag, 2000), 15–17.
75. FURT, 'Volksmusik', *Defekt* (United Kingdom: Matchless Recordings, 2002).
76. Rainer Lepuschitz, '[bracket] #2: FURT', trans. Elfi Cagala, in Berno Odo Polzer (ed.), *Almanach WIEN MODERN* (Vienna, 2000). Retrieved 6 May 2018 from http://sammlung-essl.at/jart/prj3/essl/main.jart?content-id=1465039459955&rel=de&article_id=1399965034202&x=1&event_id=1399965034205&reserve-mode=active.
77. John Oswald, 'Plunderphonics, or Audio Piracy as a Compositional Prerogative', *Musicworks* 34 (1986), 5–8.
78. FURT, in Stefano Isidora Bianchi, *Blow up*, June 2005. Retrieved 6 May 2018 from http://furtlogic.com/node/16.
79. Hannah Skrinar, 'Compositional Improvisation from the Electroacoustic Duo …', FURT *Defekt* review, 17 January 2003. Retrieved 6 May 2018 from http://www.bbc.co.uk/music/reviews/mpqv.
80. Philip Vilas Bohlman, *The Music of European Nationalism: Cultural Identity and Modern History* (Santa Barbara, CA: ABC-CLIO, 2004), 83.
81. Thomas Turino, *Music as Social Life: The Politics of Participation* (Chicago: University of Chicago Press, 2008), 3, note 2.
82. Gregory Bateson, *Steps to an Ecology of Mind: Collected Essays in Anthropology, Psychiatry, Evolution, and Epistemology* (London: Intertext, 1972), quoted in Turino, *Music as Social Life*, 3–4.
83. Trudgill, cited in Simon Frith, *Performing Rites: On the Value of Popular Music* (Cambridge, MA: Harvard University Press, 1996), 168.
84. See Marie Thompson and Ian Biddle, 'Introduction: Somewhere between the Signifying and the Sublime', in Marie Thompson and Ian Biddle (eds), *Sound, Music, Affect: Theorizing Sonic Experience* (London: Bloomsbury, 2013), 1–24.
85. Chumbawamba, 'Enough is Enough (Kick it Over)'. United Kingdom: Woodlands Studio, 2000. The track was originally released in 1993 as 'Enough is Enough' by Chumbawamba and Credit to the Nation.
86. Adam Bychawski, 'Download Chumbawamba Track for Free', *NME*, 12 July 2000.
87. See Rosa Antifa Wien, 'Newsletter boeses:oesterreich 1000', 6 October 2000. Retrieved 6 May 2018 from https://raw.at/texte/gegenschwarzblau/newsletter-boeses-oesterreich-1000.
88. See Laut.de, 'E.A.V.-Sänger beklagt Zensur durch die Medien', 24 July 2000. Retrieved 6 May 2018 from http://www.laut.de/Oesterreich/E.A.V.-Saenger-beklagt-Zensur-durch-die-Medien/24-07-2000..
89. Zellhofer, 'Steckt's den Kopf nicht in den Sand'.
90. Karl Weidinger, 'Widerstand im Mehlspeisland', 2001. Retrieved 6 May 2018 from http://www.kawei.at/site_txt_2001.htm.
91. Frith, *Performing Rites*, 165.
92. Karner, '"Austro-Pop" since the 1980s', para. 6.2.
93. Karner, '"Austro-Pop" since the 1980s', para. 4.8.
94. Frith, *Performing Rites*, 172.
95. Nicole Delle Karth, 'Chor der Nachbeter mit basso obstinato', in Baker and Boyer, *Wiener Wandertage*, 151–58, at 153.

96. 'Der Schulterträger Haiders', ORF, 2006. Retrieved 6 May 2018 from http://newsv1.orf.at/060724-2006/?href=http per cent3A per cent2F per cent2Fnewsv1.orf.at per cent2F060724-2006 per cent2F2008txt_story.html.
97. Turino, *Music as Social Life*, 17–18.
98. Baker and Boyer, *Wiener Wandertage*, illustration no. 44.
99. Volkstanz.net, 'Abtanzen für Abdanken', 2000. Retrieved 6 May 2018 from http://www.action.at/organizations/?/cgi-bin/organizations/page.pl?id=105. See also Gini Müller's evocation of Saturday protest dance and music culture in Müller, *Possen des Performativen*, especially Chapter 4, 'Lokalspezifisches theatrum gouvernemental/ posse: Wien 2000 ff.', 86–110, at 89.
100. See 'RechtsWalzer'. Retrieved 6 May 2018 from http://www.2gas.net/art.in.resistance.htm.
101. See 'Hump-Dump', in Panagl, Gerlich et al., *Wörterbuch der politischen Sprache in Österreich*, 191–92. 'Lump' might be translated as a thug or worthless prole; the dictionary definition, 'scoundrel', is too dated and polite.
102. Frederick Baker, *Widerstand in Haiderland*. Austria: Filmbäckerei, 2010.
103. Retrieved 6 May 2018 from http://www.gettyimages.co.uk/detail/news-photo/graffiti-artists-using-spray-paint-changed-a-campaign-news-photo/51952806.
104. Weidinger, 'Widerstand im Mehlspeisland'. The Haider family residence is in the Bärental region of Carinthia. The FPÖ's use in 2010 of an online game called 'Moschee baba' (developed from an existing Swiss game requiring the player to destroy mosques) was subject to a legal challenge. '"Moschee baba": Justiz lässt Minarett-Spiel sperren', *Die Presse*, 3 September 2010. Retrieved 6 May 2018 from http://diepresse.com/home/politik/steiermarkwahl/592068/Moschee-baba_Justiz-laesst-MinarettSpiel-sperren.
105. Weidinger, 'Widerstand im Mehlspeisland'. See also 'schwarz-blaue Wende' in Panagl, Gerlich et al., *Wörterbuch der politischen Sprache in Österreich*, 376–78, at 378.
106. Wolfgang Böhm, 'Sanktionen: Ein ganzes Land in Quarantäne', *Die Presse*, 30 January 2010. Retrieved 6 May 2018 from http://diepresse.com/home/meinung/marginalien/536392/Sanktionen_Ein-ganzes-Land-in-Quarantaene.
107. Photographs of some 'GegenSchwarzBlau-Accessoires' feature in Baker and Boyer, *Wiener Wandertage*. Artist activist Martin Krenn displays stickers from the protests at http://www.martinkrenn.net/?attachment_id=692.
108. Jacques Attali, *Noise: The Political Economy of Music* (Manchester: Manchester University Press, 1985), 3.
109. Turino, *Music as Social Life*, 6.
110. *Trend*, online magazine, 'Die ersten sieben Tage: Aktionen Gegen Schwarzblau in Wien'. Retrieved 6 May 2018 from http://www.trend.infopartisan.net/trd0200/t170200.html.
111. Turino, *Music as Social Life*, 14.
112. Erste Allgemeine Verunsicherung, 'Valerie, Valera: Haiders Sprung in seiner Schüssel'.
113. Georg Friedrich Haas, 'In Vain', *In Vain*, CD. Austria: Kairos, 2004, first performed in 2000 at the Klangforum, Vienna.
114. Alan Lockwood, 'Discordant Harmony: Ensemble Pi and Sarah Cahill Examine Political Activism in Music', *Time Out*, 2009. Retrieved 6 May 2018 from http://www.timeout.com/newyork/opera-classical/discordant-harmony.
115. Baker and Boyer, *Wiener Wandertage*, illustrations nos 104–6.
116. Weidinger, 'Widerstand im Mehlspeisland'. See above for the reference to Thomas Prinzhorn. Westenthascherl is an elision that suggests Peter Westenthaler, at that time a

close party colleague of Haider's in the FPÖ, and 'Hascherl', a poor soul. A number of baked items are called various kinds of 'Tascherl'. The term also evokes Haider's insulting description of French leader Jacques Chirac as a 'Westentaschen-Napoleon' (tinpot Napoleon) during his Ash Wednesday speech in 2000.

117. The pyschological implications of the term and its swift adoption into the political lexis are explained in 'Hacklerregelung', in Panagl, Gerlich et al., *Wörterbuch der politischen Sprache in Österreich*, 174–75.
118. 'Irritiert? Schockiert? Gut so. Das ist beabsichtigt. Diese Kampagne ist absurd. Rassismus ist absurd. Dennoch wird mit Rassismus wieder Politik gemacht. Dagegen: Widerstand auch unter der Gürtellinie.' Weidinger, 'Widerstand im Mehlspeisland'. The group of activists, entitled 'Monochrom', appear to have resurrected their 'Scrotum gegen Votum' tactics again in 2010. 'Die Big Brother Awards', 3 November 2010. Retrieved 6 May 2018 from http://www.monochrom.at/s-g-v.
119. Vina Yun, 'an.sage: Mission: Selbstbestimmung: Ein Kommentar', *an.schläge: das feministische magazin*, 24 June 2013. Retrieved 6 May 2018 from http://anschlaege.at/feminismus/2013/06/an-sage-mission-selbstbestimmung.
120. Rosellini notes that Mortier 'repeatedly called Haider a "fascist" and announced that he was stepping down as director of the Salzburg Festival, only to change his mind after a short time', *Haider, Jelinek, and the Culture Wars*, 159.
121. See Allyson Fiddler, 'Wie lange bleiben blaue Flecken? Erinnerungen und Gedanken aus Großbritannien zum 10. Jahrestag der schwarz-blauen Koalition', in Frederick Baker and Paula Herczeg (eds), *Die beschämte Republik: 10 Jahre nach Schwarz-Blau in Österreich* (Vienna: Czernin, 2010), 71–77. Austrians travelling abroad in 2000 could buy themselves a passport cover that stated in seven different languages 'I did not vote for our government'. Baker and Boyer, *Wiener Wandertage*, illustration no. 100.
122. Stephen Duncombe, 'Introduction', in Stephen Duncombe (ed.), *Cultural Resistance Reader* (London: Verso, 2002), 1–15, at 13.

Chapter 3

NOVEL RESPONSES
Protest in Prose

Introduction: Narratives of Resistance

The novel is understandably the least prevalent genre or art form in the field of cultural-political resistance. There have always been political novels or prose-writings that express criticism of politics in its various manifestations either expressly against particular developments or policies, or in a more concealed or allegorical fashion, perhaps by way of general resistance to an oppressive regime. But prose writers who feel the need or desire to express protest about a specific event must reckon not only with the gestation and writing time for a reasonably sized novel, but also with the publisher's production schedule and the unpredictability of both individual reception and media professional review of their work – novels that refer too exclusively to a particular political moment are sometimes deemed too narrow or too limited in their shelf life. This chapter discusses a selection of novels that use the real-life sociopolitical climate of turn-of-the-century Austria as more than just *local* colour and that consequently, albeit to varying degrees, can be described as expressing the writer's disquiet or disapproval of the *political* colour of Austrian politics of this time.

Much more common expressions of writerly protest are the numerous short pieces that were aired on the websites of the many protest organizations or delivered as contributions to the enduring weekly *Widerstandslesungen* (resistance readings; see also Chapter 2). In the age of cyber protest, it is, of course, possible for any internet user to write and 'publish' their own protest writing, poem, story, journal or blog, but the present study cannot capture this aspect of albeit fascinating, usually 'lay' responses to the black-and-blue era. Moreover, the period examined in the present volume concerns a time when user-generated internet content was still in its infancy. Common accessibility was not yet a given at the turn of the millennium and social networking sites had not yet been launched. A small number of edited publications bring together contributions by professional writers, journalists, actors and politicians, as well as in some cases ordinary members of the public. This was a particular wish of the editors of the *Wiener Wandertage* collection of 2002. Two other notable publications present a rich variety of reflections in the form of poetry, published speeches, short stories, diary entries, scenes from plays and so on. These are, first, El Awadalla and Traude Korosa's reader, ...*Bis sie gehen* (2004), which presents materials from the first four years of the resistance readings, and, second, the highly timely volume of contributions by women artists and intellectuals, entitled *Die Sprache des Widerstandes ist alt wie die Welt und ihr Wunsch* (2000).[1]

There is some overlap of material between the volumes, with a small number of pieces being printed in two of the collections. Mostly the volumes contain occasional pieces that had been penned originally for newspaper columns or for speeches. There are also a few items that were not written for these publications, or in some cases were even written before 1999, but that the editors have chosen to include, doubtless for their relevance or for their thought-provoking nature.[2] As might be expected, there are a number of high-profile or better-known writers who feature in one or more of these publications – Elfriede Jelinek, Marlene Streeruwitz and Franzobel, for example, and other literary names include Kathrin Röggla, Margret Kreidl, El Awadalla and Gerhard Ruiss. By and large, the contributions fit into certain broad category types, whether they are provided by professional writers, journalists, academics, politicians or members of the public. Thus, aside from the poems and short dramatic excerpts, the prose pieces are either essays, interviews, written versions of speeches and open letters, or they are reflective, first-person narratives sometimes written in journal- or diary-entry style. Marlene Streeruwitz, one of the 'Three Wise Women', is the author most associated with longer publications of this style, presenting her reflections of the period from 2000 to 2001 as the 184-page-long *Tagebuch der Gegenwart* and airing regular episodes of two election novels on her own internet homepage. The personal invective and supposed superior self-knowledge of her *Tagebuch* is something that earned her criticism from Hannelore Schlaffer of the Frankfurter Allgemeine Zeitung: 'she boldly picks up all the popular newspaper stories circulating in the media in 2000 and 2001 when she was writing: Haider, hatred of foreigners, surrogate mothers, the conservative turn in education, the whole fake cult of the Austrian *Heimat*, in short: life and all its wrongs, and where there's only one right way – the Marlene Streeruwitz way'.[3] Such an abundance of *Zeitzeugenliteratur* (first-hand witness literature) and *Momentaufnahmen* (literary snapshots)[4] is understandable, as contributors seek to offer personal responses or chronicles, but this chapter will deal first with a selection of more extended prose writings before concluding with a discussion of some of the many short-story protest pieces. The novels discussed here do not seem to sit comfortably within single genre descriptions, but might roughly speaking be termed: (i) a dystopian adventure novel; (ii) a love story; (iii) critical or feminist women's writing; and (iv) thrillers. This chapter might have further included novels by Gerhard Roth (*Der See*, 1995) Werner Thuswaldner (*Pittersberg*, 2000) or Milo Dor (*Wien, Juli 1999*, 1997), but it is not possible to discuss more than a small number of texts in detail in the present study.[5] The materials discussed in this chapter are all in prose form, some are shorter in length, and others are full-scale novels. The texts are full of imagination and are thus not 'prosaic' at all in the other sense of this word – they adopt 'novel' responses to discussing contemporary Austrian politics, as my chapter heading suggests.

'Aussteigen': Another Form of Protest – Ernst Molden's *Doktor Paranoiski* (2001)

Opting out of a society can very well be seen as a form of political protest, and the 'Aussteiger' or drop-out-protagonist is a common enough trope in literature, especially of the post-1968 era. However, if a novel is not readily identifiable as an expression of protest, we might wonder whether the decision to bale out of a society does not amount to the cultural equivalent of declining to vote. In other words, can it be taken as a useful and stimulating marker of protest against the prevailing political climate? Critic Susanne Messmer identifies a small but rich vein of Austrian prose writings that centre either on the central character's thoughts of escape or his actual attempts at living a life outside normal society. 'Protest gegen den Rechtspopulismus von Jörg Haider?' ('protest against Jörg Haider's right-wing populism?'), Messmer asks, and sees Daniel Kehlmann's novella *Der fernste Ort* (2001), Xaver Bayer's *Heute könnte ein glücklicher Tag sein* (2001) and Ernst Molden's *Doktor Paranoiski* as describing 'the flight from a world which requires hardworking high performers. They're getting quite close to contemporary Austria here'.[6] Kehlmann's novel is not specifically located, nor does it make any mention of contemporary social or political givens. But it would be possible to see the surreal improbabilities and Kafkaesque delusions of its insurance employee protagonist, Julian, as an expression of political denial. *Der fernste Ort* reads more like a string of almost random, Camusian events leading from the protagonist's staged death to his presumed, eventual submission to actual death. It does not suggest itself as a work of deliberate protest. The same might, at first sight, be said of the contemporaneous novel by Ernst Molden.[7]

When Molden's protagonist Dr Salzer decides to fake his own death, drop out of normal society and live instead in the forests around Vienna, he does not cite his political convictions as grounds or even express an anti-conformist desire not to become one of the FPÖ's oft-invoked, 'Leistungsträger' or 'hardworking folk and pillars of society'. Dr Salzer simply experiences a growing sense of tedium and loses any sense of joy in life, opting to fake his own death with the help of an acquaintance from the morgue from whom he receives a suitable replacement body to have burn in his flat, complete with inserted dental bridge work to ensure later false identification of the body. The first-person narrator furnishes this bizarre and truncated point of departure in a down-to-earth fashion and in a handful of pages in the first of the novel's three sections, entitled, respectively, 'wald', 'berg' and 'stadt' (forest, mountain and city). If the opening circumstances require readers to suspend their disbelief, then the rest of the novel is a challenge indeed, as the protagonist's development moves from near-dead loner (the terminus of Kehlmann's protagonist's journey) to recruited environmentalist cum anti-globalization activist in a network of underground groups residing in the forests of lower Austria and on the outskirts of Vienna. The strong narrative voice, the credibility of the narrator's slow, personal development and the realistic mode of depiction all combine to present the reader with a curious blend of convincing and compelling story on the one hand and wry parody of alternative society on the other.

The two substantial sections, 'wald' and 'berg', show the erstwhile botanist first being saved from starvation and subsequently trained up to become a member of an eco-warrior underground grouping of 'Unsterbliche' (immortals) living in the Viennese woods. He is nicknamed 'Dr Paranoiski' by the woman he is fascinated by and falls in love with, 'Rea' (or '*Realidád*. Die Wirklichkeit [reality]', whose name ironically foreshadows the novel's ending.[8] The protagonist becomes, as it were, a mobile, human form of the botanical species he has spent his former life specializing in 'Nachtschattengewächse' (Nightshades). Moving around by night in the Austrian woods and mobilizing for occasional raids, the army's various subgroupings of alternative thinkers – a women's warrior band, disenchanted youths, anti-globalization activists and even, it is intimated, extreme right-wing pockets – are all preparing, in an unlikely coalition, for what Wachtmeister Lau calls 'Tag X' ('D-Day'). Until this day of reckoning, Paranoiski and the many other initiates have to pledge to uphold the army's three main objectives: 'die Auflösung der Staaten', 'die Abschaffung des Geldes' and 'die Bewaldung der Städte' (the dissolution of states, the abolition of money and the forestation of cities). Given the almost complete absence of evaluative commentary by the narrator, it is possible for the reader to take Molden's strange scenario at face value and submit to enjoying the slow build-up of his unlikely tale:

> Right to the end of the book, the reader is not sure whether this troop is a kind of sympathetic, if somewhat militant green community or a bunch of poor nutters on the loose. The author leaves the final decision to the reader; he offers no explanation for their existence and eschews any kind of emotional statement.[9]

The narrative style is laconic, but ironies abound, and some sparse interjections allow the reader to see, too, that the narrator retains a little distance from the objectives that he has somewhat automatically signed up to. When he recruits two teenagers, 'Elvis' and 'Blondie', at the site of their intended suicide, he acknowledges that the idea of reforesting the cities does indeed sound laughable.[10]

Molden's novel is introduced by a fictive editor who explains that the account that follows is actually a transcript of three audio-cassettes he received from a man claiming to have faked his own death. This introduction and the accelerated events of the short final section, 'stadt', provide the highly unsettling framing device for the entire narrative. Just as the famous Rahmenhandlung of the classic, expressionist film *Das Cabinet des Doktor Caligari* (1920) redraws the protagonist as an inmate of an asylum and not the brave unmasker of the paranoid, murderous asylum director (and metaphorical precursor of Nazi authoritarianism), so too Salzer/Paranoiski wakes up in Chapter 29 of 31 to be told repeatedly by Dr Regina Birnbaumer, the woman who resembles his beloved Rea and wears the ring he recognizes, that he is suffering from delusions and that the tape-recording she has asked him to make is not an instruction from her putative former role as fellow underground warrior, but a common request in psychiatry practice. However, in Wiene's film and in Molden's novel, the line between reality and fantasy is blurred. The conscious overlaps between the apparently hallucinated narrative and the protagonist's knowing perception of the 'real' world of the asylum leave the reader with the feeling that Salzer's experiences cannot just be dismissed as an aberration. The hooded crow that has stayed somewhere nearby Paranoiski ever since he saves its life early on in the narrative suggests the verisimilitude of his account and reminds us of his good intentions. Yet, Salzer is not guilt-free – he has killed police guards during a raid for quantities of salt, a valuable commodity for preserving food and ironically pointing at the character's own name too (Chapter 18). Many mythical Gods – Apollo, Bacchus, the Nordic Odin and the Germanic Wotan – were said to be accompanied or warned by a wise crow or raven, although the bird is often connoted not just with intelligence, but also with death and with the Underworld. It thus seems a logical companion for Paranoiski in his own 'odyssey' into the world of the immortals, as they call themselves. All the more telling, then, that the novel ends with the narrator's – perhaps accidental – shooting of what the reader assumes is 'his' crow, as he fires his pistol into the air.

Apart from the narrator-protagonist's occasional anxious requests for clarification, for example, when charged with bringing back into the fold a group of renegades holed out in a cave, there is little hint of party-political association or of the immortals' adherence to normal political groupings: 'What are they? Right-wing extremists? I ask. Just give over with all your old-fashioned categories. Left! Right! Yes, the boys see themselves as German. But Nazis? No.'[11] However, when Paranoiski is charged with his last and most daring mission, he is updated on the political situation in Austria since his faked death:

> You'll get help in catching up on the political situation of your former state of Austria. A few things have happened since you died. The Nationals have left government, the Christian Conservatives are now ruling on their own, in a minority. There'll be elections in the autumn.[12]

Published in 2001, Molden's fictional political landscape proves prescient indeed as it pre-empts the resignation of prominent FPÖ politicians from the coalition government in 2002 following the Knittelfeldputsch, a party conference at which internal political differences came to a head and prompted the resignation of leading figures in the FPÖ.[13] The later reality differs from this earlier fiction only in that the 'Christkonservativen' or 'ÖVP' did not rule alone following the 2002 autumn election, but in a renewed coalition with the much-weakened FPÖ. Paranoiski succeeds in his mission to impersonate Gerd Wegerer, the Home Secretary and Vice-Chancellor of Austria, on live television news and secures enough air time before his inevitable arrest to proclaim a state of emergency, to inform Austrian citizens that money now has no value and to urge them to take to the woods and mountains and follow the instructions of the private army, which, he announces, has taken charge.

Ernst Molden is not a prominent name amongst the artists and writers who protested against the black-and-blue regime, but the former newspaper editor and acclaimed singer-songwriter has been a regular guest at Green Party events and has been endorsed by anti-racism events organizers.[14] There is the sense that the references to brutal, armed, secret police – like the unit who fight them in the night raid on the supermarket – and the violent beatings he receives after his capture from the television studio are disguised nods towards some of the scandals over police brutality in Austria at the time. Walter Robotka identifies in the character Gerd Wegerer what he calls 'certain similarities with a current member of the government'.[15] Molden's description of the politician and his portfolio in charge of policing and immigration, suggest to me that Wegerer is modelled on Ernst Strasser, who was Home Secretary from March 2000 to December 2004. The distortion of the onomastic's root, from 'Straße' (street) to 'Weg' (path/way) and the monosyllabic first name both point to parodic reinvention. Molden's fictional protagonist is detained and tortured by the police, but the narrative does not flesh out any of the actual domestic politics of Austria in 2000–2001. It is thus only possible for the politically knowledgeable reader – or indeed the reader who is seeking to find contemporaneous allusion – to determine associations with the concerns being voiced at the time. These included the ill-treatment of asylum-seeker detainees by the police (in the period before and after Molden's novel was published). We are reminded of the public scandals following the death of Nigerian Marcus Omofuma in police custody in 1999 and that of

Mauritian Cheibane Wague in 2003, when a video camera captured the brutality of police and emergency service staff. These, and cases such as the police abuse of Congolese asylum seeker Kambowa Mutombo in 2002, were also pursued by the human rights organization Amnesty International.[16]

It is difficult to draw lessons or messages from Molden's novel, since the text occupies a curious middle ground, oscillating between a parodic gaze at drop-out protesters whose alternative societies begin to replicate the authoritarian social structures of normal, regulated society, and an acknowledgement of the need for escape, furnished here by proxy in literary form. In taking to the woods, Molden's character can be taken as the starting point for a playful, fictive musing on the subject of authority, subjectivity and how to effect resistance in society, a kind of contemporary, tongue-in-cheek enactment of Ernst Jünger's reactionary conservative 1951 essay 'Der Waldgang',[17] or Molden's answer to Jünger's related 1977 futuristic novel *Eumeswil*.

Doktor Paranoiski takes its place, I would argue, as a variation of the anti-Heimat novel genre. The narrator sees his former self as 'ein echter Wiener, in Lodenmantel und Schal', but the body of the plot then exposes the underside of his Vienna. Molden and Salzer/Paranoiski's love of nature and fondness for the Wienerwald so feted in music, art and literature is apparent in the clear descriptions of flora and fauna, and in the authenticity of the various routes through the forests. Ironically, Salzer is given a beating by a nature watchman who comes across him in his initial tramp-like existence and accuses him of defiling 'the Austrian forest . . . as praised in song by Schubert and in paint by Waldmüller'.[18] But Molden seems to sing the virtues of 'wandern' in the Viennese woods, connoted here not as simple pastime of both the Austrian nature-lover and the tourist alike, but as yet another variation of the kind of protest by walking championed by the Thursday demonstrators, albeit secretly by night in the Viennese woods and not in full view through the streets of Vienna (see Chapter 2).

Einsteigen? Erika Pluhar's *Die Wahl* (2003)

Erika Pluhar is primarily known for her highly successful career as an actor and singer, a career that, like the protagonist of her 2003 novel, she left behind in order to pursue her writing. However, the crossovers between the author's biography and the events and characters of the novel do not stop there. Like the fictional ex-actor Charlotte Wohlig, Pluhar was also approached as a possible candidate for the 1998 presidential election, in her case by both the Green Party and by the Social Democrats.[19] If the political backdrop hints back to 1998, then, and does not address directly the legislative election of 1999/2000, the object of the protagonist's campaigning zeal is very much modelled on the criticism directed at the FPÖ and its allies both before and after the Wende, that is, for fomenting racism and promoting populist-nationalist sentiment. Like many others writing and protesting against the black-and-blue coalition government, the author and her literary representative do not shy from using terms such as 'faschistoid spirit' or fascist 'tendencies' to describe some of the developments they detect in turn-of-the-century Austria.[20]

In stark contrast to Molden's protagonist, Charlotte Wohlig's decision is to enter into the very thick of political society by running as the Social Democrat candidate for presidency. As an independent-minded person, however, she is not prepared to act as a mere party-political mouthpiece. Unlike many ordinary Austrians and political commentators at home and abroad, she does not subscribe to the view that the success of 'right-wing populism' (the inference points to the success of the FPÖ in the 1999 election) was to be attributed to the failure of the two main parties, the ÖVP and the SPÖ. In the draft of a speech sent to her daughter for comment, Wohlig concedes that the Social Democrats in Austria had been too insensitive to a changing society and too set in their ways, and further that they had failed to embrace a green agenda.[21] Wohlig's analysis continues: 'But the rise in popularity of right-wing extremism, of what's now being called "Walderism", was made possible by a discontent without cause, a discontent that could be stirred up because everything is running satisfactorily. Because, at the end of the day, our country had become a well-governed and well-appointed country, and it still is.'[22] To attribute the success of right-wing populism to the electorate's boredom with Austria's grand coalition-induced constancy and self-satisfaction does seem a little exaggerated, even though it echoes the much-peddled thesis that the FPÖ's 1999 success was in large part due to the electorate's 'protest vote' against the inertia and complacency of the two main parties. Consequently, Wohlig's clear-headed daughter counsels her to take account of some of Austria's real problems and rein in her speech. Nodding to the occasional corruption scandals and to the tarnished reputations of the larger parties, Wohlig is of the opinion that corruption will always exist, but that it is at least more easily detected in a democracy than 'in the darkness of dictatorships'.[23]

In rehearsing some of the arguments for Jörg Haider's FPÖ's success, or rather for its fictional ersatz, Pluhar is at pains not to mention this party by its proper name, referring instead to populism and right-wing extremism or, in the words of daughter, Klara, in a fax to her mother, 'the representatives of this *Mean*dom Party'.[24] Pluhar's coinages are not solely parodic strategies or aptonymic constructions (Wohlig, Klara, Mentschig), although the reader inevitably appreciates some satirical intent. The author's reticence is unsurprising, given the FPÖ's predilection for libel actions. Haider's personal lawyer and later Minister for Justice (from 2000 to 2004), Dieter Böhmdorfer, was tasked with suing dozens of Haider's critics, from newspaper editors to artists and political scientists. One of the most high-profile examples is that of the artist, singer and cabarettist André Heller, who was married to Pluhar from 1970 to 1984. In an open letter of 2000, Heller referred to the 'likes' of Haider, Böhmdorfer, Westenthaler and Riess-Passer as 'diese seelenhygienisch heruntergekommenen Politempörlinge' ('these spiritually corrupt political upstarts') and as 'Bierzeltanimateure' ('beer tent entertainers'), which made him the subject of a protracted but ultimately unsuccessful libel action.[25] It is worth noting here that the EU Report by the 'Three Wise Men' made express mention of the increased and repeated usage of libel actions by the FPÖ and pointed diplomatically to the significant, detrimental effects that this could have on freedom of speech and on citizens' willingness to express criticism of government.[26]

In what is clearly a kind of *roman-à-clef*, then, Pluhar coins easily identifiable distortions for the politicians who are referred to even if they do not feature as characters of her novel. Sepp Walder is so clearly a substitute name for Jörg Haider, the Germanic monosyllabic first name and the surname that evokes a proximity to the rural, Austrian folkish scenery and heartland.[27] The movement name 'Walderismus' is a parodic reference to 'Haiderismus' (Haiderization/ Haiderism), a term that was widely used to refer to Haider's style of politics and its influence on society in Austria and further afield. Even after Haider's death, the media were noting that 'Haiderization is still thriving, even without Haider'.[28] Another novel to have played overtly with *à clef* references is the highly successful *Opernball* by Josef Haslinger (1995), for which the subsequent film adaptation chose to convert the name of the Haider-like, right-wing nationalist party leader character to 'Jup Bärenthal' (evoking the name of the estate in Carinthia owned by the Haider family).[29] Pluhar has fun with the passing references to other familiar politicians' names too: 'Ostenberger' is derived directly from antonyms (Ost – West; Berg – Tal) and refers to Peter Westenthaler, the BZÖ Chairman from 2006 to 2008 and Haider's former secretary when both men were in the FPÖ, who changed his name from the Czech Hojač to assume his mother's more Germanic maiden name. The double-barrelled character, Sabine Spalt-Klemmer, can surely only refer to Haider's Freedom Party Vice-Chair and later Chair, Susanne Riess-Passer. Riess-Passer was Vice-Chancellor of Austria during the first ÖVP-FPÖ coalition until the early elections of 2002. She left politics following the Knittelfeld putsch and her disagreements with Jörg Haider.

The local colour and character justification originates in the political association of the novel's title ('Wahl' means election), but it is the other connotation of the German noun 'Wahl' (option) that is more salient for the love story at the centre of Pluhar's book. Candidate Charlotte Wohlig steadily falls in love with her close colleague and fellow Social Democrat, Chancellor Paul Mentschig. As might be inferred from his name, the Chancellor is truly a 'mensch' and stands by Charlotte even when compromising photographs of them are taken as they say goodbye outside her front door and when the couple sense that these will be used to blackmail her into withdrawing her candidacy. If Charlotte first had to weigh the consequences on her disabled, adult daughter of her 'choice' or 'decision' (Wahl) to stand as a candidate, she then has to consciously renew this choice as Klara is threatened and roughed up by a gang of men she encounters when out for some air with her domestic helper and wheelchair pusher, Elaine. The penultimate decision of the novel is left to Mentschig, whose career and political integrity Wohlig offers to safeguard by standing down, but in true romantic novel tradition, the hitherto silent voice of the strong man is given pride of place in the dénouement as Mentschig professes to Wohlig that through her he has rediscovered the loving man he used to be: 'I was suddenly able to love and I have no intention of giving that up again. I simply want to stand by you publicly, Charlotte, no fuss, no drama.' 'Du hast die Wahl' ('you have the choice'), Mentschig returns the final decision to Wohlig, and the novel ends with the protagonist's renewed decision to continue her candidacy.[30]

Mentschig may wish to keep pathos at bay, but the sparsely described recurring motif of nature's storms and winds presents a rather jarring suggestion of pathetic fallacy. The smells, sounds and sensations of the wind and trees are observed by Charlotte at regular intervals and provide a punctuating metaphor for the turmoil in her mind and her anticipation of the autumn, traditionally the time of elections in Austria.[31] Pluhar does, however, have the saving grace of allowing her protagonist to recognize the way in which her observations seem to be akin to the analogies found in trivial or romantic literature: 'me and my autumn storms are just too funny. How did I come to make these trashy novel analogies'.[32]

In *Die Wahl*, Pluhar contributes a very enjoyable and accessible piece of protest literature. The development of the protagonist and her thoughts and political sensitivities are presented in an appealing, modern kind of epistolary. There are large passages of direct speech, conducted in person or on the phone, but a large part of the novel consists of emails and faxes between the would-be politician mother and her highly astute and ironically very mothering daughter. When 'Lotte' cannot think what action she should take, Klara advises her to 'formulate something. Write it up. Get the whole thing straight in your head'.[33] The protagonist's modified answer – 'yes, I will write it all up or rather I'll write it down'[34] – mirrors the author's own resolve to counter her political foes, keeping things under control through writing. Outside fiction, Pluhar pens her protest in forms such as the open letter or newspaper article; in *Die Wahl*, she presents a 'Schlüsselroman' that could be said to both humanize Austrian politics[35] as well as exorcize some of its political demons.

Can Chick Lit Topple the Government? Marlene Streeruwitz's *Jessica, 30.* (2004)

There are many angles from which Marlene Streeruwitz's novel *Jessica, 30.* could be compared with Pluhar's *Die Wahl*.[36] Here, too, the protagonist is a Viennese woman whose love interest is a politician, only this time it is not an SPÖ chancellor, but an ÖVP politician with the fictitious portfolio of 'Staatssekretär für Zukunfts- und Entwicklungsfragen' (Secretary of State for Development and Future Affairs), Gerhard Hollitzer. Where Pluhar's novel ends somewhat openly but with an affirmation of love and a well-considered decision to stand for election, Streeruwitz concludes her novel with the narrator-protagonist's rather tortuous and not wholly credible resolve to seek revenge on her former lover by revealing a sex-scandal story to the German news magazine *Stern*. Both texts, then, have something of the *Entwicklungsroman* genre about them, even if the timespan allowed for the protagonists' psychological development is restricted to a matter of months, not years. Barbara Frischmuth's 1998 novel *Die Schrift des Freundes* might also bear comparison with these two novels, and sees the protagonist Anna split with her home-office civil-servant boyfriend and a clandestine data-tracking system for monitoring the immigrant community.[37]

Streeruwitz's novel consists almost entirely of the inner thoughts of the eponymous, thirty-year-old freelance journalist Jessica Somner. With the exception of a brief sequence of dialogue in the second section, *Jessica, 30.* is written in the author's own flavour of stream-of-consciousness writing, punctuated in two of its parts only by commas and characterized by the frequent changes of direction of thought and incomplete grammar that might be deemed to reflect realistically the inner monologue of any human character, and here, specifically, of a kind of crystallized, unmarried female representative of an educated thirtysomething generation. Given Streeruwitz's predilection for publications of her own observations and sociopolitical style commentaries, it is not surprising that reviewers have been tempted to align the voice of Jessica with that of Streeruwitz herself, concluding that behind the protagonist 'at every moment the presence of the author is audible, the voice of a fifty-year-old feminist dishing the dirt on countless people and topics from everyday Austrian politics'.[38] Indeed, mention is made of a great many Austrian political events and news topics of the period in which the novel is set. Jessica's thoughts whilst out running one cold morning in the Prater and then driving home to her apartment form the text of the first section, and mention is made here, and in the second part, of the coalition negotiations taking place prior to the 2002-elected coalition government being sworn in (April 2003). The final part can be calibrated amongst other things by Jessica's mention of the real-life theft of Cellini's 'Saliera' ('dieses Salzfasserl'; that salt cellar) from the Kunsthistorisches Museum in May 2003.[39]

However, the vast majority of Jessica's ruminations do not reflect the Austrian political Zeitgeist of the early twenty-first century, but consist instead of what might be thought of as an exaggerated stereotypical inner anguish of a young woman, pondering subjects such as: her body image and the concomitant thoughts of weight control and comfort eating; her current sex life and previous partners; her relationship with her divorced parents; fashion deliberations; her job search; and her circle of friends. The range of Jessica's introspection and the central focus in the novel on a failed relationship (with the philandering Gerhard) and resumption of a former relationship (with stable, loving Harti) suggests to Brenda Bethman the genre description of chick lit for Streeruwitz's novel, albeit as a kind of 'alternative fiction':

> The tension that arises from the combination of a postfeminist title character (Jessica) and form (chick-lit) with the author's second wave sensibilities results in a text that reveals the tension between second and third wave feminisms, especially in the final chapter, which depicts Jessica's evolution from the 'Ally-McBeal-Klon' (S. 21) of the first chapter to a revenge-seeking critic of patriarchy who links the Iraq war to male sexuality.[40]

Streeruwitz imbues her character with a great deal of intelligence and a Ph.D. in a feminist cultural studies topic for good measure, but in Jessica she also creates a protagonist who is full of contradictions and with whom the contemporary feminist reader will find it difficult to empathize wholeheartedly. As Ina Hartwig points out, Jessica is not so much a character as a kind of constructed intersection of opposing qualities, such as being capable of seeing clearly through oppression and being oppressed or exploited at the same time.[41] There are emotions and opinions voiced that are mutually contradictory, and Jessica's observations on contemporary politics are mostly either apolitical or more like the stuff of gossip columns. It could be argued that Streeruwitz's novel is more a deconstruction of postfeminist sensitivities than it is a political novel or protest novel per se. 'Jessica Somner, c'est moi?', Hartwig poses Flaubert's assertion of kindred association with his character, Madame Bovary, interrogatively, but answers emphatically: 'No. Marlene Streeruwitz takes a steely look at the new *condition féminine*. The thirty-something women who think their catty tactics are the way out of their political impotence do not come out of it at all heroically.'[42]

Jessica's thoughts are conveyed to the reader in Part I as she takes one of her infrequent jogs, not for pleasure but to mitigate the effects of too much binge eating of ice cream the night before. The aesthetic style of incomplete grammar, solid blocks of text without paragraphs and the complete lack of full stops mirrors the breathlessness of her running, but her mental state should be described metaphorically more as an indecisive somnambulance than as a wakeful alertness enhanced by sport. Not for nothing is the character named 'Somner', suggesting sleepiness and not the sunnier disposition that 'Sommer' might suggest.[43] The particular situation that acts as a catalyst for Jessica to get out of the rut she is stuck in and finally end her relationship with Gerhard comes in the second part of the novel, the action of which takes place in her flat. Having decided that she will not be removing her clothes or indeed allowing Gerhard to stay overnight, she resolves first to tackle him on the alleged abuse of her friend Mia, the latter having described in an unpublished book her own abuse at the hands of Gerhard in a sadomasochistic sex game. However, before Jessica takes up the subject, she ends up fellating Gerhard at first of her own volition, but then – during a bizarre phone call Gerhard has with his wife – increasingly under duress, as the stream of consciousness relates how she wants him to let go of her, but is forced to continue until Gerhard ejaculates.[44] The phone call incident is ironically timed, but the author also parallels Gerhard's abuse of Jessica with the direct speech of an ironic conversation he has with his wife about who will take on the role of establishing law and order in the new government: 'I'm not bothered if one of the Blues does that job. They'd do a better job of it, but it'd look bad abroad. We'll have to drag things out a bit longer.'[45]

In the final part of Streeruwitz's novel, we learn that it is not the prospect of exposing Gerhard's sadomasochistic games with Mia that Jessica feels will generate sufficient punishment on her former lover. Her own research has thrown up a sex scandal in which various politicians have been involved, and Gerhard has only gone and paid for the Eastern European women's pleasures with party monies, that is, with public funds. *Jessica, 30.* is prefaced with the important caveat that 'this text is a work of literary fiction. Story and characters are fictitious',[46] but as Loreley French explains, the scenario depicted foreshadows a real-life scandal that was about to break:

> Marlene Streeruwitz's novel *Jessica, 30.* appeared just some three months before politician Gerhard Roder, one-time candidate for the provincial parliament in Lower Austria and then press spokesperson for the National Parliament president Andreas Khol, was telephoning sex traffickers in Vienna on August 4, 2004, to request information on the availability and specialities of specific women.[47]

Roder, the ÖVP politician, had made a name for himself as a champion of women's issues and had even set up a citizens' initiative against child abuse. Streeruwitz's acuity for detecting the hypocrisies of contemporary society and expressing these by fictional analogy becomes more accentuated in the second and third parts of the novel. Gerhard's answer to Jessica's taunt about how the coalition will tackle the issue of sexuality and family policies must be read as an emblem of the double standards of those in power. 'How do you lot pull off that whole happy family thing?' Jessica asks. 'That's easy,' Gerhard boasts, 'the family is sacred, and prostitution is now tax-free.'[48]

In 2003, Elisabeth Gehrer, the ÖVP Education Minister, was making headlines for admonishing the thirtysomething generation for too much partying and for threatening the future financial viability of the country and its pensions funds by having too few children (see also Chapter 2). Extensive pension reforms were being discussed by the coalition government in April 2003, including the reduction of the statutory state pension and the raising of the retirement age. Jessica's thoughts even evoke the fact that Haider was distancing himself from this unpopular set of reforms.[49] Her motivation in unmasking Gerhard in the press vacillates, but the reader sees through, or at least laughs at, Jessica's denial of revenge, presented as a girl power-style feminist action on behalf of the sisterhood ('it's all for the cause of women, it's a Red Zora terrorist action, it's Tank Girl, and Angelina Jolie'),[50] sensing that Jessica wants to punish Gerhard *pars pro toto* for other men who she feels have wronged her. However, more risible yet is the fantasy logic Jessica constructs, in which, following her daydream vision, she will be the saviour of the pension reform and Thursday anti-government demonstration protesters alike:

> the best thing would be that the whole government has to stand down because of Gerhard, but that won't happen, it won't happen here, the pension reform thing would be stopped then, too, and I'd have saved our pensions, if everything went well, that would be so nice, Jessica, the Saviour, there's me standing on the Heldenplatz sending all the demonstrators home, out of the storms and the hail, because the government has to stand down anyway due to their State Secretary for Development Affairs and his sex trafficking of girls.[51]

Marlene Streeruwitz may well be parodying a genre of fiction written for young women, usually singles in their twenties or thirties, but her own bestselling riposte reached the bestseller lists too. She may send up her character's inner thoughts (as in the quotation above), but she does at least credit her protagonist with detecting the key weapon in her one-woman fight against chauvinist bullying, that is, money. The public will be incensed not by learning of the politicians' use of prostitutes after a party seminar, but by their using public monies to pay for their pleasure.[52] That Austria implicitly condones the sexual antics of men like Gerhard Hollitzer, or indeed those of 'Kardinal Groer',[53] former Archbishop of Vienna whose sexual abuses led to his dismissal by the Pope in the 1990s but to no criminal conviction, is something that Jessica laments. Hollitzer, on the other hand, compares Austria favourably to the United States or to England, praising Austrians' indifference to sexual scandal as a positive marker of society. He cites Haider as an example: 'just think of Jörgl. He can do what he likes, he could be gay, bi-sexual, he can do what he likes on the Prater fairground, nobody's interested'.[54] Indeed, the revelations about Haider's marital infidelities and his rumoured affair with then deputy BZÖ leader Stefan Petzner did little to dent Haider's popularity in the public outpouring of grief and adulation after his death. In Walter Wippersberg's *Ein nützlicher Idiot*, the spin-doctors also know that in Austria – as opposed to the United States – envy and money are more likely bait to incite public scandal and resentment than are sexual affairs: 'Sex stories go nowhere in Austria. In America, yes, but not here. Somebody could be shagging his Dachshund or his kitchen dresser, or be a child molester, it doesn't make people half as angry as when that person's earning more money than they are.'[55] Wippersberg's fictional party 'The Democrats' nevertheless decides to invent an underage rape story with which to ruin the reputation of the mayor.

More often in Streeruwitz's work, it is the play with genre conventions, the mimicry and experimentation, and not the subject matter itself, which prove to be innovative and worthy of discussion. Mario Scalla describes this text as a commentary on the history of the inner monologue. Scalla is right to designate *Jessica, 30.* as a feminist rebuttal of the fate of women in famous examples of inner monologue from Poe's Madeline in the *Fall of the House of Usher* to Schnitzler's 'Fräulein Else'.[56] Jessica does not have to resort to prostituting herself for money, but can adopt some sense of agency and control. However, the novel remains open-ended and the reader must decide whether to trust the character's professed resolve to carry out her actions. Like another of Schnitzler's monologuers, 'Leutnant Gustl', Jessica's sense of self-worth has been called into question, and the inner monologue device provides Jessica's creator and her compatriot one hundred years before with the chance to present criticisms of Austrian society. Its moral corruption comes under fire, but so too do the distracted and politically undirected minds of Austria's young women.

Jessica, 30. is not the most obvious expression of protest against the Austria of the ÖVP-FPÖ coalition, but it is nevertheless a further variation of the genre and should not just be regarded for its feminist and aesthetic interest. In *Sapporo.*, Streeruwitz presented her immediate artistic response to the 1999 success of the FPÖ (see Chapter 5). In that work too, the female character was developed in such a way as to leave it open to the audience whether she was a victim or not.[57] In choosing an ÖVP politician as a foil to her 'heroine', this literary 'Weisin'/wise woman (see Chapter 2) surely wishes to emphasize the sense of collusion and corruption between politicians of different colours and to suggest that directing attention wholly at the Freedom Party is to ignore the way in which politicians of other parties have come to champion policies previously professed by the FPÖ. Campaigns for the general election of October 2017 afforded new perspectives on this phenomenon, with the FPÖ leader H.C. Strache accusing the ÖVP of having stolen some of its party's policies, for example, on immigration and taxation (see also the Conclusion).[58] As shown in Chapter 2, Streeruwitz is one of the many writers, artists and intellectuals who clearly recognize that protest solely by means of their art form is not going to effect much change. Her participation in the protest movement as one of the 'Drei Weisinnen' and her willingness to make her opinions known in nonfiction publications and at rallies is testimony to her commitment to protest by action and not only in fiction. In declining to accept a Badener Kulturpreis in 2003, Streeruwitz was not slighting the prize or its recognition of her achievements, but was making a stand against the Foreign Minister and ÖVP politician Benita Ferrero-Waldner, who was to award the prize and give the official speech. Streeruwitz felt that Ferrero-Waldner's role thus turned the event into a kind of election campaign event. More importantly, she wanted to make an expression of sympathy with the experimental protest theatre group, the Volxtheater-Karawane, whose members had suffered ill-treatment and had been arrested in Genoa in 2001 during protests against the G8 political summit. Ferrero-Waldner's actions and public statements had only aggravated their plight.

Serializing Politics: Streeruwitz's 'Election Novel(s)' of 2006 and 2008

So ist das Leben. Wahlkampfroman. (That's How Life is. Election Novel) is the title Streeruwitz gave to her internet-published novel of some eighteen short episodes, written and posted in the run-up to the 2006 Nationalratswahl in Austria. The 2006 narrative was also published in weekly instalments in the German newspaper *Freitag*, but the 2008 episodes featured only on Streeruwitz's webpages.[59] The title of Streeruwitz's web novel and the implied title for her sequel, *Das Leben geht weiter (Life Goes on)*, immediately suggest a kind of deterministic worldview, encapsulating as they do the oft-repeated phrases of common stoic acceptance of difficulty or, conversely, the contented justification for events and circumstances being the way they are. Streeruwitz's two prose works set out to deconstruct the supposed inevitability of prevailing attitudes and political policies, and the author underpins the relevance of her novel's title as follows:

> This sentence is the first law of globalized neo-liberalism. It's become the header for all the entry limitations in society, large and small. . . . It's a society that sees economic activity as a natural phenomenon that can no longer be discussed but must just be seen as an immutable act of fate, a catastrophe of nature.[60]

In common with *Jessica, 30.*, the protagonists of the 2006 election novel and its sequel are young Austrian women, searching in vain for professional employment and opportunities. Nadine has a medical degree, but has to divide her time between part-time admin cover at a surgery and doing manicures at a beauty salon; Barbara, her cousin, is an artist, completing her degree but struggling to pay for her living expenses. Both are confronted with a lack of opportunities and with the nepotism of their respective professions. Unlike Jessica Somner, however, the fictional characters of Streeruwitz's election novels are much more politically aware and engage more critically with the political discussions of pre-election Austria. Streeruwitz's methods of political writing still centre on fictional characters who represent ordinary citizens and who function as a kind of mirror onto which to project some of the contemporary policy-making and reportage of media events and news. Thus, there is no dramatic plot featuring politicians and public figures, but rather the narrative and its development consist of snapshots from the life and everyday concerns of Nadine, Barbara and their friends, family and neighbours. The genre description functions ironically, for this is no Austrian-style 'Washington novel' giving a fictional voice and a sense of glamour to the machinations of those in power. *So ist das Leben.* makes its political points by presenting 'fiktive, literarische Schicksale' (fictional, literary fates),[61] a method the writer feels is well suited to rendering politics easier to discuss and to illustrating the (likely) impact of legislation and election campaigns on normal lives. Unlike many of its historical, literary antecedents, Streeruwitz's serial novel does not work with a sensational plot, or cliff-hanger chapter endings, although many of the episodes do end with a puzzling situation or a question. Episode 15 (2006) ends as follows: 'Irmi Kramreiter had called her brother to her parents' house to find that all the locks had been changed. To be continued.'[62] Episode 11 concludes with Nadine reflecting on whether she should once again mix some liver salt into the drinks of two right-wing politicians who are condescending and lewd to her in the bar: 'She'd know what he wanted, surely? She was one of those bright, young women who noticed such things, he said. Was that an invitation to repeat the mixture she'd administered last time? To be continued.'[63]

In addition to what might be generalized as feminist topics, the recurring major leitmotif concerns the fate of immigrants in Austria. In the 2006 story, Nadine's partner is Polish, but even as the citizen of a European Union state, he comes up against all kinds of difficulties in Austria. In 2008 Barbara has a Serbian partner, but cannot arrange for his legal entry into Austria to join her and their baby daughter after he has taken a trip to support his mother in Belgrade. Barbara expresses her irritation at what the Viennese museums have called 'Kulturschock' – an advertising campaign showing women fainting at the sight of some piece of artistic trivia. For Barbara, the frustrations of culture shock are more adequately summed up by the bureaucratic vicious circle of form-filling she must attempt if Pauli is to be able to return to Vienna:

> And culture shock. That was filling out a declaration of liability, as prescribed by Article 2, Paragraph 1, line 15 of the Law on Domicile and Residency, for which only someone with a pay slip could take on the liability for Pauli. But there was nobody left in Barbara's circle who received one.[64]

As with *Jessica, 30.*, these two episodic novels are sprinkled with references to contemporary news events and incidents. It adds enjoyment if the reader recognizes the real-life underpinning of the characters' discussions and thoughts on topics such as sex offenders and society's responses (the Natascha Kampusch story), corporate financial corruption (the BAWAG scandal) or religious improprieties (the Pope's denigrations of Islam).[65] However, the realist mode of writing ensures that readers lend credence to the allusions made, and it is not imperative that names are recognized and facts are remembered. Nadine's mother comes to stay after the latter's husband takes up with another woman, but she cannot get a job as a carer or home-help. The narrative ironizes the fact that it has become 'virtually compulsory' to employ an illegal worker from Slovakia since it had become known that this was the situation in the families of both the President and the Chancellor (*So ist das Leben.*, Episode 3). Streeruwitz bases this on reported news and reinforces the double standards of the political élite.

The election may not guide the plot of Streeruwitz's stories, but the election theme is deployed both as a device on which to pin political commentary as well as an element of the setting of her stories. *So ist das Leben.* begins with Nadine hoping to get casual work as an extra in the Chancellor's campaign photos, but she is told by the agent that her face does not look right for this kind of 'product'. Campaign news and policies are commented upon and the women debate which party to vote for in *Das Leben geht weiter.* The word 'Wahl' and its various related compounds abound. Mention is made of 'Wahlkampf' and 'Wahlkampfdiskussionen', 'Wahlplakate', 'Wahlrecht' ('electoral campaign', 'campaign discussions', 'election posters' and 'the right to vote') and even of 'Wahlzuckerl' ('election sweetener'), the latter referring in particular to a campaign promise by the right wing to lift the upper speed restriction of 130 km per hour on Austrian roads. Barbara reflects on this as she staggers away from a horrendous car accident she has witnessed on a German motorway. Knowing, in retrospect, that Jörg Haider killed himself by travelling at high speeds in 2008 makes this 'Zuckerl' particularly ironic.

In both election campaign novels, the writer inserts an older woman figure counterpart who speaks her mind and cuts through a good deal of the political vagaries. Both Tante Pauli in *So ist das Leben.* and the returning Austrian-American emigrée and wheelchair-bound aunt Rosa in *Das Leben geht weiter* are possessed of astute powers of observation and a dry sense of humour. Aunt Pauli 'always said how interesting it was that in such a Catholic country the prostitutes were only allowed to stop working once they had fulfilled their tax obligations. She said they must hope that the politicians did visit the ladies to help them to be able to meet their tax bill'.[66] This particular 'Weisin' ('wise woman') assesses the 2006 election opportunity and notes that the 'Reds', that is, the SPÖ, now had a historic opportunity to bring about real, cultural change, but that leftist men had a tendency towards melancholic brooding and would do better to desist from their middle-class desire for upwards mobility (Episode 15). Aunt Pauli sounds like she is delivering a Brechtian message of class consciousness, warning against the lure of capitalist aspiration. Aunt Rosa, who, it transpires, has studied history, describes Austria's political landscape as resembling the situation of Imperial Austria under the monarchy. It was like being in some kind of puppet show, she felt, and the various parties were defending positions not unlike their counterparts over a hundred years before.

Here, as in *Jessica, 30.*, the ÖVP is the party that attracts the most flak. 'Poverty gags people here in a different way. But it was like that in 1873, too', Rosa reflects:

In Austria it had always just been the ruling classes who had spoken, she said. The others had had no opportunity to learn *how* to speak. This was still the case. That's the ÖVP for you. They'd never moved on from the likes of Schönerer and Lueger. That was the final straw for Nadine's mother. Maybe she was right, she said, but she couldn't be doing with this constant ranting against the ÖVP.[67]

Streeruwitz uses her Auntie figure here to suggest that anti-Semitism, anti-Slav and pro-nationalist sentiment might not just be the preserve of the extreme-right parties, but at home too, in the supposed centre ground. Schüssel is even dubbed Austria's Margaret Thatcher, the champion of laissez-faire politics. However, with a proportional representation system of voting, Nadine laments that it would not be possible in an Austrian election to remove Schüssel entirely from political power (*So ist das Leben.*, Episode 18).

Streeruwitz's serial novels succeed in demonstrating the emptiness of the supposedly natural dictum – that's life, or that's just the way things are. She militates against this aphorism by using stories to suggest that there is nothing inevitable or 'natural' about the struggles of her protagonists or about the organization of political life as it is. One might consider Streeruwitz's writing here as adopting a Barthesian motivation to demythologize and to persuade her reader that situations and circumstances that seem inevitable are not in fact fixed but are determined by factors such as wealth, gender, connections and so on. Aunt Rosa refuses to be seen by an ophthalmologist after hearing how the previous patient is treated. She leaves, muttering 'Nazimethoden'. Nadine's mother, however, has been conditioned to find this level of treatment acceptable: 'Nadine's mother even said straight off that it hadn't been so bad, that you just had to put up with being treated badly if you couldn't afford anything else.'[68] Nadine's mother has absorbed the symbolic violence of privatized capital and differential welfare, and deems the system as it is to be just and fair.

There is more than a touch of dialectical politicization at work in Streeruwitz's *Wahlkampfromane*, and the two prose works do not end with an indication of where the hope for change might lie. Nadine, for example, cries throughout her plane journey home after visiting Vladi in London, reflecting on the futility of trying to explain her problems. People would just tell her not to complain and 'that life was just like that'.[69] If there is a rallying cry to be heard in Streeruwitz's texts, then it is Aunt Rosa's admonishment of Austria's apathy. In contrast to her adoptive home of the United States, she feels that the people of Austria do not recognize 'that they were governed and that one had to try to influence this'.[70] This lethargy has got the better of Aunt Rosa, who resolves to return to the United States and get far away from the Austrians, whose fixed smiles belie their cold-hearted, disdainful indifference. If international comparisons of voter statistics for parliamentary elections are anything to go by, then one must concede to Streeruwitz her transatlantic contrast as a mere piece of artistic licence. Americans are far less likely than Austrians to express an interest in influencing the legislative politics of their country, at least by showing up for the elections. However, *So ist das Leben*. works for the most part by negative example, and Streeruwitz's readership has not come to expect promising, optimistic scenarios. The author's protest against some of the burning issues in contemporary Austria comes across loud and clear, even though the second *Wahlkampfroman* remains unfinished and was abandoned by Streeruwitz because of her own disillusionment with Austrian politics and with the loneliness of the web publication format.[71]

Three Times over: Walter Wippersberg's Novel Trilogy

Walter Wippersberg's frequent political interventions are foregrounded in an interview with Christian Schacherreiter, where the author is asked whether he minds being labelled a 'political writer'. Wippersberg answers that he has no objections to this description so long as the emphasis remains on 'author' and not on 'political': 'There are political topics in my work, not exclusively, but quite often', he qualifies. 'If I were concerned with political enlightenment in the first instance, or with political intervention, then I'd work in politics directly, or in journalism. But I don't write leaders for the newspaper, I'm not a political scientist and certainly not a politician. It's my ambition to write good stories and to tell them well.'[72]

In the novels *Die Irren und die Mörder* (1998), *Ein nützlicher Idiot* (1999) and *Die Geschichte eines lächerlichen Mannes* (2000),[73] Wippersberg offers up three such 'good reads', but there can be no doubt that these soft thrillers (or, more aptly, two 'anti-thrillers' and one anti-*Bildungsroman*) are every bit as much social commentaries making acute and hard-hitting observations about Austria's fin-de-siècle political malaise. More widely known as a filmmaker, Walter Wippersberg belonged to a large body of Austrian writers, artists and intellectuals whose preoccupations have long included the commitment and desire to comment upon the increasing social acceptability of extreme-right politics as well as political processes and behind-the-scenes machinations, even before the public flashpoint represented by the 1999/2000 Wende (see also Chapter 4).

The first two novels deal with the schemings of rightist groupings. *Die Irren und die Mörder* nods eponymously to Ingeborg Bachmann's 1961 short story warning of the dangers of latent fascism in postwar Austria and itself concerns clandestine groupings of civilians who adhere to fascist political philosophies.[74] *Ein nützlicher Idiot*, on the other hand, centres on a 'legitimate' but fictional, political party called 'Die Demokraten', which bears obvious similarities in political outlook and rhetorical style to the FPÖ with its repeated claims to be the motor of democratic change in Austria.[75] The first novel makes as its object of attention an old-style fascism that remains underground and harks back to theories of racial supremacy and 'hygiene', 'mit Hinweisen auf Konrad Lorenz und Eibl-Eibesfeldt' ('with nods to Konrad Lorenz and Eibl-Eibesfeldt'), professes 'eine Art ethnischer Umweltschutz' ('a kind of ethnic environmentalism') and longs for an élitist ruler, for which role 'Herr Haider' is not deemed to be suitable, but in whose actions the conspirators see 'a small step in the right direction'.[76] The second novel puts under the author's fictional microscope the presentable new face of right-wing populism that strenuously tries to distance itself from National Socialism, although many of its attempts to do so can be seen as purely rhetorical. Finally, *Die Geschichte eines lächerlichen Mannes* takes as its protagonist and point of departure a high-ranking Social Democrat politician whose imminent elevation to the office of mayor seems unstoppable.

All three of Wippersberg's novels display elements of the thriller, but the novelist is also playful in undermining the genre. Red herrings abound in *Die Geschichte eines lächerlichen Mannes* as the protagonist and reader alike wonder about the role of the mysterious AUDI 8 car and the reader wonders whether the old wartime pistol in Martin Roller's house will be put to use. In *Die Irren und die Mörder*, Wippersberg's playfulness surfaces expressly as occasional, metafictional reminders that this is, after all, merely a novel: 'the narrator, often dubbed authorial, is not omniscient, despite the old preconception, he doesn't need to be ... Let's keep the marginal characters who don't crop up again at a distance'.[77] Suspense is a vital component, yet the author continually signposts what will happen in a fashion that paradoxically both undermines and heightens the drama. The death threat received by Martha in *Die Irren und die Mörder* is mentioned in the very first chapter, but the reader must wait until the last pages of the novel to learn that Martha does in fact meet her end, gunned down as she leaves the police station having failed to persuade a senior policeman (and probable co-conspirator) of the threat she is under from the extreme-right association to which her lover belongs. Equally, the reader learns on the very first page of *Ein nützlicher Idiot* that Axel Kessler, the naïve, apolitical party worker and fellow-traveller protagonist, will die. The final chapters of the novel accelerate in pace and Axel is conveniently disposed of as the party élite contrive to shoot him and pin the murder on the political journalist they have bidden to the scene under the guise of providing him with copy against the Democrats.[78] Left-wing anarchist leaflets scattered by the murderers at the crime scene provide further circumstantial evidence for the police apprehending the journalist nearby, and the party is able not only to silence one of its most vocal critics but also to kill off the young chauffeur-turned-personal assistant who knew far too much about the party's underhand tactics. The party leader, who remains nameless throughout, is able to dispense with the rising star woman politician Beranek, who has played a major part in winning the local Vienna elections, by threatening to make political mileage out of her family's National Socialist past. He then sheds crocodile tears in a television interview about the death of Axel, an occasion that, it is inferred, allows the party thugs to engineer 'spontaneous' demonstrations against a fictive left-wing terror.[79]

The narrative of *Die Geschichte eines lächerlichen Mannes* proceeds in a linear fashion and spans a week in the life of the eponymous man of ridicule, Martin Roller, but a short section at the end of each chapter flashes forward to the end of the week when Roller is waiting to join a party meeting that will determine his fate. Having finally found the down-and-out former childhood friend who visits him at the outset of the novel and purports to know unpleasant things about his past, Roller vents his uncontrollable anger and paranoia by brutally attacking the vulnerable, homeless man.

Predictably, then, Roller does not become mayor, and concessions, it seems, will have to be made to the Freiheitlichen, who are known in this novel by their real party name and who have set up a voluntary civilian militia in an area of the city. Veluncek, the sneering 'Blue' party member who Roller thought was spearheading attempts to blackmail him, has done nothing of the sort and will receive some portfolio of office under the new local government. Roller's mock-tragic fall from power has been brought about by his own psychological failings as he locks in on the idea of some nonexistent past failure rather than making amends for acknowledged underhand tactics and failures in his family life. Roller's longtime political running partner cum adversary, Eichinger, observes as follows, in the last paragraphs of the novel:

> He [Veluncek] will have to be allowed to be a part of the power structures, but this is unavoidable in the longer term at any rate. Such is the march of time. It's perhaps not such a bad thing: it'll make the Blues take some responsibility.[80]

Wippersberg thus concludes his trilogy in 2000 by echoing provocatively the view that many political observers had reached and that in some respects proved to be true, namely that the FPÖ was an opposition party ill-prepared and ill-suited to the demands of government and that the act of joining a government would force the party to modify some of its more radical policies. As many protesters and commentators have nevertheless pointed out, the ÖVP and the SPÖ have shown themselves to be capable of championing views that might formerly have been associated only with the more extremist parties, with regard, for example, to asylum laws. It is a further strength of Wippersberg's concluding novel that the focus widens to implicate careerist, dog-eat-dog tactics of 'ridiculous men' of all political colours, just as the first volume's title explicitly refers to the many crazed, latently violent members of society and the second volume refers *pars pro toto* to simple, expendable people who become easy victims of political skulduggery.

Despite the page-turning nature of the plots and the simplicity of style, Wippersberg's novels neither made it into paperback nor into the film adaptations for which they lend themselves very well, in part due to the 'cross-cutting' between the perspectives of two main characters, male and female, in the first two volumes, and the temporal shifts of current 'erzählte Zeit' (narrated time) and future dénouement of the concluding volume. That the readership and the publishing industry should take offence to some of the hard-hitting inferences about right-wing violence or political tactics and have thus stalled the larger success of Wippersberg's work seems an unlikely suggestion, given the huge success of Josef Haslinger's début novel *Opernball* (1995) and its film adaptation by Urs Egger in 1998. Critics have even compared Wippersberg's trilogy favourably to Haslinger's more sensationalist novel noting that 'the plot is essentially much more political and therefore probably more realistic, too'.[81] Arno Rußegger acknowledges the role of Haslinger's and Wippersberg's novels in opening up the possibilities of the crime fiction genre for the purposes of political commentary, no longer leaving such overtly political intent to the more common genre territory of the cabaret or the essay.[82]

Wippersberg's novels can be enjoyed without any specific knowledge of Austrian events. Unlike Pluhar's character names, Wippersberg's coinages are less obvious, though Loitzenthaler's proximity to the party leader suggests Peter Westenthaler as a model once more. However, the degree of interplay between Wippersberg's plots and real-life events, publications, people and newspaper stories is very high indeed, and this affords his work a heightened sense of informed protest and warning about what Austrians might be in for if a party like the FPÖ were to win elections outright.[83] In his close political reading of *Ein nützlicher Idiot*, Franz Zens provides a wealth of information for mapping many of the novel's fictional plot developments onto real-life events and FPÖ strategies.[84] These include the FPÖ's use of various, sometimes fabricated, scapegoats; of polarizations between the 'decent' people and the dishonourable (often asylum seekers); and its (albeit veiled) recourse to National Socialist terminology or to phrases that subconsciously praise National Socialist politics. Zens also identifies a small number of verbatim quotations from Jörg Haider's speeches and publications, though this is not a significant device in Wippersberg as it is in, say, Jelinek's or Fian's work, or in many of the musical and filmic items I examine in the present study. Wippersberg uses the characters of the Democrats' party leader and Meerwald, their media consultant, as conduits through which he can unmask what many political scientists and sociolinguists have analysed as the deliberate rhetorical strategies and psychopolitics of Jörg Haider and his allies: the construction of fictional threats to society such as a new 'Turkish invasion', anti-Semitic statements and inferences such as Haider's infamous use of the somewhat belittling word 'Straflager' (punishment camps) for concentration camps, [85] the collusion of pro-FPÖ newspapers, and the illegal accessing of data via party contacts and informers in the police (the 'Spitzelaffäre').[86]

If Wippersberg's fictional party leader, following Haider's example, expounds the idea of a new politics 'beyond all ideology',[87] the author himself remained anchored in an awareness of the ideas, philosophies and strategies of political life.

Wippersberg produced a trilogy of novels that entertain their readership as well as offering cautionary protest about the rising popularity of populist, demagogic political styles and the machinations that might lie behind them. The final section of this chapter looks not at prose collections like Wippersberg's trilogy, which extends to over six hundred pages in length, but at considerably shorter works of protest prose.

Keeping it Short

The most common genre in the anthologies of protest contributions is by far the prose piece written as personal commentary, as essay or speech, as diary entry or as letter, in other words not as pure fiction, but as some form of life writing or political essay. Many other contributions come in the form of poems or dramolets, and there is a much smaller number of prose fiction pieces, mostly in the form of short stories, fables and fictionalized letters. A number of the narratives centre – just as the non-fictional diary entries do – on the activities and thoughts of a demonstration participant.

Paulus Hochgatterer's 'Ready or Not, Here I Come' and Eva Jancak's 'Widerstand beim Zwiebelschneiden' are examples of first-person narratives foregrounding a moment of burgeoning politicization. In Hochgatterer's case, the narrator tries in vain to impart something of his enthusiasm for a roof-top demo to his mother, who, by contrast, 'lies on the sofa reading one of her esoteric life improvement books'.[88] Jancak's first-person narrative is also about the move towards political engagement and has a generational dimension too. This time it is an elderly woman ringing in to the radio station phone-in discussion with the new Home Secretary who inspires the narrator, a self-doubting housewife, to lay aside her feeble excuses (the line will be engaged, the politician speaks much more lucidly, she doesn't know the telephone number) and make her protest heard in future. The eponymous activity does not bring tears to her eyes; rather, the narrator's emotions and anger are prompted by the authoritarian and condescending manner in which the Innenminister puts down a caller who points out that film sequences show the police and not the protestors instigating trouble at the demonstrations. Dieter Schrage's piece 'Tomaten Widerstand' describes the protest activity of a civil servant, this time in a third-person narrative. The nameless 'Regierungsrat' has served all manner of different ministers from different parties, and although he resents the incoming new Ministerin, 'the one from the "F" party',[89] the reader does not doubt that he will execute his job professionally and properly. The story describes the character's actions in leaving work punctually, selecting precisely his chosen projectiles from the shelves of one of the more refined supermarkets and proceeding to the demonstration outside the Bundeskanzleramt, where he launches a single tomato in the direction of the

Chancellor. For this government official, it is not important whether his tomato hits its target; rather, it is the throwing, the action, that is important, and not the result.[90] When it comes to marksmanship, Schrage's character is more highly skilled in the aiming of rubber stamps, as his opening foretells: 'on behalf of the Federal Minister. First the name stamp is brought down onto the paper, and then the round one, the ministerial one in his official safe-keeping, is wielded with its usual accuracy. Done!'.[91] The civil servant is able to compartmentalize his life and there is no suggestion that he will let his personal sentiments interfere with his professionalism as he arrives at work the next day, 'as usual, at eight o'clock precisely'.[92] But the tomatoes are stowed away in the personal compartment of his desk-drawer, ready for action at next week's demonstration 'should nothing have happened'.[93] Dieter Schrage, the author of this piece, is a retired university professor and former curator of the Museum of Modern Art in Vienna. In his nonfiction piece entitled '"Zeugnis für Demo-Teilnahme". Anmerkungen zu meiner Vorlesung an der Uni Wien', Schrage details the accusations made against him by the student organization the 'Ring Freiheitlicher Studenten' and provides justification for the fieldwork he had required of his students in the course of a series of ethnography lectures on popular culture. In this piece, Schrage quotes Dr Martin Graf, from the minutes of a parliamentary meeting. Graf accuses Schrage of giving out course completion certificates to students for 'pissing against the state, maybe three times'.[94] In 2008, FPÖ politician Martin Graf became the 'Third President' of the Austrian Parliament (three are required at any given time), although his appointment to that role was the object of massive cross-party protest and public controversy due to his far-right views. He stood down from politics in 2013 and his successor was the FPÖ's Norbert Hofer (see the Conclusion).

El Awadalla is another writer who attracted parliamentary intervention by the FPÖ – again from Martin Graf, but this time for a four-page story, entitled '18. bezirk: gretl'.[95] Awadalla's story is also a third-person narrative foregrounding the moment where a person becomes politically active, although this time it is more than tomatoes that are thrown. Awadalla is known for her active role as one of the founders of the literary 'resistance readings' that took place in Vienna every week from 2000 to 2006. Awadalla often writes her poetry and prose pieces in dialect and is President of the organization ÖDA (Österreichische Dialektautoren und -archive).[96] She became more widely known after 2005, when she won Austria's *Millionenshow* TV quiz. Awadalla suspects that the publicity given to her by the TV show is a further reason for the FPÖ's dislike of her since the celebrity it brought her also raised the profile of the resistance readings she helped to organize. Unlike many of the writers and artists featured in the current study, Awadalla does not include references to real-life political agents by name or by personalizing the argumentation with quotational allusion. Her preference is to avoid providing even more attention to those politicians.[97] The frail, former peace activist, 82-year-old 'gretl' of Awadalla's story sees only one way of protesting against the right-wing government, whom she holds responsible for the fate of her elderly neighbour. Unable to afford to heat her flat, the neighbour has lain dead there for days before Gretl is able to persuade the authorities to break the door down. Gretl obtains some hand grenades via a complex process of contacts from her Kaffeehaus and then tests out her social invisibility at various locations, including regular visits to the parliament building, where she watches proceedings from the gallery. When she does lob the grenades, causing mayhem below, she immediately tries to give herself up to the duty guard. If she ends her days in prison, she will at least not freeze or starve to death, she figures. But the guard simply pushes her aside: 'come along, mother, out of the way, we're looking for a terrorist'.[98] The main theme of Awadalla's story clearly centres on the argument that elderly people – women in particular – are marginalized in contemporary society and that they are not taken seriously. She also disturbs the 'clichéd' image of the terrorist by using her elderly 18th-district widow to play this part.[99] Martin Graf tabled thirteen parliamentary questions, purportedly to establish the level of public subvention for Awadalla's work, which was dubbed an incitement to terrorism: 'It's well-nigh unbelievable that a pamphlet like this, one that can be understood as a guide to committing acts of terror against the highest representatives of the Republic of Austria, could receive financial support from the Chancellery (Art and Culture), from the city of Vienna and from the Burgenland region.'[100] The cliché of demonstrators being exclusively young people is incidentally also challenged by the contributions by pensioners in the anthology documenting the 'Wiener Wandertage'.[101] The older person's gaze is just one of a number of devices deployed in short protest prose. The child's gaze is a further strategy for constructing an ironizing perspective on the political events of contemporary Austria. Undoubtedly the top-selling protest publication in Austria is a separate short-prose publication with a difference: the *bande dessinée* or cartoon book entitled *Jörgi, der Drachentöter* (2000) by Austrian cartoonist and writer Gerhard Haderer and writer and cabarettist Leo Lukas. The present chapter concludes with a discussion of this publication.[102]

'Luca, das Widerstands-Baby' ('Luca, the resistance-baby') purports to be by a six-month-old attendant at the 'Botschaft besorgter Bürger und Bürgerinnen' ('Embassy for Concerned Men and Women Citizens').[103] Luca explains his arrival into the world as 'a consequence, as it were, of the protest which many here are calling "resistance"',[104] thus incidentally suggesting proof for the jocular view of cabarettists Thomas Maurer and Florian Scheuba that sexual relationships can be revitalized when couples' political engagement is reawakened by attending demonstrations.[105] Whether or not Luca is a real person and was taken along to the protests by a parent or parents, the whimsical simplicity of the naive perspective his 'authorship' affords brings an air of romantic contentment to the camaraderie generated by community protests. Luca is told that everyone hopes that the black-blue government will soon be over, but that if it is not, he may find himself having to take on some duties at the embassy: 'phew, quite a responsibility, and all this when I can't even crawl yet'.[106] A more dystopian view is provided by Hoppelmann Karottnig in a conversation with a child who has yet to be conceived, let alone born. Karottnig gives his story 'Wertedebatte mit einem noch zu zeugendem Kind' ('Debate on Values with a Child Who Has Yet to Be Conceived') the deliberately disingenuous subtitle 'Zur Abwechslung ein vollkommen unpolitischer Text aus Wien im Jahre 2016' ('By Way of a Change, a Completely Unpolitical Text from Vienna in the Year 2016').[107] Karottnig's story joins the ranks of protest works of a kind of soft near-future fiction category like Peter Kern's 2002 film *1. April 2021 – Haider lebt* (see Chapter 4) or the short story 'Blauer Planet?' by the group of protest artists called 'United Aliens'. 'Blauer Planet?' presents the familiar space-exploration justification of searching for intelligent life forms by reflecting this back onto planet earth in reverse. Naturally, United Aliens are keen to establish that this planet is *not* indeed 'blue' in the metaphorical sense (the colour of the Freedom Party) and rejoice in establishing that: 'According to our first explorations there is indeed a small concentration of it [intelligent life], really not to be taken for granted on this planet!'[108]

Karottnig's father-narrator addresses his now teenage child about the perennial intergenerational issues such as respect, duty, responsibilities and so on, but also argues with him/her about contemporary objects of consumerist desire, such as buying the latest mobile phone. The father is an arch-rightist and lauds the achievements of the Chancellor (Riess-Passer), who has ordered the wearing of uniforms for all children. 'Oh Jennifer-Kevin', he exclaims, for the sex of the unborn child is logically still unknown, 'where have we gone wrong. If only you could be just a bit like our Frau Chancellor.'[109] The father, whose only youthful rebellion seems to have been as one of the thirteen percent of people who refused to own a mobile phone, wishes that his offspring could be more like 'Uncle Wolf Martin'.[110] Here Karottnig expresses satirical approval of the extreme-right *Krone* journalist and poet Martin, who is infamous for his poems published on the occasion of Adolf Hitler's birthday, and for his invective against immigrants and against critical writers. Richard Weihs' story is also written as if it were a moral fable for a child's consumption. Instead, 'Das Märchen von der Stadt Auswärts' ('The Tale of the Town of Outwards') is a parody of the genre, in which the inhabitants of the town adopt a new 'Auswanderungspolitik' (emigration policy) to get rid of all the incomers. The resulting downwards spiral sees the shopkeepers having to leave as there is no business to be had. 'The last thing still functioning was the Ministry of Outward Affairs',[111] and the Oberste 'Auswart' (not a caretaker, then, but a 'don't-care-taker') is left patrolling the streets shouting 'people of Outwards, out!'.[112] Brigitte Tauer's story 'Rudi Riesenfuß' ('Rudi Giantfoot'), written in 1999 on the day on which Marcus Omofuma died during his expulsion from Austria, is another amusing, parable-style fantasy story suggesting the bigotry and xenophobic nationalism of a country of giants, whose president giant passes more and more anti-democratic laws. Rudi Riesenfuß and his family find themselves emigrating to the land of the dwarves and are much happier in their tolerant, friendly and accommodating company.[113]

Ludwig Roman Fleischer enhances what he sees as the absurdity of the black-blue government by having his tour guide explain it in the story 'Fremdenführung' ('Guided Tour') as an 'experimental pilot government deployed by MicrosoftVaticanWestinghouse to investigate how much an electorate can take in innovations'.[114] The *Widerstandslesungen* on the Ballhausplatz have become an additional spot for tour buses to stop at, 'because this post is history-pregnant [sic]'.[115] Much of the humour of Fleischer's piece comes from the increasingly drunken if rather perceptive explanations of the foibles of various leading politicians, and from the guide's poor Italian and English and his slurred Austrian-German. He urges the tourists to give the people protesting against the government ('the gonevernment, the blunderment')[116] some alcohol to warm them up: 'give the poor sausages doing their resisting thing a drop to drink. Una goccetta per li opposition fighters, so that it them warm becomes!'[117] Sylvia Treudl's piece 'Biedermensch erklärt einem Touristen, obwohl er Ausländer ist, die Welt' is a Herr Karlesque monologue, in which the first-person narrator reveals his anti-women, anti-foreigner views and his support for the return of traditional values in Austrian culture. Tourists can be tolerated so long as they pay up and share the same set of values.[118]

This outline of different narrative strategies is by no means exhaustive. We have seen moments of personal politicization, the perspectives of childhood and of older age, fantasy and sci-fi as well as the assumption of a touristic gaze. However, final mention should be made of the use of mythological figures. Elfriede Jelinek's *Das Lebewohl* (discussed in Chapter 5) is a well-known example of a dramatic piece evoking mythological figures and deploying a specific idiom for writing about heroic mythical figures in order to present its critical perspective. In terms of the short prose of protest, Monika Vasik goes a step further by using a mythological figure as her character. Vasik's 'Brief-an-den-Vater'-narrative breathes life into the statue of Pallas Athene as the mythical character composes a letter to her father in 'Allmächtiger Zeus! Lieber Papa!' ('All-Powerful Zeus! Dear Dad!'). In the first half of the short story, Pallas Athene reflects on the ups and downs of the hundred years she has spent outside the parliament building in Vienna. She writes to her father that, despite various setbacks, she had felt that since the last war she had become convinced she was having an effect on the Austrian people, but now she is resigned to having failed: 'I am the Goddess of wisdom, I had hoped to be able to teach people to use their reason. I have failed.'[119] Where United Aliens write ironically about the discovery of some intelligent life in Vienna, Vasik's mythological character despairs at the people's inability to use their intelligence and their easy manipulation by the 'shows' put on by Haider or, rather, by 'this rakish fifty year old with his boys and one or two girls'.[120] Athene has seen feminist achievements eroded and as a 'foreigner' who has never sought Austrian citizenship, she feels threatened to the point of contemplating leaving the country. Athene feels appreciated only by the tourists who stop to take their photographs in front of her and certainly not by the politicians' 'unbearable noise behind my back'.[121] Journalist Elisabeth Boyer points out in a very informative essay on the sociocultural implications and history of the statue that even when the 'erste Frau im Parlament' (first woman of parliament) was erected in 1902, much fun was made of the fact that Pallas Athene's back was turned on the parliamentarians.[122]

Vasik's story answers Boyer's questions: 'What would she say today to all the excitement around her? . . . would it bother her if she's co-opted by the people and not just by the men and women politicians?'[123] The statue outside the parliament building was the site of various protest actions, most notably the occupation by protesters of the Performing Resistance group, including the actor Hubsi Kramar (see Chapter 2). The protesters chained themselves to the statue and displayed banners protesting against the FPÖ's cultivation of contacts with the police and their illegal access to police data (in the 'Spitzelaffäre'; see above). In the second part of Vasik's story, Athene applauds the actions of protesters and states that these actions have given her hope. Perhaps her long years of standing there have been worthwhile, after all, she concludes, resolving not to leave these Austrians in the lurch: 'I am pleased that there are these other people who are often drowned out by the noise of the government's campaigns, but they are there and they speak up undeterred. They're stirring things up.'[124] Vasik's character enthuses: 'Intellectuals and artists are also recognising that they cannot stay out of political matters'.[125] The cabarettist and writer Leo Lukas and the cartoonist Gerhard Haderer have always made it their artistic business to engage with politics. Their hardback graphic novel is one of the most unusual works of Austrian protest or satirical literature following the events of 1999/2000 and certainly the one with the widest target audience.

A Graphic Response: Cartooning Haider

Racial tension is a predominant theme in the bestselling comic book entitled *Jörgi, der Drachentöter* by Austrian cartoonist and writer Gerhard Haderer and writer and cabarettist Leo Lukas. Within months of its publication in 2000, it had sold more than 40,000 copies and was reprinted. The publishers stipulate the genre as 'a picture book for children and adults',[126] but, as Kazi Stastna points out, 'oddly enough, it appeared in the non-fiction rather than the fiction category, alongside . . . *Forever Young – Das Ernährungsprogramm* . . . and *Der*

Weg zur finanziellen Freiheit'. Lukas reportedly saw this as a deliberate ploy to 'keep the book from having to be described as a "No. 1 Bestseller", seeing as non-fiction works sell many more copies than fiction'.[127]

Conceived along the lines of a lighthearted medieval tale, the narrative transmits a humorous, but fairly generic moral account of the rise and fall of an ambitious and power-seeking individual, complete with his deposition from the throne and recuperation into the fabric of the community as a future trainee chef in the castle kitchens. In purely textual-linguistic terms, the reader would be at least slightly stretched to read it as a political allegory with specific, Austrian reference, since the only character given a name is the young protagonist and would-be dragon-slayer 'Jörgi'. (Haider's given name is most convenient, given that George/Jörg is the original dragon-slayer name, at least in Christian tradition.)[128] True to the expected, formulaic pattern, the other characters are merely given type-markers: 'Der Prinz' ('the prince'), 'Der König' ('the king'), 'Der Nachtwächter' ('the night watchman') and 'Der Hofnarr' ('the court jester'). There is, however, also 'Der Chinese' ('the Chinese man'), whose food is much better than the innkeeper's, as the latter himself admits. Xenophobia becomes one of the cornerstones of Jörgi's campaign to persuade the community to side with him in trying to depose the Dragon-King who rules somewhat ineptly but peacefully over their hitherto sleepy community. The ironic exchange between the night watchman and Jörgi underlines the risible logic of Jörgi's strategic mission:

> 'Do you know why you have to keep watch every night, all alone?', Jörgi asked the night watchman.
> 'Because I'm the night watchman?', the night watchman speculated.
> 'Well yes', Jörgi said, 'but it's the dragon's fault, not yours. After all, he could have employed other night watchmen, too. Ages ago!' . . . 'And then there's the Chinese!', Jörgi added.
> 'What do you mean, the Chinese?', the night watchman asked.
> 'Erm well, because – – – because you're keeping watch here primarily because of the Chinese. Everybody knows that the Chinese are particularly dangerous!'[129]

There is much pleasure to be gained for the junior reader of this book (aged six and above according to the publisher's blurb) and young people will, without doubt, enjoy the charming and hilarious pictorial detail as well as the mixture of contemporary vernacular and archaic language, but the illustrations are, in the way of much cartoon work, the primary source of *specific*, satirical reading for the adult readers. In interacting with this book, then, adult readers must recognize pictorial codes or signs and successfully identify the real-life models upon which the personal features of the protagonists are based, in order to perform their reading as a specific satire on Austria and not simply a more generic parable about greed and racism.[130] Haderer's pictures present a linguistic and physically diminutive Jörg(i) Haider as budding dragon-slayer; the prince in the likeness of the then Chancellor, Wolfgang Schüssel (ÖVP), the princess as Heide Schmidt (formerly of the FPÖ and a founder member of the 1993 breakaway party Liberales Forum, or LIF), the latter's lady-in-waiting as Susanne Riess-Passer (Haider's successor as FPÖ Party Chair from 2000 to 2002, and Vice-Chancellor of Austria from 2000 to 2003) and court chaplain Kurt Krenn (former Bishop of St Pölten, who resigned in 2004).

After the young rabble-rouser first manufactures unrest and mobilizes this in his quest to become king, he too, like the king and the prince before him, begins to grow dragon features. And all become unhappy, downtrodden and poor in the new strife-ridden atmosphere of the village. The king's men are seen suppressing any signs of resistance in the community and the Chinese restaurateur is packing up his belongings to leave. As in Fian's work, grammatical and linguistic competence is a highly charged signifier here, too, and in the graphic novel and comic genre more broadly.[131] In this graphic novel, complicated protestations are written correctly, and the accomplishment is, of course, imputed to the cartoon characters and not to the writer or copy editor. Thus, the 'Widerstand' ('resistance') banner is spelled correctly, as is the placard 'Frieden schaffen ohne Waffen' ('make peace happen without a weapon'). 'Drachen, nein Danke!' ('dragon, no thank you') nods comically to famous anti-nuclear campaigns of the past and DRACHE, with a crossed-out 'D' to foster revenge ('Rache'), suggests a degree of political marketing and language intelligence amongst the protesters. However, the misspellings of the racist graffiti 'Wek mit denen Kinesen!' ('Gett rid of them Chinese') and 'Tödet dem Trachen!' ('kil them draggen') suggest ignorance and impressionability, while the infantile denigrations of Jörgi's inner thoughts perform a double meaning in the book. Yes, Jörgi is a young boy, whose dreams are not to become a 'Schuster', 'Schneider' or 'Lokomotivführerin' ('cobbler', 'tailor' or 'train driver') like the other boys and girls, but a 'Drachentöter' ('dragon-slayer'), and he is at first greeted with 'Weichei!' ('wimp') and even 'Schlappschwanz!' ('limp-dick') when he at first tries (and fails) to persuade others to join in with him. On the other hand, the character is drawn as an *adult* resemblance of Jörg Haider, but with a diminutive stature. The words thus also become less a realist device and more a performative marker of immaturity and wrong-headedness.

The materiality of the comic book and its layout of words and pictures provide a useful key in determining this genre's performative force. Ole Frahm draws attention to the 'precarious, different appearance of the words in comics. The words are disseminated. They are not spoken but exposed in their materiality throughout the graphic space of the page. This is true for all comics. Comics show the words without origin. The words are not utterances by somebody but material enunciations'. If, following Bert States, a framing device is necessary to 'create the sense of restored behavior – and hence a performance – that is somehow separated from normal empirical behavior', then we may see cartoonist-text writers as the quintessential performers of texts in their entrapment of utterances.[132]

The cartoon places the text within a frame within a frame, applying a graphic *mise-en-abyme* on a bordered page within the borders of a text box or a speech bubble. Moreover, this contributes to the sense that Haderer and Lukas's book is not so much a book about Jörg Haider as a book about Haider-like behaviour, 'Haiderization' and about political scenarios or texts that are 'performed' by other power-hungry individuals elsewhere. Schüssel (ÖVP) is every bit the object of ridicule in *Jörgi, der Drachentöter*, too, as he grasps opportunist moments to achieve his own rise to power before being usurped by Jörgi.[133] Readers performing the combination of text and image in their own minds are perhaps helped to 'de-demonise' Haider as Haderer intends when drawing these images. Lukas emphasizes the archetypal qualities of the book, claiming: 'Everywhere on the planet, Haider, and his many brothers (and a few sisters), are so alluring, because they appeal to the Jörg-like in very many people.'[134]

Reviewers of *Jörgi der Drachentöter* rejoice in the possibilities of him enjoying 'less destructive undertakings' and in the suggestions that 'in the end no one really needs leaders like him'.[135] After the villagers have had their moment of political epiphany and have thrown away the crown and throne, the symbols of absolute power, the previously bestial Jörgi-King now becomes redeemed, one might say, and sheds his dragon form to assume a human body once more. Initially disappointed or, rather, surprised to see apprentice Jörgi cooking simple, 'German' fare (i.e. sausages), this reader was pleased to see the Chinese chef standing behind little Jörg and smiling at his culinary progress (although a wok and some noodles might have been a nice touch). Then I reperformed my visual reading of the book and delighted in the floating (sausage) signifier featuring on most of the book's pages (observant readers will notice its presence somewhere in close proximity to Jörgi each time he is depicted). There is a rather obvious protosexual allusion here denigrating the young man with his little 'sausage'. Another possible – if rather contrived – meaning might be found in pointing to the meaning of 'Es geht um die Wurst!' ('it is crunch time') for Jörg (Haider) and for Austrian politics. Jörgi looks contemplatively towards the sausage on the very sparse, penultimate page, before answering the question 'Na, was willst du denn werden?' ('now then, what is it you want to be in life?'). The final illustration sees Jörgi successfully cooking 'that elusive sausage in its proper place – that is, in the pot',[136] but adding to it what looks like a pinch of salt. Does the reader see this as Haderer and Lukas adding a metafictional caveat (this is art, not real life) or perhaps as the artists' loaded warning that something may still be cooking up? It is tempting to draw an ambivalent conclusion, in the manner of a German pop song, 'Alles hat ein Ende, nur die Wurst hat zwei' ('Everything has an End, but Sausages have Two').[137] Exactly what plan might Jörgi be cooking up? Political analysts and the public alike speculated at great length when in 2000 Jörg Haider chose to stand down as leader of the highly successful FPÖ, allowing his deputy, Susanne Riess-Passer, to take over and consequently to adopt the office of Vice-Chancellor (Deputy Prime Minister) of Austria, preferring instead to withdraw to Carinthia and concentrate on politics in the provinces. Haider's return to chairmanship of his new, breakaway party Bündnis Zukunft Österreich (BZÖ) and the party's marked success in the Nationalratswahl of September 2008 sparked speculation as to a possible renewed higher-profile role for the controversial politician.

Another culinary illustration from *Jörgi, der Drachentöter* allows us to posit a more positive closure to the medieval fairy tale. A bunch of red radishes also features throughout the slim book, drawn as a crest on a knight's helmet. Kept whole until the final illustration, here they are sliced up to add into the meal preparation. Perhaps this is not a random choice of ingredient. In the Middle Ages, the radish apparently had a 'predominantly negative symbolic meaning as a symbol of quarrel and strife. Because the radish . . . was said to be related to evil spirits, radishes . . . were sometimes consecrated, that is, rendered harmless'.[138] The radish picture can be read etymologically too, and not just as a visual symbol. The word comes from the Latin, 'radicem' or 'radix', meaning root. The related terms 'eradicate' and 'root out' are entirely relevant to the political message of the book, it would seem, at least to this reader-performer: the radishes have been chopped, xenophobia has been eradicated and radicalism (also etymologically related) has been deflected.

Conclusion: A Space for Reader Engagement

I began this chapter by noting the unlikely format of the novel as a medium for protest art. It is not possible to include discussion here of all of the relevant novels – and short stories – that could be said to demonstrate resistance or protest against the black-and-blue turn in Austrian politics. The selection here shows a range of interactions with the post-Wende direction of Austrian politics, including the adventure novel with its alternative society (Molden), a love story against the odds but set very much in a real-life Austria (Pluhar), and a collection of feminist interventions looking at women's relationships and real-life social problems against a background of issues affecting contemporary society (Streeruwitz). Wippersberg's three novels play, in volumes one and two, with some of the conventions of the political thriller and, in volume three, with the expectations of a psychological novel or *Entwicklungsroman* by presenting decline and inner degeneration as opposed to the forwards development and sense of bourgeois completion afforded by the traditional *Bildungsroman*. Aesthetically, the novelists' tools vary a great deal, but common elements include the use of *à-clef* techniques to suggest that fictional characters are based on real-life public figures. The novels presented here contain some humorous elements, but the overriding mode is not comic. The satirical impetus seems to be better housed in the shorter protest pieces against *schwarz-blau*, including the graphic novel (Lukas and Haderer). Whether or not humorous expression in art acts merely as a substitute for political action, a kind of pacifier to dampen subversion, is a topic that has been widely debated.[139] We cannot, in any case, evaluate the works discussed here for some kind of tangible effect or mobilizing quality, and suggest that the sales figures do not signal their political impact.[140] What is of interest in the present study is the literary text itself, the themes at play, the techniques deployed and the interpretations that open up when a reader engages with those texts.

There are countless essayistic reactions and protest markers against developments in Austrian politics brought about by the fateful elections of 3 October 1999. Indeed, the essay and the open letter are much-invoked means of protest in democratic societies all over the world. It is interesting to see how professional writers and concerned members of the public alike turn instead or as well to creative writing or the writing of fiction as a means of expressing their concern – a means, as it were, of practising resistance. 'Writing is precisely *the very possibility of change*, the space that can serve as a springboard for subversive thought, the precursory movement of a transformation of social and cultural structures', the French feminist thinker Hélène Cixous tells us, referring in particular to the powerful space that writing can offer to women.[141] But writing fiction is not taking direct action or protesting visibly in public spaces. We must suppose that the writers considered here *pars pro toto* for the genre of protest prose in Austria as a whole would not advocate replacing public protest with writing stories as a sole means of voicing criticism. In creating and utilizing the *Widerstandslesungen* as a hybrid form of reading-literature-as-public-protest, many of these writers recognize the need to wrest creative writing or fiction from its normally contained and placid home between the covers of a book. Fortunately, the publications remain for readers to enjoy regardless of the ways in which they may – or may not – be read and acknowledged as works of protest, and surely attest that political fiction is still alive and well in Austria in the twenty-first century.

Notes

1. Baker and Boyer, *Wiener Wandertage*; Awadalla and Korosa, *...Bis sie gehen*.
2. See, for example, Friederike Mayröcker's poem 'wenn ich hinter dem Haus gehe und wühle', in Milena Verlag, *Die Sprache des Widerstandes*, 284, first published in Friederike Mayröcker, *Das besessene Alter: Gedichte 1986–1991* (Frankfurt am Main: Suhrkamp Verlag, 1992).
3. 'Mutig greift sie in den Blättern alle populären Themen auf, die zur Abfassungszeit 2000 und 2001 in den Medien kursieren: Haider, den Ausländerhaß, die "Leihmütter", die konservative Ausrichtung der Pädagogik, den verlogenen Heimatkult, kurz: das Leben "im Falschen", in dem es nur ein Richtiges gibt, Marlene Streeruwitz.' Hannelore

Schlaffer, 'Habermas und Uschi Glas. Mein fremdbestimmter Körper: Marlene Streeruwitz führt Tagebuch', *Frankfurter allgemeine Zeitung*, 31 January 2003. Retrieved 6 May 2018 from http://www.faz.net/aktuell/feuilleton/buecher/rezensionen/belletristik/marlene-streeruwitz-tagebuch-der-gegenwart-habermas-und-uschi-glas-193438.html.

4. Jelinek calls one political reflection 'Moment! Aufnahme! 5.10.99', in Isolde Charim and Doron Rabinovici (eds), *Österreich: Berichte aus Quarantanien* (Frankfurt am Main: Suhrkamp, 2000), 100–9; academic Katharina Pewny calls her reflection 'Lesben kennen keine Gnade: Widerstand' a 'Momentaufnahme aus dem regnerischen März 2000', in Milena Verlag, *Die Sprache des Widerstandes*, 158–60, at 158.
5. Werner Thuswaldner, *Pittersberg* (Munich: Albert Knaus Verlag, 2000) explores the right-wing scene of Nazi veterans and younger neo-Nazis in Carinthia. Milo Dor's *Wien, Juli 1999* (Paul Zsolnay Verlag, Vienna, 1997) presents Vienna against the rise of a new political 'movement' with a charismatic leader. In Gerhard Roth's novel *Der See*, there is a failed assassination attempt on a character whose description also fits that of Jörg Haider. The FPÖ launched a parliamentary enquiry against Roth as a consequence. See 'Autoren: Wie die Nazis', *Der Spiegel* 19 (1995), 214. Retrieved 6 May 2018 from http://www.spiegel.de/spiegel/print/d-9184929.html.
6. 'Die Flucht aus einer Welt, in der "fleißige Leistungsträger" gefragt sind. Damit kommen sie Österreichs Gegenwart sehr nahe.' Susanne Messmer, 'Stille Tage im Wienerwald', *Die Tageszeitung*, 22 January 2002. Retrieved 6 May 2018 from http://www.taz.de/index.php?id=archivseite&dig=2002/01/22/a0119.
7. Ernst Molden, *Doktor Paranoiski* (Vienna: Deuticke, 2001). Molden is primarily known as a singer-songwriter. His father, Fritz Molden, was a highly influential newspaper editor and active resistance fighter in World War II.
8. Molden, *Doktor Paranoiski*, 94.
9. 'Bis zum Schluß des Buches ist sich der Leser nicht im klaren darüber, ob diese Truppe nun eine sympathische, wenn auch grün-militant angehauchte Gemeinschaft ist oder ein herumlaufender Haufen armer Irrer. Die letztendliche Entscheidung überläßt der Autor dann auch dem Leser selbst, denn er bietet keinerlei Erklärung für ihre Existenz und verweigert jegliche emotionale Stellungnahme.' Walter Robotka, 'Militanter Naturschutz: Ernst Molden, *Doktor Paranoiski*', *Evolver*, 3 January 2002. Retrieved 6 May 2018 from www.evolver.at/site/review.php?id=12139.
10. Molden, *Doktor Paranoiski*, 138.
11. '"Was sind das? Rechtsextreme?" frage ich. Hören Sie doch auf mit Ihren altmodischen Kategorien. Links! Rechts! Ja, die Knaben fühlen sich deutsch. Aber Nazis – nein.' Molden, *Doktor Paranoiski*, 175.
12. 'Du kriegst Nachhilfe in der Innenpolitik deines ehemaligen Staates Österreich. Seitdem du tot bist, sind ein paar Dinge passiert. Die Nationalen sind aus der Regierung gebrochen, die Christkonservativen regieren allein, in der Minderheit. Im Herbst sollen Wahlen sein.' Molden, *Doktor Paranoiski*, 193–94.
13. See 'Knittelfeld,' in Panagl, Gerlich et al., *Wörterbuch der politischen Sprache in Österreich*, 220.
14. See Samir Köck, 'Ernst Molden: "Ich hatte das Bedürfnis, alt zu sein"', *Die Presse*, 26 June 2016. Retrieved 6 May 2018 from https://diepresse.com/home/leben/mensch/5003243/Ernst-Molden_Ich-hatte-das-Beduerfnis-alt-zu-sein. Molden expresses the view here that singer-songwriters should generally steer clear of politics.

15. '[G]ewisse Ähnlichkeiten mit einem zeitgenössischen Regierungsmitglied.' Robotka, 'Militanter Naturschutz'.
16. Amnesty International, 'Amnesty International Report 2003: Austria', 28 May 2003. Retrieved 6 May 2018 from http://www.refworld.org/docid/3edb47cd4.html.
17. Reviewer Wolfgang Koch dislikes the glaring ironies of Molden's novel, but finds this literary allusion and others in the novel to be well chosen. Wolfgang Koch, 'Mytho-Wesen in Waldsaga', *Wiener Zeitung*, 19 October 2001.
18. 'Österreichischen Wald … wie ihn Schubert besungen hat und Waldmüller gemalt.' Molden, *Doktor Paranoiski*, 48.
19. See Senta Ziegler, 'Pluhar wird Bundespräsidentin', *News*, 20 February 2003, 132.
20. Erika Pluhar, *Die Wahl* (Hamburg: Hoffmann und Campe, 2003), e.g. 89, 157 and 225.
21. Pluhar, *Die Wahl*, 155.
22. 'Aber der Zulauf zum Rechtsextremismus, zum – wie es jetzt bereits genannt wird – "Walderismus", der geschah auf Grund grundloser Unzufriedenheit, die geschürt werden konnte, weil alles zur Zufriedenheit lief. Weil unser Land letztlich ein wohlregiertes, wohlbestalltes, gut bestelltes Land geworden war und immer noch ist.' Pluhar, *Die Wahl*, 155–56.
23. '[I]m Dunkel diktatorischer Staatsformen.' Pluhar, *Die Wahl*, 156.
24. '[D]ie Vertreter dieser traurigen *Fies*heitspartei.' Pluhar, *Die Wahl*, 173 (emphasis added).
25. 'Warum Haider kneift', *Die Zeit*, 40, 28 September 2000. Retrieved 6 May 2018 from http://www.zeit.de/2000/40/Warum_Haider_kneift. The comments Heller made are reported on in English in Karl Pfeifer, 'Der FPÖ-Feldzug: Geschichten aus den Wiener Gerichtssälen', *haGalil onLine*, 10 November 2000. Retrieved 6 May 2018 from http://www.klick-nach-rechts.de/austria/haider-1.htm.
26. Ahtisaari, Frowein and Oreja, 'Report'; see paras 97 and 98.
27. Jelinek's Heinrich Böll prize acceptance speech of 1986 sets a precedence for nature-related parodic distortions of politicians' names. Jelinek, 'In den Waldheimen und auf den Haidern'.
28. 'Der Haiderismus lebt auch ohne Haider weiter.' Susanne Knaul, 'Israel: "Der Haiderismus lebt auch ohne Haider weiter"', *Die Presse*, 12 October 2008. Retrieved 6 May 2018 from http://diepresse.com/home/politik/innenpolitik/421941/index.do?from=suche.intern.portal.
29. See Robert Acker, 'Josef Haslinger's Opernball: From Best Seller to Film Thriller', in Margarete Lamb-Faffelberger (ed.), *Literature, Film and the Culture Industry* (New York: Peter Lang, 2002), 160–69, at 168.
30. '[I]ch konnte plötzlich lieben. Und ich denke nicht daran, es wieder aufzugeben, … Ich will mich schlicht und einfach, unpathetisch und unaufgeregt, *zu dir bekennen*, Charlotte.' Pluhar, *Die Wahl*, 237 and 240; emphasis in original.
31. Pluhar, *Die Wahl*, for example at 43, 171, 188, 229, 237, 248.
32. 'Ich und mein Herbststurm sind wirklich zum Lachen. Wie komme ich nur auf diese Groschenroman-Analogie.' Pluhar, *Die Wahl*, 165.
33. '[F]ormuliere. Schreib auf. Kläre das Ganze mal in deinem Kopf.' Pluhar, *Die Wahl*, 202.
34. 'Ja, … aufschreiben werde ich jetzt. Oder besser *nieder*schreiben'. Pluhar, *Die Wahl*, 206.
35. Konstanze Fliedl, 'Damenwahl', *Falter*, 21 March 2003.

36. My discussion of Pluhar's *Die Wahl* and Streeruwitz's *Jessica 30.* was originally published as Allyson Fiddler, 'Of Political Intentions and Trivial Conventions: Erika Pluhar's *Die Wahl* (2003) and Marlene Streeuwitz's *Jessica, 30.* (2004)', *German Life and Letters* 64(1) (2011), 133–44.
37. See Allyson Fiddler, 'Shifting Boundaries: Responses to Multiculturalism at the Turn of the Twenty-First Century', in Katrin Kohl and Ritchie Robertson (eds), *A History of Austrian Literature 1918–2000* (Rochester, NY: Camden House, 2006), 265–89.
38. '[I]n jedem Augenblick [bleibt] die Anwesenheit der Autorin vernehmbar ..., einer über fünfzigjährigen Feministin, die zahllose Themen und Personen der österreichischen Tagespolitik durchhechelt.' Leopold Federmair, 'Das ungenierte "Und": Marlene Streeruwitz beschreibt Österreich als Sumpf', *Neue Züricher Zeitung*, 14 July 2004.
39. Marlene Streeruwitz, *Jessica, 30.* (Frankfurt am Main: Fischer Taschenbuch, 2006), 232, (first published in 2004).
40. Brenda Bethman, 'Generation Chick: Reading *Bridget Jones's Diary*, *Jessica, 30.*, and *Dies ist kein Liebeslied* as Postfeminist Novels', *Studies in 20th and 21st-Century Literature* 35(1) (2011), 136–54, at 148. Retrieved 6 May 2018 from https://doi.org/10.4148/2334-4415.1743.
41. Ina Hartwig, 'Jessicas Lauf gegen die Weiblichkeit', in Jörg Bong, Roland Spahr and Oliver Vogel (eds), *'Aber die Erinnerung davon': Materialien zum Werk von Marlene Streeruwitz* (Frankfurt am Main: Fischer Taschenbuch Verlag, 2007), 136–48, at 146.
42. 'Nein. Marlene Streeruwitz blickt eiskalt auf die neue *condition féminine*. Die dreißigjährigen Frauen, die aus ihrer Unmündigkeit nur mit Zickenmethoden ausbrechen zu können meinen, schneiden dabei nicht besonders heroisch ab.' Hartwig, 'Jessicas Lauf gegen die Wirklichkeit', 146.
43. 'Somnus' is the Latin word for sleep; 'Jessica', on the other hand, if it derives from the Hebrew name Iscah in the Bible, suggests 'one who sees'. This is fitting as Jessica comes to comprehend the situation around her. Retrieved 6 May 2018 from http://www.behindthename.com/name/jessica.
44. Streeruwitz, *Jessica, 30.*, 150.
45. '"Mir würde das nichts machen, wenn das einer von den Blauen wird. Die machen das sicher besser, aber es schaut schlecht aus im Ausland und wir müssen uns noch ein bisserl hinziehen".' Streeruwitz, *Jessica, 30.*, 150.
46. 'Dieser Text ist ein Werk literarischer Fiktion. Figuren und Handlungen sind frei erfunden', Streeruwitz, *Jessica, 30.*, 4.
47. Loreley French, 'Prostitution and Sex Trafficking of Women in Austria: The Legalities and Illegalities of the Sex Trade Meet Marlene Streeruwitz's *Jessica*', in Rebecca S. Thomas (ed.), *Madness and Crime in Modern Austria* (Newcastle: Cambridge Scholars Publishing, 2008), 150–73, at 150.
48. 'Wie bringt ihr das auf die Reihe, das mit der glücklichen Familie? Das ist doch ganz einfach. Die Familie ist heilig und die Prostitution wird wieder steuerfrei.' Streeruwitz, *Jessica, 30.*, 145.
49. Streeruwitz, *Jessica, 30.*, 193.
50. '[E]s ist für die Sache der Frauen, es ist eine Rote-Zorra-Aktion, es ist tank girl, und Angelina Jolie.' Streeruwitz, *Jessica, 30.*, 230.
51. '[D]as Beste wäre, die ganze Regierung muss zurücktreten wegen dem Gerhard, aber das passiert nicht, hier passiert das nicht, dann wäre das mit der Pensionsreform auch gestoppt, und dann hätte ich die Pensionen gerettet, wenn dann alles gut ausgeht,

aber das wäre schön, Jessica, die Retterin, ich stehe auf dem Heldenplatz und schicke alle Demonstranten nach Hause, weg aus dem Unwetter und dem Hagel, weil diese Regierung sowieso zurücktreten muss, wegen ihrem Staatssekretär für Zukunfts- und Entwicklungsfragen und seiner Mädchenhändlerei.' Streeruwitz, *Jessica, 30.*, 233.
52. Streeruwitz, *Jessica, 30.*, 228.
53. Streeruwitz, *Jessica, 30.*, 103.
54. '[D]enk an den Jörgl. Der kann machen, was er will, der könnte schwul sein, der könnte bi sein . . . der kann in der Praterstraße machen, was er will, das interessiert niemanden.' Streeruwitz, *Jessica, 30.*, 163.
55. ' "Sex-Affären bringen nichts in Österreich. In Amerika ja, aber bei uns nicht . . . Bei uns da kann einer seinen Dackel pudern oder seine Kuchlkredenz oder ein Kinderschänder sein, das regt die Leut lang net so auf, wie wenn er mehr verdient als sie".' Walter Wippersberg, *Ein nützlicher Idiot* (Salzburg: Otto Müller Verlag, 1999), 177.
56. Mario Scalla, 'Formvollendete Fragen. Über das Verhältnis von literarischer Form und gesellschaftlicher Aktualität in den Texten von Marlene Streeruwitz', in Bong, Spahr and Vogel, *'Aber die Erinnerung davon'*, 149–63.
57. See Marlene Streeruwitz, '15.9.2000: Standard-Interview', in Streeruwitz, *Tagebuch der Gegenwart*, 110–11.
58. Kirstie Knolle and Shadia Nasralla, 'Austria's Far-Right Party Accuses Conservatives of Stealing Campaign Ideas', 5 September 2017. Retrieved 6 May 2018 from https://uk.reuters.com/article/uk-austria-election/austrias-far-right-party-accuses-conservatives-of-stealing-campaign-ideas-idUKKCN1BG2IL.
59. Regrettably, neither the 2008 nor the 2006 episodes are now housed on the author's webpages. See *Freitag* newspaper for the 2006 novel: https://www.freitag.de/autoren/der-freitag/so-ist-das-leben. I am grateful to Marlene Streeruwitz for pdf files of both works. Streeruwitz's office informed me (email correspondence of 6 July 2016) that the author was considering publishing more online episodes of her election novel for the occasion of the rerun of the Austrian presidential elections (scheduled at the time for 2 October 2016). See also the Conclusion to this volume.
60. '[D]ieser Satz [ist] der erste Hauptsatz des globalisierten Neoliberalismus … und [wurde] zur Überschrift über die kleinen und großen Zulassungsbeschränkungen in einer Gesellschaft …, in der wirtschaftliches Handeln als Naturereignis nicht mehr besprechbar geworden ist und als unveränderbare, schicksalhafte Naturkatastrophe gesehen werden soll.' Streeruwitz, quoted in *Freitag* 33, 18 August 2006. Retrieved 6 May 2018 from https://www.freitag.de/autoren/der-freitag/so-ist-das-leben.
61. Streeruwitz. Retrieved 6 May 2018 from https://www.freitag.de/autoren/der-freitag/so-ist-das-leben.
62. 'Die Irmi Kramreiter hatte ihren Bruder in das Haus der Eltern geholt und alle Schlösser waren ausgewechselt. Fortsetzung folgt.'
63. 'Sie wisse doch sicher noch, was er wolle. Sie sei doch eine von diesen intelligenten jungen Frauen, die sich so etwas merkten . . . War das eine Aufforderung gewesen, die Mischung vom letzten Mal zu wiederholen? Fortsetzung folgt.'
64. 'Und Kulturschock. Das war das Ausfüllen der Haftungserklärung gemäß §2 Abs. 1 Z 15 NAG, auf der nur jemand mit Lohnzettel die Haftung für den Pauli übernehmen konnte. In der Umgebung Barbaras gab es aber niemanden mehr, der einen Lohnzettel hatte.' *Das Leben geht weiter.*, Episode 2. Marlene Streeruwitz, *Das Leben geht weiter*, unpublished manuscript, originally published at http://www.marlenestreeruwitz.at.

65. The Bank für Arbeit und Wirtschaft AG nearly collapsed amidst a fraud scandal in the early 2000s; Natascha Kampusch, aged eighteen on her escape in 2016, had been held captive since the age of ten by her kidnapper, Wolfgang Přiklopil; during an address in 2006, Pope Benedict XVI (Joseph Ratzinger) made comments intimating that Islam was a fundamentally fanatical religion.
66. '[H]atte immer gesagt, dass das schon interessant sei, dass in einem so katholischen Land, die Prostituierten erst zu arbeiten aufhören durften, wenn sie ihre Steuervorschreibung erfüllt hatten. Und dass man dann hoffen musste, dass die Politiker zu den Damen gingen, damit die ihre Steuer dann auch abzahlen konnten.' Streeruwitz, *Das Leben geht weiter*, Episode 4, 2006.
67. 'Armut mache hier anders mundtot. Aber auch das war wie 1873. In Österreich hätten halt immer nur die höheren Herrschaften geredet. Da hatten die anderen keine Gelegenheit, das Reden zu lernen. Und das dauere halt an. Diese ÖVP. Die sei doch von den Schönerern und den Luegers nicht weggekommen. Das war der Mutter von der Nadine dann zu viel. Sie habe ja vielleicht recht, meinte sie. Aber sie könne dieses Geschimpfe auf die ÖVP nicht haben.' Streeruwitz, *Das Leben geht weiter*, Episode 7. Georg von Schönerer (1842–1921) was a member of the Austrian nobility, an anti-Semitic extremist and pan-Germanist. Karl Lueger (1844–1910), another anti-Semitic politician, founded the precursor to the ÖVP, the Christian Social Party, in 1891.
68. 'Auch die Mutter von Nadine sagte gleich, daß es doch nicht so schlimm gewesen wäre. Daß man es eben aushalten müßte, schlecht behandelt zu werden, wenn man sich nichts anderes leisten könne.' Streeruwitz, *Das Leben geht weiter*, Episode 5, 2008.
69. '[D]aß das Leben eben so sei.' Streeruwitz, *Das Leben geht weiter*, Episode 18.
70. '[D]aß sie regiert würden und daß man das beeinflußen mußte.' Streeruwitz, *Das Leben geht weiter*, Episode 7.
71. I am grateful to Helga Kraft for an email exchange (25 March 2009) sharing these insights into Streeruwitz's work.
72. 'Es gibt bei mir – nicht nur, aber oft – politische Stoffe. Ginge es bei mir aber in erster Linie um die politische Aufklärung oder die politische Einmischung, dann würde ich entweder direkt politisch arbeiten oder journalistisch. Ich bin kein Leitartikler, kein Politologe und schon gar nicht Politiker. Mein Ehrgeiz ist es, gute Geschichten gut zu erzählen.' Walter Wippersberg, '"Mein Ehrgeiz ist es, gute Geschichten, gut zu erzählen": Walter Wippersberg im Gespräch mit Christian Schacherreiter', *Porträt: Walter Wippersberg*, special issue, *Die Rampe* (2003): 7–18, at 18.
73. All published with Otto Müller Verlag, Salzburg. Wippersberg died in 2016, leaving behind a body of films, screenplays, novels, children's books, essays and a controversial nonfiction book defending the rights of smokers: *Der Krieg gegen die Raucher: zur Kulturgeschichte der Rauchverbote* (Vienna: Promedia, 2010).
74. The prefatory quotations in Gerhard Roth's *Der See* are also grouped together under the Bachmann-inspired heading, 'Im Land der Mörder'.
75. Franz Zens demonstrates the validity of this claim and points out that it is not likely that Wippersberg's fictional party is based on the single-issue, short-lived Austrian political party 'Die Demokraten'. Franz Zens, 'Fiktion und FPÖ: mögliche Anspielungen auf Darstellungen freiheitlicher Politik in drei Texten von Josef Haslinger, Milo Dor und Walter Wippersberg, unpublished Diplomarbeit, University of Vienna, 2002 (at 54).
76. '[E]inen kleinen Schritt in die richtige Richtung.' Wippersberg, *Die Irren und die Mörder*, 24.

77. 'Der oft so genannte auktoriale Erzähler ist, einem alten Vorurteil zum Trotz, nicht allwissend, braucht es nicht zu sein. . . . Aber halten wir die Randfiguren, die nicht wieder auftauchen, auf Distanz.' Wippersberg, *Die Irren und die Mörder*, 21.
78. Zens ('Fiktion und FPÖ') notes that the journalist and FPÖ critic Wolf Purtscheller was smeared by the FPÖ as the Oberwart bomber at a time when it was not yet known that Franz Fuchs was responsible for killing the four members of the Roma community in 1995.
79. Wippersberg, *Ein nützlicher Idiot*, 248.
80. 'Man wird ihn [Veluncek] an der Macht teilhaben lassen müssen, aber das wäre auf längere Sicht sowieso nicht zu vermeiden, das ist der Zug der Zeit. Und vielleicht auch gar nicht so schlecht: Die Blauen müssen auf diese Art ja auch Verantwortung übernehmen.' Wippersberg, *Die Geschichte eines lächerlichen Mannes*, 211–12).
81. '[W]eil der Plot . . . wesentlich politischer und damit veilleicht auch realistischer ist.' Andreas Pittler review in *Der Standard*, quoted in the collection of press reviews at: http://members.aon.at/wippersberg/idiot.html.
82. Arno Rußegger, 'Walter Wippersberg: Ein nützlicher Idiot'. Retrieved 6 May 2018 from http://www.literaturhaus.at/index.php?id=3315&L=percent2Fprocpercent2Fself per cent2Fenviron.
83. 'Real sind die Rahmenbedingungen der Handlung, womit eine Analyse der aktuellen politischen Situation gelang, fiktiv ist das Ende . . . Eine spannende literarische Warnung' ('the contextual framework of the plot is real and has succeeded in giving us an analysis of the contemporary political situation. The ending is fictional. It's an exciting literary warning'). Katharina Kratzer in *Kleine Zeitung*, Retrieved 6 May 2018 from http://members.aon.at/wippersberg/idiot.html.
84. Zens, 'Fiktion und FPÖ'.
85. Haider used the term in a parliamentary speech in 1995. Several newspapers that accused him of thereby trivializing Nazi crimes were sued by the FPÖ. The case eventually went as far as the European Court of Human Rights, which judged that the newspaper group had been wrongly fined by the Austrian State and that financial compensation had to be made. See European Court of Human Rights, 'Case of Wirtschafts-Trend Zeitschriften-Verlags GmbH v. Austria', 27 October 2005. Retrieved 6 May 2018 from http://portal.nasstar.com/75/files/Wirtschafts-v-Austria per cent20ECHR per cent2027 per cent20Oct per cent202005.pdf.
86. See 'Spitzelaffäre', in Panagl, Gerlich et al., *Wörterbuch der politischen Sprache in Österreich*, 399-400.
87. '[J]enseits aller Ideologien.' Wippersberg, *Ein nützlicher Idiot*, 21.
88. '[L]iegt auf der Couch und liest eines ihrer esoterischen Lebensbewältigungsbücher.' Paulus Hochgatterer, 'Ready or Not, Here I Come', in Baker and Boyer, *Wiener Wandertage*, 91–98, at 91. Eva Jancak, 'Widerstand beim Zwiebelschneiden', in Milena Verlag, *Die Sprache des Widerstandes*, 78–80. Both Hochgatterer and Jancak work in psychiatry as well as pursuing literary careers.
89. '[D]ie von der F' [Freiheitlichen Partei]. Dieter Schrage, 'Tomaten Widerstand', in Awadalla and Korosa, *...Bis sie gehen*, 42–46, at 42.
90. Schrage, 'Tomaten Widerstand', 45.
91. '"Für die Bundesministerin – i.A." Den Namensstempel auf das Papier gebracht und dann mit gewohnter Treffsicherheit den amtlichen, in seiner dienstlichen Verwahrung sich befindenden Rundstempel. Fertig.' Schrage, 'Tomaten Widerstand', 42.

92. '[W]ie gewohnt, pünktlich um acht Uhr.' Schrage, 'Tomaten Widerstand', 46.
93. '[S]ollte nichts eingetreten sein.' Schrage, 'Tomaten Widerstand', 46.
94. '[V]ielleicht dreimal gegen diesen Staat zu pinkeln.' Dieter Schrage, ' "Zeugnis für Demo-Teilnahme": Anmerkungen zu meiner Vorlesung an der Uni Wien', in Baker and Boyer, *Wiener Wandertage*, 398–401, at 399.
95. El Awadalla, '18. bezirk: gretl', in El Awadalla, *wienerinnen: geschichten von guten und bösen frauen* (Vienna: Sisyphus, 2006), 89–92.
96. El Awadalla and Grace Latigo's dialect cabaret extract, 'Monolog', is published in Milena Verlag, *Die Sprache des Widerstandes*, 258–59.
97. 'Interview with the Author', Vienna, 16 December 2008.
98. '[G]eh muatterl, machens platz, wir suchen einen terroristen.' Awadalla, '18. bezirk: gretl', 92.
99. El Awadalla explains some of the background to the FPÖ-generated scandal in an interview with Martin Tschiderer. These quotations feature in Gerald Grassl, 'Granaten unterm Strickzeug: Die Wiener Schriftstellerin El Awadalla als Terror-Patin?', *Augustin*, 225, 9–22 April 2008, 6–7. Retrieved 6 May 2018 from http://www.augustin.or.at/ documents/article-docs/article-2910/augustin_225.pdf.
100. 'Es ist eine schiere Unglaublichkeit, dass ein solches Pamphlet, welches als Anleitung zum Terror gegen höchste Repräsentanten der Republik Österreich verstanden werden kann, vom Bundeskanzleramt (Kunstförderung), der Stadt Wien und dem Land Burgenland finanziell unterstützt wurde.' The submission, led by FPÖ politician Martin Graf, is available at: https://www.parlament.gv.at/PAKT/VHG/XXIII/J/J_03915/imfname_103551.pdf. The complaints against El Awadalla were not upheld.
101. Schrage quotes an elderly student whose grandchild is proud of her demo-attendance, Schrage, ' "Zeugnis für Demo-Teilnahme", 401. See also the contribution by one of the Three Wise Women (Drei Weisinnen), Anneliese Gesswein, 'Wortbruch Schüssels', in Baker and Boyer, *Wiender Wandertage*, 41–44.
102. It is not possible to discuss the wealth of political cartoons in newspapers of the era. A sample of Othmar Wicke's 'Blaubär und Propeller' (mimicking Haider and Schüssel) can be seen at: http://www.otwic.com/textfiles/portfolio.pdf. An earlier version of my analysis of protest in short format works such as *Jörgi, der Drachentöter* as well as pieces by Antonio Fian (see Chapter 5) appeared as Allyson Fiddler, 'A Political "Brief": Performativity and Politicians in Short Works of Austrian Satire', in Brigid Haines, Stephen Parker and Colin Riordan (eds), *Aesthetics and Politics in Modern German Culture: Festschrift in Honour of Rhys W. Williams* (Oxford: Peter Lang, 2010), 179–93.
103. Luca Kilian Kräuter, 'Luca, das Widerstands-Baby', in Baker and Boyer, *Wiener Wandertage*, 456–57, at 457.
104 '[S]ozusagen eine Folge des Protestes, den hier viele als "Widerstand" bezeichnen.' Kräuter, 'Luca, das Widerstands-Baby', 457.
105. Thomas Maurer and Florian Scheuba, 'Widerstand', in Baker and Boyer, *Wiener Wandertage*, 247–49.
106. 'Puh, ne ganz schöne Verantwortung und das, wo ich ja noch nicht einmal krabbeln kann.' 'Luca, das Widerstands-Baby', 457. Luka Kilian Kräuter, the 'Widerstands-Baby', is indeed a real person. He and his parents, Manuela Kräuter and Jens Karg, are interviewed in Frederick Baker's retrospective film on the Austrian Wende: Baker, *Widerstand in Haiderland* (08:33).

107. Hoppelmann Karottnig, 'Wertedebatte mit einem noch zu zeugendem [sic] Kind: Zur Abwechslung ein vollkommen unpolitischer Text aus Wien im Jahre 2016', in Awadalla and Korosa, ...Bis sie gehen, 89–90. The volume's mini-biography of Karottnig indicates that he is an activist, writer and translator (Awadalla and Korosa, Bis sie gehen, 178).
108. '[E]rsten Untersuchungen zufolge existiert dort sogar eine kleine Konzentration davon [intelligent life], auf diesem Planeten wahrhaft keine Selbstverständlichkeit!' United Aliens, 'Blauer Planet', in Baker and Boyer, Wiener Wandertage, 246–47, at 246.
109. '[W]as haben wir nur falsch gemacht. Wenn du nur wenigstens ein bisserl so sein könntest, wie die Frau Bundeskanzlerin.' Karottnig, 'Wertedebatte', 89.
110. 'Onkel Wolf Martin.' Karottnig, 'Wertedebatte', 90.
111. 'Das Letzte, was schließlich noch funktionierte, war das Auswärtige Amt.' Richard Weihs, 'Das Märchen von der Stadt Auswärts', in Awadalla and Korosa, ...Bis sie gehen, 41–42, at 41. Weihs is an author, musician and actor.
112. 'Auswärtser raus!' Weihs, 'Das Märchen von der Stadt Auswärts', 42.
113. Brigitte Tauer, 'Rudi Riesenfuß muß flüchten', in Milena Verlag, Die Sprache des Widerstandes, 249–57. The volume indicates that Tauer has worked as a secretary, journalist and adult educator (Milena Verlag, Die Sprache des Widerstandes, 363).
114. Ludwig Roman Fleischer, 'Fremdenführung', in Awadalla and Korosa, ...Bis sie gehen, 148–51, at 148. Fleischer is the author of thirteen novels and countless short stories, as well as dialect books and occasional pieces.
115. Fleischer, 'Fremdenführung', 148.
116. 'Wegierung, Wegirrung.' Fleischer, 'Fremdenführung', 151.
117. 'Gebt's den armen Widerstandswürschteln was zum Piperln! Una goccetta per li opposition fighters, so that it them warm becomes!' Fleischer, 'Fremdenführung', 150.
118. Sylvia Treudl, 'Biedermensch erklärt einem Touristen, obwohl er Ausländer ist, die Welt', in Milena Verlag, Die Sprache des Widerstandes, 308–12. The title might translate as 'Mr Petty-Bourgeois Explains the World to a Tourist, Even Though the Latter is a Foreigner'. Treudl has published poetry and prose, and has edited numerous anthologies, most notably as an editor for the feminist publishing house, the Milena Verlag, in the 1980s and 1990s.
119. 'Ich bin die Göttin der Weisheit, habe gehofft, daß ich die Menschen den Gebrauch ihres Verstandes lehren könnte. Ich bin gescheitert.' Monika Vasik, 'Allmächtiger Zeus! Lieber Papa!', in Milena Verlag, Die Sprache des Widerstandes, 63–69, at 65. Vasik is a practising doctor. She continues to publish poetry and short stories. Her most recent collection of poems is Himmelhalb (Vienna: Verlagshaus Hernals, 2015).
120. '[D]ieser schnittige Fünfziger mit seinen Buberln und den paar Mäderln.' Vasik, 'Allmächtiger Zeus!', 65.
121. '[D]er unerträgliche Lärm hinter meinem Rücken.' Vasik, 'Allmächtiger Zeus!', 66.
122. Elisabeth Boyer, 'Die Pallas Athene muß beschützt werden', in Baker and Boyer, Wiener Wandertage, 115–24.
123. 'Was würde sie heute zu all der Aufregung um sie sagen? ... Ob es sie wirklich stört, wenn sie auch vom Volk vereinnahmt wird und nicht nur von PolitikerInnen?' Boyer, 'Die Pallas Athene muß beschützt werden', 124.
124. 'Ich bin froh, daß es diese anderen gibt, die vom Lärm der Werbeaktionen der derzeitigen Regierung oft übertönt werden, aber sie sind da, sie melden sich unbeirrt zu Wort. Sie rütteln auf.' Vasik, 'Allmächtiger Zeus!', 68.

125. 'Auch Intellektuelle und KünstlerInnen, erkennen plötzlich wieder, daß sie sich nicht aus dem politischen Leben heraushalten können.' Vasik, 'Allmächtiger Zeus!', 68.
126. '[E]in Bilderbuch für Kinder und Erwachsene.' Gerhard Haderer and Leo Lukas, *Jörgi, der Drachentöter* (Vienna: Ueberreuter, 2000).
127. Kazi Stastna, 'Jörgi, the Dragon Slayer', *Central Europe Review* 3(10) (2001). Retrieved 6 May 2018 from www.pecina.cz/files/www.ce-review.org/01/10/books10_stastna.html.
128. The dragon-slayer narrative is ubiquitous, assuming a 'master type' position in Propp's morphology of folk tales. See Üto Valk's entry on 'Monogenesis' in *The Greenwood Encyclopedia of Folktales and Fairy Tales*, ed. Donald Haase, 3 vols (Westport: Greenwood, 2008), vol. 2, 636.
129. ' "Weißt du, warum du jede Nacht ganz alleine Wache halten musst?" fragte Jörgi den Nachtwächter. / "Weil ich Nachtwächter bin?", mutmaßte der Nachtwächter. / "Schon", meinte Jörgi, "aber die Schuld liegt nicht bei dir, sondern beim Drachen. Schließlich hätte er längst noch andere Nachtwächter einstellen können!" . . . "Und die Chinesen!", fügte Jörgi hinzu. / "Wieso die Chinesen?", fragte der Nachtwächter. / "Weil, weil – – – weil du ja hauptsächlich wegen der Chinesen überhaupt Wache halten musst. Das weiß doch jeder, dass Chinesen ganz besonders gefährlich sind!" ' Haderer and Lukas, *Jörgi, der Drachentöter*, n.p.
130. The book is listed on the pages of the International Children's Digital Library Foundation (ICDL Foundation) at: http://childrenslibrary.org/servlet/WhiteRavens?searchText=erwachsen.
131. See the distinctive phonetic rendition of Adolf Hitler's intonation in Walter Moers's trilogy of Hitler comic books, for example, in the title *Adolf: Äch bin wieder da* (Frankfurt am Main: Eichborn, 2001).
132. Ole Frahm, 'Too Much is Too Much: The Never Innocent Laughter of the Comics', *Image and Narrative* 3 (October 2003). Retrieved 6 May 2018 from http://www.imageandnarrative.be/inarchive/graphicnovel/olefrahm.hrm. Bert States, 'Performance as Metaphor', in Philip Auslander (ed.), *Performance: Critical Concepts in Literary and Cultural Studies*, 4 vols (London: Routledge, 2003), vol. 1, 108-37, at 117–18.
133. It was in fact Schüssel who was dubbed the 'dragon slayer' by philosopher Rudolf Burger, who thought that history would see him as the one to have finished off Haider. See Walter Mayr, 'Österreich: Die Stunde des Drachentöters', *Der Spiegel*, 2 December 2012. Retrieved 6 May 2018 from http://www.spiegel.de/spiegel/print/d-25832002.html.
134. Haderer and Lukas, cited in Stastna, 'Jörgi, the Dragon Slayer', n.p.
135. Barbara Rassi, 'Review of Haderer, Gerhard and Leo Lukas (2000) *Jörgi, der Drachentöter*', *Rethinking History: The Journal of Theory and Practice* 6(3) (2002), 365–67, at 367.
136. Stastna, 'Jörgi, the Dragon Slayer', n.p. If the sausage is read as a sexual signifier, we might interpret the symbol as a marker of little Haider's phallic stage and the final outcome as an ironic resolution or as an emasculation.
137. Stephan Remmler, 'Alles hat ein Ende, nur die Wurst hat zwei' (1986) and covered since by other artists.
138. See 'Radish', in Udo Becker, *The Continuum Encyclopedia of Symbols*, trans. Lance W. Garmer (London: Continuum, 1994), 243.
139. See, for example, Marjolein 't Hart and Dennis Bos, 'Humour and Social Protest: An Introduction', *International Review of Social History*, 52, supplement 15 (2007):

'Humour in itself never changes circumstances. In addition, humour may even lessen discontent among the oppressed, which might inhibit the mobilization into action. In this regard, jokes are often viewed as safety valves, just as the early modern authorities regarded carnival or charivari', 1-20, at 7.

140. As noted, Streeruwitz's *Jessica, 30*. and Lukas and Haderer's *Jörgi der Drachentöter* were both bestselling publications. This suggests that purchasers enjoyed reading them or perhaps that the books were well marketed, but it says nothing about their impact on readers' opinions or actions. An amazon.de customer feels that Molden is too complex an author to have penned a mere allegory of the political situation in Austria. 'Militanter Naturschutz', https://www.amazon.de/product-reviews/3216305392/ref=acr_dpproductdetail_text?ie=UTF8&showViewpoints=1.

141. Hélène Cixous, 'The Laugh of the Medusa', in Dennis Walder and Open University (eds), *Literature in the Modern World: Critical Essays and Documents* (Oxford: Oxford University Press, 1990), 316–25, at 319–20.

Chapter 4

PROJECTING PROTEST
Resistance on Screen

Introduction: Lights, Camera, Protest!

In contrast to the novelist, the filmmaker who wishes to react to a set of political circumstances can do so within a short timeframe and bring his or her work to wider public attention via screenings or internet postings almost immediately. Creating a work of feature-film length or a film with the cinematographic qualities of narrative or of art-house cinema naturally takes a good deal longer. The difficulties of financing film production and distribution are substantial, and in a small country such as Austria they become more acute still. This chapter will discuss a number of feature-length films that can be seen as expressing protest at political circumstances in turn-of-the-century Austria, but the initial focus will be on the sizeable body of short-length protest films that were made as direct responses to the formation in February 2000 of the black-and-blue regime.[1]

Many of these films were made, then, before the tangible financial and politicocultural effects of the new, neoliberalist government took effect. Taking stock of the state of Austrian film in 2001, critic Michael Omasta notes the sad ironies of policy timing, with Austria's swingeing cultural budget cuts and reduction of institutional support coming at a time when, after many years of international invisibility, Austrian film was finally making a name for itself at the major film festivals and the Austrian state was capitalizing on this increased profile: 'If you took the lively interest shown by Austria's cultural politics after Haneke's triumphal success [at Cannes] as a measure, you would think that its film-making had long since been anchored in the Austrian conscience as an immutable factor in the country's identity-formation.'[2] Michael Haneke is doubtless the best known of Austria's directors, though his work has been mostly shot abroad and with French actors. His many successes include his Jelinek adaptation *La Pianiste* (Grand Prix, Cannes 2001) and *Das weiße Band* (*The White Ribbon*, 2009), for which he received the Cannes Film Festival's ultimate accolade, the Palme d'Or. The assumption that Austria is fully behind its film industry and its high-profile directors such as Haneke, Barbara Albert, Ulrich Seidl – and more latterly Stefan Ruzowitsky and Hans Weingartner – would be completely wrong, Omasta asserts:

> Quite the opposite is the case. First off, the bourgeois-right-wing populist government has drastically reduced the amount paid for so-called large-scale film financing (from around 24 million DM per year in 1999 to just short of 15 million); secondly, at the beginning of the year the government office with responsibility for young filmmakers, the avant-garde and for a large part of documentary film was removed at one stroke.[3]

Statistics made available by the organization 'Statistik Austria' would seem to suggest that the public financing of Austrian films rose over the first decade of the twenty-first century.[4] However, it is plain that the wave of short protest films in Austria in 2000 and 2001 did not have potential or actual budget cuts as their primary inspiration.[5] Professional and lay filmmakers alike were motivated to make their cinematic statements of dissent by the reality of the election results and the coalition formation in February 2000. Their films protest against the unthinkable having come true – the FPÖ was now in government.

Brief Encounters: 'Die Kunst der Stunde ist Widerstand'

'Die Kunst der Stunde ist Widerstand' is the name under which the various series of short protest films were aired. The slogan was first used as a print or sticker action by the activist group 'getto attack' and then appeared as a banner on the walls of the University of Applied Art in Vienna. The significance of the name and its adoption by the resistance filmmakers works on several levels, as cultural theorist Gerald Raunig explains. He points out that resistance, in the Austria of February 2000 and beyond, palpably *becomes* art just as artistic protests themselves intervene in political events. This creates a kind of space in which the division between the two is, as it were, temporarily cancelled out.[6] Thus, the slogan reads 'Die Kunst der Stunde *ist*' and not '*heißt* Widerstand' ('Resistance *is* the art of the moment' and not 'the art of the moment *is called* resistance'). The temporal allusion (to an 'hour'/'Stunde') implies an ironic distancing, Raunig suggests, from the pretentious and highfalutin pathos of grander institutions whose claim is to a lasting political position of emotional concern and not just one of the 'Stunde' or 'moment', as we might say in English. The equation of cultural resistance with political resistance as in the German motto above features in Stephen Duncombe's explanation of terms: 'Cultural resistance can also be thought of *as* political resistance', he notes, adding more pessimistically, 'cultural resistance can be seen as an escape from politics and a way to release discontent that might otherwise be expressed through political activity'.[7]

The term 'Widerstand'/'resistance' is itself not unproblematic in Austria, as I have noted in Chapter 2, especially in view of its immediate association with the notion of resistance against National Socialism, as in 'Widerstandskämpfer' or resistance fighter. In 2000, the letters pages of the newspapers were filled with irate *resistance* to the word 'resistance', Raunig reminds us, and underlines the irony that in emphasizing only the 'heroic days' of 1944/1945, the public omitted to evoke the underground resistance of February 1934, that is, the *communist* resistance against the authoritarian system of what became dubbed 'Austrofascism'.[8] The notion of resistance will take on more heightened meaning in the case study of Frederick Baker's protest film triptych *Erosion und Wi(e)derstand* below.

The film material discussed in the following originates in a series of protest films screened at the Diagonale festival in Graz in 2000, where the films received the 'Förderpreis für innovatives Kino'. After the 2000 festival, the series grew in size, and a different combination of films featured at the next Diagonale in 2001. Varied programmes of these resistance films were shown at a number of international festivals thereafter, from Nyon to Berlin and London. In attempting to impose some categorization onto this body of films, it is clear primarily from the context of their screening and the title of their series that they are by definition films with what might be called rhetorical structural forms. There are, of course, narrative elements, even in some of the shortest films here, but it goes without saying that we must expect these protest films to be trying to persuade their viewers of a particular conviction – against the black-and-blue coalition, and in particular, though not exclusively, against the 'blue' politics of the FPÖ. The films are made both by people in the media and film industry and by amateurs or activists who are simply exploiting the film medium to express their protest. Almost all of the fifty or so films that were shown as part of the 'Kunst der Stunde' programmes are unavailable commercially as individual films – they could, however, be distributed for screening, by seeking the rights from Vienna's independent video archive Medienwerkstatt Wien, and are now finally collectable in video format.[9] A small number of the films were made before the February coalition was inaugurated.

Many of the films use self-generated or found footage of the protest marches themselves, or consist entirely of documentary-style footage of such marches and demonstration events. Some of the films may have emerged out of the sheer urge to bear witness, either because of the magnitude of the demonstration and the desire to capture something of the filmmaker-activist's feelings about the demo, or indeed because in capturing on film scenes of police provocation or dubious arrests, the films also provide evidence and thus intervene directly in the political process. An example of this would be the 26-minute *Opernball 2000: Chronik einer Amtshandlung* (by the Schnittpunkt production team); this even calls itself a chronicle (of an official act) and captures shots of policemen in hooded civilian clothes (a mode of undercover disguise that the police initially denied having utilized). The Epilogue informs the viewer that a scandal ensued following this and other similar police interventions, and that the Green Party subsequently tabled questions in Austria's parliament to elicit clearer information.[10]

Some of the documentary-demo-films also capture interview snippets in order to present the voice of protesters or, in some cases, to expose the opinions of those against whom they are protesting. Examples include a couple of films by the cultural activist group Volxtheater Favoriten and its 'Kulturkarawane', a kind of itinerant journey of cultural activism that moved around Austria (and visited Italy, too, for the G8 summit). Their collaborative film *Neubewertung* (dir. Volxtheater Favoriten/Videogruppe, Rosa Antifa Wien and Martin Gössler, 12 minutes) was shot against the backdrop of tanks and military information stands at an army display, with men and women in uniform, and with crowds coming to visit the stands around Vienna's Hofburg.[11] The footage features activists holding donation boxes and asking passers-by if they would like to donate towards 'European Security' (the banners they are wearing are labelled with this too). The activists then engage in conversation and inform the passers-by that they are collecting for 'Wehrdienstverweigerer', or men who refuse to do their national service. The responses are antagonistic, but entirely expected at this kind of event. The film collaborators and protest event organizers intend to provoke, but also to make the visitors think that peace might be a better form of security than war. The filmmakers otherwise largely allow the images to speak for themselves. A veteran from World War II shows the photograph of himself in uniform that he always carries in his breast pocket in case he should bump into an old comrade, suggesting that military pride is still alive many decades later. Young children are seen being allowed to play with the firearms at the displays, thus pointing to the way in which the very young become inured and even drawn to state violence by tactile exposure to the symbols of military weaponry.

Filmically, this piece is not doing anything aesthetically unusual to achieve its provocation. Its parodistic undercutting of the military ethos relies to a fair extent on the dialogues in the film. Other pieces work more heavily with irony, not necessarily in terms of their content, but by using the screen space unusually or by manipulating the soundtrack, for example. Dieter Auracher's three-minute film *Parallelaktion* alternates between extracts of the Austrian evening news with Chancellor Schüssel, each time featuring the soundbites of the government's strategy focusing on 'Gelassenheit aber Festigkeit' (being 'calm but firm').[12] As the screen shows a calm Chancellor on the news and a digit counter to screen right registering the number of times that Schüssel rehearses his mantra of being 'gelassen', the alternating 'action' is that of serried ranks of riot police lining the streets. The name of the film describes the aesthetic device – cutting between two parallel types of action – and summarizes the tactical ploy of undermining the kind of 'action' or strategy that the government is pursuing; that is, supposedly professing a softly-softly approach in the studio whilst engendering violence and heavy-handedness on the streets. Thematically, too, Auracher could be alluding to the kind of ironic 'Parallelaktion' of Robert Musil's *Der Mann ohne Eigenschaften* (1930), to the societal forces shaping contemporary Austria (and that Musil in his day was also critiquing), and implying that Schüssel's best intentions might lead to something far worse.[13]

Die Herren (by Ewa Einhorn and Misha Stroj, 3.5 minutes) also uses interview footage and similarly mobilizes political rhetoric against the grain, adopting it here, too, as a kind of leitmotif.[14] Following a scandal when at an FPÖ rally in 2000, Ernest Windholz, the regional party leader for Niederösterreich, used the Waffen-SS phrase 'Meine Ehre heißt Treue!' ('loyalty is my honour'), a number of FPÖ politicians were interviewed by the filmmakers, and the film plays with some of their unapologetic or even supportive answers. The response that is repeated and varied in length, however, is that of the Transport Minister, Michael Schmid, who just shrugs and says 'Ich bin Verkehrsminister' ('I'm the Transport Minister'), as if this entitles him to remain silent. He is, the filmmakers imply and the viewers infer, guilty by association and by his self-imposed silence. Einhorn and Stroj begin their film with what might be read as a narrative device of mystery, 'somewhere in Europe, June 2000', as an ironic marker of a kind of undercover documentary (not wishing to stipulate where these interview events took place); they end very much with a documentary-form strategy, an intertitle informing the readers that 'the Gentlemen are members of the Freedom Party of Austria and of the Austrian People's Party. Since February 2000 these parties have formed the coalition government of Austria'.[15] My feeling is that the directors did not wish to suggest that the events could have taken place anywhere in Europe, but the 'somewhere in Europe' tag seems ironically generic when reviewing these artistic statements almost two decades later, given the rise in populist parties in many European countries (see the Conclusion). The film is not subtitled, nor indeed is it intended as a piece of information or education broadcasting for the Austrian or the foreign public, but the factual, uncommented verb phrase describing the function of 'Die Herren' is tactically disingenuous – contemporary viewers of these protest films knew who the 'Gentlemen' were. The ironically contrasting, mock-polite term 'Die Herren' implicitly invites the viewer to join with the filmmakers' disgust at the idea of these men actually being in power. The eponymous 'gentlemen' remain anonymous and vague in number, and can stand *pars pro toto* for all the so-called 'gentlemen' in government.

The device of linguistic reworking, reappropriation or ironic manipulation of political rhetoric is a common strand in the 'Kunst der Stunde ist Widerstand' series. Another common device in the short protest films, as in the short prose writings discussed in this study (see Chapter 3), is the use of children's perspectives or the representation of the political situation in Austria through the lens of childhood. Noteworthy here are the five short films by Thomas Horvath and Niki Griedl, all of which feature short scenarios of children playing or going about their activities.[16] Each time, the picture is bleak and stylized, most of the films using a child's voice singing a song, saying a rhyme or asking a question in an emotionally neutral manner. So, for example, in *Grenze*, we see ten children walking along the edge of a field accompanied by the music of the famous and now rightly disavowed children's song 'Zehn kleine Negerlein' ('Ten Little Niggers'). The text is replaced by a child singing sweetly a more modern, more final kind of disappearing song, in that the numbers do not reduce from ten to one (in the 'Ten Green Bottles' style that English-speaking children are familiar with), but at one fell stroke: 'ten little foreign children asking for asylum, not one child was taken in, there were just too many of them'.[17] The line of children disappears from the picture in one sudden cut. In another of their films, entitled *Schaukel*, it is the melody of Beethoven's 'Ode to Joy', the European Union's anthem, that is sung as 'lah-lah-lah' by the voiceover child. In *Tempelhüpfen*, the child's game of 'hopscotch' sees the young girl throwing her stone on the chalked-out structure and the song accompaniment is 'Fünfzehn Staaten in Europa lebten im Verband; eines machte einen Ruck an den rechten Rand; Vierzehn Staaten in Europa fühlten sich geneckt; wenn sich das nicht ändern wird, dann ist der eine weg' ('fifteen European states in association; one of them lurched to the right, an extremist nation; fourteen European states felt this took the mickey. If things don't get better soon, it's out with tricky dicky'). The political song does not, of course, 'belong' with the children's game, although in any of its worldwide variants, the game of hopscotch might be said to be about territory demarcation in terms of the boxes the child is allowed to hop in or out of. Thus, the filmmakers add a simple and ironic song casting Austria's aberrant behaviour in 1999/2000 as that of a naughty child who will be rightly ostracized by his or her peer group. Each of Horvath and Griedl's short films ends with a still shot of large writing with alternating blue-and-black coloured letters saying simply 'Politik ist kein Kinderspiel' ('politics isn't a kids' game'). The visuals have a kind of post-apocalyptic sadness about them with rather lifeless, inert children, almost as if the filmmakers are imputing an adult wisdom and world-weariness to the children, whilst elsewhere their elders and supposed betters are larking around with *infantile* political policies and platforms.

Martin Reinhart's one-minute film *Pinocchio* foregrounds its putative juvenile target audience by flagging up the name of Carlo Collodi's eighteenth-century tale, which has been the subject of many children's books and filmic reworkings.[18] The visuals are clearly all stills – shots of two specific election posters featuring then party leader Jörg Haider, and all taken from roughly the same angle and from roughly the same distance. The stills are strung together with perhaps a quarter of a second for each image. The fast speed, the slight differences in length and angle, and the different states of repair of the posters – from tears to graffiti – give a jerkiness to this 'moving picture' that does not actually move. In its way, Reinhart's film is also an experimental celebration of the still picture (Reinhart's pioneering avant-gardist compatriot Peter Kubelka is lauded for this in his structuralist films of the 1960s), but *Pinocchio* says something similar – aesthetically – about movement being 'relative to the eye of the viewer' and 'not something that takes place on the "movie-Screen"'. It is, as Kulbeka explained to Bernadette Wegenstein, a kind of contract, which the viewer should be made aware of.[19] Described as a 'filmmaker, film historian and inventor' on his staff page at Vienna's University of Applied Art,[20] Reinhart underscores the innovative editing in this short film. *Pinocchio* performs a kind of deconstructionist journey as Haider's image is subjected to various graffiti (see also Chapter 2) or is only partially present, having been torn from the poster board itself. We are reminded that images (*and* verbal sign systems such as the political slogan for that matter) require our complicity to believe in them. The enduring version of Haider is, of course, the title allusion to the woodcarver's mendacious puppet.

The soundtrack might be absorbed by the non-German speaker as simply a happy-sounding, rather dated family or children's song, but it will be recognizable to a middle-aged and older generation of German-speakers as the soundtrack to a favourite animated TV series of 'Pinocchio'. The nondiegetic music thus reinforces the visual inference of Haider's growing graffiti nose, as the particular poster's writing has also been defaced to say 'he *did* lie to you' and not '*he* did not lie to you' (the 'nicht' of 'Er hat Euch nicht belogen' is erased)[21] and Haider is interpellated as the 'kleines Püppchen' ('little puppet') of the song. The jerky effect of the editing gives a kind of visual suggestion of a wooden puppet's uneven movements rather than the smooth flow and continuity precision one would normally expect from an animation film. Equally, the original song's words seem perfect to infantilize Haider's pursuit of 'freedom' and his so-called 'Freedom' movement: 'Little doll, cheeky boy, you dream of freedom and fame, of riches and heroism, why my friend?'[22] The election posters stem from the national election of 1995 for which the FPÖ had styled itself not so much as a party but as a movement, hence calling itself in those days (in a runic font) 'Die Freiheitlichen'.[23] Austrian viewers sense the multiple layers suggested by the poster slogan of 1995 and its reuse in a protest film of 2000. The Freedom Party campaigners' allusion in 1995 is to the lies they suggested had been spun by the other parties (the ÖVP and the SPÖ in particular) and the wider reference is to the accession by Austria to the European Union (also in 1995). The posters are clearly shot in situ and the graffiti signals to the 2000 spectator that Haider's party's own 'lies' were being protested against in 1995 just as they are in 2000, when the posters are joined together to make a moving picture. Rosa

Antifa Wien (RAW), the left-wing, anti-fascist, anti-homophobia group, writes about the various electoral promises of the FPÖ and the realities that ensued after February 2000 under the banner ' "Er hat Euch nicht belogen"?', invoking this memorable slogan from years previous and pointing to broken election promises and worsening social conditions.[24] However, the Pinocchio symbol was not only a chosen allusion of countercultural groups and protesters. Even the ÖVP used a Pinocchio-style picture of Jörg Haider in a vile piece of negative campaigning. Their Carinthian election poster cast Haider with an initial runic 'F', as Finocchio. They then issued the unlikely denial that they did not know 'finocchio' was an Italian slang word for homosexual.[25]

Much more avant-gardist, and reminiscent of a kind of 1950s and 1960s Viennese actionism, is the body performance of multidisciplinary visual artist Bernadette Huber's film piece, the two-minute *Wie böse ist Österreich?* (1999).[26] The film features a running banner along the bottom of the screen, with printed quotations of some of the mock retractions or unpleasant rhetorical avoidances for which Jörg Haider was infamous. Each time, the text drives in from right to left in bursts of three or four words in a style reminiscent of tickertape, giving the necessary time to make the reader's encounter with these statements newly potent, since the Austrian viewer-protester is doubtless already familiar with them. Haider, however, does not feature either by attribution to the quotations or as a visual image. One quotation, for example, is 'Wenn Sie so wollen – dann war es halt – Massenmord' ('It was mass murder, if you will'), Haider's rejoinder to a journalist questioning why he used the term 'Vorfälle' and shied away from words like 'Vergasungen und Massenmord' ('gassing and mass murder'; see also Chapter 2).[27] The final part of Huber's film is a kind of birth scene, as a tiny Austrian flag is 'born' out of a vagina and the red-white-red then turns to *blue*-white-*blue*. The newly born Austria of February 2000 is an innately rightist-populist one, Huber's visuals imply. The birth is accompanied by the final few bars of the Austrian national anthem (which features in several of the protest films) as the text then enjoins the viewer, more neutrally, with the film's title: 'Informieren Sie sich. Wie böse ist Österreich?' ('Get Yourselves Educated, How Evil is Austria?').

'Die Kunst der Stunde ist Widerstand' had seen itself as a collective of film-makers who were trying to form new ways of getting their political message out and helping to create a kind of counterpublic. As the grouping became successful with having its programme series shown at festivals, and as the first wave of protests passed and the coalition government became older news, the 'Kunst der Stunde' took on the trappings of conventional film distribution, with its own office and agent. Reactions to the work of 'Kunst der Stunde' from the 'offizielle Filmszene' were mixed, with Hans Hurch, the Viennale festival director, reportedly dismissing the videos as by and large 'historische Dokumente und filmisch-ästhetisch uninteressant' ('historical documents, uninteresting in filmic terms').[28] Most of the films in the series have no afterlife outside the brief span of time in which they were most relevant and when audiences were most receptive to hearing and seeing works of protest in their cinemas, theatres or bookstalls. They are not all aesthetically insignificant, however, and some of the short films discussed above are testimony to the ways in which film devices can be harnessed to make political questions more effective.

This taxonomy of the different genres and techniques in the 'Kunst der Stunde' film programmes must unfortunately remain all too brief. The comedic element should, however, receive a mention, since humour is deployed in numerous films, as it is in the prose writings discussed in this book. For example, there are the two films featuring actor and cabarettist Hubsi Kramar, a frequent and very well-known Hitler impersonator. In 2000, Kramar tried to attend the high-society Viennese ball dressed as a very convincing Adolf Hitler and was unceremoniously arrested and escorted from the scene by the police and questioned for having committed an act of revival of Nazism, known in short in Austria as 'Wiederbetätigung'. One view on humour as an artistic strategy is that it acts in a kind of conciliatory, even cathartic fashion, thus assuaging anger and protest. Kramar feels that humour helps to keep protest alive.[29] In veteran Austrian film director Franz Novotny's *Frühling in Wien* (1.5 minutes), Kramar-Hitler is seen rehearsing his political speech in front of a mirror, only the lines are not Hitler quotations from the Nazi period, but are contemporaneous FPÖ lines.[30] *Torte statt Worte* (Klaus Hundsbichler, 5.5 minutes) is the pop video of the Austrian hard-rock band Drahdiwaberl's title song from the album *Torte statt Worte* of 2000 (see also Chapter 2). The music video features on the fourth programme of the 'Kunst der Stunde' collection.[31] The film begins with Kramar-Hitler announcing 'Ich bin wieder da' ('I'm back') and receiving the eponymous pie in the face. The video bills Kramar as a famous 'Tortologe' or cake scientist called Masoch Sacher, punning on the name of the nineteenth-century writer Leopold von Sacher-Masoch, from whose name the term 'masochism' derives but also on the famous Viennese chocolate cake, the 'Sachertorte', and the hotel that gives it its name.

The protest series include two films by the well-known trio of Austrian cabarettists who perform under the name Maschek and who specialize in adding voiceovers to found footage. In *Der graue Star 2: Die Wehrmacht* (2001, 8 minutes), a group of former Wehrmacht soldiers reminisce – via Maschek's voiceovers – about their wartime routines and their life in Argentina after the war where it was rather too hot and there were too many mosquitoes. *Unser schönes Kärnten* (2001, 6 minutes) uses footage from the 1970s to create the discord between what is seen and what is said.[32] The voiceovers deliver in slow, country-bumpkin Carinthian accents a marketing bid for the region to host the Olympics and boast of Carinthia's world-class facilities as the film shows shabby facilities, including public swimming baths.[33] The claim to have 'moderne computerunterstützte Zeitnehmung' ('modern, computer-aided timekeeping') is synchronized with a shot of a large floral clock. Maschek, derived from 'die Maschekseite', a term coming from the Hungarian and meaning the reverse or other side, are satirical cabarettists whose popularity has grown enormously since the days of the turn-of-the-millennium protests. These are clearly not one-off protest films intended only for the festival circuit like many others in 'Kunst der Stunde', but are instead continuations of Maschek's work for performances and television appearances. Their vein of political humour still draws large audiences in 2018, for example, via social media, but also as a regular feature of the weekly *Willkommen Österreich* television show series hosted by Christoph Grissemann und Dirk Stermann. A final example of a comedy clip from the 'Kunst der Stunde' series, *Demo Stewardess* (Studio West, 2000, 3 minutes), is not by famous filmmakers or artists, but by a Salzburg film collective and is taken from the third programme or series of films. It is a dry parody of airline safety announcements. The bearded, drag stewardess provides the minimalist, stylized actions to the voiceover advice, recommending, for example, that if a fist comes towards you, you should shout 'Widerstand' ('resistance') and that if you should want to use a stick, you must ensure that this is only one-tenth the size of the police batons.

A Longer 'Take': Frederick Baker, *Erosion und Wi(e)derstand*

Frederick Baker is an Austro-British filmmaker and journalist with a track record in documentary films with a political edge.[34] The German title of his three-part, twenty-minute protest film hints at one of the planks of Baker's cinematic actionism – Widerstand means resistance, but 'Wieder' (with an 'e') means 'again', so Wiederstand, a deliberately misspelled construct with a parenthetical 'e', implies something like 'standing up again'. Baker reports that he was much criticized for using the term 'resistance',[35] but the initial part of his film, 'AUSTRIA 05 2000', shot and shown separately in 2000, makes explicit reference to the resistance to Nazism during the Third Reich by explaining the symbolism of the letter plus number pattern 'O', '5'. The name 'Austria' was banned during the Nazi years and O plus 5 (the fifth letter of the alphabet being 'e', and 'Oe' (or Ö) being the beginning of the word Österreich) became a symbol of Austrian resistance. By the time of the shooting of the 2002 section, a perspex cover has been added to the famous wartime resistance graffiti next to the front door of Vienna's St Stephen's Cathedral, and Baker's film finishes with a Spanish tour guide explaining the significance of the 'O5' plaque to a group of visitors. In this first part of the film, Baker also shows contemporary graffiti, this time against the black-blue coalition, for example, a large 'Widerstand' sprayed on the side of the Café Ritter or a 'No Jörg' on the horizontal white bar of a 'no entry' traffic sign.

Some of the aesthetic devices Baker uses in this segment include fast time lapse and frozen frames against an indy-style song track written by the Fratelli Brothers and featuring the words 'resistance' and a ruptured, repeated 'Wieder- Wieder- Wiederstand'.[36] The predominant tool that Baker deploys in the later parts of his film, shot in 2002 when Austria had to call another election after less than two years of the coalition government, is something that he terms 'projectionism'. Having captured images from 2000 (for example, graffiti or film sequences of the Thursday night demonstrations), he then proceeds to project them during the actual filming of the later part of the film in 2002. The graffiti may have been removed, but Baker reimposes it via his projector and recaptures this on film. The graffiti can, as it were, be reinscribed in his film at any time. The images can be projected back onto their 'original' locations or they can be screened on new, original surfaces. Baker projects the large, red 'Widerstand' graffiti back onto the wall of the Café Ritter, but also projects his demonstration films onto anti-riot policemen. Baker writes of the manner in which projection can engender meanings as follows: 'Projection seeks a dialogue with surfaces that have something to say, do two or three jobs, walls that don't just hold up buildings . . . Projectionism prefers the word surface, to the word screen. Screen also means to select out of or to shield off.'[37] Like the Austrian projectionist artist Julia Starsky, Baker too is concerned that the image and the surface onto which it is projected work together to produce meaning and that the projectionist's surface should not be used as a mere 'wallpaper'. Starsky's projections during the protests of 2000 used the surface of the Federal Chancellery building against which to beam manipulated slogans and phrases. Although a film of her work *Zufallsindoktrinator* (dir. Julia Starsky and Julius Sternenhimml, 5.5 minutes) was shown as part of Programme 4 (2001) of the 'Kunst der Stunde' protest films, I have discussed Starsky's physical, everyday art interventions in Chapter 2 alongside some of the graffiti interventions of the time.

With an original background in archaeology, Frederick Baker sees his work as adopting a similar yet reverse process methodology. 'Archaeologists', he points out, 'usually work by digging down from the "present" to reveal the "past"' and goes on to argue that 'projectionism is paradoxical, it does the same but the opposite way – it excavates by addition'.[38] In Baker's filmic excavation, the traces of meaning are complex and various. Baker certainly charts the 'erosion' of the resistance movement, from the heightened days of February 2000 to 2002 when Schüssel's People's Party gained 15 per cent and the Freedom Party lost 16 per cent. The third part of the triptych is shot on the election night of 24 November 2002 and records some of the disappointment of the protesters. They were right to be concerned as the People's Party in fact renewed its coalition with a much-diminished Freedom Party. Moreover, as one of the demonstrators explains to camera, there is not much ground for celebration – Schüssel is as bad as Haider, having taken on some of the worst excesses of FPÖ politics and made them his own. There are, however, few words in Baker's film, and simple introductory text stills serve to situate the documented action that features in each of the three parts. Baker's work manages to convey its message of political protest very keenly nevertheless. A feature of Baker's technique is the sparse handful of interviewer questions from behind the camera, most notably and ironically to a number of young ÖVP party members who are celebrating Schüssel's party's restored success at the 2002 elections. The offscreen interviewer's slightly accented German and *faux naivité* allow him to ask a group of loud revellers if they are demonstrating, to which the response is that demonstrating is only something that lefties do – what they are doing is celebrating: 'Demonstrieren tun nur Linke.' In another sequence at the party headquarters' marquee, a jubilant solo ÖVP activist is happily dancing about in front of Baker's camera, but decides to walk away when the filmmaker asks him if he knows that the music blasting out from the speakers, the rock anthem much used at sports events and political rallies ('The Final Countdown' by the band Europe), is the same music that Jörg Haider uses for his appearances. No further commentary by filmmaker-cum-participant observer Frederick Baker is necessary.

In conclusion, Baker's work 'projects' or throws out ways for protest to 'wiederstehen', to be revitalized, to arise again, and it lodges this idea as a metaphorical call to the politically minded film viewer.[39] *Erosion und Wi(e)derstand* also makes its meaning as a metafilmic piece, stressing its status as film and dispensing very much with the trappings of illusionism by foregrounding and featuring the devices of its making – the camera, the film projector and the screen. Baker embeds avant-gardist projectionist methods into his film to reinforce his political message to the viewer to continue resisting. His film piece is aesthetically challenging not because it is difficult to watch, but because it invites us to ask questions about surfaces and what lies beneath them, and about the images and challenges of resistance in a contemporary, political context.

Portmanteau Protest: The Anthology Film *Zur Lage* (2002)

Zur Lage is a feature-length documentary film collaboration between four different Austrian filmmakers, all well known in their own right – Barbara Albert, Michael Glawogger, Ulrich Seidl and Michael Sturminger.[40] Broadly speaking, Austria's dramatic change of government is the filmmakers' prompt to explore the 'State of the Nation', with the film bearing the laconic subtitle 'Österreich in sechs Kapiteln' ('Austria in Six Chapters'). Each of the four directors has a different concept and style, but the overall principle has clearly been to keep interview questions to a minimum and simply allow people to talk. The first of the 'chapters' consists largely of in-car footage of the drivers who pick up the hitchhiking Glawogger as he makes his way around Austria. They talk about their private lives and problems, and they talk, too, about Austrian history and politics. One long-haired young man, at turns plagued by and wallowing in his apparent resemblance to a pop star, thinks that Hitler's policies were actually quite right, if only he could have got the foreigners out peacefully. Another interviewee is indiscriminate in his condemnation of contemporary politicians: Wolfgang Schüssel (ÖVP politician and Chancellor since the ÖVP-FPÖ government of 2000) is a 'bow-tie wearing idiot', and Haider (who had resigned as leader of the FPÖ in February 2000, but was continuing to serve as governor of Carinthia) is a 'clown'. The same driver offers an analogy between the *Vielvölkerstaat* of Austria-Hungary, a state uniting a multitude of peoples, and the contemporary move towards a 'Europe of the Regions'. In his explanation of the dissolution of the Habsburg Empire, the driver says that everybody had wanted to get out of the 'Vielvölkerkerker' ('prison for a multitude of peoples'), but that it had in fact not been a prison. Indeed, he points out that the European Union, which everyone is now striving to be part of, is not dissimilar, given its single currency, members who are individual nations, and policy of freedom of movement.

The style of *Zur Lage* is deliberately disjointed, with continuity editing at a minimum, but the material engages the viewer through the sheer honesty of the people in it and the almost total lack of compunction shown that what they might be saying is in any way problematic. The most shocking parts are undoubtedly the man and woman talking to camera in the prologue and epilogue of the film (some of Ulrich Seidl's contributions). In one of the epilogue takes, the woman is on the brink of describing her attitudes as Nazi. In a bizarre, near-comic reversal, she notes that there are people who are more Nazi or who think about these issues more emphatically than she and her partner, but she laments that these people do not dare open their mouths. In another of Seidl's sections, a notorious writer of newspaper readers' letters is interviewed at his home. The film captures the man's furious jogging around the inner perimeter of his garden and displays his rigid sense of order and tidiness. He brushes vigorously at the leaves on the pavement outside his house and shows the camera his neatly labelled piles of shirts, a system that his mother had devised for him. Where a writer such as Elfriede Jelinek has lampooned a kind of fascistic, political 'hygiene' and worldview in her novels and dramas, the documentary material of *Zur Lage* makes xenophobic and racist attitudes all the more disturbing because they are presented in documentary fashion without critical comment or linguistic irony. The sender of readers' letters complains of the 'Muslimization' of Austria and remarks that all these people need to do is to keep having children and soon Austrians will be in the minority and will have no say in their own country.[41]

A number of clever cuts bring out thought-provoking juxtapositions and ironies in the film material. Barbara Albert cross-cuts between a smug middle-class woman, possibly a housewife, complaining from her armchair that the foreigners should be forced to work, and shots of a Turkish-Austrian woman working at a factory conveyer belt, assembling computers. Moreover, as the latter points out, she in fact comes from Vienna, having been born there, whereas the many who flock to the capital from the other Austrian *Länder* are the real 'Einwanderer' ('immigrants'). Although Albert's original question is not in the soundtrack, she has clearly asked her interviewees what they would wish for in life. The middle-class woman is unhappy in her marriage, but explains that she would not leave her husband after seven years of marriage and all the work they have put into the house. Her wish – to get the house better insulated and thus reduce their bills – is in stark contrast to that of a physically disabled woman interviewee whose disability does not feature on her list of three wishes. She answers immediately: 'sofort eine neue Regierung' ('a new government, immediately'). Her second wish would be to live with her boyfriend and her third would be a better future together. A memorable and suggestive piece of editing comes in one of Sturminger's house visits, where the TV presenter Dieter Chmelar first hears from the younger generation (the grandson of the family) that Haider's (anti-immigrationist) ideas are quite good. The film cuts to the kitchen table where the three generations of the family sit together, and the grandson, as well as the film viewer, hear the grandmother's tale of her persecution at the hands of the Nazis for having a foreign (Polish) lover.

Where the documentary strategies of *Zur Lage* see many ordinary people sometimes unwittingly and sometimes consciously voicing their xenophobic or at best dubious attitudes towards the immigrant community, many of the social realist films of Austria's new wave also grapple with the issue of migration in contemporary Austria in their fiction-based plots. 'The casual reference to contemporary social reality has a long tradition in Austrian films, particularly with regard to the topic of migration', Manfred Hermes argues in a short survey of the state of the new 'Vienna School' of filmmaking.[42] Feature films by Barbara Albert, Goran Rebić, Jessica Hausner, Ulrich Seidl and indeed Michael Haneke are among the many examples of contemporary Austrian cinema to approach issues of social integration and dispossession and to problematize more fruitfully the complexities of migrant integration and Austrian identities. Of Haneke's Paris narrative *Code inconnu* (2000), Michael Omasta notes that the film indeed 'seems more decisively aimed at home-grown politics in general than any of Haneke's Austrian productions: in the age of Haider, the film's piercing discourse about multicultural entanglement in a Western metropolis feels angry and sad, yet undefeated'.[43] However, the latter part of this chapter deals not with the better-known fiction films to have come out of Austria in the last decade or so that use political actualities such as migration or social deprivation as part of their settings or plot developments, but instead discusses three feature-length films that arguably have the Austrian political Wende as their raison d'être and can be said to have a more overt agenda of satirical questioning or protest. These films all utilize the documentary mode, either in the almost lyrical sparingly interventionist, oral history-cum-film-essay style of Ruth Beckermann's *Homemad(e)* (2001), by distorting the documenting process towards satirical ends as in Walter Wippersberg's *Die Wahrheit über Österreich* (2000) or by integrating a feigned investigative mode in the fictionalized, futurist documentation of Peter Kern's political farce *1. April 2021* (2002).[44]

Ruth Beckermann's Microcosmic Perspective: *Homemad(e)* (2001)

In an interview accompanying the DVD edition of her film, Ruth Beckermann talks about the coincidence afforded by Haider's election success in 1999 as some kind of mere ironic serendipity, but despite all appearances of noninterventionist filming and simplistic documentary aesthetics, her filmic gaze is nevertheless highly politically focused. Ostensibly a piece of cinematic flaneurism, *Homemad(e)* is much more than a quaint observationist snapshot of the people who live and work in or frequent the restaurants and cafés of the Marc-Aurel-Straße in Vienna's first district. The director and occasional but unobtrusive interviewer is also a resident of the street, and the filming takes place over a period of one year – September 1999 to September 2000 and within a space of 200 m² in Vienna's first district.[45] Many if not all of Beckermann's previous films had previously foregrounded the process of journeying and indeed use physical travel – in directions 'nach dem Orient' ('to the East') or 'nach Jerusalem' ('to Jerusalem'), for example – as the platform from which the filmmaker launches a metaphorical or philosophical voyage of exploration. *Homemad(e)*, on the other hand, has been described as a 'mini cinema journey, in which the film has obliged itself not to move – for a change, it is the others who come and go'.[46] Beckermann's films explore the structures and markers of identity and territory, and deal in particular with questions about what it means to be Jewish and how personal and public memories are communicated.

Up until the political turning point marked by the coalition government formation of February 2000 at nearly sixty minutes into the film, the images and unscripted discussion to camera circle around the daily lives and individual concerns of a number of the 'characters', including the film's charming central figure, the elderly textile merchant and shopkeeper Adolf Doft, who lives in the Marc-Aurel-Straße with his wife. A less frequent interlocutor is the politically exiled Iranian restauranteur who lives opposite and who mildly rebukes both Beckermann and Doft for not having set foot on his premises for a coffee or a meal. The people Beckermann encounters relate how the district has changed over the years, and the regulars at the Café Salzgries bemoan the passing of its former proprietor Ernst Göschl, whose constant company at the tables of the café had fostered frank but friendly exchange of opinion between people of all social and racial backgrounds and political persuasions.

A number of stories are recounted by Herr Doft and other Jewish visitors and residents of the street about how difficult it had been to settle or resettle in Vienna after World War II and how there had been a shared unwillingness and sheer inability to talk with other people, let alone with their own sons and daughters, about the suffering experienced during the war and during their internment in concentration camps. It is Doft's sober but poignant account of how his mother and four siblings were killed that lends the film one of several moments and layers of titular reference. Doft predicts that in a hundred years, when people are told that innocent people were burnt, shot and buried alive, nobody will believe it. They would call him 'meschugge' in utter disbelief, he says, using the Hebrew loan word meaning 'mad' or 'crazy'. Beckermann's film is about 'home', but, like many of her other works, it is also an exploration of the presence of the past, functioning as a filmic working through of the past, or 'Vergangenheitsaufarbeitung'. The parenthetical 'e' gives Beckermann's title the dual references to home and to the sense of keeping alive Doft's – far from crazed – memories and those of other victims of Nazi atrocities. The implied suggestion that Austria itself may be lapsing back into the 'madness' of xenophobia is certainly intentional in Beckermann as it is in the title of the short film by Elke Mayr for the 'Kunst der Stunde', entitled *Mad in Austria*.[47] The film is an anti-commercial or counter-image to the prevailing patriotic strapline 'made in Austria' much loved by Austrian manufacturers to emphasize that their goods represent wholly Austrian produce.

Christina Guenther alludes to the connotations of Beckermann's titular 'deterritorialized foreign word', which evoke not just the personal, home-focused project of the latest of the filmmaker's 'Vienna films' but also 'a set of associations which includes both madness and anger'.[48] Nevertheless, the general tenor of the film can be read as affirmative. Although tinged with a sense of nostalgia for the vibrant Jewish community that used to flourish in this area of Vienna, Beckermann's film provides vivid evidence and eyewitness confirmation of a sense of multicultural community and friendly, supportive coexistence. The discussions in and around the Kaffeehaus in the latter part of the film, in particular those with some of Beckermann's circle of literary and artistic friends, centre not just on the addressee's 'usual', daily routine or plans, but on the new addition to many people's commitments – protest activity against the new regime, in the form of the Thursday demonstrations or 'Wandertage'. However, Beckermann's film resists becoming a montage of intellectual 'talking heads' (Harald Friedl's *Das Land ohne Eigenschaften* of 2000 might be said to adopt such an approach). The names of 'famous' interviewees are acknowledged in the final credits just as the other residents of the neighbourhood are.

Dagmar Lorenz interprets the resonance of *Homemad(e)* in a rather less optimistic vein, as Guenther acknowledges. For Lorenz, the title 'implies that even the limited trust in a familiar environment and confidence in a home-made film production may be sheer madness in a country where in October 1999 every third citizen cast a vote for the extreme right'.[49] But Beckermann chooses to end this film about her own home neighbourhood not with Doft's testimonial against the Holocaust or with his solemn confirmation that he will never be able to show forgiveness. Instead, Doft's words affirm the importance of family, friends and 'a good neighbour'. Beckermann's film captures some of the moments of rest of many of her friends and neighbours who took part in the initial protest activities of 1999–2000. The photographer Lisl Ponger talks to the camera about her need and desire to photograph the protests, the filmmaker Franz Novotny speaks of the short protest films he is busy making, the essayist Franz Schuh expounds some of the issues that he will go on to write about in his work, and the journalist Karl Pfeifer shows his letter protesting against the anti-Semitic poems by Wolf Martin published in *Die Kronenzeitung* and the feeble response he has received from Alfred Gusenbauer, the then leader of the Social Democratic Party. Beckermann captures these moments in a performative *mise-en-abyme* as the larger work that envelopes these moments – namely her own film – stands as its own marker of protest, but also as a lasting testimony to the civic community and a gentle paean to that community in miniature for which the Marc-Aurel-Straße must stand *pars pro toto*.[50]

This chapter concludes by discussing two films that use the documentary mode to satirical ends.[51] They might be said to represent two types of 'fake' documentary or mock-documentary, in the first instance within a film that styles itself with all the codes and conventions of a classic information film (Wippersberg's *Die Wahrheit über Österreich*) and, in the other (Kern's *1. April 2021 – Haider lebt*), a film whose near-future setting marks it as fiction, but that foregrounds the investigative activities of a young German filmmaker protagonist (played by August Diehl) setting out to make a 'documentary' film about contemporary Austria and to hunt down the now-vanished political leaders Jörg Haider and Wolfgang Schüssel. Both films might also be said to draw a certain amount of impetus from a comedy of the postwar period, namely from Wolfgang Liebeneiner's state-sponsored film *1. April 2000* (1954), which enjoyed a revival around the turn of the millennium. Liebeneiner's charming and amusing story mirrors the true, historical setting of a still occupied Austria, but invents a futuristic scenario for protesting Austria's national character as innocent, musical and peace-loving. Austria's Prime Minister attempts to prove to the leader of the 'galactic union' (the fictionalized 'United Nations') that Austria's long history is marked by acts of Christian defence (in the form of the Crusades, for example), a preference for music and culture over war-mongering and by territorial gain through royal intermarriage rather than by military aggression. Austria's ultimate objective in the film is that it should be granted its status as a sovereign, independent state. *1. April 2000*, made one year before Austria did indeed sign its state treaty and see the four Allied powers withdraw from its territory, makes no mention of the period 1938–45 and reads, as critics and reviewers have noted, more like a tourist advertisement for Austria, covering everything from music and dancing to the Lippizaner horses of Vienna, while mobilizing a cast of the most famous Austrian actors of the day and a plot with numerous romantic strands to delight its home audience.[52]

Where Kern's film references Liebeneiner's in its title, Wippersberg might be said to satirize more the actual raison d'être of the earlier film. Accordingly, Wippersberg's film concludes by having his fictional, historian anchor man reassure his (Austrian) viewer-addressees that the proof he has just brought before them can now allow them to sleep unperturbed and no longer give credence to the – falsified – histories that postwar historiography has insistently peddled. 'We Austrians don't politicize, we're an artistic people', the presenter confirms, having unveiled to the film audience numerous examples of corrective, historical 'evidence'.[53] Liebeneiner's characters predominantly narrate stories of Austrian history from previous centuries and political eras, but the stated objective of Wippersberg's fake documentary is to investigate Austria's participation in twentieth-century wars and ultimately to disprove in particular the allegations of anti-Semitism and of enthusiastic National Socialist sympathy.

The Truth about Austria? *Die Wahrheit über Österreich*

Die Wahrheit über Österreich: oder wie man uns belogen hat (2000) might be said to deal with the many reverberations of what is often seen as the founding myth of postwar national identity formation: the Moscow Treaty's absolution of Austria in 1943 as the 'first victim of Hitlerite aggression'. Austria's victim status and the subsequent moments when Austrians have been brought together by events that have disadvantaged them or besmirched their reputation abroad are starting points for many other critical works of culture, satirical or otherwise, and the film discussed here also revisits moments of sporting victimization (see the discussion of Karl Schranz in Chapter 5), as well as moments of international political condemnation such as that instigated by the Waldheim affair of 1986 (see Chapter 1). What gives Wippersberg's film new purpose and clearly locates it as a protest triggered by the events of 1999/2000 is its foregrounding, at the outset of the film, of the European Union's sanctions against Austria following the coalition government's inauguration in February 2000. After a brief visual montage of images, including Kurt Waldheim, a Jewish man hiding in a wardrobe, Jörg Haider giving a 'thumbs up' and a victory sign, and Benita Ferrero-Waldner smiling, a certain, fictional 'Prof. Dr. Bernhard Hopfgärtner' then introduces the weighty topic that will form the basis of 'his' 55-minute documentary film. Sitting in front of a fluttering Austrian flag, he alludes first to the famous description of Austria by Pope Paul VI in 1971 as an 'island of the blessed' and juxtaposes this sharply with the interference by the then fourteen states of the European Union in Austrian affairs: 'Austria. Praised not long ago as an island of the blessed, now suddenly the subject of gossip. Foreign states have even tried to tell us who should be allowed to govern this land and who should not.'[54] The central ruse of the film is to have 'Prof. Dr. Hopfgärtner' lay claim to his research having uncovered the 'true' history and to his being able to prove this new version of events via a sequence of documents and documentary films that he has uncovered in the KGB archives following the fall of the Soviet Bloc. Using the standard devices of a television history documentary, then, Wippersberg has his actor 'historian' show us newly found, black-and-white film 'documentaries', interview snippets with various living witnesses who have been tracked down, and academic expert testimonies from university professors of literature and history. Wippersberg thus mobilizes the whole panoply of documentary devices in his satire. However, the imitation of documentary conventions becomes more and more hilarious as the scenarios presented are coded as absurdly exaggerated, the acting is pointedly shaped for the camera to record the relevant evidence and the aesthetic markers are ironically laden, for example, with the crackly white vertical lines of old footage overlaid to suggest that the film reel is authentically 'of its time'. Thus, the Viennese are shown to have resisted Nazism and to have found ingenious places for large quantities of Jews to hide in their apartments, sheltering on average, as the statistics now prove, around two Jews per head of population. A retired university professor, with the suitably suggestive name Professor Dr Attila Baranovicz and dressed in his traditional, folksy Lederhosen and 'Lodenmantel', is about to comment that this proves to him that Austria really was 'overrun' with Jews at the time. But the documentary film being made within Wippersberg's satire swiftly censors Baranovicz midword ('Ich hab' ja damals schon gesagt, dass Österreich total verju . . .'), so that we complete his reprehensible thoughts for ourselves.

As a professor at the Viennese film academy since 1990, the director of many films and author of screenplays as well as novels, essays and plays, Wippersberg is well versed in the theory of genre itself, but his following is most decidedly a popular one, as can be seen by the near-cult status of his earlier mock-ethnographic film about the people of Upper Austria, entitled *Das Fest des Huhnes* (*The Festival of the Chicken*, 1992), released first in 2003 by the ORF, then on DVD as part of the 'Standard/Hoanzl' edition of top Austrian films. Both of these made-for-television films can be said to question the formation and projection of knowledge and images of knowledge, but the self-reflexive element of the later film is more complexly layered. *Das Fest des Huhnes* works hard at sending up some of the traditions and characteristics of the director's home region of Upper Austria, but it also obliges home viewers to open their eyes to the westernized assumptions of anthropologists and ethnographers as they set out to apply their supposedly sophisticated methods of analysis and inference on the African tribes they explore and explain for European audiences.

Jane Roscoe and Craig Hight comment on 'mock-documentary', Wippersberg's preferred film genre, that it 'assumes a sophisticated viewer able to recognise and participate in the form's largely parodic agenda; in other words, a viewer both familiar with the codes and conventions of documentary and ready to accept their comedic treatment'.[55] Wippersberg's conceit in *Die Wahrheit über Österreich* is to revisit Austria's victimization myth by using a mock-documentary mode to intervene in the documentary mode itself, but with the ultimate purpose of confirming (not negating) the original, i.e. confirming the negative print of Austria's history. Thus, the director sends up those who would wish to try to exonerate Austria or belittle their crimes by developing an increasingly absurd set of 'documentary' counternarratives about how Austria's history has been mediatized and anchored in postwar memory-building. The film performs a kind of double bind, then, cleverly spoofing the inscribing of an alternative, 'uncovered' or unmasked, 'true' version of history and thus emphatically reconfirming the extant, accepted 'truth about Austria'. In terms of the generic codes, Wippersberg mobilizes a full range of historical documentary techniques, and his lampooning is accentuated yet further by using Joachim Höppner as the actor to play his anchor man. Höppner's voice is extremely well known both from his own television and film roles, but also as the dubbed voice of many a famous American film actor too. Imitating well-known Austrian television histories such as Hugo Portisch's *Österreich I* and *Österreich II*, *Die Wahrheit über Österreich* parodies the close, almost conspiratorial relationship between presenter and viewer, makes mock recourse to the discourses of science and objectivity, and also invokes specific knowledge that only Austrians or Austria-watchers will be familiar with.

Accordingly, the film is brought right up to date by asking, satirically, just how international opinion could come to view the FPÖ as an undemocratic party and to see its 'great' leader, Jörg Haider, as an arch-conservative xenophobe, hater of modern, critical art and Nazi apologist. What is presumably bona fide archival footage of Haider at Harvard University is cut together with contrived and constructed 'interviews' with Haider's supposed fellow-student friend, now Finance Minister of Nigeria, confirming Haider's liberal views on art (his black African friend mentions the course on modern art for beginners that Haider took at Harvard). A Viennese *Heurigen* waitress confirms that Haider and the avant-garde painter and performance artist Hermann Nitsch were in fact great friends as she shows the camera one of the pieces of art they created together (paint that has clearly been flicked at the wall of the wine tavern). The 'evidence' becomes more and more outlandish and culminates in the presenter's assertion that there was really more than one Haider, and that it was his doppelgänger who voiced some of the outrageous statements, not the real Jörg Haider, who would never have dreamed of saying some of these things. Haider's infamous, euphemistic description of concentration camps as punishment camps ('Straflager') in 1995 or his praise for the 'ordentliche Beschäftigungspolitik' ('proper employment policy') of the Third Reich are proven by the fictional announcer to have been made on days when Haider was busy on other official business. Hopfgärtner rallies further to Haider's defence by pointing out that Haider could hardly allege that these remarks were made by somebody pretending to be him as the public would have thought him mad. The anchor man even uses some of the trademarks of Haider's own discourse, for example, in his adoption of mock-conciliatory words such as 'meinetwegen' ('if you like') when making some small concession to camera.[56] The mockumentary thus comes full circle as Austria is 'proved' once more to have been the victim of the malicious intervention of other countries. This time, it is the European Union that conspires to prevent Austria's natural leadership of the union and to thwart great Austrian leaders such as Haider. Hopfgärtner's historical tour d'horizon concludes with an exposé of how Austrians could have been tricked into believing the documentary images of mass pro-Hitler hysteria and throngs of fanatical Austrian Nazis: he points out how cleverly the Nazi propagandists edited their footage, claiming that scenes were shot in Vienna when a close-up in fact shows a sign for Tempelhof Airport in Berlin, or when the 'real' footage of the Heldenplatz shows one or two disinterested onlookers and a whining stray dog rather than the familiar images of massed Viennese with their arms outstretched in the Nazi salute. The footage consists of a montage of Hitler's speech and shots of the crowd gathered on the Heldenplatz for the outdoor concert of a much-beloved tenor, so the announcer argues. But Hopfgärtner's own heavy editing, botched cutting and absurd scenarios underscore Wippersberg's parodic intentions. Wippersberg's film plays self-referentially with the genre of the historical documentary, but its purpose is not to negate the value of documentary media. Instead, his film acts as a further reminder of the need to keep reading Austrian history, to be wary of attempts to whitewash the viewer or reader of that history and to stay alert to the attempts – by FPÖ politicians, perhaps, or by others – to trivialize the crimes of the past or indeed to perpetrate new ones. Wippersberg's films guard against the delusional power of political myth-making and the irrational mobilization of emotion to stir up nationalist sentiment, in this case ironically assisting his viewers finally to sleep unperturbed by the falsifications of history. Wippersberg's films are placed here as signs of protest. Ulrike Steiner would seem to concur with this in her description of Wippersberg's 'Doku-Fakes':

> It's not a matter of demonizing the media. It's a matter of strengthening our immune system. After all, there must be a reality behind the 'media contaminated' society, the structures of which can be laid bare. What's at stake is the ability to differentiate between the 'true' and the 'distorted' representation of facts. In this sense, Walter Wipperberg's docu-fakes are a vaccine against the impact of global mechanisms of delusion.[57]

Dystopian Prophecies: *1. April 2021 – Haider lebt*

Peter Kern was a very well-known actor and film director who tended to polarize his audiences with his often uncomfortable, polemical work. The political satire I discuss here had its cinema release in the autumn of 2002, just as campaigning for the next general election was under way and the first, short-lived ÖVP-FPÖ coalition government was coming to a close. With Martin Strutz, the then head of the Carinthian FPÖ, calling – unsuccessfully – for a ban on the film, Kern's low-budget, self-financed dystopia gained notoriety and excellent publicity even before it had been seen on the big screen. The fictional Jörg Haider and Susanne Riess-Passer being gunned down by a Wolfgang Schüssel character singing the Austrian national anthem in the film's absurdist conclusion was clearly something that was calculated to offend. Riess-Passer is ecstatic at having been reunited with her beloved 'Jörgeli', a scene described by the enthusiastic fictional film director protagonist in the most ironic and vulgar intertextual reference, as being brilliant and reminiscent of the ending of *Jud Süß* (the most vicious piece of anti-Semitic, Nazi propaganda). It seems pertinent to note that many famous actors and writers collaborated on Kern's film and reputedly for low or no wages. This must be seen as a sign of their support for an often controversial director and actor who is well known for foregrounding political topics, including the gender-political theme of homosexuality. More importantly, the willingness of well-known Austrian actors such as Traute Hoess (as Riess-Passer), Günter Tolar (Schüssel), Heinrich Herki (as Haider) or Hilde Sochor (who plays an elderly Social Democrat voter) and the appearance of high-profile Austrian writers in the film too (for example, Peter Turrini, Robert Schindel and Marlene Streeruwitz) are indicative of the creative support and solidarity being shown to Peter Kern in his satirical protest against the political climate of Austria in the early twenty-first century.

Kern uses the conceit of projecting his Austria forward to a date when the country has just come out of a twenty-year rule by the right-wing coalition, but is now under foreign occupation and has become 'Austria-America'. Conceived of at the time of the escalating Iraq crisis, Kern's film prophetically pre-empts the American and British invasion of Iraq and the overthrowing of Saddam Hussein. It is rumoured that Haider is not dead, but has in fact gone into hiding, as has his collaborator Wolfgang Schüssel. Fairground attractions exist that entertain their public by telling historical narratives and using the scary ghouls of Schüssel and Haider. The 'Haider-Monster' turns out to be the real thing, and when the young German filmmaker August Maria Kaiser (played by August Diehl) from the fictional 'Freies deutsches Fernsehen' (Free German TV) finally catches up with him, in the closing moments of the film, the Riess-Passer and Haider characters discover that the German filmmaker is in fact their clandestine love child whom they had given up for adoption. Haider says to Riess-Passer that sometimes instead of spitting on him at the fairground, the people are full of hope and ask (and here he uses the terminology that is redolent of National Socialism) whether this is now the 'Endsieg' ('final victory') of which they had spoken. Kern also incorporates moments that suggest Haider's homosexual relationships. Following a libel action brought by Haider's widow in 2009, German and Austrian newspapers were under an injunction not to describe Haider as homosexual or bisexual,[58] but to the gay filmmaker Kern, the implication in his 2002 film is certainly not an insult. When the young documentary filmmaker discovers a CD-Rom Haider has secreted into a roadside shrine as a recorded message to his followers, Kern is able to use a montage of real-life television interview footage of Haider to political effect. In the first interview, Haider is describing the situation on the ground after the invasion of foreign troops as a kind of civil war, and since the names of countries and forces are omitted, we assume that Haider is describing Austria after the Americans' occupation and not, say, the situation in the former Yugoslavia. The second clip is after Haider's resignation as party leader in 2000, when he effectively ceded the Vice-Chancellorship of Austria, retreated to his home region of Carinthia, but remarked that like the marathon runner that he is, he was used to having to take a long time to get to his ultimate goal and that he would not rule out becoming Chancellor of Austria one day.

The fun poked at Haider's reputation as a sporty family man and at his manner of self-styling as a kind of quasi-religious leader is evident here, as it is in many other political lampoons (see, for example, Jelinek's *Das Lebewohl* in Chapter 5). Riess-Passer refers to Haider's followers as the 'faithful' and comments to Kaiser and cameras: 'Now you see how the people loved Jörgeli. He lives on eternally in the people; in me, too.'[59] Kaiser's increasing frustration at their wild-goose chase and his Austrian crew member's confession that he liked Haider and had heard all his speeches, results in Kaiser's frustrated provocation that since they could not find Haider, they would just let him die. A kind of funeral, complete with burial cross and chief mourner (Riess-Passer), is then staged for the film within the film (a still of this sequence is used for the DVD edition cover). The real Jörg Haider died on 11 October 2008 after driving at high speed and with a high level of alcohol in his bloodstream on his way home from late-night socializing with his deputy Stefan Petzner, who later announced emotionally on live radio that he had had a 'special relationship' with Haider. Petzner was removed from his role as successor leader to Haider's party and the BZÖ vehemently refuted that Haider was gay. Although Kern's 'April Fool' pre-dates Haider's death by some six years, then, the implication that his following was nothing short of cultic and worshipful was to find uncanny expression in 2008 in the mass outpouring of grief, the vigils held and the veneration directed at the deceased leader of the BZÖ.[60] His party even campaigned in the regional elections of the following spring with the highly successful slogan 'Ihm zuliebe BZÖ' ('BZÖ, for His Sake') and gained 45 per cent of the vote. The titular reassurance that 'Haider is alive!' means that Kern's film has if anything become more political and provocative in the post-Haider period. To assert by analogy that right-wing extremism lives on is a line that Kern takes in his 2009 film *Blutsfreundschaft* (*Initiation*), fully cognizant of the campaigning strategies of the FPÖ under the current, good-looking, male, populist leader H.C. Strache. *Blutsfreundschaft* is about a fictional, neofascist political party called the RWT ('Partei für Recht, Würde und Tugend' – 'Party for Justice, Dignity and Virtue') and a homosexual relationship between a former Nazi and a young, sixteen-year-old party member who reminds the old man of the lover he betrayed during the war. The topic of the film is controversial enough, but the public scandal surrounding the film was caused more by its advertising campaign than by its content. Film posters purporting to advertise the party were billed with a slogan based on comments and slogans of the FPÖ, for example, in Strache's comments rejecting support for gay marriages. Because the poster seemed to be about a political party (and not a film) and contained the deliberately provocative statement 'Soziale Wärme statt Woame', echoing a Viennese pronunciation of the colloquial, pejorative term 'warm', meaning gay (thus, social warmth or provision, not homosexuals), the advertising company refused to display the film posters. It was not until a banner was superimposed on the poster stating that Kern's film *Blutsfreundschaft* would be in the cinemas soon that limited advertising could proceed. Kern and others argued that it did not seem fair that their satire was being rejected, but that the FPÖ itself could carry on advertising with the most offensive homophobic and xenophobic slogans and was not rebuked or restrained for doing so.[61] Like some of the other artists and intellectuals discussed in this book, Kern was also politically active in more conventional ways, for example, running as a Green Party candidate in the Viennese local elections in 2009.

In the 2002 film we are concerned with here, the provocative and intertextually resonant title is just one part of what Claus Philip describes as Kern's general filmic strategy of pointing up truth in amongst the fake ('erzählen vom Wahren im Verfälschten'). This is a deliberate tactic by the filmmaker whose dictum Philipp quotes: 'by playing like this I can present real-life circumstances in a condensed form'.[62] A major plank of Kern's ludic subterfuge in *1. April 2021* is to have the viewer learn something of how things have been in Austria as a result of twenty years of ÖVP-FPÖ. Riess-Passer comments on how the German 'Chancellor' Stoiber – the Bavarian hardliner also well known for his antiimmigrationist stance – worked so well with them towards planning the eventual 'annexation of Austria' and in getting the 'Ausländerfrage' ('the immigrant question') under control.[63] To Kaiser's incredulous question as to whether there were in fact any foreigners in Austria during her period in office, the fictional Riess-Passer explains that they had completely solved the problem by giving over the UNO-City entirely to immigrants. They were allowed twelve-hour passes out of their delimited compound if they occasionally wanted to use the shops of Vienna, and the Viennese would occasionally travel to the UNO-City to visit restaurants and eat couscous. The director's political points are anything but subtle. One admiring commentator gives the film the equally blunt alternative subtitle 'Haider Lives: 1. April 2021 (aka *Who the Fuck is Haider*)' and calls it 'an all-out agitprop assault' and 'an ultra-campy farce about a far-right Euro politico'.[64]

Kern does not mind his work being labelled 'trashy': 'I don't find it insulting because "trash" is a marker of quality for me. People do tend to dismiss you very quickly, though. My "rubbish" is very carefully narrated.'[65] The conscious crafting of *1. April 2021* does not mean that Kern employs sophisticated camera angles, lighting or editing. Kern even pokes mild fun at the idea of cinematic codes and would seem to have no pretensions to emulating an art-house style, having his cipher filmmaker Kaiser admonish his cameraman on a number of occasions for adopting an 'arty' camera angle or for focusing on something that is not germane to the film. The rebuke comes full circle too when the cameraman goads his producer-director who is about to stage Haider's burial site for the camera: 'Ah, so this is what you call documentary?'[66] In my opinion, Kern's 'conscious crafting' lies in the way in which his film works in a metareferential fashion. It does this aesthetically by referencing the making of film and the styles of filmmaking in a kind of *mise-en-abyme*. Itself a kind of resistant text, the film also plays with the very theme of resistance. Since the Americans have outlawed the use of dialect, the use of Viennese vernacular is laughingly seen as an act of resistance. A secret society even meets up to sing *Volkslieder* to keep Austrian traditions alive. The camera team are led to a secret location in the woods where, in a parodic reference to Truffaut's adaptation of Ray Bradbury's novel *Fahrenheit 451*, starring Austrian-born actor Oskar Werner, well-known contemporary writers are walking up and down reading out loud passages from books and endeavouring to commit them to memory. Kern is clearly not setting up the futuristic American version of Austria to be better than the ÖVP-FPÖ-governed one. As with Bradbury's dystopian America, the viewer of *1. April 2021* infers that independent thinking furthered by reading will be every bit as frowned upon in the new, fantastical Austria, but we note that it is the continuance of *Austrian* culture – some of it read out in dialect – to which the Austrian writers dedicate their outlawed reading.

An early sequence in Liebeneiner's 1954 April Fool film supposedly documents to the courtroom the provenance of the Austrian flag. Leopold V, Duke of Austria, removes his belt after the Siege of Acre (during the Third Crusade) to reveal a white unbloodied band in the middle of his bloodstained tunic and producing a red-white-red effect. (This is one of the many legends that purport to explain the Austrian flag's provenance.) In what might be a nod by Kern to the earlier, unlikely act of burgeoning national consciousness, the Riess-Passer character performs her own act of resistance, she tells us, by occasionally hanging out a bloodied towel on her balcony. Riess-Passer mutters 'rot weiß rot' as she sees the wound on the cameraman's face. He has sustained this cut after being attacked by the zombified Austrians patronizing the former 'Café Jelinek', now known as the 'Have-a-nice-day Coffeeshop'. The kindly patriot Riess-Passer wants to tend to the cameraman's wounds, and Kern's omniscient camera now focuses on the very unrealistic dripping of red blood onto the white towel before it is hung out amidst Riess-Passer's explanation of what she sometimes does, 'damit die Leute sehen – hier ist eine, die lebt im Widerstand' ('so that people can see – here's somebody living a life of resistance'). Like most of the art works discussed in this book, Kern's film is clearly an expression of the artist's disquiet over the FPÖ's – admittedly shared – acquisition of executive power, but in common with many others, Kern does not spare the left wing from his contempt. In *1. April 2021*, the SPÖ are a spent force, and when Kaiser and his team track down the character Sepp Hinterhiersel, a supposed legend of the Left's resistance, what they find is an old soak and his female companion whose current 'resistance' amounts to the smoking of cannabis. 'Das ist unser Widerstand' ('this is our resistance'), the old lady tells Kaiser, 'Sie machen zwei Züge und die Sozis sind wieder an die Macht' ('take two drags on this and the socialists are back in power'). She harks back to the 1970s and claims to hear Bruno Kreisky's voice calling from the trees. The attempt on Jörg Haider's life, for which old Sepp is famed, is fittingly unheroic too, as the former waiter had attempted to serve Haider a glass of poisoned wine, but mixed the glasses up and gave it to Peter Westenthaler instead.

The 'plot' of Kern's political satire is clearly nothing short of absurd, but the hammed-up accents, deadpan delivery, wooden acting and contrived suspense of the search for Haider and Schüssel are not the necessities of a low-budget film, but are deployed very deliberately by Kern to produce an ironic excess that is quite effective in its blunt style of questioning. In a pointed twist to the standard legal caveats that sometimes precede films, the viewer is informed at the outset that the film is only fantasy and that the real people of the same names as the film characters will never do what the film shows them doing. However, should the viewer identify similarities between any living people and fictional characters bearing the same name, then this is only because nightmares have their basis in reality. If the narrative is deliberately improbable, then the cheap, video style of Kern's film is also a calculated tool in enabling the director to create independent art relatively quickly and to do so in a politically perceptive manner. Dietmar Schwärzler comments of *1. April 2021*: 'its cheap video aesthetics produce emotional (mostly humorous) aspects and at the same time touch on sociopolitical patterns of perception'.[67] Schwärzler is right to locate in Kern's art a renewal of the political qualities promised by video film when it was first used and promised to be: 'a quick, political medium giving artistic independence'.[68] Kern's peculiar low-budget cocktail of humorous, dystopian social criticism is punchy and raw, but it makes its protest heard as loudly as any of the other films discussed here and deserves a much wider reception.

Conclusions: Reel Alternatives

Cinematic responses to the political events in Austria around the turn of the millennium show a rich variety of techniques and topics, despite the very specific and narrow nature of their raison d'être. The short protest films themselves display a remarkable variety of strategies for putting across an essential sense of immediate protest. If it were information about Haider or about the 'Haider phenomenon' that one were seeking, then apart from the many books available on this topic, one would turn to a more standard documentary film than the creative and fake documentary mélanges discussed here. It has not been my concern to discuss the political history of this period itself or the psychology of the individual politicians, but instead to address creative works of film and ask how they put across their own form of protest or resistance. Films that seek primarily to educate their public and impart information about Haider and his success or the way in which he and his collaborators worked are few and far between. That there was no stomach for investigative or probing documentaries about Haider during his lifetime[69] is evidenced by the fact that it was British-Austrian filmmaker Frederick Baker who made a film in 2000 entitled *The Haider Show* for the BBC. Baker encountered many hurdles in his search for archive materials and a lack of collaboration from the ORF. It would be to a documentary film such as this that one would turn for an explanation of some of the psychological underpinning of the FPÖ's populism and for a range of background context that is particularly informative for non-Austrian viewers.

A film such as Harald Friedl's *Land ohne Eigenschaften* (also 2000) provides a beautifully constructed, almost lyrical film-essay on the topic of how Austrians see Austria. Bearing the same name as Robert Menasse's essay *Das Land ohne Eigenschaften* and featuring Menasse as one of a string of intellectuals and artists who talk in the film about growing up in Austria or about what for them are key features of Austrian identity, Friedl's film muses on the question of Austrian national identity in the way that so many works of literature and art have throughout the twentieth century. Austria's history, its territorial changes and its complex relationship with Germany are just some of the reasons motivating the perpetual drive to define, contest or defend the way in which Austria presents itself at home and abroad. Friedl's film is thus not really classifiable as a film that reacts to and protests about the Wende of 1999/2000, although there are moments that show the Zeitgeist of protest. In one of the final sequences of the film, Menasse reiterates Thomas Bernhard's analogy of the Austrian mentality being like a 'Punschkrapfen' cake, 'pink on the outside, brown on the inside, and neutralized, as it were, by alcohol'.[70] The author then explains to camera that this metaphor has now served its time. He does not need to explain the political colour coding to Austrians and implies that the combination of 'pink' veneer (social democracy) concealing the (Nazi-connoted) brown interior should give way to a more relevant contemporary analogy (and cake variety). The 'Mohnzelten' ('poppy-seed cake'), Menasse explains, as he breaks one open for the viewer to see, is brown on the surface (the association with Nazism needs no explanation) and black (conservative) on the inside.

The result of this chapter should not be to imply that Austrians or Austrian filmmakers are only interested in Austrian topics or in protest,[71] but for a good many the political turn to the right was truly the epicentre of their creative work around the turn of the twenty-first century. The short protest films of the 'Kunst der Stunde ist Widerstand' series provide an insight into the huge variety of instant filmic responses, and the shorter constituent parts of *Zur Lage* equally constitute different filmmakers' 'takes' on measuring what many Austrians felt about the political developments. Baker's 'reverse archaeology' method of projectionism offers an intelligent activist intervention in the process of filmmaking as protest, and indeed Beckermann's oral history and 'snapshot' documentary of the Aurel-Straße ironically digs much further back into Austrian history to provide a layer of contextualization to protesters' concerns about their home country's extreme-right-wing abuses of political power. The final two filmic responses from Wippersberg and Kern utilize and blur the genre of documentary in very different and deliberately thought-provoking ways. Filmic protest, it would seem, is very much alive in the twenty-first century. The films discussed here may have served to educate or to rally and to provide crystallized talking points. They can certainly still entertain their viewers and they provide a dimension to explaining recent Austrian social and cultural history to which the textbooks and political histories can hardly do justice.

Notes

1. The short film material discussed here has previously been published as Allyson Fiddler, 'Lights, Camera, ... Protest! Austrian Film-makers and the Extreme Right', *Journal of European Popular Culture* 2(1) (2012), 5–18.
2. 'Nimmt man das rege Interesse der österreichischen Kulturpolitik unmittelbar nach Hanekes triumphalen Erfolg als Gradmesser, könnte man glauben, das hiesige Filmschaffen sei als wesentlicher Beitrag zur Stiftung "österreichischer Identität" schon längst unverrückbar im öffentlichen Bewusstsein verankert.' Michael Omasta, 'Der österreichische Film: eine Momentaufnahme', *EPD Film* 15(7) (2001), 28–33, at 29.
3. 'Das Gegenteil ist der Fall. Zum einen hat die bürgerlich-rechtspopulistische Bundesregierung die Mittel zur so genannten großen Filmförderung drastisch reduziert (von rund 24 Millionen DM anno 1999 auf knapp 15 Millionen jährlich); zum

anderen wurde Anfang des Jahres die bislang fur die Belange der Filmavantgarde, des Nachwuchsfilms und eines Gutteil des dokumentarischen Fillmschaffens zuständige Abteilung im Bundeskanzleramt handstreichartig aufgelöst.' Omasta, 'Der österreichische Film', 29. Omasta was writing for a German audience, hence the Deutschmark figures.
4. Statistik Austria's information on public funding; see, for example, Statistik Austria, 'K10. Filmförderung und Filmfinanzierung aus öffentlichen Mitteln 1981 bis 2008', 2010. Retrieved 6 May 2018 from http://www.statistik.at/web_de/statistiken/bildung_ und_kultur/kultur/kinos_und_filme/021253.html.
5. However, Ruth Mader's short political film *Null Defizit* (2001) uses one of the new government's slogans as its title, and the director asserts: 'es ist ein Film über die neue Art des "finanziellen Gesundschrumpfens" im neuntreichsten Land der Welt. Ich versuchte zu zeigen, dass nicht bei allen Menschen Sparmaßnahmen angemessen sind' ('it's a film about the new kind of quest for 'financial fitness' in the world's ninth richest country. I tried to show that austerity measures are not appropriate for everyone'). See Beate Hennenberg, 'Ich will auf Missstände im neuntreichsten Land der Welt aufmerksam machen', *Leipzig Allmanach*, 20 June 2001. Retrieved 6 May 2018 from http://www.leipzig-almanach.de/film_interview_mit_ruth_mader_deren_streifen_null_defizit_in_diesem_jahr_fuer_cannes_nominiert_wurde_beate_hennenberg.html.
6. I paraphrase here Raunig's explanations of the origins and connotations of the motto. See Gerald Raunig, *Wien Feber Null: eine Ästhetik des Widerstands* (Vienna: Turia und Kant, 2000), especially Chapter 18, 'Die Kunst der Stunde ist Widerstand', 114.
7. Duncombe, Introduction to 'Adorno', 6.
8. Raunig, *Wien Feber Null*, 115.
9. Retrieved 6 May 2018 from http://www.medienwerkstatt-wien.at/files/titles/kunst-der-stunde.htm. There are four programmes of films. Individual films are referenced in the bibliography under the director's name and the programme number they have been allocated by Medienwerkstatt Wien.
10. Angelika Schuster and Tristan Sindelgruber from Schnittpunkt have since codirected other documentary-style films with political themes. *Operation Spring* (Austria 2005) investigates the undercover police raids on African immigrants in 1999. This was their submission to the Thessaloniki documentary festival of 2006. See http://www.filmfestival.gr/docfestival/2006/index.php?page=filmdetails&ln=en&box=tributes&id=358.
11. Gini Müller explains that this was part of a series of actions protesting against military parades going back to 1995. Müller, *Possen des Performativen*, 100. Information from the Stadtkino in 2009 (retrieved 6 May 2018 from http://lichtblick.action.at/About_Africa_Programm09.html), describes Martin Gössler as an independent filmmaker.
12. Dieter Auracher works as a graphic designer in Vienna. He is not well known as a filmmaker, although he has worked on many films and videos, according to the biography in the online databank of the Lower Austrian history project. Retrieved 6 May 2018 from https://www.gedaechtnisdeslandes.at/personen/action/show/controller/Person/person/auracher.html.
13. Philip Payne asks: 'Might it not be the case that Musil himself saw the *Parallelaktion* as a kind of "Earth Secretariat" gone terribly wrong – an enterprise that starts out with the best intentions to bring benefits to the whole nation and ends up bringing the whole of Europe closer to war?.' Philip Payne, 'Introduction: The Symbiosis of Robert Musil's Life and Works', in Philip Payne, Graham Bartram and Galin Tihanov (eds), *A Companion to the Works of Robert Musil* (Rochester, NY: Camden House, 2007), 1–52, at 37.

14. The collaboration is between Polish born Ewa Einhorn (http://www.torinofilmlab.it/people/225-ewa-einhorn) and Viennese Fine Arts graduate Misha Stroj (https://iscp-nyc.org/resident/misha-stroj).
15. 'Die Herren sind Mitglieder der Freiheitlichen Partei Österreichs sowie der Österreichischen Volkspartei. Seit Februar 2000 bilden diese Parteien die österreichische Regierungskoalition.'
16. Niki Griedl boasts a number of popular Austrian films and television programmes in his entry for the International Movie Database as cinematographer or cameraman. Retrieved 6 May 2018 from http://www.imdb.com/name/nm2102371.
17. 'Zehn kleine Fremdenkinder baten um Asyl, Keins wurde angenommen; alle waren zuviel.'
18. Reinhart's film is item four on Programme 2 of the 2000 Medienwerkstatt Wien series. Retrieved 6 May 2018 from http://www.medienwerkstatt-wien.at/files/titles/kunst-der-stunde.htm. It can also be watched on YouTube at http://www.youtube.com/watch?v=9MxJBIktO4o with English subtitles. *Pinocchio* continued to have success as an animated film, showing again at the 2009 'Diagonale' festival. Retrieved 6 May 2018 from http://2009.diagonale.at/fetchfile/press%20kit_120309.pdf.
19. The quotations are Bernadette Wegenstein's glosses on Kubelka. See Bernadette Wegenstein, 'The Embodied Film: Austrian Contributions to Experimental Cinema', in Randall Halle and Reinhild Steingröver (eds), *After the Avant-Garde: Contemporary German and Austrian Experimental Film* (Rochester, NY: Camden House, 2009), 50–68, at 52.
20. See 'About Martin Reinhart'. Retrieved 6 May 2018 from http://artscience.uni-ak.ac.at/people/herr__martin_reinhart.
21. Information about the making of this film is not available, but the logical premise is that the filmmaker's stills are largely found footage, having come across all these graffitied posters and not vandalized them for the sake of his film.
22. 'Kleines Püppchen, freches Bübchen, du träumst von Freiheit und vom Ruhm, vom Reichtum und vom Heldentum, mein Freund warum?' (subtitles from YouTube).
23. The Demokratiezentrum, Vienna explains the background to this poster and to the 1995 national elections. Retrieved 6 May 2018 from http://www.demokratiezentrum.org/index.php?id=25&index=1233.
24. Rosa Antifa Wien, '"Er hat Euch nicht belogen"?'. 9 February 2000. Retrieved 6 May 2018 from https://raw.at/texte/gegenschwarzblau/er-hat-euch-nicht-belogen.
25. See Kurt Krickler's review of the press, 'Jörg Haider: Wird Kärnten noch wärmer?' Retrieved 6 May 2018 from http://www.hosiwien.at/haiderouting/ln-berichte/jorg-haider-wird-karnten-noch-warmer.
26. See Huber's homepage. Retrieved 6 May 2018 from http://www.bernadettehuber.at/frame1.htm.
27. This particular interview from 18 February 1985 and hundreds more of Haider's statements can be found in Czernin, *Wofür ich mich meinetwegen entschuldige*, 15–17.
28. Hurch, reported in 'Kunst der Stunde ist Widerstand', 15 March 2003. Retrieved 6 May 2018 from http://no-racism.net/article/329.
29. See Hannah Fröhlich, 'Hubsi Kramars Gratwanderungen', *Augustin*, 29 April 2000, which reports that Hubsi Kramar 'ist nicht zornig. Er weiß, daß Widerstand ein hohes Lustpotential braucht, um lebendig zu bleiben' ('is not angry; he knows that resistance requires a high quotient of fun to keep itself alive'). Retrieved 6 May 2018 from http://www.augustin.or.at/zeitung/artistin/hubsi-kramars-gratwanderungen.html.

30. Novotny's film is under Programme 1 of the Medienwerkstatt Wien series. Retrieved 6 May 2018 from http://www.medienwerkstatt-wien.at/files/titles/kunst-der-stunde.htm.
31. See also *Weltrevolution* (2008), Klaus Hundsbichler's film about lead singer Stefan Weber and his controversial band Drahdiwaberl. Weber died in 2018.
32. Originally a trio, Maschek comprised Peter Hörmanseder and Robert Stachel, as well as Ulrich Salamun.
33. Carinthia, Jörg Haider's political home territory, has been the focus of many satirical works. See also the discussion of the Olympics bid and Franzobel's *Olympia* in Chapter 5.
34. Baker made a film about Haider for the BBC called *The Haider Show* (broadcast on 28 October 2000); see http://news.bbc.co.uk/1/hi/programmes/correspondent/990373.stm. He drew on Klaus Ottomeyer's investigation of the pyschology behind Haider's party: Klaus Ottomeyer, *Die Haider-Show: Zur Psychopolitik der FPÖ* (Klagenfurt: Drava, 2000). Baker experienced significant problems in accessing materials from the ORF at the time.
35. Discussion with Frederick Baker, Vienna, 16 December 2008.
36. http://www.imdb.com/name/nm1096708 has an entry for the Fratelli Brothers. They are not to be confused with the Glaswegian rock band formed in 2005.
37. Baker, *The Art of Projectionism*, 62.
38. Baker, *The Art of Projectionism*, 69.
39. Baker's 2010 retrospective film, *Widerstand in Haiderland*, looks back at the momentous events and protests of ten years earlier.
40. Barbara Albert, Michael Glawogger, Ulrich Seidl and Michael Sturminger, *Zur Lage* (Austria: Lotus Film-GmbH, 2002).
41. The number of Muslims in Austria is in fact relatively small. The 2001 census puts the proportion of Muslims at 4.2 per cent (compared to 2 per cent in 1991). Martin Reisigl and Ruth Wodak, *Discourse and Discrimination* (London: Routledge, 2001) show that without immigration, the Austrian population would have decreased, thus putting the social welfare system in jeopardy. By 2009, the numbers had increased again by around 50 per cent, amounting to 6 per cent of the population: Alexander Janda and Mathias Vogl (eds), 'Islam in Österreich', a report for the Österreichischer Integrationsfonds, 2010, 4.
42. 'Die beiläufige Bezugnahme auf aktuelle soziale Tatsachen hat gerade beim Thema Migration in österreichischen Filmen eine lange Tradition.' Manfred Hermes, 'Die Neue Wiener Schule: der aktuelle österreichische Film und sein sozialer Realismus', *EPD Film* 4 (2004), 10–11, at 10.
43. Omasta, 'Der österreichische Film', 12.
44. Peter Kern, *1. April 2021: Haider lebt* had its cinema release in 2002 and was issued as no. 87 of the *Der Standard* collection 'Der österreichische Film' (Austria: Hoanzl) in October 2007. Peter Kern died aged sixty-six in 2015.
45. Bert Rebhandl, interview with Ruth Beckermann, 9 September 2007, 'Extras', on Ruth Beckermann, *Homemad(e)* (Vienna: Ruth Beckermann-Filmproduktion, 2007).
46. Bernard Benoliel, 'Along the Paths of Time', in Ruth Beckermann Filmproduktion (ed.), *Texte von, Texts by, Textes de Ruth Beckermann, Bernard Benoliel, Christa Blümlinger, Hélène Cixous, Paulus Hochgatterer, Siegfried Mattl, Bert Rebhandl*, information and accompanying essays as part of the Ruth Beckermann film collection 8 DVD set (Vienna: Ruth Beckermann Filmproduktion, 2007), 77–134, at 78. Note that Beckermann's film titles often signal the journey motif, as in *Ein flüchtiger Zug nach dem Orient* (1999) or *Nach Jerusalem* (1990).

47. Elke Mayr, *Mad in Austria* (0.5 minutes), Programme 4 of 'Die Kunst der Stunde ist Widerstand', 2001. See also *Commercial Breakdown* (dir. Nina Bauer, Jasmin Trabichler, Amina Handke, Manuel Maxl, Elke Mayr, Simona Shimanovich and Axel Stockburger, 4 minutes), Programme 1 of 'Die Kunst der Stunde ist Widerstand', 2001.
48. Christina Guenther, 'The Politics of Location in Ruth Beckermann's "Vienna Films"', *Modern Austrian Literature* 37(3/4) (2004), 33–46, at 42.
49. Dagmar Lorenz, quoted in Guenther, 'The Politics of Location', 45 (fn. 10).
50. Beckermann's positive, first-district microcosm stands in marked contrast, then, to Ulrich Seidl's vision of suburban hell in his film of the same year, *Hundstage* (2001). Seidl's documentary techniques bring disturbing credibility to images and fictionalized stories of sexual exploitation, crime and self-gratification in Viennese suburbia.
51. An earlier version of my comparison of these two films appeared as Allyson Fiddler, 'Fooling around with Film: Political Visions of Austria – Past, Present and Future', in Allyson Fiddler, John Hughes and Florian Krobb (eds), *The Austrian Noughties: Texts, Films, Debates*, special issue, Austrian Studies 19 (2011), 126–41.
52. For an insight into how the film was viewed upon its release, see Ernst Kieninger (ed.), *1. April 2000* (Vienna: Filmarchiv Austria, 2000).
53. 'Wir Österreicher sind kein politisierendes, wir sind ein musisches Volk.' Wippersberg's film was first broadcast on 8 November 2001. The ORF aired a director's cut version on 10 February 2002. On 5 February 2016, it was broadcast in memory of Wippersberg, who had recently died, but more importantly as a marker of state celebration, the ORF used it in 2015 as one of six films in its sixtieth-anniversary celebration, 'lange Nacht des dok.film' (*sic*). On all occasions, the film had a very late-night slot.
54. 'Österreich. Eben noch als eine Insel der Seligen gepriesen, dann auf einmal ins Gerede gekommen. Und ausländische Staaten haben sogar versucht, uns vorzuschreiben, wer dieses Land regieren dürfe und wer nicht.'
55. Jane Roscoe and Craig Hight, *Faking it: Mock-Documentary and the Subversion of Factuality* (Manchester: Manchester University Press, 2001), 184.
56. Hence the title of Czernin's collection of Haider quotations and extracts: Czernin, *Wofür ich mich meinetwegen entschuldige*.
57. 'Es geht nicht um Dämonisierung der Medien, sondern um Stärkung der Immunkräfte. Es muss schließlich eine Wirklichkeit hinter den "medienkontaminierten" Gesellschaft geben, deren Strukturen freizulegen sind. Es geht um die Unterscheidungsfähigkeit zwischen "richtiger" und "verzerrter" Wiedergabe realer Sachverhalte. So gesehen, sind Walter Wippersbergs Doku-Fakes ein Impfstoff, der gegen die Auswirkungen globaler Verblendungszusammenhänge wirkt.' Ulrike Steiner, 'Weltbilder verrücken – Die Doku-Fakes von Walter Wippersberg' in *Die Rampe, Porträt: Walter Wippersberg* (2003), 99.
58. This is reported widely in the press. See, for example, 'Österreich: Toter Haider gewinnt Prozess' or Elke Galvin, 'Gericht schützt posthum Haiders Privatsphäre', *Kleine Zeitung*, 19 November 2009 (the latter is no longer available online, possibly due to the number and tenor of reader comments).
59. 'Nun sehen Sie wie das Volk Jörgeli liebte. Im Volk lebt er ja ewig; fur mich ja auch.'
60. Some of this outpouring was itself turned into satire. A cabaret evening in Vienna was sourced from messages written into a condolence book for a fictional Jörg Haider ersatz called 'Horst Binder'. See a 'best of' video: Agentur Brendt, 'Die Heimaterde sei dir leicht: eine Kondolenz Lesung'. Retrieved 6 May 2018 from https://www.youtube.com/watch?v=5-CVTd3TeiU.

61. See Thomas Trenkler, '*Blutsfreundschaft*: Mit den Waffen der Rechtspopulisten', *Der Standard*, 20 October 2009. Retrieved 6 May 2018 from http://derstandard.at/1254311841330/Blutsfreundschaft-Mit-den-Waffen-der-Rechtspopulisten.
62. 'Mit dem Spiel kann ich reale Verhältnisse komprimieren.' Claus Philipp, 'Retter der Erniedrigten und Beleidigten: Peter Kern', *Der Standard*, 19 April 2007. Retrieved 6 May 2018 from http://derstandard.at/2847809/Retter-der-Erniedrigten-und-Beleidigten-Peter-Kern.
63. The Christian Social Union (CSU) politician Edmund Stoiber was indeed a candidate for the job, having narrowly beaten his Christian Democratic Union (CDU) competitor, Angela Merkel, to become the CDU/CSU candidate in 2002. The national election was very closely fought, the Social Democrats winning, and Gerhard Schröder was re-elected as Chancellor.
64. Olaf Möller, 'Undefeated', *Film Comment* (July/August 2007), 18–19, at 19.
65. 'Darüber bin ich nicht beleidigt weil "Trash" für mich ein Qualitätsbegriff ist. Trotzdem wird man schnell abqualifiziert. Mein "Müll" ist bewusst erzählt.' In Philipp, 'Retter der Erniedrigten und Beleidigten'.
66. 'Aha, das nennt man eine Dokumentation?'
67. 'Dessen billige Video-Ästhetik kreiert affektive (großteils lustige) Momente und berührt gleichzeitig gesellschaftspolitische Wahrnehmungsmuster.' Dietmar Schwärzler, 'Zukunftsvisionen. Ein Heimatfilm: Peter Kerns *1. April 2021: Haider lebt!*', *Der Standard*, 3 October 2007. The text also features on the box of the DVD edition.
68. '[E]in schnelles, politisches Medium . . . das künstlerische Unabhängigkeit gewährt.' Schwärzler, 'Zukunftsvisionen'.
69. The ORF released a DVD in 2008: Gerhard Jelinek (dir.), 'Das war Jörg Haider'.
70. '[A]ussen rosa, innen braun . . . und durch Alkohol gleichsam neutralisiert.' Harald Friedl, *Land ohne Eigenschaften* (Austria: Harald Friedl, 2000) (70:43 onwards). See also Robert Menasse, *Das Land ohne Eigenschaften: Essay zur österreichischen Identität* (Frankfurt am Main: Suhrkamp, 1992).
71. For contrastive filmmaking, see, for example, Nikolaus Geyrhalter's four-hour ethnographic panorama *Elsewhere* (2001), for which the director visited twenty different locations throughout 2000. He documents the autonomous and varied modes of living in places as far apart as China, Finland, Siberia or Nigeria. The process of globalization, Geyrhalter feels, will inevitably encroach on even the most remote populations.

Chapter 5

STAGING RESISTANCE
Dramatic Themes and Interventions

Introduction: Playing for Political Points

Dramatists have long been amongst the most active and controversial cultural commentators on Austrian politics. One does not need to look far to find examples of playwrights whose works have expressly dealt with the state of the Austrian nation at important political junctures. Thomas Bernhard's infamous play *Heldenplatz* (1988) was commissioned by Claus Peymann, the then director of the Burgtheater, ostensibly to mark the hundredth anniversary of the country's prestigious state theatre. However, the play premièred on the anniversary date of the annexation of Austria to Nazi Germany in 1938 and is shot through with the trauma of Austria's anti-Semitic past. Its pre-première hype was calculated to stir up media interest, and the public controversy that ensued was heated and protracted. The election of Kurt Waldheim to the office of President in 1986 had taken place amidst large-scale international scrutiny, as the former UN Secretary General's apparent amnesia over the exact details of his wartime activities in the Wehrmacht gradually unravelled. Just as Waldheim and the year 1986 had functioned as a catalyst for literary and public engagement with the subject of Austria's attitude to its own political representation and indeed to the ever-recurrent topic of Austria's failure to deal adequately with its war guilt and anti-Semitism, so too did the FPÖ's rise to coalition government function as a springboard for dramatists' attention in 1999/2000.

Theatre and politics are indeed frequent companions. Plays can enlist political themes as material to be mimicked, travestied or simply to be documented, and the results can range widely from comedy to tragedy, from realist to absurdist.

The dramatis personae can include fictional political characters or indeed characters named after real politicians, whether dead or alive. Alternatively, plays can reflect on a political situation (deliberately or inadvertently) and promote some kind of message or call to action. The reader or spectator is often indispensable in accomplishing or 'performing' this kind of reading by recognizing the contemporary, sociopolitical allusions. In the materials considered in the present chapter, a range of different strategies is deployed. The reader or spectator's ability to read between the lines is not required for the sometimes bluntly titled dramolets of Antonio Fian, with which this chapter begins, but the concluding discussion of Robert Menasse's *Das Paradies der Ungeliebten* (2006) requires an allegorical reading.

Like novels, however, full-length plays often take a while to conceive of and to commit to writing. Moreover, in order to be realized as a drama, the material then usually requires a long list of team members to direct, produce, costume and act out, and a theatre venue or other performance space to boot. For these reasons alone, there is not an extensive list of what we could call plays of resistance to the black-and-blue coalition. The genre of drama might include cabaret and sketches, for which Austria (and Vienna in particular) has a long and prominent history. Cabaret materials are not often published or, indeed, recorded in written form, and thus do not feature here as a genre; indeed, the same applies to television materials.[1] However, there are short dramas, or 'dramolets' such as those by Antonio Fian, that are very much conceptualized as prompt, satirical responses to Austrian politics and are indeed very similar in conception to cabaret sketches. Often published first in newspapers, these texts can reach their audiences very quickly. A longer dramolet discussed in this chapter is the specifically labelled 'Haider monologue' by Elfriede Jelinek, *Das Lebewohl (Les Adieux)*, for which the première was an open-air staged reading, delivered as part of the anti-government protests in the summer of 2000.[2]

The second and longer part of my chapter on drama is dedicated to an analysis of a particular topic and its intersection with drama. In Austria around the time of the Wende, sport and sporty looks became part of both a heightened discourse of political and élite self-marketing, but also a lens through which intellectuals and writers chose to view contemporary Austrian society. I therefore take a closer look at a number of writers who use sport to varying degrees in their playwriting to advance their critique and protest against Austria's turn to the right. The authors and texts chosen stem from the lead-up to the millennium, in the form of Jelinek's 1998 *Ein Sportstück* and from the coalition year itself, namely Franzobel's *Olympia* (2000) and Marlene Streeruwitz's *Sapporo*. (published in 2002 but first staged in 2000).[3] Franzobel is a prolific novelist, but has also written many plays. Streeruwitz's early career was built on the dramatic form, but has concentrated on writing novels since 2000. Robert Menasse has only penned a couple of dramas, but is a much-fêted novelist and essayist. There are other plays and dramatic dialogues that clearly protest against the state of affairs in Austria, but that do not use sport as a foil and thus are not discussed here. One need only look to Peter Turrini and his *Ich liebe dieses Land* (2001), set in Germany but with obvious criticisms of his Austrian homeland.[4] Although published a little later than most of the materials covered in this book, the play I have chosen to complete the deliberations on this subject is by one of Austria's foremost essayists and writers. Robert Menasse's *Das Paradies der Ungeliebten* (2006) is a commissioned piece, but one that has not yet been performed in Austria. Despite its setting in 'Denmark', the play is clearly an allegory of Austria and of the rise of the extreme right.

Acting Political: Staging Politicians

Antonio Fian: Giving Politics Short Shrift

That contemporary politicians require acting skills as well as good oratory would seem to be confirmed by the existence of successful politicians who had a previous career in film or stage acting. One thinks immediately of former US President and erstwhile Governor of California Ronald Reagan, or indeed of the Austrian-American incumbent of that post, the 'governator', Arnold Schwarzenegger, who served two terms in office spanning 2003 to 2011. There are fewer examples of politicians-turned-actors, though it was a career direction mooted by satirical commentators to counter the wave of conservative cultural policy reforms brought in as a result of Austria's 2000 government coalition between the People's Party (ÖVP) and the right-wing Freedom Party (FPÖ). 'The cultural policy objectives of the coalition, re-elected in 2002' are summarized in a report by Veronika Ratzenböck and fellow collaborators as having been focused on: 'outsourcing of public cultural institutions and a reduction of the cultural budget. Greater emphasis [was] placed on prestige culture, the creative industries and the promotion of economically oriented projects (such as festivals to increase tourism)'.[5] Dramatist Peter Turrini jibed that all the failed artists-turned-politicians were avenging themselves after 1999 on Austrian culture and artists.[6] As a way of countering this 'Turrini-Theorem', Rayk Wieland suggests diverting these 'Untalente' (talentless folk) by offering them the chance to publish a slim volume of their poems or a little theatrical role. It is well known that when he was young, Haider had wanted to become an actor, and so, Wieland urges, 'the regional theatre in Linz should not be above tempting Haider out of provincial government: it would be one small step for the ensemble, and one giant step for mankind'.[7]

This observer is not aware of any theatrical roles that Haider did indeed take up, but as many have commented, Haider's ability to perform for the camera, his rhetorical abilities, his adaptability to different contexts and audiences, and his persuasive style all made him a natural for the stage. Asked if he thought Haider was a good actor, Turrini points out that all actors are liars – they pretend to be another person and seek to be believed: 'how else can they constantly be another person? Actors always bring across a sense of agreeing with you. Anyone who talks to Haider feels like they've been deeply understood by him. It's just one big performance'.[8] There are, however, a number of stage characters or roles designated as 'Haider' (or other politicians), and I turn now to look at examples of short dramas that 'stage' politicians, first of all from the popular novelist, essayist and dramatist Antonio Fian and then – more extensively – from Elfriede Jelinek.

Fian is best known for his collections of 'dramolets',[9] in which he targets his skill for mimicry at the utterances and actions of public figures. Literary and media figures are often the subject (or object) of Fian's dramolets,[10] but I am most interested here in protagonists who are named after real-life politicians. In examining how Fian's literary material performs these public personae – that is to say, how Fian's dramolets interact with utterances or political performances politicians have themselves made – focus is placed on how one of the writer's favourite targets, Jörg Haider, is realized as a fictional character. The following considers a number of transformations of politicians into what we might call materials for performance by us as readers, if not necessarily on a real stage. 'Works of literature, after all, are quasi-*speech-acts*; they require readers to give the substance of fully operative conventions to language that lacks it.'[11]

With the dramolets of Antonio Fian, it is clear that we are not dealing with *pièces à clef*, since his are, for the most part, not evasively named characters who happen to bear resemblances to real people. In this sense, as Konstanze Fliedl describes, they 'savagely or mockingly negat[e] the self-referentiality of art'. 'The polemical writer pays no heed to discreet anonymity', she points out, observing that 'from this perspective, the legal problem of the *roman* or *pièce à clef* is reversed, so that empirical persons become no more than the arbitrary appendages of their names, and it is the name that has gained the textual status of a unique character'.[12] One of Fian's most explicit Haider satires is entitled *Jörg Haider arbeitet an seiner Aschermittwochrede*.[13] The title alludes to the scandal following the speech that Haider made on Ash Wednesday 2001 in which he slandered Ariel Muzicant, the leader of Vienna's Jewish community, contriving a pun suggesting the irony of his first name's evocation of a washing powder, following his alleged 'dirty' practices of stirring up anti-Austrian sentiment abroad. Fian only rarely provides contextual, 'factual' information, but with this dramolet, the stage direction ('Vorhang') ('curtain') is followed by a line or two of 'Material', in which he states the source for his reworking. This dramolet also bears an epigraph quotation from the ÖVP politician Andreas Khol opining that he has never experienced Haider being directly anti-Semitic: 'he was always careful never to make this mistake'.[14] The action takes place in Haider's study and consists of Haider plus a chorus, working together on his forthcoming speech. The dialogue alternates between the chorus chanting ideas for the speech and Haider's reactions to these. The quickfire litany of suggested targets of blame ('roaming musicians, Sinti, Roma / Jew, Gypsy / they're all to blame') is interspersed with ironic performances of what the epigraph has described as Haider's careful avoidance of mistakes: 'Haider: too general, too / easy to attack, too little / care ... Lueger, no / I am different / careful, me, and / no mistakes.'[15] Fian deploys here a similar linguistic strategy to that of Elfriede Jelinek in her Haider drama. In referring to the performed words of Haider's actual, political speech and ironically mutating and *re*-performing these in fragmented quotations in his dramolet, Fian's writing enacts a satirical, literary and linguistic mirroring of Haider and his speechwriter Herbert Kickl's anti-Semitic-sounding lines.[16] Jacques Lajarrige describes how this literary process enacts or is tantamount to a kind of literary trial: 'as for [Fian's] dramolets, their fundamentally dialogic nature promotes a powerful *mise en abyme* of ironic modes of speech. This brings the relevant parties to book, so to speak'.[17]

I draw attention here to an earlier dramolet as it gives evidence of the early 'Haider watching' alluded to in Chapter 1 and to a phrase that was reworked in a musical protest piece (see Chapter 2). In *Der Einbruch des Akrostichons in die österreichische politische Kultur. Ein Ausblick* (*Perspectives on the Advent of the Acrostic in Austrian Political Culture*), it is the FPÖ politician Reinhard Gaugg and his manner of speaking who stand trial. The former Deputy Mayor of Klagenfurt's infamous 1993 interview answer to the question 'Was sagt Ihnen das Wort "Nazi"?' ('What does the word "Nazi" mean to you?') was 'neu, attraktiv, zielstrebig, ideenreich' ('new, attractive, zealous, imaginative'). The dramolet features a membership candidate presenting himself at a political party headquarters, and it is the applicant's dialect rendition of various personal mnemonics from which the humour primarily derives. Most of his answers are to the interviewer's satisfaction, even with the candidate's poor spelling (for example, 'Sozi' – 'solche Orschlecha zertritt i'; ('such orseholes zquelch I' [I tread on such arseholes]), and the interview performance is deemed 'exzellent'. Despite applauding his innovative renditions of such acronyms as 'Wiener' and 'Busek',[18] the interviewer nevertheless rejects the applicant for his anti-democratic views and reminds him of the party's motto, 'Demokratiefeindlichkeit ist keinesfalls tolerierbar, alles Trachten unserer Republik!' ('anti-democratic thought is not to be tolerated; such is the striving of our Republic!').[19] The recorded, live reading of this piece lends more weight to the idea that these dramolets are conceived with what might be termed an epistemology of writing/reading in mind and are not primarily designed for physical performance. The live track does not demonstrate audibly that the audience has picked up on the ironic implications of the unstated central acrostic of the party motto, which spells out 'D-i-k-t-a-t-u-r'.[20] Similar to the micro-dramas of Wolfgang Bauer, Fian's texts often contain lengthy passages of stage directions – a device more for the pleasure of the reader than for the irritation of the director. In the 'Akrostichon' dramolet, the stage directions describe not only the office with its 'altdeutsche Möblierung' ('old Germanic furnishings') and bright blue walls, but also state: 'aus Windmaschinen frischer Wind' ('a fresh breeze blows from wind machines'). Stage props could include a wind generator (as opposed to a simple office fan), and the spectator might make some kind of connection, but unless the dramaturg or director stages this in a surreal fashion, perhaps with a banner stating 'frischer Wind' streaming from the machine, then the theatre audience would not pick up on Fian's reference to the self-styled 'new era' or fresh atmosphere that this party is purporting to be bringing about.[21]

In the tradition of Austrian satirical drama, be it by Nestroy, Kraus, Horváth or Jelinek, this dramatist's aesthetic antennae are tuned to investigate and stage language or discourse phenomena anew. In the example just cited, Fian plays with the acronym; in *Rilke bei Schüssel*, he has Chancellor Schüssel speak to the poet Rainer Maria Rilke in verse. In an anachronistic move, Rilke (1875–1926) has been summoned to help the Chancellor in convincing the people how good their lot is as Schüssel knows that a great poet is the very man to help him. German grammar, a favourite Fian device, is used to comic effect as Rilke's famous lines are interrupted twice. Rilke has to persist to finish his line ('for poverty is luminous from within'),[22] as each time he says 'denn', Schüssel mistakes this for 'den' and interrupts Rilke to point out that 'it's *die* Armut, Rilke, poverty is always feminine'.[23] In *Alarmist und Besonnener. (Einübung in die Normalität)*, the propagandistic coinage 'umvolken', to describe the influx of immigrants, or being 'swamped' by immigrants, is ridiculed not by a protracted discussion of the facts or otherwise of the situation, but by highlighting the difficulty of conjugating such a ludicrous verb. 'Der Zweite' asks: 'And who to discuss this with? ... Is the past participle of "umvolken" "umgevolkt" or "umvolkt"?'[24] A coinage that came to prominence under the National Socialists, the term has experienced renewed use in recent years, provoking considerable controversy and protest. FPÖ ideologue Andreas Mölzer spoke in 1992 of how the Austrian people were facing the threat of ethnic change. In 2004, another prominent FPÖ politician, Johann Gudenus, criticized the number of foreigners becoming Austrian citizens, saying that this was a kind of systematic 'Umvolkung' ('racial repopulation') of Austria.[25]

Fian's publications satirize politicians, and in so doing ask questions about the motivation behind their political agenda. It is not the 'real' Jörg Haider, then, who is the subject matter here, but instead a number of short artistic fictionalizations or literary enactments of him or his utterances. In the days following the untimely death of Haider in a road accident on 11 October 2008, epithets were scattered liberally in death notices and news items: 'the head of the BZÖ apparently "died like James Dean", he was a "Robin Hood", "the greatest political genius since Bruno Kreisky"'.[26] Some of the 'roles' are ones that Haider chose for himself and are testament to his showmanship and ability to play to a particular public. Psychologist Klaus Ottomeyer analyses these in his *Die Haider-Show* (2000), beginning with a chapter on 'Robin Hood in Österreich'.[27] These roles are no longer available for a living Jörg Haider to adopt, although they can and will still be ascribed to him posthumously, whether justifiably or not. However, his words and political deeds can still be scrutinized for their ethical stance, and Haider was rightly taken to task for the many veiled racist, or anti-Semitic and anti-immigrationist statements he made, as well as for quips that can be interpreted as provocative, positive evaluations of Nazi policies.[28]

Elfriede Jelinek Protests Haider's 'Farewell'

The contribution made by Elfriede Jelinek in the field of cultural resistance to right-wing nationalism in Austria is constant and unrelenting. It is coupled with an overriding preoccupation in her work with Austria's National Socialist atrocities. The term 'resignation' has a dual resonance in the analysis that follows. It refers to the growing expression of frustration and despair in the face of political developments that comes to the fore in Jelinek's writing, but it also refers to Jörg Haider's *actual* resignation as leader of the FPÖ in February 2000. After negotiation talks between the ÖVP and the SPÖ broke down, Wolfgang Schüssel, leader of the ÖVP, invited the FPÖ to form a coalition government under his chancellorship. Haider's resignation was seen by many at the time as a tactical withdrawal in response to widespread unrest at the prospect of his becoming deputy chancellor. His deputy, Dr Susanne Riess-Passer, then assumed both of these roles. Haider was ostensibly confined to Carinthian politics, but of course was continuing to guide the national conduct of his party from behind the scenes.[29]

There are certain parallels in the applicability of the term 'resignation'. Jelinek's writing expresses resignation, but only as a textual *strategy*, an ironic provocation to the reader. Irony has been a prominent device in Jelinek's aesthetic toolkit throughout her entire oeuvre: the title of her 1999 collection, *Macht nichts*, for example, should be read as a punning injunction, implying both 'it doesn't matter' ('*es* macht nichts') and 'do nothing!'. Jörg Haider may have resigned his post, but his too was a mock resignation. Many artists and political observers alike argue that Haider merely withdrew to Carinthia in order to re-emerge to a more triumphant role in Austrian politics.[30] Jelinek's comments are thus intended to prick at the reader's conscience to 'do' something. It might then seem strange that Jelinek reacted to the coalition government of the FPÖ and the ÖVP by banning her plays from being staged in Austria,[31] precisely where her critical voice should be heard. However, Jelinek contended at the time that to continue to allow her plays to be produced in Austria would have been to endorse the political situation. She underlines a contrast between her stance and that of the revered Austrian actress Paula Wessely, who continued to be a favourite with the public through the Nazi years and even acted in propagandistic films:[32]

> I can't criticize the likes of Paula Wessely for supporting and even furthering a regime that should be opposed and then go and do the same myself, whereby I obviously don't mean to compare the Third Reich with what we have now. I absolutely do not want to put my colleagues under pressure to do the same thing, it's just my personal way of protesting. High culture in the performing arts has a kind of flagship function. By permitting critical high culture, the powers that be get the chance to claim for themselves a sense of tolerance which is lacking elsewhere.[33]

Jelinek's dramatic monologue *Das Lebewohl* is not the first of her dramas to have featured a leading politician as its protagonist. The idea of repressing the past or of claiming to have forgotten past events is an important theme in Jelinek's short drama *Präsident Abendwind* (1986), a commissioned response to Nestroy's *Häuptling Abendwind oder Das greuliche Festmahl* (1862). Nestroy inverts the Romantic idea of the noble and portrays his natives as nationalistic and as aspiring to notions of diplomacy and civilization. The cannibals' fixation on matters culinary and their thick Austrian accents are markers of satirical attack that both playwrights have in common. Parallels between Waldheim and Abendwind are quite easy to spot, as Jacques Lajarrige has noted. In the figure of Hermann, the would-be son-in-law courting Abendwind's daughter, Lajarrige sees the ambitions of the up-and-coming Jörg Haider: 'one can't help thinking here of the ambitions of the FPÖ and of its ultranationalist leader Jörg Haider, or of the latter's slogans against immigrants and against the Slovene minority in Carinthia'.[34] It is certainly possible to see a Haider caricature in *Präsident Abendwind*, but in *Das Lebewohl*, the speaker is quite expressly Jörg Haider, the stage directions even referring to the speaker as the 'Sprecher des "*Haider*monologs"'.[35]

Whereas the intellectual background of *Präsident Abendwind* is Viennese-Austrian (Nestroy) and also French (Nestroy's intertext was Jacques Offenbach's operetta *Vent du soir ou l'horrible festin* of 1857), in Jelinek's satire on Jörg Haider, *Das Lebewohl*, the inspiration is taken both from Greek mythology, in the form of Aeschylus' *Oresteia* and from mundane contemporary discourse, in the form of a text written by Haider on the occasion of his resignation from party leadership of the FPÖ, entitled 'Glücksgefühl nach bangen Stunden'.[36] The crimes narrated in the *Oresteia* are the murder of Agamemnon by his wife Clytaemnestra and the latter's murder by her son, Orestes, who thus avenges his father's death. There are no such dramatic developments in Jelinek's text, but the themes of guilt, vengeance, past crimes, reverence for the father or male principle and disregard for the maternal are clearly shared with the play's Greek precursor. Although the nature of the deed or the crimes is not made explicit, it is quite clear that Jelinek's character has in mind the atrocities of the Holocaust when he at first refuses to admit his own guilt or that of his father's generation.

The speaker then concedes this guilt and explains that they have apologized for these 'abscheuliche, einmalige Verbrechen' ('unprecedented, abhorrent crimes') and have said 'nie wieder!' ('never again'). However, the sentiment progresses to one of regretful necessity and an implied sense of dignity in having carried the deed through: 'and should we have offended anybody, we regret it, but are we not right? . . . We dared to execute the deed we had contrived'.[37]

There are precedents for staging Aeschylus' *Oresteia* in the cause of exploring questions of guilt and of *Vergangenheitsbewältigung*.[38] However, in Jelinek's use of the *Oresteia*, the playwright's concern is not with Clytaemnestra's guilt, but with the character and significance of the Orestes figure as an analogy for Jörg Haider. Jelinek sees part of Haider's political motivation as seeking some kind of retribution for the postwar condemnation of his own father, an early member of the Nazi Party in Austria when it was still illegal.[39] Melanie A. Sully argues that 'whatever the assessment of Haider's grasp of history, it is clear that he had a built-in mechanism which rallied to the defence of the fathers from the war generation . . . The rehabilitation and passionate defence of the NS fathers was deeply ingrained in many of Haider's background'.[40] Jelinek has her dramatized Haider-speaker echo Orestes, saying: 'It is your word that destroys me now, father! I avenge you like the morning storm. But now there is another wind that blows. Can you feel it blowing, father?'[41]

It is not the case that Jelinek has been deliberately prompted into offsetting Haider's putative relationship with and feelings for his father with her own literary engagement with her father, as there are indeed signs of Jelinek's fictional reworkings of her father's biography in many of her earlier works and not merely in the later ones. Furthermore, there is a striking contrast between the lives of these two men, and especially between the treatments each received in and by the Third Reich. In addition to providing a fictional voice for her dead father in the monologue 'Der Wanderer' (*Macht nichts*), Jelinek or 'die Autorin' also addresses her dead father in the play *Ein Sportstück*, where she expresses an internalized guilt over his death, or 'murder' in the asylum: 'I myself took part, whilst my papa was killed . . . You should turn up right now and accuse me of something'.[42] These expressions of remorse have no parallel in Aeschylus, whereas Euripides in his *Orestes* portrays the hero as much more troubled over his murder of his mother. In fact, the frenzied rhetoric of Jelinek's speaker arguably has more in common with the 'mental collapse' of Orestes in Euripides' play, even though there is no central act of matricide at the heart of Jelinek's text.[43]

What inspiration, then, does Jelinek take from the theme of matricide in her intertext? There are passages in *Das Lebewohl* that may have been drawn from Aeschylus and that centre on Orestes' design to murder his mother precisely as vengeance for this father, or for the male principle ('Vengeance for the father! Vengeance! Destroy the land, kill the mother!')[44] or that bemoan women's cunning. The following passage conflates Orestes' anger over his father's treatment at the hands of women (or more specifically his wife) with the fictional Haider's irritation at being succeeded by a woman (Dr Susanne Riess-Passer). He leaves the women to the Chancellor who succeeds him (Wolfgang Schüssel is, of course, implied here): 'He did not endure the fornication in his house for long; but now it is I who leave this house, the paramour is his. Riess-Passer, Frau Dr. Riess to me. Mother! We have witnessed how women's cunning in this land has betrayed my father, the land: a woman. Little fat woman. Little fat woman, rich and evil. Never conquered was I: by a man.'[45] Although there is no physical murdering of women, there is a metaphorical murder or erasure of the feminine in the misogynist tone of the speaker's words. The dramatized Haider is in good company with Orestes, of whom Gilbert Murray has said that: 'There are not many tragic heroes with such an extreme anti-feminist record.'[46] The speaker professes amazement at his successor's ability to speak so authoritatively, but then criticizes her for merely reproducing his own words. At this point, Jelinek's writing performs Lacanian psychoanalytic theories which argue that women are forced to emulate men's words in order to have any kind of access to language and to the powerful institutions and structures of the symbolic order:

> Beautiful boy, just look at how masterfully this wench acts at the press conference! That woman! I didn't think she had it in her. Isn't it just super, the way she speaks? Ensnaring the people with her web of cunning, she talks and talks, she just talks completely without notes, but what is it she says? It does not matter. For it is not what Apollo commanded. It's from me, of course, but it is nothing. When I say it, it is different. When she says it, it is nothing.[47]

In an interview, Jelinek has explained her interest in the *Oresteia* as a text that marks the progression from matriarchal to patriarchal society. Indeed, Bachofen, Freud and more recently Cixous have all used the *Oresteia* as an illustration of this premise.[48] Cixous underlines how Aeschylus' text signals the victory of the name of the father over the blood ties of the mother. It is the purging of his name that must take precedence. If Freud saw Aeschylus' text as signalling an advance in civilization, then both Cixous and Jelinek are concerned with deconstructing and thus questioning the nature of this civilization. Cixous' theatre-based work has concerned itself with 'an understanding of history as a struggle between competing economies, described as "masculine" and "feminine"',[49] and one could see Jelinek's text as exploring another angle or stage in the sexual economy. Jelinek argues that there is a sublimated homosexuality in Haider's following. She characterizes it as follows:

> The weak, the alien, that which 'does not belong to us' is excluded or banished. It's no coincidence that Haider brought a former Olympic downhill skiing champion into parliament [Patrick Ortlieb]. He works, like all proto-fascist movements do, with the

aesthetic cult of the body, the homoerotic male alliance that manifests itself in sport. It is, as it were, the sanctioned sexual act with the young, bronzed *Führer*, who graciously administers his favours.[50]

Rather than the chorus of Old Men, of Slave women, or Furies in the three respective parts of Aeschylus' trilogy, Jelinek chooses to form a chorus of adoring 'schöner Knaben', dressed, she requests, either in 'kindlichen, pludernden Spielhöschen' (kiddies' rompers) or in Lederhosen, who listen reverently and strew rose petals over the speaker. They are the visible, though mute, addressees of the monologue which is peppered with references to them, such as 'it is your tears, you fellows' or 'colleagues, boys, comrades'.[51] They are praised by the speaker as follows: 'I had to endure how my family, my family, my beautiful, good, clever, brilliantly blond family, were made – by brutally violent people – to share my suffering. But my passion is much more for you, boys, you glorious, good men.'[52] Surrounded by his adoring, faithful disciples, the speaker takes on the air of a divine force, referring to himself as 'me, the favourite of the gods' and 'the dear lord'.[53] This overblown rhetoric is a reflection of the discourse Haider himself used in his resignation as party leader and consequently also in foregoing the Vice-Chancellorship of Austria.[54]

The sensitive reader must surely find Haider's diary entry text quite remarkable in tone, even without having read Jelinek's parodic reworking of it in *Das Lebewohl*. There are passages that suggest a sense of superiority, self-importance, even of a divine calling to fulfil an ineluctable destiny. After the press conference at which Jörg Haider announced his decision, it would appear that the leading figures in the FPÖ went back to Susanne Riess-Passer's home to continue their discussions. Consider the following account of Riess-Passer's comportment and of the emotional reactions of Haider's political companions:

> For if I had looked out into the group and seen the tears in the eyes of many a long-serving fellow campaigner, who knows if I mightn't have weakened. Deputy Chancellor Susanne Riess-Passer acted masterfully and I was pleased to assist her. I did so all the more readily because I knew how much she really wanted to rebuke me for my decision, but her discipline and her intellect accepted what was inevitable. We resolved to meet up again privately at Susanne Riess-Passer's. Some of my faithful followers were with us.[55]

To this reader, and doubtless to others, Haider's attitude to his successor comes across as avuncular and patronizing. Riess-Passer is the only colleague who merits being referred to by her first name only, a special treatment that some will justify as gentlemanly: 'Böhmdorfer, out of bed. Susanne was worried about the justice minister. I too spoke with Michael Krüger, whose state of health will keep him tied to his bed in the coming weeks.'[56] In Jelinek's text, the respect that women and mothers are due is relative to that granted to men ('everyone should honour their father and their mother, but more their father')[57] and the 'family values' promoted by the Freiheitlichen are rendered with terminology that is redolent of the 'Kinder, Küche, Kirche' rhetoric of the Third Reich: 'Mother, homeland, hearth, we worship and protect them, we are cut from the best cloth.'[58]

Haider's use of phrases such as 'Einige meiner Getreuen' ('some of my faithful followers') or 'ein Glücksgefühl nach bangen Stunden' ('a joyous feeling after anxious hours') is somewhat archaic, not to say religiose in places, and Jelinek's satire indeed posits him as a redeemer figure.[59] The essayist Franz Schuh has commented on the 'christologische Moment' in the debate about Austria's political 'resurrection' and asks rhetorically: 'Has he [Jörg Haider] not always seen himself as redeemer?'[60] In keeping with the pseudo-religious tone of his text, Haider styles himself as a kind of martyr, a martyr to the hateful, left-wing press, in particular to the television journalists of the *Zeit im Bild* news programme:

> Three left-wing journalists let rip about me, their hatred was just dripping out of the television set. They hadn't counted on this. The object of their hate-filled desire had escaped them. What should their journalistic raison-d'être consist of now? There would be no one they could direct their leftist ideological hatred and malice at so pointedly as they had at me.[61]

Haider's act of self-sacrifice is one in the face for the press and, by his implication, a service to his fellow citizens, who will now be spared the vitriol of the media. Apart from a few examples of archaic and elevated language in Haider's text, the general tone of the language is everyday, in keeping with the 'day-in-the-life-of' genre in which it is written. What makes it so useful for Jelinek's purposes is that it is so full of the kind of cliché that characterizes politicians' rhetoric and of the trivial and banal details to be expected in a diary text. Jelinek's linguistic methodology in *Das Lebewohl* aims at a kind of alienation effect. By embedding Haider quotations in the predominant register of pathos from her Greek intertext, she aims to make the politico-speak of Haider and others seem even more laughable and banal. The speaker explains: 'I am there as regional governor and I can help to build a good team; I shall set the log alight now; it has been burning since I left my mother's womb.'[62] The juxtaposition in the same sentence of words such as 'Pressekonferenz' and 'Weib' (woman or wench), or 'Team' and 'Scheit' (log of wood), promotes a comic alienation, as does the anachronism of a mobile phone: 'My family send me encouraging text messages, those blond people, good people, doubts and stresses: away! begone! Shall I eat my newborn, this movement of people, now or later? No. It is strong. No movement, not without me.'[63]

A constant feature in Jelinek's writing, puns and wordplay are put to good if sparing effect too in *Das Lebewohl*. The *Zeit im Bild* reference becomes an opportunity for the speaker to stress that their 'time' will come and that they are 'in the picture': 'Let's put it like this, the picture remains, the time passes by, but we are in the picture, we have been for some time. The times will become ours, too, one day. Please hold the line.'[64] Jelinek takes Haider's own idiom that the Freedom Party people are cut from a different cloth (or, in fact, wood, in German) and turns it back on her 'blockhead' Haider-speaker to comic effect: 'We are made of different wood. The Chancellor seemed reassured when I said this. He knocked on my head: a different wood.'[65] Aeschylus too provides Jelinek with archaic textual material for rather contrived punning. The verb 'einschirren' ('schirren', 'anspannen', to harness) allows a sideswipe at the subservient role of women: 'Mein Vater noch ganz im Joch des Leidens eingeschirrt, das Geschirr wäscht die Frau, ganz klar, sie ist gut drauf und hoch motiviert' ('My father is washed out under the yoke of suffering, but the dishes are washed by the woman. Of course they are – she's happy and highly motivated.'[66]

A further effect of the conflation of linguistic registers is to enhance the madness of the text and its speaker. The short, clipped phrases and exclamations and the frequent rhetorical questions reinforce the themes of power and of camaraderie in the path towards victory ('we have fought and now we may victory celebrate').[67] The speaker's monomaniac, paranoid egotism ('No more movement, not without me')[68] reaches its climax in the final lines of the monologue as his speech becomes more and more frantic and self-centred. His plea for justification and acknowledgement becomes crazed and juvenile as he calls out to his father and mother. The egotism seems to become pathological, an impression that is created by the frequency and by the positioning of the word 'ich' as the regression and breakdown are accomplished not merely in the subject matter, but also in the text's syntax:

> 'Die Freiheit vertreib: ich, das Dunkel seh gar nicht: ich . . . In den Spiegel schauen können will: ich auch mich. Zögern will nicht auch: ich. Mein Vater sein will auch: ich. Sag nicht Mutter! Sag Vater! Sag nicht Mutter! Sag Vater! Und zieh dein Schwert! . . . Alle niedermachen will auch: ich . . . Die Freiheit sein will auch: ich. Vaters Kind sein will auch: ich. Sags Mutter, sags Vater, sags Mutter, sags Vater. Sag ich. Sag doch: ich! Die ganze: Zeit!' (Freedom shall be banished by: me, darkness is not even seen by: me . . . being able to look into the mirror: I want to be able to see myself, too. Hesitation will not be for: me. To be my father is what: I want. Do not say mother! Say father! Not mother, but father! And draw your sword! . . . Butchering them all is for: me. Embodying freedom is also for: me. Being father's child: that's also for: me. Say it mother, say it father, say it mother, say it father. I say it. It is I saying it. The whole – time!)[69]

By putting the sentence subject, 'ich', in the final position and by repeating the same sentence structure over and over again, Jelinek both replicates something of the emphasis of the poetic syntax ('und jetzt dürfen wir feiern den Sieg') and heightens the sense of egotism. The separation of the subject from the verb phrase by a colon underlines this egotism, while assisting the actor in achieving the kind of non-naturalist delivery that Jelinek seeks.[70] The final word, 'Zeit', breaks the pattern and spoils the cadence, but it returns the monologue to the real threat of the Haider phenomenon, that is, to the advent of a new political or postpolitical era. The playwright comments on this 'Zeitenwende', saying: 'It's perhaps rather pretentious to call it this [a historic turning point], too dramatic maybe, but something has happened that none of us would have thought possible, namely that the extreme right should have come to power precisely in one of the perpetrator countries.'[71] Jelinek's creative writing implies, in fact, that the language of fascism is merely repressed and still distinctly audible in contemporary far-right discourse. Barbara Kosta notes how the Haider figure's language 'is inflected constantly with fascist undertones that intimate continuity between the rhetoric of Haider's party and that of Austria's fascist past'.[72]

The speaker's mythological counterpart, Orestes, is absolved by the goddess Athena and by the court that hears his crime. Jelinek chooses a marked contrast to her intertext at this point and leaves her Haider-speaker in a state of madness, of temporary exile and political limbo. As for the function and purpose of Jelinek's text, it would seem to echo the purpose of Greek tragedy. Simon Goldhill describes Greek tragedy as 'an event that places the tensions and ambiguities of a rapidly developing political and cultural system in the public domain to be contested'.[73] Jelinek's dramatic monologue *Das Lebewohl* was premièred outside on the Ballhausplatz and not inside the Burgtheater. Her self-imposed ban on the Austrian state stage doubtless attracted more critical attention and made a more widely acknowledged contribution to the Wende protests of 2000 than did the *Lebewohl* drama itself. However, as the dramatist points out, even today, the theatre can be seen as 'ja im Allgemeinen ein Ort, wo der Staat sich repräsentiert' ('generally a place where the state presents itself to the public') and where political discussion can be promoted. Jelinek's ban thus signals anything but political resignation: 'I have to withhold my language in order to be able to keep hold of it. That sounds melodramatic, I'm sure, but as I cannot leave, at least my plays can leave in order to have an effect (hopefully) somewhere else.'[74] In September 2000, the month in which *Das Lebewohl* was published, the European Union's 'wise men' adjudicated and asked the fourteen 'Furies', or EU Member States, to lift the diplomatic sanctions placed against Austria after the formation of the ÖVP-FPÖ coalition (see Chapter 1). Elfriede Jelinek's own 'sanction' against Austrian state theatres lasted until 2002.[75] She is, however, one of many artistic and intellectual 'furies' who continue to plague extreme-right politicians and who campaign hard to keep the memory of Austria's past crimes from being forgotten.

Sport and the Drama of Austrian National Identity

Not only was there a heightened use of sporting imagery in political rhetoric around the millennium, but essayists and writers also chose to use sport as a thematic means or starting point for advancing their own cultural-political critique of contemporary Austrian politics. Four plays will be discussed here: Jelinek's *Ein Sportstück* (1998), Franzobel's *Olympia: eine Kärntner Zauberposse samt Striptease* (2000), Marlene Streeruwitz's *Sapporo. Eine Revue* (2002) and Robert Menasse's *Das Paradies der Ungeliebten* (2006).[76] Streeruwitz uses a sporting idea as the impetus for her critique, but it is not a major theme of her work. Both *Olympia* and *Sapporo.* are presented by their authors expressly as contributions to the political debate surrounding the inauguration of the ÖVP-FPÖ government in 2000. Jelinek's drama pre-dates the historic elections of the autumn of 1999, but her plays and novels have for many years drawn attention to the ascendancy of extreme right-wing politics in Austria, and her play *Ein Sportstück* is very much a response to the growth in popularity of the FPÖ. Menasse's play posits corruption and populism as a wider European phenomenon, but uses the anniversary year of its commission (2005) to repeat the Thomas Bernhard phenomenon of penning a play that accuses his homeland of ongoing xenophobia and latent Nazism.

Following Benedict Anderson's conception of the nation as an 'imagined political community', nationality is no longer described merely in terms of a spatially and temporally fixed political identity, but as a cultural artefact or mental construct.[77] Thus, as Austrian sociolinguist Ruth Wodak explains, national identity implies a 'complex of similar conceptions and perceptual schemata, of similar emotional dispositions and attitudes, and of similar behavioural conventions, which bearers of this "national identity" share collectively and which they have internalised through socialisation (education, politics, the media, sports or everyday practices)'.[78] Sport, then, is an important means of socialization and very much part of what may be thought of as national culture. Alongside all the traditional manifestations of 'culture', Austrians themselves also see sport – and skiing in particular – as an expression of their national culture. In purely economic terms, skiing is a key cultural 'product' for the Austrian economy:

> If you look beyond the nostalgic self-understanding of Austria as a 'cultural nation', defined by New Year's Day concert, the Salzburg festival, the Burgtheater and the Vienna State Opera, you find, interestingly enough, the widely shared conception that skiing is also a typically Austrian cultural property. Austria is obviously – 'culturally' speaking – a nation of skiers.[79]

Skiing events provide an excellent photo opportunity for politicians and other 'Prominente' (celebrities) to be photographed and filmed amongst the young, fit sportsmen and women and to be associated with the many successes of the Austrian team. The skiing world championships in St Anton of February 2001 offered the occasion for a sublimated celebration of the first anniversary of the ÖVP-FPÖ regime and functioned as a popular, mediatized distraction from the demonstrations in Vienna marking a year of protests against the coalition. Both the Chancellor and the Vice-Chancellor, Wolfgang Schüssel (ÖVP) and Susanne Riess-Passer (FPÖ), were given pride of place near the finishing line to ensure that the camera could not miss them. Franzobel has commented on such blatant use of sport for political capital as follows: 'Sport is used in this country essentially to spread nationalism, sport dominates the television schedules. In sport it's not just a matter of pretending everything is business as usual, the new regime is casually celebrated through sport, too.' He adds the provocative analogy: 'Sport has a considerable part in helping to strengthen new governments – after all, Hitler was allowed to stage an Olympic Games in 1936!'[80]

The huge expression of 'Pisten-Patriotismus' to which such sporting events give rise thus does not go totally without check, and journalists and academics add their own analyses and attempts to relativize its function.[81] For Roman Horak, sport is very much a factor that contributes to the process of nation-building, or 'innere Staatsbildung', a process that he describes as 'the growing awareness of belonging to the state of Austria, conveyed via large-scale sporting events'.[82] This process is valid for large nations and for small ones, as Anton Pelinka points out, and he emphasizes the unifying function of the sporting event: '"we" are so unified – when it comes to the success of our skiing nation, then all our differences are set aside'.[83] Commentators agree that the expression of patriotism is often, if not always, most pronounced in young nations, which are still trying to establish, justify or strengthen their own nationhood, and it is in this light that Austria's national consciousness is theorized: 'In Austria's defence it might nevertheless be pointed out that exaggerated patriotism is quite typical for young nation states. And the Second Republic is really not that old yet.'[84]

Historical analyses agree on the list of decisive sporting events in the identity formation of Austrian national identity. At the Winter Olympics of 1956, Toni Sailer became the first ever competitor to win three alpine gold medals. This phenomenal success came within a year of the signing of Austria's State Treaty (May 1955) and is theorized as helping to anchor the Austrian people's identification with the newly founded Second Republic, the neutral postwar state of Austria. In this respect, it can be contrasted with the significance of Germany's defeat of Hungary in the football World Cup final of 1954. This latter victory has been seen as a reawakening of a more aggressive nationalism and as symbolizing the triumph of capitalism over communism at the height of the Cold War.[85] There are numerous other moments of sporting pride for Austrians in the field of skiing, but two of the more celebrated successes are Franz Klammer's gold-medal performance at the Innsbruck Winter Olympics of 1976, gaining him the popular epithet 'Kaiser', and the success of Hermann Maier ('Herminator') at the Nagano Winter Olympics in 1998. Of course, it is not only positive sporting stories that influence national self-consciousness; negative moments play their part too. The ultimate instance of this in Austrian history would have to be the case of

Karl Schranz, who was barred from competing in the 1972 Winter Olympics in Sapporo, the location that gives the title to Streeruwitz's play.

Austria's relationship with Germany is a key component in terms of how its national identity is defined. Here too, sport has played a pivotal role. The publicist and essayist Armin Thurnher points out that economic takeovers of Austrian companies by German ones do not impinge on the national consciousness in the way that defeats at the hand of German teams do.[86] It is not surprising, then, that great significance has been attached to the 1978 World Cup in Córdoba. The Austrian team only came seventeenth overall, but it won a far greater victory to Austrian minds – it beat Germany by three goals to two. There are many ways of understanding the impact of this result, but sports historians have tied it in with the victimization myth (see also Chapter 1). It has been termed a 'myth' due to the at best dubious validity of this description. The victim myth has often been used to denote the expression of feelings of victimization more generally and has come to be seen as a defining feature of postwar Austria's self-identity. Austrian reaction to international disapproval following the election of Kurt Waldheim in 1986 may be seen in this light, as can the defensive outpouring of hurt national pride after the European Union placed sanctions against it in 2000 in protest over the inclusion of the FPÖ in the new government. For Austrians, the Córdoba victory could be seen as 'a defining moment in the evolution of their nation' and as a sign of a 'victimized' country fighting back:

> most Austrians were clearly eager to dissociate themselves from guilt by association – or outright complicity – with the monstrous crimes of Hitler's New World Order. They readily accepted the Moscow Declaration's designation of Austria as the 'first victim' of the Third *Reich*, if only because they realized that it was impossible to be both a victim *and* a German at the same time. Hence the significance of . . . Córdoba, which to many Austrians represented the ultimate triumph of the vanquished over those who had long deprived them of their historic identity.[87]

Although Austrian skiers did extremely well at the World Alpine Ski Championships in Vail, Colorado in 1999, the Austrian football team suffered a humiliating 9-0 defeat to Spain in the same year. Naturally, it was this image and experience of sporting failure that Jörg Haider chose to provide him with an appropriate metaphor for the political situation when he stated in January 2000 that the players had failed and that the captain should seriously consider a new team. This was his choice of analogy for the failure of the SPÖ-ÖVP and his pitch for the inauguration of an ÖVP-FPÖ coalition.[88] But sporting metaphors were a staple part of Haider's political vocabulary, as Armin Thurnher makes clear. From party political broadcasts in which Haider cast himself as the nation's fitness trainer to personal criticisms of the physique of his political opponents, Haider took every opportunity to stress his sporting credentials and use these to political ends. Haider's sporting pastimes (running, skiing and mountaineering) added to his cultural currency as a fit, dynamic leader and were used to full effect in his media self-presentation. He is the prime example of what Thurnher has coined 'Feschismus', a neologism using the Austrian-German word 'fesch', meaning 'pretty, dashing, sporty-looking'.[89] With only a slight vowel difference from 'Faschismus', the term sums up the impact and logic of the new, fresh, fit image of Austrian politics that is redolent, Thurnher implies, of the fascist preoccupation with the racially 'healthy' and beautiful body:

> By fescists . . . I mean people who consciously position their looks and their bodies as fit and new in contrast to the worn-out bodies of the old political ragbags. To do so they draw on the victory symbolism and background of alpine mountaineering. . . . Their aim is not the renewal of representative democracy but rather its abolition. It's no longer a matter of trying to even out society to help the weaker, the alien or the other. What's important for them is the mandate of the victor, of the physically stronger.[90]

Jelinek's Sporting Spectators and Perpetrators

The most significant and hardest-hitting of the plays using sport in their social and political analysis is Elfriede Jelinek's *Ein Sportstück*. This play does not directly correlate to real-life incidents or people in the way that her *Lebewohl* material or Fian's dramolets do. Nevertheless, *Ein Sporstück* must be seen as protesting against the political ethos being peddled by Austria's competing political leaders in the late 1990s. In this play, as indeed in Franzobel's *Olympia*, sport is enacted not as a civilizing force, as some sociologists have theorized it, but as the embodiment of war in peacetime and, ultimately, as a symptom of protofascist enthusiasm for the strong, healthy body and an implied or actual condemnation of the weak and the sick. The idea that sport provides some kind of safety valve to society and that its forms of violence are mostly symbolic and rational (e.g. the jeering of spectators, and the tackling of opponents in rugby) is not one with which Jelinek would have much sympathy. For sociologist Norbert Elias, sport could be seen as part of 'a long-term shift in the patterns of violence expression and control in modern industrial societies. This shift has led to a lessening in the desire to attack others . . . and an internalization of a taboo on interpersonal violence as part of long-term socialization processes'.[91] Others have arrived at more negative conclusions as to a putative long-term shift towards a more civilized society. James Curtis, for example, makes analogies between war and sport, arguing that it is as ill-founded to see modern sports as more civilized because the violence in them is channelled and expressed in more prescribed ways as it is to see a war as somehow more 'civilized' if it is motivated by rational and utilitarian objectives (e.g. territory or raw materials) and not by affect (hatred and anger).[92]

Philosophers of sport have seen in Nietzsche's celebration of Greek culture the idea of sport as a sublimation of violence. The Greeks' recourse to competition in cultural and sporting contests prevented them, so the theory goes, from regressing into what Nietzsche calls 'the abyss of a horrible savagery of hatred and lust for destruction'.[93] Elfriede Jelinek, on the other hand, sees sport not as a guarantor of peace and civilization, but as a manifestation of this very 'lust for destruction'. The text of her play enacts this destruction in an ironic and estranged way. Her characters kick and beat their victims on the ground, they play football with torn-off shins attached to trainers, but, as the stage directions tell us, this is done in a random and very casual way. Violence is not presented in a dramatic, emotional or instinctive way, and Jelinek's staging of sport – indeed, her entire theatre aesthetics – mitigate against the idea of sport as itself a kind of dramatic form.[94] Nietzschean philosophers of sport speak of the seductive power of the sporting spectacle on the fan community, arguing that 'because of its Dionysian (affective) unity, the fan-community is an irresistible target of demagoguery'.[95] The demagogue figure of Jelinek's drama is the former leader of the FPÖ, Jörg Haider, whose political 'movement' is parodied and made into literal, athletic movement: 'Here, for example, you see right away the gentleman of this political movement, the one who's really moving us at the moment. He stands there on the street with his sweaty marathon headband, gasping like Christ on the Cross.'[96] In Jelinek's analysis, sport functions in a similar way to religion, as an institutionalized distraction from proper political debate and as another promoter of a false sense of (national) community. Of course, describing sport as a kind of modern-day religion is itself nothing new,[97] but ironizing the crucifixion as a sporting posture is certainly provocative.

Jelinek's commitment to the memory of the mass murders of the Holocaust is never far away in her new inscriptions of violence. Acts of violence become infused with moments and images of cultural memory such that the author does not need to spell out the associations with the crimes of National Socialism. The 'Opfer' ('Victim') of *Ein Sportstück* talks of how his gold fillings had been ripped from his mouth[98] and the Holocaust is described euphemistically as a kind of strict, demographic 'diet. Everything was at stake, about a hundred thousand . . . who kicked the bucket only so that we could start the game all over on another, happily refurbished, field'.[99] In the context of this preoccupation with the crimes of fascism, sport must be understood in Jelinek's writing as a kind of substitute form of community, a legacy of the sense of cultural belonging promoted by the National Socialists. For Matthias Konzett, Jelinek has shown that 'the illusion of collective identity, that figured so prominently in fascist ideology . . . has not been critically and fundamentally questioned. It has merely been displaced onto the consumer who lays claim to a distorted sense of community by obsessively substituting leisure for reflection, spectacle for history and amnesia or melancholy for mourning'. Sport is debunked by Jelinek as a new kind of 'spirituality', which 'feeds not only consumerism but actively contributes to the cultural alienation of those who do not or cannot share this spirit of leisure, health and fitness'.[100]

Sport, it is argued, has become a vicarious mode of living, replacing rational thought and substituting for a more reflective mode of being, or as one of Jelinek's 'victims' defines it: 'Sport is the organisation of human immaturity, amalgamated in seventy thousand people, and then poured out over a couple of million more back home.'[101] Thurnher is more emphatic about the link between sport, its hold over 'the masses' via television and the manipulation of mass society in fascism:

> What was formerly called fascism in the political world, the vision of obedient masses, can be found every year at the skiing event of the year, in Kitzbühel. 200 million watching their screens. The stylish sporty masses are bubbling over, the snow canons have done a great job. The Hahnenkamm mountain swells up in the background. Should we call it ski fascism? Let's say: feschism.[102]

The extreme thrill of risking death or injury can also transfer to the armchair sportsperson who experiences the sensation of escaping death when watching the downhill skier crash to her death. The butcher character of Jelinek's previous play *Stecken, Stab und Stangl* comments in an observation adapted from real-life Austrian sporting history when Ulli Maier's fatal skiing crash was captured on live TV that 'one of our most able downhill skiers . . . crashed into a post and snapped off her head. . . . Instinctively, we, the millions of television viewers at home, said goodbye to life for a moment, too'.[103]

Murder, as legitimized through war, is expressed as a sporting activity in the 'sports competition' of the Bosnian war, presided over by its UN 'referee'.[104] But in Jelinek's framework, murderous crimes of peacetime are also expressions of a sporting mentality or expressions of a protofascist mindset. The sense of belonging to a community that is promoted by sport finds its sinister expression in the xenophobia of the community that produces graffiti such as 'Roma, zurück nach Indien!' ('Roma – go back to India!'), Jelinek argues, and leads her to the provocative if at first sight baffling condemnation of racist murderers in *Stecken, Stab und Stangl* as 'sportsmen, perhaps even defensive or military sportsmen'.[105] By implication, Franzobel uses similar connotations by terming the persecuted Jews 'Anti-sportler' or 'Nicht-sportler' and has his politician figure, Pluderich Gautsch, state that 'we killed too few of them, too few, not all of them. It should be called parte caust, not holom. We failed. All anti-sportsmen. All of them should have been put up against the wall. We should have destroyed the anti-sports behaviour, stamped it out. They've got no reason to live, these weaklings'.[106]

Franzobel and the Olympian Spirit

The printed text of Franzobel's play features a number of comical photographic collages that juxtapose sporting images and war photos to reinforce the idea of sport as a surrogate war. There is a form of war taking place within the play as two of the characters try desperately to sabotage the games due to take place in the fictional region of Tamtam. Fian's choice is to invent a location for his political scenario; in Menasse's play, the Austrian action will be displaced to Denmark. The first of Franzobel's saboteurs is Joker Zenobia Gilchrist, a fairy or sylph character taken from the Austrian 'Zauberposse' tradition which gives the play its ironic genre description 'eine Kärntner Zauberposse samt Striptease' ('a Carinthian magical farce compete with striptease'). She has been sent to Tamtam to sabotage the games, but her magic cap has been stolen and she is forced to work as a *Gastarbeiter* in a bar. Pluderich Gautsch, the fascist politician, finds the name she assumes, Zenerl Pachutova, an affront, compared to his own 'rein deutscher Sportlername' ('pure German, sportsman's name'). Not only does *he* rape her, but the second would-be saboteur, 'Simon', the jilted husband of Fritzi, and 'anti-Sportler' (or, by implication, Jew), clearly would like to do something similar to the barwoman, but fails. This kind of sexual violence finds a parallel in Streeruwitz's revue *Sapporo*. Here, Nina Kossak comes to audition for the role of TV presenter. She disturbs the masculine equilibrium of the group and, it is implied, is gang raped by her co-presenter and the producers. Her name is changed to Nina *Deutsch* for her television recordings as cookery and Volksmusik show hostess. Despite these experiences, Nina stays with the group and the play ends with her reflecting on what has happened to her and on the nature of her relationship as a victim to the male perpetrators. Streeruwitz may be using these words to say something about the difficulty for women to break out of oppressive relationships, but Nina's reflections on 'damals' take on something of a broader, historical significance, as the stage directions have her turn to the audience and state: 'You know. The perpetrators. They will be the same. The perpetrators will always be the same.'[107]

Franzobel's play promotes one of the same lines of investigation as Jelinek's work in debunking the National Socialists' preoccupation with the healthy body as a precondition for the healthy mind. Franzobel has Fritzi's trainer, the sex-changed Tigerlili, humorously overturn this correlation. Tigerlili's unfortunate linguistic tick or Freudian slip bursts forth when she explains to the journalist Cola Edi how she and Fritzi cope with the pressure of representing the nation: 'A whole nation is watching you. You've got to learn to cope with this pressure first.... But we work with psychologists. Heil Hitler!'[108] The mutilation and degeneration of human bodies seen in *Sportstück* is also promised by the promoters of the Olympics in Franzobel's *Olympia*. What is offered is a kind of grotesque circus: 'Suppurating, splintered bones, torn tendons, careers coming to an end, unfulfilled dreams, aspirations, misery, sacrifice, suffering, and people faring a lot worse than this.'[109] One reviewer of the play suggests that: 'After you have seen *Olympia* you will only be able to sneer at the expression "a healthy mind in a healthy body".'[110] Thurnher points out that in 1999, the Carinthian

FPÖ was forced to withdraw a campaign poster that stated 'a healthy mind can only be found in a healthy body'.[111]

The idea of sport as consuming the body of the sportsperson – via injury, muscle degeneration and harmful drugs – is made literal in *Olympia* as the central sporting character, the skier Fritzi, mutilates her own body, cuts off her ears and consumes them. Finally, she crashes to her death. In Franzobel's 2002 novel *Lusthaus oder die Schule der Gemeinheit*, the character Manker muses on the effect of sport not on the body, but on the mind. Manker is annoyed by how much disruption the athletes' training causes. Once again, sport is something that substitutes for or prevents rational thought: 'If you thought about how many neighbours, local residents and family members were robbed of their peace and quiet by the senseless training going on. How many thoughts were made impossible by it . . . And an Olympic Games was the culmination of this cycle of thought-impediment . . . today's equivalent of a book burning. No wonder Hitler staged an Olympics.'[112]

Olympia does not deal with a date that has gone down in Austrian sporting history, but with one that failed to do so. The programme cover of the Klagenfurt Ensemble première contains a quotation from the *Kärntner Tageszeitung*, which posits the importance of the date of 19 June 1999, the day on which a decision would be made about which region would win the bid to hold the Winter Olympics. From the viewpoint of a Carinthian, it would be perhaps the most important date since 10 October 1920. It would signal 'a chance for Carinthia to become not the blank space that it was on the international map but an area full of glorious colour'.[113] The idea that, in the event of a successful bid by Carinthia to hold the Winter Olympics, this date might come to have the same importance for Carinthia as the plebiscite in 1920 that saw its population voting to join Austria and not the new Yugoslav state is clearly risible, and Franzobel's play is an extensive parody of these delusions of grandeur. The fascistic politician, Gautsch, is aware of the economic potential of the Tamtam games, but despairs at the poor forward planning and at the region's inability to market itself through its cuisine: 'In the Olympic village the crisis continues to spread. Wie had to fly in whores from Ikutien and Kalmükistan . . . and worst of all, not one single participant has yet to taste our famous Tamtam cheesy pasta.'[114] As the producer of the play's première production points out, the Carinthians' disbelief at the failure of their Olympic bid fits into the general Austrian pattern of would-be victim: 'In not having been given consideration as a candidate for the Winter Olympics of 2006 we see ourselves as victims of political corruption and criminal intrigue, and we do rather like to see ourselves in the role of the victim. At any rate, the topic is still a very current one.'[115] By choosing a saboteur from the fairy kingdom, Franzobel deliberately belittles the Opfermythos, and by including one who is styled as possibly coming from the Jewish community, he touches on a scapegoat of Austrian and German historical significance.

On the whole, Franzobel has a much greater personal interest in sport than the other dramatists considered here, and a genuine interest in football in particular, as his publication of essays, *Mundial: Gebete an den Fußballgott*, testifies and as the humorous biography on its cover suggests: 'Born during the early rounds of the 1967 championships, Franzobel featured in the schools regional league for Lenzing High School as centre-half ... He has not missed a single game played by the Austrian national team since 1970.'[116] The dustcover even offers a footballing explanation of the author's chosen nom de plume, Franzobel, 'whose pseudonym consists of the result of a football match, namely France against Belgium: Fran2:0Bel'.[117] In advocating an international sports boycott of Austria instead of the EU's rather ineffectual sanctions, Franzobel was only partly joking. He knew that this would have a far greater impact on Austria.[118] It was an action that was demanded by Israel's Sports Minister in 2000,[119] but not one that was widely acted upon. Belgium intervened in the leisure market, discouraging ski tourism to Austria. Had all protesting EU Member States taken similar action to discourage their citizens from taking holidays in Austria, this might have had a significant impact.[120]

Streeruwitz: Sporting Memory and Political Analogies

Sapporo. was billed as Marlene Streeruwitz's response to the new political situation of Austria in 2000 and promoted by the then Steirischer Herbst Director, Peter Oswald, as part of his campaign to repoliticize the Graz festival.[121] The title alludes to the location of the Winter Olympic Games of 1972, but it functions metonymically as signalling another sporting example of Austria's myth of victimization.[122] Schranz was barred from competing by the International Olympic Committee after he had chosen to ignore warnings about the use of his name and his photograph in advertising. The skier came back to Austria to a tumultuous welcome on the Heldenplatz, appearing with Chancellor Bruno Kreisky on the balcony to accept the empathy and shared indignation of thousands of his compatriots. In Streeruwitz's play, the ex-skier's future in part evokes the real-life career of Hansi Hinterseer, the skier who became a folk singer (Streeruwitz's character wears white, Hinterseer's trademark colour). An implied parallel is intended between the 'exclusion' of Jörg Haider from the new government and the exclusion of Schranz from the Olympic Games, both men thereby attaining a quasi-martyr status.

The bulk of the action of Streeruwitz's 'revue' is made up of the preparations for a new television programme, to be hosted by ex-skier Dominik Redler, the discussions between the group of male friends who are to produce the show and their audition of Nina Kossak for the role of co-presenter. Their radical new idea is to put together a cookery programme with folk music entertainment. Peter Gerlich writes of 'the empty ceremony of the presentation of Austrian folklore and gastronomic culture by the mass media',[123] and Streeruwitz ironizes these two strong mediators of the Austrian 'Heimat' by putting them together into one show and by having her new media types see themselves as 'die wahre Avantgarde' ('the true avant garde') who will put paid to all the 'Scheißdreck aus dem 18. Jahrhundert' ('eighteenth-century rubbish'). The FPÖ's democratic populism is clearly the focus of the dramatist's satire, and the producer of 'Kochen mit Musik' ('Cooking with Music'), Severin Hravath, explains that 'art was just know-it-alls sucking up to some money-bags or other. But now we have democracy'.[124] According to the 'Feschist' Hravath, the young and those who would like to think of themselves as such need 'guiding principles like fatherland, joy, peace, love, honour, loyalty'.[125] Much as Haider's cultural adviser, Andreas Mölzer, advocated the cultural celebration of such traditional values, Hravath advises the team to build these ideas into their lyrics. With the last concepts of 'Ehre' and 'Treue', Streeruwitz is pointing in the direction of the Waffen SS motto, 'Meine Ehre heißt Treue'. Hravath emphasizes the importance of a fit, good-looking body and professes the message of 'Feschismus': 'fescism: negotiation is always bodily. . . . For politics. I mean. A good-looking guy always comes across better'.[126] Some of the racist sentiments and ideas voiced within FPÖ circles also have echoes in *Sapporo*. Hravath's words echo the fear of 'Umvolkung' propounded by Andreas Mölzer, who warned against what he saw as the genetic undermining of Austria from the south and the east.[127] Hravath tells Pugatschnigg, his editor and producer: 'We won't say such things, but it's completely clear. Everyone longs for racial purity . . . for territory for peaceful natural expansion . . . People aren't stupid. They can sense it for themselves.'[128] Cookery is an ideal topos to expose the absurdity of expounding a 'pure' Austrian identity, and Pugatschnigg's suggestion of starting off the programmes with 'Serbische Bohnensuppe' ('Serbian bean soup') is an ironic nod to Austria's history as a 'Vielvölkerstaat'.

Very different use is made of folk songs in Franzobel and in Streeruwitz. Franzobel's highly provocative texts were set to well-known Carinthian melodies in the Klagenfurt production, such that the fairy (herself a 'Tschusch')[129] sings the following as she strips: 'The little town of Tamtam, stuffed full by God and built on cheesy noodles and Tamtam meat, should it now languish, bloated in filth? So we ask you, dear God, free us from the Gypsies and foreigners.'[130] Streeruwitz's Volkslieder are originals in text and in melody, but rather than using the shock tactics of Franzobel, they seek to send up the traditional Volkslied by both exaggerating the sugariness of the messages and by promoting a defiant, anti-foreigner patriotism. 'Wir bringen der Heimat herrliche Lieder' ('We Bring Songs of Glory for the Homeland') praises Austria to the hilt and rejects all things foreign: 'French – we don't speak it, Champagne – we don't press it. We have Veltliner wine . . . we have our own songs. We don't need anyone else.'[131] The effect of the songs during performance was stage-managed.

Members of the audience were given the free gift of a cigarette lighter (sponsored by banks and newspapers) on the way in to the auditorium and were encouraged by the dimming of the lights during one of the schmaltzy songs to sway with the flames aloft in the air (in 'Schunkel', or side-to-side swaying style). Streeruwitz explains this trickery as follows: 'Using this kind of gag quite superficially would be a way of making it clear from the stage that you'd been lured into a trap.'[132] There are parallels between the unthinking participation of the audience 'crowd' and that of the sporting participant in Jelinek's text. One of Jelinek's hooligans recites, as he brutalizes the victim on the ground: 'My repression mechanism has run out of power because group dynamic forces are exerting their power.'[133]

As Streeruwitz and Franzobel have shown, and as Haider's opportunistic contrasting of the fitness of his own party and the country's need to get fitter suggests, poor sporting results can be just as much a catalyst for identity formation as good results. In both Jelinek and Franzobel, however, there is a much deeper understanding and more sinister depiction of the pursuit of fitness and of the role of community as forged in and through sport. Sport might be thought to provide a legitimate and harmless outlet for the expression of national pride, a highly important and desirable asset for a relatively young nation for whom the patriotic blueprint could so easily be tainted by its National Socialist precursor. The dramatists and thinkers discussed here provide a timely warning against such a slippage and promote a more socially aware understanding of sport and of Austrian culture in general. The Austrian body politic is also what is at stake in the final play I look at here, Robert Menasse's *Das Paradies der Ungeliebten*.

Menasse: Something is Rotten in the State of Austria

Das Paradies der Ungeliebten (2006) has little to do with sport as a dramatic theme or subject matter. The sporting connection, alluded to in the very titles of the other three plays, features somewhat confusingly in the dramatis personae of Menasse's 2006 publication. Mostly made up of politicians and journalists, the characters are named after members of the winning Danish side from the UEFA Euro 1992 championships. Thus, Peter Schmeichel does not play the part of a goalkeeper, but is instead the leader of the right-wing populist party (here the LdU, though the acronym's similarity to the FPÖ's precursor, the VdU or Verband der Unabhängigen, seems obvious). Flemming Povlsen is not an attacking forward, but the incumbent Chancellor and leader of the Social Democrat party. The would-be Chancellor, installed in that office by the play's close, is Christian Christiansen, not a defending footballer, then, but the leader of the Christian Social Party and the serving Vice-Chancellor.

The location for the action is given as 'Dänemark', but even without seeing its indication in inverted commas, the false or at least flexible location is clear to anyone reading the play or seeing it staged. Commissioned by the then Director of the Burgtheater, Klaus Bachler, as a commemorative piece for the 2005 anniversary festivities in Austria, Menasse's play was apparently already conceived of in the 1990s. It offers up obvious satirical parallels to the political machinations of the time and to the Austrian political players of that period. However, unlike the scandal generated by Thomas Bernhard's 1988 commission for the *Burg*, *Heldenplatz*, the scandal surrounding Menasse's work played out almost entirely in the newspapers and public debates and not additionally as a byproduct of the play's reception. Indeed, the play was denied its planned Viennese première, and speculation abounded as to why this was the case.[134] Claus Peymann championed Bernhard's work in the mid 1980s, but Klaus Bachler did not stand by this debut play by the highly renowned novelist and political essayist Menasse, citing a number of reasons for his decision.[135] These included his appraisal of the play as being too cabarettistic and even of having lost its political bite, since it looked like it was referring to the political intrigue of pre-ÖVP-FPÖ coalition Austria some five years before. Ironically, then, the implication is that this is one resistant text that came too late to be deemed interesting enough to be staged.

Menasse acknowledges the correlations with existing politicians, referring, for example, to Christiansen as 'in inverted commas, the [Wolfgang] Schüssel character, in terms of his political role'.[136] Schmeichel's concern to dress well for every different occasion, his search for jokey phrases to belittle his opponents (often suggested by his Arabic man-servant Achmed) and, indeed, Menasse's textual allusions to real-life speeches or events all point to the figure of Schmeichel being based on Jörg Haider. Schmeichel's irate reaction in Scene 7 to newspaper articles reporting a politician's description of him as being 'außerhalb des Verfassungsbogens' ('outside constitutionally acceptable politics') might refer, for example, to events in 1995, when Andreas Khol, then leader of the ÖVP, accused Haider's FPÖ of wanting to rewrite the constitution and found a 'Third Republic' of Austria.[137] Schmeichel's description of his country as this 'Mißgeburt eines Staates' ('freak nation') is a reference to Haider's early 1990s pan-Germanic lamentation of Austria as an ideological monstrosity or miscarriage.[138] However, in the writer's own opinion, it is the figure of the actor-turned-Christian Socialist-politician Lars Olsen that caused the biggest difficulties for his patron Klaus Bachler. Menasse is at pains to point out that from a dramaturgical point of view, his play needed the device of this newcomer to politics and the inflated, theatrical language he adopts. Menasse recounts: 'The Burgtheater's Herr Bachler just said Morak, Morak, Morak incessantly and out of sheer fear of his financial sponsor – Herr Morak. I kept explaining to him that it was not [a representation of Franz] Morak, but he just replied "Morak".'[139]

It was a political turn of fate that allowed the Danish football team to participate in the European Championships in the first place. The Danes only gained their place at the last minute when the civil war broke out in Yugoslavia and the country withdrew from the competition. In Menasse's play, there is much more to these 'ostensibly untainted tropes of Denmark and soccer', as they become a fictional overlay for a play about the 'denunciation of political corruption'. Heide Schlipphacke notes that Menasse 'stages the engrained fascism of European politics in a nation generally considered innocent of the crimes of Nazism'.[140] At the time of writing the play, Denmark's right-wing nationalist party, the Danish People's Party, was only providing a minor supporting role in coalition and had yet to experience its considerable increase in electoral share.[141] However, Denmark has certainly since joined the list of European countries with highly successful populist or far-right political parties. Menasse was working on his material when staying in Amsterdam, and drawing parallels with some of the details around controversial Dutch far-right politician Pim Fortuyn is not difficult. Pim Fortuyn appointed a black immigrant from Cape Verde as his assistant, an action that was used to counter the allegations of anti-immigrationism and anti-multiculturalism levelled at Fortuyn's party. Menasse was reportedly thinking through the subject of how, when a particular individual is deemed to be dangerous or particularly influential in politics, the possibility (or in some quarters the deemed desirability) of an assassination can rear its head. In the play, the journalist Brian Laudrup hatches a plan to find an AIDS sufferer who is willing to kill Schmeichel, but the plan does not come to fruition. In real life, however, and to Menasse's great surprise, the assassination of Pim Fortuyn did take place, during the 2002 election campaign in the Netherlands.[142]

The violence that attaches to sport and politics in the other plays examined here (most particularly in Jelinek's *Ein Sportstück*) is mostly of a psychological nature in *Das Paradies der Ungeliebten*. One exception is reported through the dialogue, but does not feature in the action: a fellow journalist from Laudrup's left-wing paper has been beaten into a coma. The journalists feel sure that Schmeichel's lackeys are behind this brutal act (the journalist had been undertaking investigative research on their party), but they are realistic that the police will simply put it down to 'Rowdies'. After all, when the Jewish cemetery was desecrated two weeks before, the police investigation concluded that 'the incident was not politically motivated'.[143] The police are in the pay of Schmeichel's party, it is implied, via the figure of Møller Nielssen, the chief of police. Nielssen's dedication is so total that he goes so far as obeying Schmeichel's order to fire a revolver at his own head. The bullet is a blank, but Møller's devotion is dogged and total. Schmeichel mocks him by woofing quietly as Møller leaves the room. In Scene 7, Schmeichel has already recounted his own father's experiences of military training under Hitler, along with the doubtless apocryphal story that all the trainees were instructed to shoot dead the dog that they had been training and looking after individually. His father had told him: 'We all shot our dogs, giving back to them what we had learned through them: love, unconditional loyalty, obedience.'[144]

Recalling the spirit of his dead father is just one of several somewhat distorted references to Shakespeare's *Hamlet* that feature in Menasse's play. The topic of political intrigue, the setting in Denmark and the assassination plotting are all ironic allusions. Olsen even refers to himself as 'Polonius' as he falls out from behind the curtains where he and Møller have been stashed by Schmeichel in order that they overhear and subvert the hoped-for assassination attempt by Laudrup on Schmeichel. Unlike Shakespeare's Polonius, Olsen is not accidentally killed. In Menasse, the action takes on farcical, not tragic tones, the playwright even dubbing his approach 'Shakespeare played for ridicule'.[145] The play's enigmatic title could be interpreted as an oblique reference to Shakespeare. The 'paradise of the unloved' is the name of a snake farm that Chancellor Povlsen has seen during the travels he is undertaking in order to appear to be caring about the recent flood victims in the south of the country. Snake or serpent is a favoured term in Shakespeare for treachery, and Hamlet is told by the ghost in Act 1, scene 5, that 'the serpent that did sting thy father's life/ Now wears his crown'. Nobody loves snakes, Menasse's Chancellor points out, but the weary Chancellor is full of admiration for the snake farm paradise created by university scientists for these unloved creatures. The analogous unloved creatures are the country's political elite – these 'snakes' enjoy all kinds of privileges in their paradise of power and influence, but are almost universally despised. The author explains that 'the title "Paradise of the Unloved" is nothing more than the generic term for all the clichés or general ideas of life in the political elites'.[146]

Tempting though it is to see this ironic or feared paradise solely as an allegory for the 'unloved' state of Austria, as evidenced by the EU sanctions and the near-universal opprobrium directed at its politicians in and around 2000, Menasse's play clearly has a far wider reach. Menasse's footballing champions, the 'Europameister', stand – symbolically – for the political elite of Europe, and his play is clearly intended as a warning parable against the spread of far-right politics and of corrupt practices, such as the silencing of democratic media and the subjugation of police powers to political ends. The future does not look rosy at the close of *Das Paradies der Ungeliebten*. Claus Christiansen (the Christian Social) has got into power with Schmeichel's help, and the journalists are now having to clear out their offices. The neverending rain of the stage directions means that in the final scene, all of the play's characters are left building up defences with sandbags against the physical floods, but of course against the implied political deluge too. Lars Olsen's Shakespearean flourish distorts Hamlet's last words, and the character tells us not that 'the rest is silence', but that we should be silent: 'The rest is: be silent!'[147] Reflecting on a renewed turn to political topics in contemporary Austrian literature, Uwe Matuschka-Eisenstein feels that in the case of Robert Menasse, 'the writer's power as the spearhead of protest culture appears exceptional'.[148] Written with the intention of contributing to the 2005 Austrian commemorations of sixty years since the end of World

War II and fifty years since the signing of the Austrian State Treaty, Menasse's protest is clearly not a saccharine piece of nostalgia or retrospective wisdom, but a play with political bite and a lasting message.[149] It is regrettable that Menasse's *Paradies* has not been staged in Austria, receiving its première in Darmstadt to very little reception at home. Perhaps a play does not always need a theatre to effect a lasting contribution. Menasse, a great advocate for a post-nationalist Europe, continues to make his point in journalistic essays and in his creative writing. For one reviewer of his *Paradies*, the point Menasse made was a very sore one indeed. Menasse had pointed towards a generalized tendency towards populism and opportunism in Europe, making Denmark not so much an allegory of Austria, but of a generalized European condition: 'Translators and dramaturgs from different countries saw in the play the description of their own respective country's circumstances, for example the Berlusconi regime in Italy or the right-wing movements in Germany. These reactions show that Robert Menasse had hit a sore point of many European democracies.'[150]

Conclusion: Locating Theatrical Protest

The playwrights discussed here set their action in a variety of different physical and geographical locations, but Austria is clearly the political locus or starting point of the protest expressed in their plays. Jelinek eschewed the theatre as institution for the first airing of her *Das Lebewohl* material. The author had a political statement to make by refusing to engage with state-sponsored cultural institutions. Menasse's *Paradies* material was denied the Austrian staging for which it was commissioned. Franzobel's *Olympia* and Streeruwitz's *Sapporo*. only made it onto regional Austrian stages in the first year of protests against the ÖVP-FPÖ coalition government. Collections of Fian's dramolets have been presented together on stage, but they have mostly 'played' on the pages of Austria's newspapers and in the heads of their readers. Arguably, it is in the social reverberations around these texts – the press coverage, the arguments about whether or where they should be produced – that their real value as cultural and intellectual catalysts is most effective. Reading the plays also gives a new perspective on political and social developments as well as providing lasting enjoyment to those who read them *after* the political times in which they are set, as indeed we do here.

Theatres themselves had a not insignificant 'role' to play in the physical business of making anti-coalition protests heard and seen. As institutions, the theatres were set to suffer from the financial cuts in the arts sector, but their stages offered up protest in a number of ways. First and foremost, the theatres were venues for protest discussions, with artists, intellectuals and arts managers holding debates at the Burgtheater, for example. Demonstrators broke into the

Burgtheater during a production to stage their own politico-artistic protest.[151] Students from the University of Applied Art brought with them a large banner that they affixed to the roof of the Burgtheater. It said: 'Die Kunst der Stunde ist Widerstand' (see also Chapter 4). In 2000, resistance was becoming a kind of performance art form in itself. The actionist theatre group Volxtheater-Karawane became nomadic – as the name suggests – and toured its protest events and political actions around Austria and to larger political rallies such as the G8 summit in Genoa. The physical, public arena was most definitely a space for political performance events for groups such as these that really needed no actual theatre institutions to act in. Moreover, as activist-performer and academic Gini Müller explains, it was the very public nature of the streets as performance location that could make accidental spectators into like-minded, fellow players or possibly into opponents or antagonists ('zufällige MitspielerInnen, gegebenenfalls GegenspielerInnen').[152]

Aware of the limited potential of the theatre to change its audience members' viewpoints, the Volkstheater director Emmy Werner nevertheless felt it was vital to put on an extensive programme of readings, discussions and critical productions, and to work hard to open the eyes of even just a few ticket holders. The series of events staged under the title 'Unruhiges Österreich' ('Troubled Austria') was for Werner not so much a protest against the inauguration of the coalition government, but rather an expression of protest against a change in the Zeitgeist and in the social policies of the day. The theatre quickly introduced resistant performances and readings of existing plays whose message or subject matter would be recognized as anti-regime. Thus, Carl Merz and Helmut Qualtinger's classic postwar monologue, *Der Herr Karl* (1961), was read at the theatre in 2000, as was Elias Canetti's essay 'Hitler nach Speer' (1971). The voice of the immigrant newspaper-seller from Robert Schneider's monologue *Dreck* (1993) was also to be heard again as part of the series as well as excerpts from work by Ingeborg Bachmann, Thomas Bernhard and Elfriede Jelinek.[153]

There is a handful of other published and performed plays that have been motivated by the political events in Austria 2000. In my view, this would include a new commission such as Peter Turrini's *Ich liebe dieses Land* (2001), even though it is set in Berlin and also premièred there. Another example would be Gerd Jonke's new version of Aristophanes' *Die Vögel* (2000). The première of Jonke's play was in Klagenfurt, Carinthia, very much the heartland of the FPÖ. Under the directorship of Ernst Binder, the play received mostly negative reactions, although the playwright denied that Jörg Haider had been a model for his lampooning.[154] The play was picked up again in 2002 by the Viennese Volkstheater, directed this time by Georg Staudacher. The political satire was deemed rather too obvious by most of the reviewers. Jonke's version of Aristophanes' avian utopian city 'Cloud Cuckoo Land' was called 'Himmelblau' ('Sky Blue') and was, according to Hans Haider from *Die Presse*, an 'FPÖ-Terrorstaat'.[155]

The majority of the performed acts of protest against the ÖVP-FPÖ coalition were not, however, fully fledged, staged works of dramatic writing; rather, they took the form of actions, installations and performance art pieces that could be enacted in open, public spaces. Chapter 2 probes some of the better-known examples of these performances, whereas this chapter has analysed a small corpus of published stage plays whose subjects or settings have drawn on sporting themes or analogies. This provides an additional point of comparison between the playwrights' approaches. A highly fertile topos around the period of investigation, sport, fitness and the body beautiful become mobilized as part of the virility cult and self-representation of a largely younger generation of Austrian politicians. Of course, sport continues to be manipulated off the pitch or outside of the stadium, and its politicization is not a phenomenon that is by any means restricted to Austria or indeed to the late twentieth and early twenty-first century. When the current leader of the FPÖ, H.C. Strache, mentioned in a 2015 TV interview that he had played a bit of football with one of the Viennese clubs as a lad, the Wiener Sportklub (WSK) chose to distance itself immediately. WSK tweeted a pre-emptive photo reminder that its football kit bore the 'Refugees Welcome' logo and warned that it did not want to be appropriated by the FPÖ or associated with its politics.[156] At that point, nobody could have foreseen that only a little over two years later, the country itself would be more than just *associated* with the FPÖ's politics and that H.C. Strache would be the Vice-Chancellor (Deputy Prime Minister) in another ÖVP-FPÖ coalition. The concluding pages of this book identify some of the main political factors leading to this outcome and ask whether the present political situation in Austria is likely to spawn yet more cultural protest.

Notes

1. An extract from the cabaret 'Zwei echte Österreicher' is included in Maurer and Scheuba, 'Widerstand', 247–49. In it, a woman proposes a toast to Jörg Haider because her marriage has been rejuvenated by the couple's activities on resistance marches. 'Dorfers Donnerstalk' was a regular satirical series on ORF television from January 2004 and is available on DVD.
2. Elfriede Jelinek, 'Das Lebewohl (Les Adieux)', in *Das Lebewohl, 3 kl. Dramen* (Berlin: Berlin Verlag, 2000), 7–35, first published in *Theater heute* 5 (2000), 36–41. *Das Lebewohl* was first performed on 22 June 2000 by the actor Martin Wuttke as part of the regular Thursday demonstrations in Vienna against the new government and under the auspices of the Wiener Festwochen (Vienna Festival). The play had its stage prèmiere under Ulrike Ottinger's direction at the Berliner Ensemble later in 2000.
3. An earlier version of my discussion of these three plays was published as Allyson Fiddler, 'Sport and National Identity in the "New" Austria: Sports Plays by Jelinek, Franzobel and Streeruwitz', in Janet Stewart and Simon Ward (eds), *Blueprints for*

No-Man's Land: Connections in Contemporary Austrian Culture (Oxford: Peter Lang, 2005), 111–30.
4. Peter Turrini, *Ich liebe dieses Land: Stück und Materialien* (Frankfurt am Main: Suhrkamp, 2001). For discussion of the play, see also Fiddler, 'Shifting Boundaries', 265–89.
5. See the report by the European Institute for Comparative Cultural Research (ERICarts): Veronika Ratzenböck, Franz-Otto Hofecker and Anja Lungstraß, 'Austria', in *Compendium of Cultural Policies and Trends in Europe*, 9th edn (2008). Retrieved 6 May 2018 from www.culturalpolicies.net/web/austria.php?aid=1.
6. Peter Turrini, 'Für Österreich', *Freitag*, 18 February 2000. Retrieved 6 May 2018 from https://www.freitag.de/autoren/der-freitag/fur-osterreich.
7. '[D]as Linzer Landestheater sollte sich nicht zu schade sein, Haider mit einer Offerte aus dem Landeshauptmannamt zu locken: ein kleiner Schritt für das Ensemble, ein großer Schritt für die Menschheit.' Rayk Wieland, 'Die Welt als Wille zur Vorstellung', in Hermann L. Gremliza (ed.), *Braunbuch Österreich. Ein Nazi kommt selten allein* (Hamburg: Konkret, 2000), 151–58, at 152.
8. 'Alle Schauspieler sind Lügner ... wie sollen sie sonst ständig ein anderer sein? Schauspieler geben ihrem Gegenüber immer das Gefühl der Übereinstimmung. Jeder, der mit Haider redet, hat nachher das Gefühl, zutiefst von ihm verstanden zu werden. Es ist Theater, was da abläuft.' Peter Turrini, 'Ist Jörg Haider ein guter Schauspieler?', *Tagesspiegel*, 29 February 2000. Retrieved 6 May 2018 from http://www.tagesspiegel.de/kultur/ist-joerg-haider-ein-guter-schauspieler-herr-turrini/126264.html.
9. All published with Droschl: *Schratt* (Graz: Droschl, 1992), *Was bisher geschah. Dramolette 1* (1994), *Was seither geschah. Dramolette 2* (1998), *Alarm. Dramolette 3* (2002) and *Bohrende Fragen. Dramolette 4* (2007). The term 'dramolet' is adopted here to reflect Fian's own preference and because the English term 'short drama' does not adequately suggest the very short length of Fian's pieces.
10. See Jacques Lajarrige, 'Antonio Fian als Satiriker der österreichischen Literaturszene', in Jeanne Benay and Gerald Sticg (eds), *Österreich (1945–2000): Das Land der Satire* (Berne: Peter Lang, 2002), 241–67.
11. Sandy Petrey, *Speech Acts and Literary Theory* (New York: Routledge, 1990), 72.
12. Konstanze Fliedl, 'A Field Guide to Names in Literature: Notes on Austrian Onomastics', *Austrian Studies* 15(1) (2007), 155–68, at 164.
13. *Jörg Haider Works on His Ash Wednesday Speech*. Fian, *Alarm*, 64–67.
14. '[E]r hat immer sorgfältig versucht, nie diesen Fehler zu machen.' Fian, *Alarm*, 64.
15. 'Chor: Musikante Sinti Roma / Jud Zigeuner / alle schuld' and '[z]u allgemein zu/ angreifbar zu wenig / Sorgfalt ... Lueger nein / Ich anders / Sorgfalt ich und / keine Fehler".' Fian, *Alarm*, 65 and 64. Karl Lueger was the openly anti-Semitic Mayor of Vienna from 1897 to 1910.
16. Kickl has been appointed as Interior Minister (or Home Secretary) under the latest ÖVP-FPÖ coalition (December 2017) and is already generating controversy. See Jon Stone, 'Austria's Far-Right Interior Minister Sparks Outrage after Saying Migrants Should Be "Concentrated"', *The Independent*, 15 January 2018. Retrieved 6 May 2018 from https://www.independent.co.uk/news/world/europe/austria-far-right-fpo-migrants-concentrated-herbert-kickl-a8159541.html.
17. 'Was [Fians] Dramolette betrifft, erlauben sie durch den sie grundierenden Dialogismus eine aussagestarke 'mise en abyme' ironisierender Redeweisen, wodurch die Betroffenen gleichsam vor Gericht erscheinen.' Lajarrige, 'Antonio Fian als Satiriker', 266.

18. Erhard Busek (ÖVP) was Vice-Chancellor (or Deputy Prime Minister) of Austria and ÖVP Chairman from 1991 to 1995.
19. Antonio Fian, *Der Einbruch des Akrostichons in die österreichische politische Kultur. Ein Ausblick*, in Fian, *Was bisher geschah*, 116–17.
20. Fian's own public reading of this can be listened to on the CD *Café Promenade* (Graz: Droschl, 2004).
21. On Fian's stage directions, see Franz Haas, 'Die Komik und die Kürze in den Texten von Antonio Fian', in Wendelin Schmidt-Dengler, Johann Sonnleitner and Klaus Zeyringer (eds), *Komik in der österreichischen Literatur* (Berlin: Erich Schmidt, 1996), 300–8, at 304.
22. 'Denn Armut ist ein großer Glanz aus innen.' Fian, 'Rilke bei Schüssel', in *Bohrende Fragen*, 120–22, at 121. The English translation of Rilke is Susan Ranson's, from Ben Hutchinson and Susan Ranson (eds), *Rainer Maria Rilke's The Book of Hours: A New Translation with Commentary* (New York: Camden House, 2008).
23. '[D]ie Armut, Rilke, Armut immer Femininum!' Fian, 'Rilke bei Schüssel', in *Bohrende Fragen*, 121.
24. 'Und mit wem soll man diskutieren? . . . Ob das P.P. von "umvolken" "umgevolkt" heißt oder "umvolkt"?' In Fian, *Bohrende Fragen*, 68–70, at 68.
25. See 'Umvolkung' in Panagl, Gerlich et al., *Wörterbuch der politischen Sprache in Österreich*, 433–34. The term was used in Nazi propaganda. My translation is an approximation.
26. 'Der BZÖ-Chef sei "gestorben wie James Dean", ein "Robin Hood", das "größte politische Genie seit Bruno Kreisky".' Thomas Mayer, 'Haider: Kein James Dean', *Der Standard*, 13 October 2008.
27. See Ottomeyer, *Die Haider-Show*, 10–18.
28. See 'Haider watch': www.smoc.net/haiderwatch. Walter Ötsch analyses Haider's political style in *Haider Light: Handbuch für Demagogie* (Vienna: Czernin, 2002).
29. My discussion of *Das Lebewohl* has previously appeared as part of Allyson Fiddler, 'Staging Jörg Haider: Protest and Resignation in Elfriede Jelinek's *Das Lebewohl* and Other Recent Texts for the Theatre', *Modern Language Review* 97(2) (2002), 353–64.
30. See the press reaction to Haider's resignation – for example, Isabelle Daniel, 'Der lange Marsch nach Wien', *News*, 3 March 2000.
31. See Elfriede Jelinek, 'Meine Art des Protests', *Der Standard*, 7 February 2000, 27.
32. Jelinek's play *Burgtheater* satirizes the Wessely-Hörbiger family of actors and takes issue with their account of their own activities during the Third Reich. See Allyson Fiddler, 'Demythologising the Austrian "Heimat": Elfriede Jelinek as "Nestbeschmutzer"', in Moray McGowan and Ricarda Schmidt (eds), *From High Priests to Desecrators: Contemporary Austrian Literature* (Sheffield: Sheffield Academic Press, 1993), 25–44. The monologue spoken by the 'dead' actress in 'Erlkönigin' (the first part of the *Macht nichts* trilogy) is a continuation of Jelinek's dramatization of Paula Wessely, who died in May 2000.
33. 'Ich kann auch nicht eine Paula Wessely dafür kritisieren, dass sie ein System, das abzulehnen ist, unterstützt und sogar trägt und dann dasselbe machen, wobei ich natürlich das Dritte Reich nicht mit dem vergleichen will, was wir jetzt haben. Ich will damit auf keinen Fall die Kolleginnen und Kollegen unter Druck setzen, das Gleiche zu machen, es ist eben meine persönliche Art des Protests. Die Hochkultur in den performing arts hat natürlich immer auch Repräsentationsfunktion. Indem sie kritische Hochkultur zulassen, gibt man den Machthabern die Chance, sich eine Toleranz zuzuschreiben, die

sie andernorts vermissen lassen.' See Pia Janke, interview with Elfriede Jelinek, 'Tragödie und Farce in einem', *Der Standard*, 17 June 2000, supplement magazine, 1. Although Jelinek is careful here to uncouple historical fascism from contemporary nationalist movements, in her creative writing she does make productive and ironic analogies between the two.

34. 'On ne peut s'empêcher de songer aux ambitions du FPÖ et de son leader ultranationaliste Jörg Haider ou aux slogans de ce dernier contre les immigrés et les minorités slovènes de Carinthie.' Jacques Lajarrige, 'Formation et appropriation d'un mythe: le cannibalisme et la littérature autrichienne de Nestroy à Jelinek', *Cahiers d'Etudes Germaniques* 26 (1994), 151–62, at 159.
35. Jelinek, *Das Lebewohl*, 9, emphasis added.
36. Jörg Haider, 'Glücksgefühl nach bangen Stunden', *News*, 8 March 2000. Jelinek mentions Walter Jens' translation of Aeschylus and the Austrian *News* magazine in her acknowledgements. See *Aeschylus: Die Orestie*, trans. Walter Jens (Munich: dtv, 1981).
37. '[U]nd wenn wir jemand gekränkt haben, wir bedauern, aber haben wir nicht Recht? . . . Wir wagten, die Tat, die wir ersannen, auch auszuführen.' Jelinek, *Das Lebewohl*, 13–14.
38. John Chioles, 'The Oresteia and the Avant-Garde: Three Decades of Discourse', *Performing Arts Journal* 45 (1993), 1–28.
39. See Janke, 'Tragödie und Farce in einem'. This view of Haider is voiced in biographical writing on Haider; see, for example, Christa Zöchling, *Haider: Licht und Schatten einer Karriere* (Vienna: Molden, 1999).
40. Melanie A. Sully, *The Haider Phenomenon* (New York: Columbia University Press, 1997), 135.
41. '[Z]u grunde richtet mich jetzt dein Wort, Vater! Ich räche dich, dem Morgenwind vergleichbar. Und jetzt weht auch schon ein andrer Wind. Spürst dus, Vater, wie er weht?' Jelinek, *Das Lebewohl*, 30.
42. 'Und ich habe selber dabei mitgemacht, als mein Papa umgebracht worden ist . . . Papi. Du sollst jetzt bitte auftreten und mir einen Vorwurf Machen.' Jelinek, *Ein Sportstück*, 184–85. English translations are from Elfriede Jelinek, *Sports Play*, trans. Penny Black with translation assistance and a foreword by Karen Jürs-Munby (London: Oberon, 2012). Here at 157–58.
43. Euripides, *Orestes and Other Plays* (Harmondsworth: Penguin, 1972). For an account of the different treatment of Orestes by Euripides, see John R. Porter, 'Madness and Σγνεςις in *Orestes*', in John R. Porter, *Studies in Euripides' Orestes* (Leiden: Brill, 1994), 298–313.
44. 'Rache für den Vater! Rache! Tötet das Land, tötet die Mutter.' Jelinek, *Das Lebewohl*, 26.
45. 'Er hat die Unzucht im Hause ertragen nicht lang, doch nun verlaß ich das Haus, ich geh, die Buhlschaft, sie bleibt ihm. Riess-Passer, Frau Dr. Riess für mich. Mutter! Wir sind Zeugen gewesen, wie die Frauenlist des Landes meinen Vater verriet, das Land: eine Frau. Kleine dicke Frau. Kleine dicke Frau, reich und böse. Das Land besiegt: eine Frau. Ich niemals besiegt: von einem Mann.' Jelinek, *Das Lebewohl*, 27.
46. Gilbert Murray, 'Hamlet and Orestes: A Study in Traditional Types', in Robert A. Segal (ed.), *Ritual and Myth: Robertson Smith, Frazer, Hooke, and Harrison* (New York: Garland, 1996), 309–33, at 317.
47. 'Schöner Knabe, schau du einmal her, wie souverän dies Weib in der Pressekonferenz agiert! Diese Frau! Hätt ich gar nicht von ihr gedacht. Ist es nicht einfach super, wie

sie spricht? Umgarnt mit dem Netz der List schon das Volk, sie spricht, sie spricht, vollkommen frei spricht sie, doch was sie sagt? Es ist egal. Nicht ist es, was Apoll befahl ... Es ist von mir zwar, doch es ist nichts. Wenn ich es sage, ist es anders. Wenn sie es sagt, ist es nichts.' Jelinek, *Das Lebewohl*, 20.

48. See Simon Goldhill, 'The Influence of the *Oresteia*', in *Aeschylus: The Oresteia* (Cambridge: Cambridge University Press, 1992), 93–99.
49. Morag Schiach, *Hélène Cixous: A Politics of Writing* (London: Routledge, 1991), 4.
50. 'Das Schwache, Fremde, das, was "nicht zu uns gehört", wird ausgegrenzt oder vertrieben. Nicht zufällig hat Haider ja einen ehemaligen Olympia-Abfahrtssieger [Patrick Ortlieb] ins Parlament geholt. Er arbeitet, wie alle faschistoiden Bewegungen, mit dem ästhetischen Körperkult, mit dem homoerotischen Männerbund, der sich im Sport manifestiert, es ist sozusagen der erlaubte sexuelle Akt mit dem braungebrannten jungen ... "Führer", der huldvoll seine Gunst gewährt.' Volker Oesterreich, 'Ironie unter der Straßenwalze', interview with Elfriede Jelinek, *Berliner Morgenpost*, 27 February 2000. The homophile appeal is arguably also present in Euripides' *Orestes*, where the bond between Pylades and Orestes is foregrounded.
51. '[E]ure Tränen sinds, ihr Knaben' and 'Mitarbeiter, Knaben, Kameraden.' Jelinek, *Das Lebewohl*, 17 and 18.
52. 'Ich *mußte miterleben, wie meine Familie*, meine Familie, die Schönen, die Guten, Gescheiten, die vor Blondheit Strotzenden, von brutal Gewalttätigen *in Mitleidenschaft gezogen* wurde. Doch meine Leidenschaft gilt viel mehr noch euch, Burschen, ihr Herrlichen, Guten.' Jelinek, *Das Lebewohl*, 16–17; italics indicate phrases, words or word roots taken from Haider's own text.
53. '[M]ich Götterliebling' and 'der liebe Herr bin ich.' Jelinek, *Das Lebewohl*, 16 and 33.
54. Haider, 'Glücksgefühl'.
55. 'Denn hätte ich dabei *in die Runde ge*blickt und *die Tränen* in den Augen vieler *meine*r langjährigen *Mit*streiter gesehen, *wer weiß, ob ich nicht schwach geworden wäre* ... Vizekanzlerin Susanne Riess-Passer [agierte] ganz souverän, und ich hatte Freude, ihr zu assistieren. Ich tat es umso lieber, weil ich wusste, wie sehr sie mir eigentlich *Vorwürfe* wegen meiner Entscheidung machen wollte, aber ihre *Disziplin* und ihr *Intellekt akzeptierten das nicht Verhinderbare* ... Wir beschlossen, noch bei Susanne Riess-Passer *privat zusammen*zukommen. *Einige meiner Getreuen* waren mit dabei.' Haider, 'Glücksgefühl'.
56. 'Böhmdorfer aus dem Bett. Susanne machte sich Sorgen wegen des Justizministers. Auch ich habe mit Michael Krüger gesprochen, dessen Gesundheitszustand ihn in den nächsten Wochen ans Bett fesseln wird.' Haider, 'Glücksgefühl'. The sexual connotations here are deliberate and point to some sexual antics that came to light in journalistic conversations. For intimations of the details, see, for example, http://www.raketa.at/vom-schnackseln-und-anpinkeln.
57. 'Verehren soll jeder Vater und Mutter, doch mehr den Vater.' Jelinek, *Das Lebewohl*, 13.
58. 'Die Mutter, das Land, den Herd, das verehren wir und schützen wir, wir sind vom besten Zuschnitt.' Jelinek, *Das Lebewohl*, 29.
59. The two other short dramas in Jelinek's collection *Das Lebewohl, 3 kl. Dramen* are entitled *Das Schweigen* and *Der Tod und das Mädchen II*, and together the collection may be seen as paralleling the three movements from the Beethoven sonata, to which Jelinek alludes in her subtitle. The movements of Beethoven's Sonata in E flat major, Op. 81a, 'Les Adieux', are entitled 'Das Lebewohl (Les Adieux)', 'Abwesenheit (L'Absence)' and

'Das Wiedersehen (Le Retour)'. The sonata was dedicated to Archduke Rudolph, who in 1809 went into exile to escape the siege on Vienna by the French. The sleeping princess of Jelinek's final drama is to be read as Austria and the prince who awakens her as Jörg Haider.

60. 'Hat er [Jörg Haider] sich nicht seit eh und je als Erlöser gesehen?' Franz Schuh, 'Unglückliches Österreich: eine Innenansicht', in Isolde Charim and Doron Rabinovici (eds), *Österreich: Berichte aus Quarantanien* (Frankfurt am Main: Suhrkamp, 2000), 19–32, at 27.
61. '*Drei linke Journalisten* ließen sich so über mich aus, dass der *Hass* nur *triefend* aus dem TV-Gerät herausquoll. Damit hatten sie nicht gerechnet. Das *Objekt ihrer hasserfüllten Begierde war ihnen abhanden gekommen*. Worin soll da noch ihr journalistischer Lebenssinn bestehen? An niemandem mehr würden sie linksideologischen Hass und menschliche Niedertracht . . . so gezielt ausleben können wie an mir.' Haider, 'Glücksgefühl'; italics indicate phrases, words or word roots subsequently used in *Das Lebewohl* by Jelinek.
62. '*Als Landeshauptmann bin ich dabei und kann mithelfen, ein gutes Team zu schaffen*, brennen laß ich jetzt schon das Scheit! Es brennt ja, seit ich den Schoß verließ der Mutter.' Jelinek, *Das Lebewohl*, 25–26.
63. '*Meine Familie hat mir ermutigende SMS übers Handy geschickt*, die Blonden, Guten, Druck und Zweifel: weg! Fort! Freß ich mein Neugebornes, die Bewegung jetzt? Oder später? Nein, sie ist stark. Keine Bewegung mehr, keine ohne mich.' Jelinek, *Das Lebewohl*, 18.
64. 'Laß es dir sagen, das Bild bleibt, die Zeit geht, doch wir sind im Bilde, schon lange, schon immer. Die Zeit wird auch noch unsere werden, bitte warten Sie!' Jelinek, *Das Lebewohl*, 22–23. *Zeit im Bild* is the main state TV news programme.
65. '*Wir sind aus einem anderen Holz*. Der Kanzler *schien beruhigt*, als ich dies sagte. Er schlug an meinen Kopf: ein andres Holz.' Jelinek, *Das Lebewohl*, 28.
66. Jelinek, *Das Lebewohl*, 33–34.
67. '[W]ir haben gefochten, und jetzt dürfen wir feiern den Sieg.' Jelinek, *Das Lebewohl*, 12.
68. 'Keine Bewegung mehr, keine ohne mich.' Jelinek, *Das Lebewohl*, 18.
69. Jelinek, *Das Lebewohl*, 34–35.
70. Excerpts from the street performance by Martin Wuttke can be heard on Jelinek's own website. Retrieved 6 May 2018 from http://www.elfriedejelinek.com under 'Das Lebewohl'. For the playwright's demands of actors and her understanding of the theatre, see, for example, Elfriede Jelinek, 'Ich möchte seicht sein', in Christa Gürtler (ed.), *Gegen den schönen Schein: Texte zu Elfriede Jelinek* (Frankfurt am Main: Verlag Neue Kritik, 1990), 157–61; or Elfriede Jelinek, 'Sinn egal: Körper zwecklos', in *Stecken, Stab und Stangl, Raststätte, Wolken. Heim. Neue Theaterstücke* (Reinbek: Rowohlt, 1997), 7–14.
71. 'Es ist vielleicht ein hochtrabender Ausdruck, zu pathetisch, aber es ist etwas geschehen, dass niemand von uns für möglich gehalten hätte. Dass gerade in einem der Täterländer die extreme Rechte wieder an die Macht kommt.' Jelinek, quoted in Janke, 'Tragödie und Farce in einem'. Jelinek calls the electoral victory of the far right 'vielleicht das Ende des Politischen überhaupt . . . das Politische, das darin besteht, daß Menschen sich über etwas verständigen, einander zuhören, Vorschläge einbringen, diskutieren, und dann wird abgestimmt' ('perhaps the end of political life *tout court* . . . political life consisting of people coming to an agreement on something, listening to each other, offering

suggestions, discussing, and then coming to a vote'); see Jelinek, 'Moment! Aufnahme! 5. 10. 99', in Charim and Rabinovici, *Österreich: Berichte aus Quarantanien*, 100–9, at 105.
72. Barbara Kosta, 'Elfriede Jelinek's *Das Lebewohl [The Farewell]*: An Austrian Tragedy', in Matthias Konzett and Margarete Lamb-Faffelberger (eds), *Elfriede Jelinek: Writing Woman, Nation and Identity: A Critical Anthology* (Madison, NJ: Fairleigh Dickinson University Press, 2007), 157–73, at 167.
73. Goldhill, *Aeschylus: The Oresteia*, 21.
74. 'Ich muss [meine Sprache] ihnen entziehen, um sie erhalten zu können. Das klingt sicher pathetisch, aber: Da ich also nicht gehen kann, können wenigstens meine Stücke weggehen, um woanders (hoffentlich) irgendwie zu wirken.' Jelinek, 'Meine Art des Protests'.
75. Teresa Kovacs, 'Sanktion und Selbstzensur: Elfriede Jelineks Aufführungsverbote für Österreich'. Retrieved 6 May 2018 from https://jelinektabu.univie.ac.at/sanktion/zensur/teresa-kovacs/#_ednref58.
76. Elfriede Jelinek, *Ein Sportstück* (Reinbek: Rowohlt, 1998). Franzobel, *Olympia. Eine Kärntner Zauberposse samt Striptease* in Franzobel's collection of two plays, *Volksoper Olympia* (Weitra: Bibliothek der Provinz, 2000). Marlene Streeruwitz, *Sapporo.*, in Barbara Engelhardt, Theres Hönigk and Bettina Masuch (eds), *TheaterFrauenTheater* (Berlin: Theater der Zeit, 2002), 156–81. Robert Menasse, *Das Paradies der Ungeliebten: Ein Schauspiel* (Frankfurt am Main: Suhrkamp, 2006).
77. See Benedict Anderson, *Imagined Communities: Reflections on the Origin and Spread of Nationalism*, revised edn (London: Verso, 2000), 6.
78. Ruth Wodak et al., *The Discursive Construction of National Identity* (Edinburgh: Edinburgh University Press, 1999), 4.
79. 'Wenn man vom nostalgischen Selbstverständnis einer "Kulturnation Österreich", das von Neujahrskonzert, Salzburger Festspielen, Burgtheater und Staatsoper bestimmt wird, absieht, besteht in Österreich interessanterweise die weitverbreitete Auffassung, daß auch der Skilauf typisch österreichisches Kulturgut sei. . . . Österreich ist offenbar – "kulturell" betrachtet – eine Ski-Nation.' Herbert Hofreither, '"Kulturnation" Österreich: Anmerkungen zu Image, Identität, Sport, Film und Literatur', *Modern Austrian Literature* 32 (1999), 19–39, at 21. Peter Gerlich presents public opinion poll statistics that demonstrate the importance of music and sports as factors in promoting national identification. See Peter Gerlich, 'National Consciousness and National Identity: A Contribution to the Political Culture of the Austrian Party System', in Anton Pelinka and Fritz Plasser (eds), *The Austrian Party System* (Boulder: Westview Press, 1989), 223–58, at 246–48.
80. 'Sport wird in diesem Land wesentlich zur Verbreitung von Nationalismen gebraucht, Sport dominiert das Fernsehprogramm, im Sport wird nicht nur so getan, als wäre alles normal, im Sport wird wie nebenbei auch die neue Regierung gefeiert. Sport dient wesentlich zur Festigung von Regierungen – auch Hitler durfte noch 1936 eine Olympiade veranstalten!' Franzobel, 'Chronologie der laufenden Scheiße', in Charim and Rabinovici (eds), *Österreich: Berichte aus Quarantanien*, 59–71, at 70–71.
81. Rainer Nikowitz, 'Lauter Sieger', *Profil* 6 (2001) asks: 'Ganz Österreich siegt und verliert mit seinen Skihelden. Aber ist unser Pisten-Patriotismus am Ende ein bisschen übertrieben?' ('The whole of Austria wins and loses alongside its skiing heroes. But isn't our piste patriotism a bit excessive?')

82. '[D]as wachsende Bewusstsein der Zugehörigkeit zum Staate Österreich in der Vermittlung durch große Sportereignisse.' Roman Horak, 'Philharmoniker und Älpler. Wie Sport beim "inneren Staatsbildungsprozess" hilft', *Der Standard*, 9 February 2002.
83. '[S]o einig sind "wir", wenn es um den Erfolg der Schination geht: alle Gegensätze sind aufgehoben.' Anton Pelinka, 'Sport definiert "uns". Zum patriotischen Hochgefühl der Schination Österreich', *Profil* 6 (2001).
84. 'Übersteigerter Patriotismus ist allerdings, so viel sei zur Ehrenrettung Österreichs gesagt, typisch für junge Nationalstaaten. Und so alt ist ja die Zweite Republik noch nicht.' Nikowitz, 'Lauter Sieger'.
85. The symbolism of Germany's 1954 victory has found cultural representation, for example, in Fassbinder's 1978 film *Die Ehe der Maria Braun* and in F.C. Delius' novella *Der Sonntag, an dem ich Weltmeister wurde* (Reinbek: Rowohlt, 1994). For an analysis of the impact of the match on the German national consciousness, see Arthur Heinrich, *Tooor! Toor! Tor! 40 Jahre 3:2* (Berlin: Rotbuch Verlag, 1994).
86. Armin Thurnher, *Das Trauma, ein Leben: österreichische Einzelheiten* (Vienna: Paul Zsolnay Verlag, 1999), 16.
87. Charles Ingrao, 'Foreword', in Peter Thaler, *The Ambivalence of Identity: The Austrian Experience of Nation-Building in a Modern Society* (West Lafayette: Purdue University Press, 2000), vii–ix, at viii.
88. Thurnher, *Das Trauma, ein Leben*, 137.
89. '[H]übsch, flott, sportlich aussehend.' Jakob Ebner, *Wie sagt man in Österreich? Wörterbuch der österreichischen Besonderheiten*, 2nd edn (Mannheim: Duden, 1980), 70.
90. 'Als Feschisten ... bezeichne ich Leute, die ihr Aussehen und ihre Körper bewußt als fit und neu gegen die abgeschlafften Körper der alten politischen Säcke positionieren. Sie bedienen sich dabei der alpinen Siegersymbolik und deren Milieus ... Ihr Ziel ist nicht die Erneuerung, sondern die Abschaffung der repräsentativen Demokratie. Es gilt nicht mehr der Ausgleich von Interessen zugunsten der Schwächeren, der Anderen, der Fremden. Gelten soll das Diktat des Siegers, des physisch Stärkeren.' Armin Thurnher, 'Apartes Österreich: Notizen aus den paradoxen Tagen vor und nach der Wende in Österreich', in Charim and Rabinovici, *Österreich: Berichte aus Quarantanien*, 33–45, at 42. See also Ottomeyer, *Die Haider-Show*, especially Chapter 2, 'Der männliche Sportler und die symbolische Überwindung der Klassengesellschaft', 19–50.
91. Robert Pearton contextualizes Elias' position in, 'Violence in Sport and the Special Case of Soccer Hooliganism in the United Kingdom', in Roger Rees and Andrew W. Miracle (eds), *Sport and Social Theory* (Champaign, IL: Human Kinetics, 1986), 67–83, at 71. See Norbert Elias, *The Civilizing Process: The History of Manners* (Oxford: Blackwell), 1978.
92. James Curtis, 'Isn't it Difficult to Support Some of the Notions of *The Civilizing Process?* A Response to Dunning', in Rees and Miracle, *Sport and Social Theory*, 57–65, at 60.
93. Lawrence J. Hatab, 'The Drama of Agonistic Embodiment: Nietzschean Reflections on the Meaning of Sports', *International Studies in Philosophy* 30 (1998), 97–107, at 100–1. Hatab cites Nietzsche's posthumous fragment, 'Homer's Contest'.
94. On sport as dramatic form, see Joseph K. Kupfer, 'Waiting for DiMaggio: Sport as Drama', in Judith Andre and David N. James (eds), *Rethinking College Athletics* (Philadelphia: Temple University Press, 1991), 109–19.
95. Steven Galt Crowell, 'Sport as Spectacle and as Play: Nietzschean Reflections', *International Studies in Philosophy* 30 (1998), 109–22, at 111.

96. Jelinek, *Sports Play*, 51. 'Hier zum Beispiel sehen Sie gleich den Herren von dieser einen Bewegung, welche uns derzeit besonders bewegt, wie er mit verschwitztem Marathonband, keuchend wie Christus am Kreuz . . . auf der Straße steht.' Jelinek, *Ein Sportstück*, 26.
97. See Eric Dunning on the 'essentially religious' nature of top-level sporting events. Eric Dunning, 'The Sociology of Sport in Europe and the United States: Critical Observations from an "Eliasian" Perspective', in Rees and Miracle, *Sport and Social Theory*, 29–56, at 43.
98. Jelinek, *Ein Sportstück*, 74.
99. Jelinek, *Sports Play*, 53-54. 'Abmagerungskur, in der wir alles aufs Spiel gesetzt hatten, an die Hunderttausend . . . durch unsere Auslöscheimer verloren, nur damit wir jetzt erneut spielen dürfen, aber auf einem anderen, glücklicherweise ganz neu hergerichteten Feld.' Jelinek, *Ein Sportstück*, 29.
100. Matthias Konzett, *The Rhetoric of National Dissent in Thomas Bernhard, Peter Handke, and Elfriede Jelinek* (Rochester, NY: Camden House, 2000), 115 and 112.
101. Jelinek, *Sports Play*, 67. 'Der Sport ist die Organisation menschlicher Unmündigkeit, welche in siebzigtausend Personen gesammelt und dann über ein paar Millionen daheim vor den Bildschirmen ausgegossen wird.' Jelinek, *Ein Sportstück*, 49.
102. 'Was man in der Politik früher Faschismus nannte, die Vision der fügbaren Masse, findet sich jährlich beim österreichischen Schiereignis des Jahres, in Kitzbühel. 200 Millionen an den Schirmen. Die fesche Masse brodelt, die Schneekanone hat ganze Arbeit geleistet. Es schwillt der Hahnenkamm. Soll man es Schifaschismus nennen? Sagen wir: Feschismus.' Thurnher, *Das Trauma, ein Leben*, 12.
103. '[E]ine unserer tüchtigsten Abfahrtsläuferinnen [. . . ist] in einen Pfahl hineingestürzt und [hat] sich dabei den Kopf abgerissen . . . Unwillkürlich nahmen für einen Augenblick auch wir Millionen Fernsehzuschauer Abschied vom Leben.' Elfriede Jelinek, *Stecken, Stab und Stangl*, in *Stecken, Stab und Stangl, Raststätte, Wolken. Heim. Neue Theaterstücke* (Reinbek: Rowohlt, 1997), 15–68, at 24–25.
104. Jelinek, *Ein Sportstück*, 147.
105. 'Sportler . . . Vielleicht sogar Wehrsportler bzw. Abwehrsportler.' Jelinek, *Stecken, Stab und Stangl*, 29.
106. '[W]ir haben zu wenig umgebracht, zu wenig, nicht alle. Es müßte heißen parte caust, nicht holom. Wir haben versagt. Wir hätten alle Antisportler. Alle hätten wir an die Wand stellen müssen. Das Nichtsportlertum vernichten, ausrotten. Die haben gar keine Lebensberechtigung, diese Weichlinge.' Franzobel, *Olympia*, 25.
107. 'Wissen Sie. Die Täter. Die werden gleich bleiben. Die Täter werden immer gleich bleiben.' Streeruwitz, *Sapporo.*, 181.
108. 'Eine ganze Nation schaut auf einen. Mit diesem Druck muß man erst fertigwerden . . . Aber wir arbeiten mit Psychologen. Heil Hitler!' Franzobel, *Olympia*, 36.
109. 'Eitrige Knochenabsplitterungen, gerissene Sehnen, zu Ende gehende Karrieren, unerfüllte Träume, Sehnsüchte, Elend, Opfer, Leid, Menschen, denen es noch schlechter geht.' Franzobel, *Olympia*, 12.
110. 'Nachdem Sie *Olympia* gesehen haben, werden Sie über den Ausspruch "Gesunder Geist in einem gesunden Körper" nur noch lächeln können.' Tatjana Greif, 'Tödlicher Sport', *Dnevnik*, 7 February 2000.
111. '[N]ur in einem gesunden Körper wohnt ein gesunder Geist.' Thurnher, *Das Trauma, ein Leben*, 137. The phrase is thought to smack of the National Socialist cult of the healthy body.

112. 'Wenn man bedachte, wie viele Nachbarn, Anrainer und Familienmitglieder von diesen sinnlosen Trainings um ihre Ruhe gebracht wurden. Wieviele Gedanken so verunmöglicht wurden . . . Und eine Olympiade war das Ende dieses Gedankenverunmöglichungs-Zyklus . . . die heutige Form der Bücherverbrennung. Kein Wunder, daß der Hitler eine veranstaltet hat.' Franzobel, *Lusthaus oder die Schule der Gemeinheit* (Vienna: Paul Zsolnay Verlag, 2002), 116–17.
113. '[D]ie Chance, daß sich Kärnten auf der internationalen Landkarte von einem bisher weißen Fleck zu einem Gebiet voller Farbenpracht entfalten kann.' Cover of Klagenfurter Ensemble programme for *Olympia*, Klagenfurt, 1999. On the significance of the Carinthian plebiscite of 10 October 1920 and its reflection in postwar Austrian culture, see Allyson Fiddler, 'Carinthia, Interculturalism, and Austrian National Identity: Cultural Reflections on 10 October 1920', *German Life and Letters* 58(2) (2005), 195–210.
114. 'Im olympischen Dorf grassiert der Notstand. Wir mußten Nutten aus Ikutien und Kalmükistan einfliegen lassen . . . und das Schlimmste ist, noch immer hat kein einziger Teilnehmer die berühmten tamtamer Kasnudeln gekostet.' Franzobel, *Olympia*, 41.
115. 'Durch die Nichtberücksichtigung bei der Kandidatur für die Olympischen Winterspiele 2006 sehen wir uns als Opfer politischer Korruption und krimineller Machenschaften, und in der Opferrolle sehen wir uns ja nicht gerade ungern. Auf jeden Fall ist dieses Thema immer noch aktuell.' Quoted in T.K., 'Eine kollektive Degeneration', *Die Brücke*, 4 February 2000.
116. 'Franzobel . . . geboren während der ersten Frühjahrsrunde 1967, war mit der Hauptschule Lenzing im Schülerligabezirksfinale als Vorstopper . . . Seit 1970 hat er kein Spiel der österreichischen Nationalmannschaft verpasst.' Franzobel, with illustrations by Carla Degenhardt, *Mundial: Gebete an den Fußballgott* (Graz: Droschl, 2002). The essays are not so much analyses of football as broader cultural investigations attached to or provoked by sport (not just football).
117. '[D]essen Pseudonym aus dem Ergebnis eines Fußballspiels Frankreich gegen Belgien entstand: Fran2.0Bel.' Franzobel, *Mundial*. Franzobel's name is actually a portmanteau constructed out of his father's first name, 'Franz', and his mother's maiden name 'Zobl'. See Andreas Herzog, 'Gespräch mit Franzobel', *Neue deutsche Literatur* 45 (1997), 11–21, at 21.
118. See Franzobel, 'Chronologie der laufenden Scheiße', 70.
119. Ben Segenreich, 'Israel initiiert Sport-Boykott Österreichs', *Der Standard*, 8 February 2000. Retrieved 6 May 2018 from http://derstandard.at/161784/Israel-initiiert-Sport-Boykott-Oesterreichs.
120. 'Belgians being asked to boycott Austrian ski resorts', the BBC reported. 'US Acts over Austrian Far-Right', *BBC News*, 4 February 2000. Retrieved 6 May 2018 from http://news.bbc.co.uk/1/hi/world/europe/631376.stm.
121. See APA, '"Es ist höchste Aufmerksamkeit angezeigt"', *Der Standard*, 5 September 2000. Reviews broadly agree that *Sapporo*. failed in this regard. See, for example, Ronald Pohl, 'The Heavy, Heavy Trottel-Sound', *Der Standard*, 28–29 October 2000, 18; and Werner Krause, 'Wär's doch ein Seufzer nur', *Kleine Zeitung*, 28 October 2000, 82.
122. See Nikowitz, 'Lauter Sieger'. Franzobel places Schranz in a long line of famous humiliations: 'Ein Weltreich verloren, Nazis, Südtirol, und zum Schluss noch Karl Schranz' (Franzobel, *Mundial*, 102; 'a world empire lost, Nazis, South Tyrol and now even Karl Schranz').
123. Gerlich, 'National Consciousness and National Identity', 253.

124. '[D]ie ganze Kunst war nur Besserwisserei im Arsch von irgendeinem Geldsack. Aber jetzt haben wir Demokratie.' Streeruwitz, *Sapporo.*, 172.
125. 'Heimat. Glück. Frieden. Liebe. Ehre. Treue.' Streeruwitz, *Sapporo.*, 162.
126. 'Es wird immer um den Körper verhandelt . . . Für die Politik. Ich meine. Ein fescher Kerl kommt besser an.' Streeruwitz, *Sapporo.*, 174.
127. See Thurnher, *Das Trauma, ein Leben*, 141 on this and on Haider's racism in general.
128. 'Wir werden so etwas nicht sagen aber es ist doch klar. Alle sehnen sich nach Aufrassung . . . Nach ruhigem Lebensraum . . . Die Leute sind ja nicht blöd. Die können das dann schon selber spüren.' Streeruwitz, *Sapporo.*, 163.
129. This is a derogatory Austrian German term for a foreigner (often of Slavic origin). See Ebner, *Wie sagt man in Österreich?*, 185.
130. 'Das Tamtamerloch, das unser Herrgott gstopft schon hat, und angebaut durch Tamtamerfleisch und Kasnudln, das soll gefüllet schmachtn jetzt in schuldiger Sauerei? Drum bitt di Herrgott, mach uns von de Tschuschn frei.' Franzobel, *Olympia*, 46–47.
131. 'Französisch sprechen wir nicht, Champagner kelltern wir nicht. Wir haben den Veltliner . . . Wir haben unsere Lieder. Niemanden anderen brauchen wir.' 'Veltliner' refers to 'Grüner Veltliner', a popular Austrian white wine. Streeruwitz wrote the lyrics, the music was written by Max Nagl and Roland Jaeger, and the CD of the songs *Sapporo. Eine Revue von Marlene Streeruwitz* was produced by Steirischer Herbst and sold at the theatre (CD no. 150830-2).
132. 'Ganz vordergründig sich dieser Form von Witz zu bedienen, wäre eine Möglichkeit, um nachher von der Bühne herunter klar zu machen, man sei in eine Falle gegangen.' Interview with Heinz-Norbert Jocks, 'Über die Macht des Patriarchats', *TheaterFrauenTheater*, 146–55, at 153. On the two occasions that I saw the production, there were different audience reactions. On the first night, the audience was caught by this strategy, and on the second, the discomfort and reluctance of the audience to be drawn into celebrating national pride was clearly visible.
133. 'Mein Hemmungsmechanismus ist zur Zeit außer Kraft gesetzt, weil gruppendynamische Kräfte auf mich einwirken.' Jelinek, *Ein Sportstück*, 55.
134. For an extensive account of the background to the refusal to stage the play, see Beilein, *86 und die Folgen*, 113–14.
135. Antonio Fian penned a satirical sketch in which Robert Menasse watches a quiz show contestant on television trying to guess from a description of the contents of the rejected play who is the author of *Das Paradies der Ungeliebten*. See Antonio Fian, *Menasse sieht Millionenshow*, Der Standard, 28 November 2006. Retrieved 6 May 2018 from http://derstandard.at/2053234/Robert-Menasse-sieht-Millionenshow.
136. '[U]nter Anführungszeichen die Schüssel-Figur, von seiner politischen Rolle her.' Quoted in Uwe Matuschka-Eisenstein, 'Literatur und Politik: eine Analyse des politisch versierten Autors Robert Menasse und seines Schauspiels *Das Paradies der Ungeliebten*', Diplomarbeit dissertation (Vienna: University of Vienna, 2011), 102.
137. 'Bombenbogen', *Falter*, 10 June 2015. Retrieved 6 May 2018 from https://www.falter.at/archiv/FALTER_20150610A881016037/bombenbogen. Khol is credited as having cointed the term 'Verfassungsbogen'. See Hans Rauscher, 'Verfassungsbogen'. Retrieved 6 May 2018 from http://derstandard.at/2000028856723/Der-Verfassungsbogen.
138. Menasse, *Das Paradies der Ungeliebten*, 36.
139. 'Herr Bachler vom Burgtheater hat ununterbrochen Morak, Morak, Morak gesagt vor lauter Angst vorm Herrn Morak, der sein Subventionsgeber war und ich hab ihm

dauernd erklärt das ist nicht der Morak und er hat wieder Morak gesagt.' Matuschka-Eisenstein interviews the author, who provides these insights into his play and its reception, (Matuschka-Eisenstein, 'Literatur und Politik', 126). Franz Morak's previous career path was as an actor and singer, but he then served as ÖVP Secretary of State for the Arts and the Media from 2000 to 2007.

140. Heidi M. Schlipphacke, *Nostalgia after Nazism: History, Home, and Affect in German and Austrian Literature and Film* (Lewisburg: Bucknell University Press, 2010), 221.
141. In the 2015 national elections, the DPP obtained just over 21 per cent of the vote, gaining 37 of the 179 seats in Parliament.
142. Matuschka-Eisenstein, 'Literatur und Politik' covers the background to the author's conception of the play extensively (see especially 83).
143. '[D]ie Tat hatte keinen politischen Hintergrund.' Menasse, *Das Paradies der Ungeliebten*, 14.
144. 'Wir alle haben unsere Hunde – erschossen! ... ihnen damit zurückgegeben, was wir durch sie gelernt hatten: Liebe, bedingungslose Treue, Gehorsam.' Menasse, *Das Paradies der Ungeliebten*, 36.
145. 'Shakespeare auf lächerlich.' Interview with Matuschka-Eisenstein, 'Literatur und Politik', 125.
146. 'Der Titel, *Das Paradies der Ungeliebten* ist nichts anderes [als] der zusammenfassende Begriff für sämtliche Klischees oder allgemeine Vorstellungen vom Leben in den politischen Eliten.' Matuschka-Eisenstein, 'Literatur und Politik', 120.
147. 'Der Rest ist: Schweigt!', Menasse, *Das Paradies der Ungeliebten*, Scene 23, n.p.
148. '[D]ie Macht der Schriftsteller als Speerspitze der Protestkultur erscheint ... außergewöhnlich.' Matuschka-Eisenstein, 'Literatur und Politik', 12.
149. See Dagmar Travner's criticisms of the official state commemorations and of the coalition's approach to culture: Dagmar Travner, 'Rechte Nichtkultur versus subversive "Unkultur"', in Becker and Wassermair, *Kampfzonen in Kunst und Medien*, 46–52.
150. 'So sahen denn auch die Übersetzer und Dramaturgen verschiedener Länder in dem Stück die Beschreibung der jeweils eigenen Zustände, etwa die Berlusconi-Regierung in Italien oder die rechten Bewegungen in Deutschland. Diese Reaktionen zeigen, dass Robert Menasse mit dem *Paradies der Ungeliebten* einen wunden Punkt der europäischen Demokratien getroffen hat.' Frank Raudszus, 'Es ist etwas faul im Staate D...: Uraufführung von Robert Menasses "Paradies der Ungeliebten" im Staatstheater Darmstadt', *Egotrip*, 18 October 2006. Retrieved 6 May 2018 from http://www.egotrip.de/?p=11408.
151. Henryk M. Broder, 'Wut im Land des Lächelns'. Retrieved 6 May 2018 from http://www.spiegel.de/spiegel/print/d-15737872.html.
152. Müller, *Possen des Performativen*, 101.
153. See Silvia Kornberger, 'Das Wiener Volkstheater als Teil politischer Widerstandskultur', dissertation, University of Vienna (Munich: GRIN, 2011).
154. Ralf Leonhard, '"Wie ein Kind": Ein unübertroffener Interpret seiner selbst: Zum Tod des "gesitteten Sprachkünstlers" Gert Jonke aus Österreich', *Die Tageszeitung*, 6 January 2009.
155. Hans Haider, 'Anti-"Himmelblau": Wiener Volkstheater als parteipolitische Anstalt', *Die Presse*, 21 January 2002.
156. 'Wiener Sportklub distanziert sich von Strache', *Die Presse*, 18 August 2015. Retrieved 6 May 2018 from http://diepresse.com/home/sport/fussball/national/4801500/Wiener-Sportklub-distanziert-sich-von-Strache.

Conclusion

THE COLOURS OF 2016 AND 2017
Green, Blue ... Turquoise

The year 2016 was a momentous one for the political direction of the United Kingdom and the United States, but Austria also felt the weight of developments abroad. The United Kingdom's referendum-generated preference for leaving the EU in June 2016 (52 per cent of those who voted were in favour) was frequently alluded to in Donald Trump's campaign to become the US President – an election that he won on 9 November 2016. Trump saw the United Kingdom's vote for 'Brexit' as a sign of Britain putting itself first and as a harbinger of the philosophy he felt the Americans would adopt by electing him and thus endorsing his policy of 'America First'. The reason I begin these short concluding deliberations with the political context of the European Union and of the United States is because they are widely believed to have had some influence on the electoral outcome of the Austrian presidential elections of 2016, although this is not something that can be empirically quantified. In contrast to the voters in these polls, the comparatively tiny electorate of Austria (with 6.4 million eligible voters in December 2016) did not – yet – choose the candidate or option that would herald another new turn or Wende in their political development and signal a narrowing of their concerns towards domestic protectionism, or towards 'Österreich zuerst' ('Austria First'), as the Freedom Party's rallying call of the early 1990s had demanded. The Austrian presidential election was followed with keen interest by the international media.

Following the normal practice for presidential elections, the initial wider round pooled two candidates to go head to head in a deciding election on Sunday 22 May. This election broke the usual practice of clear-cut, Sunday-night results in Austria and an announcement had to wait until Monday morning, when the sizeable quantity of postal votes was added. The near-draw of the night before turned into a victory for former Green Party leader Alexander Van der Bellen, with an extremely narrow margin of just 0.6 per cent (50.3 per cent, compared to the FPÖ candidate Norbert Hofer's 49.7 per cent). On the Thursday before the first head to head of the presidential elections, the anti FPÖ sentiment had started to translate into unofficial civil action. An impromptu demonstration took place in Vienna with around 700 protesters assembled on the Ballhausplatz. They carried banners with anti-fascist and anti-racist slogans expressing their determination that there should be 'Kein Nazi in der Hofburg' ('no Nazi in the Hofburg Palace').[1] The chosen day of the week for this demonstration was apposite, not accidental – it echoed the Thursday demonstrations against the coalition government of the Freedom Party of Austria and the Austrian People's Party inaugurated in February 2000.

However, the concentrated suspense of the May election was as nothing compared to the extended aftermath of this close result. The party that Hofer represents, the Freedom Party of Austria, subsequently submitted a challenge to the country's constitutional court due to possible, if not proven, irregularities in the administration of the vote, and the resulting legal decision was an annulment of the May elections, with a rerun scheduled for October 2016. Yet, when the glue on the postal vote envelopes proved to be faulty, the election was postponed to 4 December and the campaigning stepped up significantly on both sides. Pre-election commentators wondered whether voter fatigue would produce a markedly reduced participation. In fact, despite the near-year-long process, the annoyance of repeated attempts at running the election and the inauspicious timing for the second Sunday of Advent, there was a slightly higher turnout. This time the result was more convincing, and Van der Bellen was named Austria's next President with a margin that had increased significantly since the spring (the final figures were Van der Bellen 53.8 per cent and Hofer 46.2 per cent).[2]

The international media interest in Austria's elections was so keen because of the possibility that Austria might elect a far-right candidate as head of state. Since the inauguration of the Second Republic and with only one exception in the form of the independent Rudolf Kirchschläger (two continuous periods of office spanning 1974 to 1986), Austria had always had either an SPÖ or an ÖVP president. Sentiment ran high enough at home in Austria, but foreign journalists were moved to formulate the possible outcome in rather blunter terms: 'An anti-immigration and Eurosceptic candidate is hoping to become the first far-right European head of state since Adolf Hitler in a re-run of the Austrian presidential election.'[3] Like his party leader Heinz-Christian Strache, Hofer is also a hardliner. Despite his calmer, smiling interview style, his pronouncements bear the hallmarks of his party background – he is anti-gay marriage, he wants to stop the 'Invasion der Muslime' ('invasion of Muslims')[4] in Austria and is also anti-European Union, although his statements on the matter are hedged in terms of it being something that the people should decide (much like the British supposedly have with the Brexit result, although at the time of writing it is still not clear what the realities of this Brexit decision are). Hofer is also a member of a student fraternity organization, the *Burschenschaft* Marko-Germania zu Pinkafeld. These fraternities subscribe to a men-only, fatherland-worshipping, conservative German worldview and wear their colours with pride.

Alexander Van der Bellen chose to campaign for the rescheduled election with a slogan that made his internationalist credentials clear. A vote for Van der Bellen was 'für das Ansehen Österreichs' ('for the reputation of Austria'). A vote for the other candidate was, by implication, a choice that would bring Austria into disrepute, much like the FPÖ's coalition participation in 2000 had done. In the same vein, it was not the potential economic implications of the United Kingdom exiting the European Union that troubled many in Austria. After all, the United Kingdom and Austria share a relatively low trade volume and the impact of Brexit is likely to be small. Of much greater concern was the signal it would give to others wishing to pursue withdrawal from the European Union, as a report for the Austrian Society for European Politics asserted.[5] Van der Bellen saw Brexit as a 'tragic mistake' and knew that by and large in a broadly pro-EU country such as Austria (which has only been a member since 1995), the noises made by Hofer and the Freedom Party about a possible Austrian Exit, or 'Öxit', were of significant concern to the Austrian electorate. Van der Bellen refers to the paradox of the Brexit vote – namely that in seeing the Brits opting to leave, Austrian voters were suddenly a lot clearer about the good sense and necessity of retaining their membership of the European Union.[6]

Despite the international sigh of relief that followed Norbert Hofer's defeat, the election had still produced a result in which nearly half of Austria's electorate (46 per cent) had voted for a far-right candidate. More surprises were to come in 2017. Hofer's bullish optimism on the first head-to-head election night in May 2016 projected that either Austria would see him as its new President or that they would have an FPÖ chancellor in two years' time. Setting his personal sights on the next presidential election in 2022, Hofer went on to promise that four years after the scheduled national elections of 2018, Austria would then indeed have a Freedom Party president, as well as a Freedom Party chancellor in H.C. Strache. These elections, scheduled for the autumn of 2018, were subsequently brought forward to October 2017 following a breakdown in working relations between the coalition partners and more pointedly after the ambitious new ÖVP leader, Sebastian Kurz, took control of the leadership in mid May 2017.

In 2016, the personality politics around Kurz, the very young pretender to the lead role of the ÖVP, had not yet become a major driving force, although the personal appeal of the FPÖ's Norbert Hofer, a rhetorically skilled, handsome, 46-year-old former aeronautical engineer, probably played a part in his strong presidential challenge to Alexander Van der Bellen. The overriding reason for the FPÖ's renewed popularity in the national election campaign of 2017 was undeniably the refugee crisis that had emanated mainly from the Middle East (predominantly Syria) and impacted significantly on Austria. Whereas in 2014 the number of applications for asylum in Austria was 28,064, the calendar year 2015 showed a total of 89,098 applications, an increase of nearly 215 per cent.[7] 'In relative terms', the EU Commission explains, 'the largest increases in the number of first time applicants were recorded in Finland (over nine times as high), Hungary (over four times) and Austria (over three times)'.[8] Austria faced huge challenges over how to cope with the influx of refugees and asylum seekers. The FPÖ had never strayed from its anti-immigration platform, not in the late 1980s and early 1990s when Jörg Haider came to prominence, nor from 2002 to 2005 (when it had a succession of five different leaders) and certainly not since 2005, when H.C. Strache took charge. The difference in today's political landscape is that other parties are now promoting strong anti-immigration policies too.

Having initially been against border controls, Austria changed its policy in 2016 – under its then grand coalition of black and red – and began to build barriers to impede the refugees' entrance to Austria, for example, by erecting fences with Slovenia, or in contemplating the reintroduction of border controls on the Brenner Pass with Italy. Expressing the desire to lower the numbers of migrants made the then Chancellor, Werner Faymann (SPÖ), popular with some but deeply unpopular with others, and arguably led to his standing down and ceding office to Christian Kern in May 2016. The question of immigration became a strong campaign issue in 2017 not just for the FPÖ, but also for Sebastian Kurz's rebranded People's Party. Kurz missed no opportunity to stress that his was a new political 'movement', his party even contesting the election under the personalised banner of the 'Liste Sebastian Kurz – die neue Volkspartei', still with the short form ÖVP, but with the new colour of turquoise. Although there were plenty of other points of similarity between their manifestos, it was the migration issue that was singled out by H.C. Strache's FPÖ posters. Strache expressed his anger with a partially concealed accusation that Kurz had even stolen ideas from the FPÖ. Thus, the final wave of FPÖ posters encouraged the electorate to vote for the man who was the 'Vordenker statt Spätzünder' ('the pioneer, not the latecomer'). The posters then qualified the areas in which this was the case: 'In dealing with refugee crises, border protection, and Islamization.'[9]

Whither Protest Art?

If between 2006 and 2017 the far-right in Austria did not manage to take up a role in government other than at a regional level, this does not mean that art in Austria has had nothing to protest about.[10] Indeed, as I was keen to stress in the Introduction to this volume, protest art, political writing or filmmaking can adopt a variety of forms and express its disagreement with political events or philosophies of any colour, and is not regime-dependent. Some of the work discussed in this book could have been interpreted merely as art against racism or as feminist writing, as drama that speaks truth to power or as critical culture that is determined to keep alive the issue of Austria's Nazi war guilt. The refugee crisis itself has offered ample thematic material for many artists, even before the coalition of the ÖVP and the FPÖ was inaugurated in December 2017. The theme has yielded music, plays and novels on human experiences of migration and refuge seeking in Austria.[11] Most prominent among the artists to have tackled the topic is Elfriede Jelinek, whose play *Die Schutzbefohlenen* (2013) looks at the refugee crisis and associated manifestations in Vienna (including the refugee protests of 2012 and 2013, when Vienna's Votivkirche was occupied). Jelinek's text incorporates intertextual references to the rights of migrants and to the discourse around them from different eras, referencing as one of her sources Aeschylus's *Die Schutzflehenden (Suppliant Women)*.[12] In an ironic turn, Jelinek's protest play about the plight of asylum seekers became itself the object of protest when a group of activists from the extreme-right movement 'Die Identitären' (the Identitarian Movement) stormed its performance in the University's main lecture hall in April 2016. The group also succeeded in climbing onto the Burgtheater's roof to display protest banners when the production was staged there later the same month. ('Die Identitären' is an extreme-right youth movement that emerged in France, has found popularity in Germany and Austria, and subscribes to ethnically separatist views.)

Political art is alive and well in Austria. But this book has not set out to discuss a genre simply dubbed 'political art' or protest art *tout court*. It has sought to track down examples from multiple genres that have dealt with the Austrian Wende of 1999/2000 in particular. The examples discussed here have spanned the approximate period 1998–2006. Whether or not the events and personalities of the millennial political upheaval will continue to feature in the prose, drama, film, music and art installations of the future remains to be seen. After all, works of art are still being generated about the Waldheim scandal of the 1980s. One thinks of Robert Schindel's 2013 novel *Der Kalte* or of Ruth Beckermann's 2018 film *Waldheims Walzer*. Many of the artists and intellectuals discussed in this volume of course continue to conceive works of art and cultural expression that feed off and react to the contemporary political context of Austria. Marlene Streeruwitz picked up her electoral novel idea (see Chapter 3) in 2016 and penned further episodes of *So wird das Leben*. In September 2017, in the run-up to the general election, Streeruwitz published three acts of a short satirical drama entitled *Die letzten Tage der Zweiten Republik*.[13] A novel by Austrian journalist Tony Glassberg, *Land im Sumpf* (2017), posits what happens when a neo-Nazi movement comes into power. There will be other examples to collect as time goes by.

Major political upheaval can be seen as a catalyst to mobilizing artists, just as it also galvanizes the physical expression of protest by civic society. In the United Kingdom, Ali Smith's novel *Autumn* (2016) was hailed as 'the first Brexit novel' and Howard Jacobson's novella *Pussy* (2017) as one of the first pieces of fiction to respond to the election of Donald Trump.[14] Trump has made it, if not by name then by obvious allusion, into Elfriede Jelinek's writing too, in her 2016 play *Am Königsweg*, just as controversial political figures of Austria have also featured (Waldheim, Haider and Hofer). Jelinek reworked some of her *Lebewohl* material of 2000 (see Chapter 5) into a new short piece entitled *Das Kommen* (2016). Its publication on her webpages features an image of the cornflower, the blue flower chosen by the FPÖ as one of its symbols.[15] The cornflower has a complicated and controversial history in Austria. When the Nazi Party was banned in Austria (before the Anschluss), it was a coded symbol worn by the party's adherents. Nobert Hofer apparently instructed his friends not to wear one in the run-up to the December presidential election, doubtless to deflect criticism.[16] If *Das Lebewohl* was boldly referred to as a 'Haidermonolog', the identity of the redeemer figure of *Das Kommen* is puzzled over by the speaker: 'Wasn't there somebody there? Somebody who will come again? Let's see now, it's not Jesus).'[17] The fact that he ruminates on being 'nicht weiter Ingenieur . . . nicht weiter im zweiten Glied' ('no longer an engineer, no longer in the back seat') can be interpreted as an allusion to Nobert Hofer's professional background and to the power wranglings between Hofer and Strache that have been the topic of speculation.[18] Responding to admonishments that her critical voice was lacking in the resistance against a possible new coalition with the FPÖ, Jelinek offers some creative thoughts on what on earth she might possibly have to say, under the title 'Mein Alterswerk, da geht es hin, da fliegt es rum' ('My Late Work, Off it Goes, Off it Flies'). The first-person narrator compares 2017 with 2000, saying 'back then they all walked around on a Thursday, nobody walks anywhere now, they get about on their bikes and cover up their faces, which is illegal'.[19] Then she concedes 'no, that's not true, a large mass of people has already risen up against the new government and has produced a fabulous sea of light'.[20] The reference here is to a demonstration organized by SOS Mitmensch on 3 November 2017 to protest against FPÖ politicians being awarded key ministerial roles. Since then, however, there has also been an enormous, illuminated, night-time rally or 'Lichtermeer' ('sea of light') to stand in solidarity with migrants. It was occasioned by the death of human rights activist and refugee champion Ute Bock and took place on 2 February 2018.

Austria is not seeing a systematic wave of protest marches specifically against the new coalition, but there have been demonstrations and rallies where protests against the latest 'turn' to the right have been voiced. The first was a dedicated march against the new government, held on 13 January 2018, which drew a 20,000-strong crowd. There are often demonstrations against the annual high society ball of the Vienna State Opera and 2018 was no exception. This year, the protesters marched under the motto 'Gegen die Regierung der Reichen' ('against the government of the rich').[21] The Akademikerball, the annual ball of the FPÖ since 2012, and the successor ball to the Wiener Korporationsring for Austria's affiliated fraternities or *Burschenschaften* also saw large protests (26 January 2018). This year's protests have been augmented by media and social media alarm on discovering that the song books still used, for example, by the *Burschenschaft* Germania zu Wiener Neustadt contain violently anti-Semitic songs.

The lack of international shockwaves against the latest iteration of black/turquoise and blue is in large part attributable to the general shift to the right and the progress of populist parties or populist strategies in many European countries. The March 2017 general election in the Netherlands did not see a victory for Geert Wilders' Freedom Party (Partij voor de Vrijheid), but the party's second place result did entail an increase in seats. Germany's far-right Alternative für Deutschland (founded only in 2013) is currently the third-strongest party (receiving 12.6 per cent in the 2017 elections). France's presidential election of 2017 saw centre-right, relative newcomer Emmanuel Macron win by a large margin, although the far-right Front National's Marine Le Pen had enjoyed high poll ratings early on. Le Pen has pledged to relaunch and revitalize the party in 2018. In the cases of Viktor Orbán's Fidesz (Hungarian Civic Alliance) and the Polish Law and Justice Party (Prawo i Sprawiedliwość), conservative nationalists and populists are already in government in Hungary and Poland. The European Union has been slow to try to stem autocratic practices in these countries.[22] Italy has recently voted overwhelmingly (over 50 per cent) for a variety of parties who are Eurosceptic. The anti-establishment Five Star Movement (founded in 2009) is the biggest winner, but it will need to form a coalition in order to govern. It seems likely that this will be an alliance comprised of the nationalist Lega party, Berlusconi's Forza Italia, a centre-right party, and Fratelli d'Italia (Brothers of Italy), a party of the radical right.

In Austria, there are currently plenty of protest activities and burgeoning protest groups that are visible at physical events and, very importantly, are highly active on social media. The new initiative Omas gegen Rechts (Grannies against the Right) has become a highly vocal platform of older women who, as the group rightly say, represent a marginalized voice in society. Their membership document underlines their democratic principles and outlines their aim to fight against anti-Semitism, racism, misogyny and fascism.[23] Student groupings, anti-fascist groups, feminist organizations and ordinary citizens are attending marches, just as they did after the 1999 elections. It remains to be seen what creative symbolism may come into being during the latest protests in Austria or whether unrest over the new coalition will develop into anything more than periodic demonstrations and rallies.

Of course, artists and writers have no power to make decisions of policy or of government, nor, indeed, can their work be shown to have a measurable influence on politicians or on those who elect them. But we can at least have confidence that novelists, filmmakers, playwrights, musicians, poets and essayists will continue to use their creativity to resist developments that normalize the expression of far-right sentiment. Their work entertains audiences, but it also encourages them to think and to make their own protest known. The art of resistance that boomed in the early twenty-first century has given Austria renewed confidence in its civil society and grassroots activism and has delivered an impressive array of aesthetically rich and highly thought-provoking works of art and literature.

Notes

1. APA/Helmut Fohringer, '700 Teilnehmer bei Anti-Hofer-Demo in Wien', *Die Presse*, 19 May 2016. Retrieved 6 May 2018 from http://diepresse.com/home/politik/bpwahl/4992255/700-Teilnehmer-bei-AntiHoferDemo-in-Wien.
2. The full results are available on Austria's government webpages. Retrieved 6 May 2018 from http://wahl16.bmi.gv.at.
3. World Breaking News, 'Austria May Be about to Elect Europe's First Far-Right Leader since Hitler', 4 December 2016. Retrieved 8 March 2017 from https://www.wbnews.info/2016/12/austria-may-be-about-to-elect-europes-first-far-right-leader-since-hitler. This is no longer available online; others report in similar terms, but replace the provocative analogy 'since Hitler' to 'since WWII'. See Eric Frey, 'Austria is Poised to Go Far … Right', *Vice News*, 3 December 2016. Retrieved 6 May 2018 from https://news.vice.com/en_ca/article/ned8bb/austria-could-soon-elect-western-europes-first-far-right-head-of-state-since-wwii.
4. Christa Zöchling and Jakob Winter, 'Der Volksempfänger: Was uns bei Norbert Hofer Angst macht', 18 May 2016. Retrieved 6 May 2018 from https://www.profil.at/oesterreich/volksempfaenger-was-norbert-hofer-wahl-biographie-portrait-6368391.
5. Kurt Bayer, 'Brexit und Österreich: Wie sollte Österreich reagieren?', *Policy Brief* 17 (2016). Retrieved 6 May 2018 from http://oegfe.at/wordpress/wp-content/uploads/2016/06/OEGfE_Policy_Brief-2016.17.pdf.
6. These are the terms in which Van der Bellen speaks of the Brexit effect, in 'Van der Bellen beklagt Brexit', *Süddeutsche Zeitung*, 13 February 2017. Retrieved 6 May 2018 from http://www.sueddeutsche.de/politik/oesterreich-van-der-bellen-beklagt-brexit-1.3377900.
7. Bundesministerium für Inneres, 'Asylstatistik'. Retrieved 6 May 2018 from http://www.bmi.gv.at/301/Statistiken.
8. 'Asylum Statistics', *Eurostat: Statistics Explained* (data extracted on 2 March 2016 and on 20 April 2016). Retrieved 6 May 2018 from http://ec.europa.eu/eurostat/statistics-explained/index.php/Asylum_statistics.
9. 'Im Umgang mit Flüchtlingskrisen, Grenzschutz und Islamisierung.' APA, 'Neue FPÖ-Plakate zeigen Strache als "Vord-enker"', *Der Standard*, 25 September 2017. Retrieved 6 May 2018 from https://derstandard.at/2000064731197/Neue-FPOe-Plakate-zeigen-Strache-als-Vord-enker.

10. The FPÖ had been in coalition with the SPÖ in the Burgenland Regional Parliament since 2015.
11. See McMurtry, Áine, and Deborah Holmes (eds), *Austria in Transit: Displacement and the Nation State*, special issue, *Austrian Studies* 26 (forthcoming 2018).
12. Published first on the author's webpages (2013), then as Elfriede Jelinek, *Die Schutzbefohlenen*, in *Theater heute* 7 (2014), 3–19.
13. Retrieved 6 May 2018 from http://www.marlenestreeruwitz.at/wahlkampfroman-2016-so-wird-das-leben. See Streeruwitz's homepage for this drama with its titular allusion to Karl Kraus's *Die letzten Tage der Menschheit* (1915–22), a monumental collection of 220 scenes. Retrieved 6 May 2018 from http://www.marlenestreeruwitz.at/aktuell.
14. Alex Clark, 'Writing Wrongs', *The Guardian*, 'Review', 11 March 2017, 2–3. A study of how literature is responding to Brexit has recently been published as Robert Eaglestone (ed.), *Brexit and Literature: Critical and Cultural Responses* (London: Routledge, 2018).
15. Elfriede Jelinek, *Das Kommen*, author's homepage, 2016. Retrieved 6 May 2018 from http://www.elfriedejelinek.com.
16. TheLocal.at, 'FPÖ's Hofer Rejects Cornflower Symbol', 30 November 2016. Retrieved 6 May 2018 from https://www.thelocal.at/20161130/austrian-freedom-party-hofer-rejects-cornflower-symbol.
17. 'War da nicht einer, der nun wiederkommt? Mal schauen, Jesus ist es nicht.' Jelinek, *Das Kommen*.
18. 'Hofer hat bessere Imagewerte als Partei-Chef Strache', *Der Kurier*, 6 December 2016. Retrieved 6 May 2018 from https://kurier.at/politik/inland/heinz-christian-strache-legt-im-vertrauensindex-deutlich-zu-norbert-hofer-hat-aber-bessere-imagewerte/234.483.406. The term 'zweites Glied' could be interpreted as a nod to Hofer's injured leg. Hofer walks with a cane following a crash in a light aircraft.
19. '[D]amals sind die alle am Donnerstag herumgegangen, heute geht keiner mehr, sie fahren alle mit ihren Rädern und verhüllen ihre Gesichter, was verboten ist.' Elfriede Jelinek, 'Mein Alterswerk, da geht es hin, da fliegt es rum', author's homepage, 17 November 2017 (titled 'Neue Regierung '17' on the sidebar). Retrieved 6 May 2018 from http://www.elfriedejelinek.com.
20. '[N]ein, das stimmt nicht, es ist bereits eine große Menschenmenge gegen die neue Regierung aufgetreten und hat ein wunderbares Lichtermeer erzeugt.' Jelinek, 'Mein Alterswerk'. Jelinek alludes to the law in Austria introduced in October 2017 prohibiting the wearing in public of anything that fully covers the face. Cyclists wearing scarves against the cold have been challenged as well as burqa-wearing Muslim women.
21. Vanessa Gaigg, 'Opernballdemonstration dieses Jahr gegen die Regierung', *Der Standard*, 5 February 2018. Retrieved 6 May 2018 from https://derstandard.at/2000073661991/Die-Opernballdemonstration-richtet-sich-dieses-Jahr-gegen-die-Regierung.
22. Harmen van der Veer and Maurits Meijers, 'Hungary's Government is Increasingly Autocratic: What is the European Parliament doing about it?', *Washington Post*, 3 May 2017. Retrieved 6 May 2018 from https://www.washingtonpost.com/news/monkey-cage/wp/2017/05/03/hungary-is-backsliding-what-is-the-european-parliament-doing-about-this/?utm_term=.c969aa992225.
23. See their homepage at: https://www.omasgegenrechts.com/uber-uns.

REFERENCES

Acker, Robert, 'Josef Haslinger's Opernball: From Best Seller to Film Thriller', in Margarete Lamb-Faffelberger (ed.), *Literature, Film and the Culture Industry* (New York: Peter Lang, 2002), 160–69.
Aeschylus, *Die Orestie*, trans. Walter Jens. Munich: dtv, 1981.
Ahtisaari, Martti, Jochen Frowein and Marcelino Oreja, 'Report'. Adopted in Paris, 8 September 2000. Retrieved 6 May 2018 from http://www2.ohchr.org/english/bodies/hrc/docs/ngos/HOSI-1.pdf.
Albert, Barbara, Michael Glawogger, Ulrich Seidl and Michael Sturminger, *Zur Lage*. Austria: Lotus Film-GmbH, 2002.
Andersen, Kurt, 'The Protester', *Time*, 14 December 2011. Retrieved 1 May 2018 from http://content.time.com/time/specials/packages/article/0,28804,2101745_2102132_2102373,00.htmln.
Anderson, Benedict, *Imagined Communities: Reflections on the Origin and Spread of Nationalism*, revised edn. London: Verso, 2000.
APA, 'Neue FPÖ-Plakate zeigen Strache als "Vord-enker", *Der Standard*, 25 September 2017. Retrieved 6 May 2018 from https://derstandard.at/2000064731197/Neue-FPOe-Plakate-zeigen-Strache-als-Vord-enker.
APA/Helmut Fohringer, '700 Teilnehmer bei Anti-Hofer-Demo in Wien', *Die Presse*, 19 May 2016. Retrieved 6 May 2018 from http://diepresse.com/home/politik/bpwahl/4992255/700-Teilnehmer-bei-AntiHoferDemo-in-Wien.
Artnet, 'Haider's Cultural Scene in Carinthia', 3 September 2000, retrieved 8 April 2018 from http://www.artnet.com/magazine/ news/ artnetnews/artnetnews3-9-00.asp.
Attali, Jacques, *Noise: The Political Economy of Music*. Manchester: Manchester University Press, 1985.
Auracher, Dieter, *Parallelaktion* (3 minutes), 2000, programme 2. Retrieved 6 May 2018 from http://www.medienwerkstatt-wien.at/files/titles/kunst-der-stunde.htm.
Awadalla, El, *wienerinnen: geschichten von guten und bösen frauen*. Vienna: Sisyphus, 2006.
Awadalla, El, and Traude Korosa (eds), *...Bis sie gehen: vier Jahre Widerstandslesungen*. Vienna: Sisyphus, 2004.
Bailer, Brigitte, 'They were All Victims: The Selective Treatment of the Consequences of National Socialism', in Günther Bischof and Anton Pelinka (eds), *Austrian Historical Memory and National Identity* (New Brunswick, NJ: Transaction, 1997), 103–15.
Baker, Frederick, *Erosion und Wi(e)derstand*, (20 minutes). Austria: Frederick Baker, 2003.
———, *The Art of Projectionism*. Vienna: Czernin, 2008.
———, *Widerstand in Haiderland*. Austria: Filmbäckerei, 2010.

Baker, Frederick, and Elisabeth Boyer, *Wiener Wandertage: eine Dokumentation*. Klagenfurt: Wieser, 2002.
Bayer, Kurt, 'Brexit und Österreich: Wie sollte Österreich reagieren?', *Policy Brief* 17 (2016). Retrieved 6 May 2018 from http://oegfe.at/wordpress/wp-content/uploads/2016/06/OEGfE_Policy_Brief-2016.17.pdf.
Becker, Konrad, and Martin Wassermair (eds), *Kampfzonen in Kunst und Medien: Texte zur Zukunft der Kulturpolitik*. Vienna: Löcker, 2008.
Becker, Udo, *The Continuum Encyclopedia of Symbols*, trans. Lance W. Garmer. London: Continuum, 1994.
Beckermann, Ruth, *Homemad(e)*. Vienna: Ruth Beckermann-Filmproduktion, 2007.
Beilein, Matthias, *86 und die Folgen: Robert Schindel, Robert Menasse und Doron Rabinovici im Literarischen Feld Österreichs*. Berlin: Erich Schmidt, 2008.
Beller, Steven, *A Concise History of Austria*. Cambridge: Cambridge University Press, 2006.
Benoliel, Bernard, 'Along the Paths of Time', in Ruth Beckermann Filmproduktion (ed.), *Texte von, Texts by, Textes de Ruth Beckermann, Bernard Benoliel, Christa Blümlinger, Hélène Cixous, Paulus Hochgatterer, Siegfried Mattl, Bert Rebhandl*, information and accompanying essays as part of the Ruth Beckermann film collection 8 DVD set (Vienna: Ruth Beckermann Filmproduktion, 2007), 77–134.
Bethman, Brenda, 'Generation Chick: Reading *Bridget Jones's Diary*, *Jessica, 30.*, and *Dies ist kein Liebeslied* as Postfeminist Novels', *Studies in 20th and 21st-Century Literature* 35(1) (2011), 136–54.
Beyes, Timon, 'Uncontained: The Art and Politics of Reconfiguring Urban Space', *Culture and Organization* 16(3) (2010), 229–46.
Bianchi, Stefano Isidora, 'Interview with FURT', *Blow up* (June 2005). Retrieved 6 May 2018 from http://furtlogic.com/node/16.
Boehringer, Michael and Susanne Hochreiter (eds), *Zeitenwende: Österreichische Literatur seit dem Millennium: 2000–2010*. Vienna: Praesens, 2011.
Bohlman, Philip Vilas, *The Music of European Nationalism: Cultural Identity and Modern History*. Santa Barbara, CA: ABC-CLIO, 2004.
Bong, Jörg, Roland Spahr and Oliver Vogel (eds), *'Aber die Erinnerung davon.' Materialien zum Werk von Marlene Streeruwitz*. Frankfurt am Main: Fischer Taschenbuch Verlag, 2007.
Bonilla, Yarimar, 'The Past is Made by Walking: Labor Activism and Historical Production in Postcolonial Gaudeloupe', *Cultural Anthropology* 26(3) (2011), 313–39.
Bourriaud, Nicolas, *Relational Aesthetics*, trans. Simon Pleasance and Fronza Woods, with the participation of Mathieu Copeland. Dijon: Les Presses du réel, 2002.
Boyer, Elisabeth, 'Die Pallas Athene muß beschützt werden', in Baker and Boyer, *Wiener Wandertage*, 115–24.
Brambilla, 'B.E.N.I.T.A.', *Little Terror Creek* (CD). Austria: Lunadiscs/Knallcore and Bloodshed 666, 2002.
Bushell, Anthony, *Polemical Austria: The Rhetorics of National Identity: From Empire to the Second Republic*. Cardiff: University of Wales Press, 2013.
Bychawski, Adam, 'Download Chumbawamba Track for Free', *NME*, 12 July 2000. Retrieved 6 May 2018 from http://www.nme.com/news/chumbawamba/3836.
Charim, Isolde and Doron Rabinovici (eds), *Österreich: Berichte aus Quarantanien*. Frankfurt am Main: Suhrkamp, 2000.
Chioles, John, 'The Oresteia and the Avant-Garde: Three Decades of Discourse', *Performing Arts Journal* 45 (1993), 1–28.

Chor der Nachbeter mit basso obstinato, 'Politlitanei von Nicole Delle Karth', Collage und Chor der Nachbeter mit basso obstinato. Austria: Gas, 2000. Retrieved 6 May 2018 from http://www.2gas.net/musikw.htm.

Chorvereinigung Gegenstimmen (eds), *Hohes Haus Musik: Kantate in F Dur*. Vienna: Alwa & Deil, 2002.

Chumbawamba, 'Enough is Enough (Kick it Over)'. United Kingdom: Woodlands Studio, 2000.

Cixous, Hélène, 'The Laugh of the Medusa', in Dennis Walder and Open University (eds), *Literature in the Modern World: Critical Essays and Documents* (Oxford: Oxford University Press, 1990), 316–25.

Conny Chaos und die Retortenkinder, 'KHG', Retorte Rockt! (4-track Demo-CD). Austria: Broken Heart Records, 2004.

——, 'Lisi Gehrer'. Austria: Broken Heart Records, 2004.

Crowell, Steven Galt, 'Sport as Spectacle and as Play: Nietzschean Reflections', *International Studies in Philosophy* 30 (1998) 109–22.

Curtis, James, 'Isn't it Difficult to Support Some of the Notions of *The Civilizing Process*? A Response to Dunning', in Roger Rees and Andrew W. Miracle (eds), *Sport and Social Theory* (Champaign, IL: Human Kinetics, 1986), 57–65.

Czernin, Hubertus (ed.), *Wofür ich mich meinetwegen entschuldige: Haider, beim Wort genommen*. Vienna: Czernin Verlag, 2000.

Delle Karth, Nicole, 'Chor der Nachbeter mit basso obstinato', in Baker and Boyer, *Wiener Wandertage*, 151–58.

Die Ärzte, 'Halsabschneider', B-side of *Wie es geht*. Single. Germany: Hot Action Records, 2000

Dor, Milo (ed.)., *Die Leiche im Keller: Dokumente des Widerstands gegen Dr. Kurt Waldheim*. Vienna: Picus, 1988.

Drahdiwaberl, 'Torte statt Worte', *Torte statt Worte*. Austria: Drahdiwaberl Music, 2000.

Drahdiwaberl, Klaus Hundsbichler, *Torte statt Worte* (5.5 minutes), 2001, programme 4. Retrieved 6 May 2018 from http://www.medienwerkstatt-wien.at/files/titles/kunst-der-stunde.htm.

Duncombe, Stephen, Introduction to 'Adorno, on the Fetish-Character in Music and the Regression of Listening', in Stephen Duncombe (ed.), *Cultural Resistance Reader* (London: Verso: 2002), 275–303.

——, 'Introduction', in Stephen Duncombe (ed.), *Cultural Resistance Reader* (London: Verso, 2002), 1–15.

Dunning, Eric, 'The Sociology of Sport in Europe and the United States: Critical Observations from an "Eliasian" Perspective', in Rees and Miracle, *Sport and Social Theory*, 29–56.

Eaglestone, Robert (ed.), *Brexit and Literature: Critical and Cultural Responses*. London: Routledge, 2018.

Ebner, Jakob, *Wie sagt man in Österreich? Wörterbuch der österreichischen Besonderheiten*, 2nd edn. Mannheim: Duden, 1980.

Eidlhuber, Mia, 'Du sollst recherchieren! Die gängigen Vorwürfe an Haider und was Sie darüber wissen sollten', *Die Zeit*, 17 February 2001, 1–5.

Einhorn, Ewa and Misha Stroj, *Die Herren* (3.5 minutes), 2001, programme 4. Retrieved 6 May 2018 from http://www.medienwerkstatt-wien.at/files/titles/kunst-der-stunde.htm.

Elias, Norbert, *The Civilizing Process: The History of Manners*. Oxford: Blackwell, 1978.

Erste Allgemeine Verunsicherung, 'Kurti', B-side, *Burli/Kurti*. Austria: EMI Austria, 1988.

——, 'Valerie, Valera: Haiders Sprung in seiner Schüssel'. Promo Single CD. Germany: Blanko Musik, 2000.
Euripides, *Orestes and Other Plays*. Harmondsworth: Penguin, 1972.
Federmair, Leopold, 'Das ungenierte "Und": Marlene Streeruwitz beschreibt Österreich als Sumpf', *Neue Züricher Zeitung*, 14 July 2004.
Fian, Antonio, *Schratt*. Graz: Droschl, 1992.
——, *Was bisher geschah. Dramolette 1*. Graz: Droschl, 1994.
——, *Was seither geschah. Dramolette 2*. Graz: Droschl, 1998.
——, *Alarm. Dramolette 3*. Graz: Droschl, 2002.
——, *Café Promenade*. Graz: Droschl, 2004.
——, 'Menasse sieht Millionenshow', *Der Standard*, 28 November 2006. Retrieved 6 May 2018 from http://derstandard.at/2053234/Robert-Menasse-sieht-Millionenshow.
——, *Bohrende Fragen. Dramolette 4*. Graz: Droschl, 2007.
Fiddler, Allyson, 'Demythologising the Austrian "Heimat": Elfriede Jelinek as "Nestbeschmutzer"', in Moray McGowan and Ricarda Schmidt (eds), *From High Priests to Desecrators: Contemporary Austrian Literature* (Sheffield: Sheffield Academic Press, 1993), 25–44.
——, *Rewriting Reality: An Introduction to Elfriede Jelinek*. Oxford: Berg, 1994.
——, 'Staging Jörg Haider: Protest and Resignation in Elfriede Jelinek's *Das Lebewohl* and Other Recent Texts for the Theatre', *Modern Language Review* 97(2) (2002), 353–64.
——, 'Carinthia, Interculturalism, and Austrian National Identity: Cultural Reflections on 10 October 1920', *German Life and Letters* 58(2) (2005), 195–210.
——, 'Sport and National Identity in the "New" Austria: Sports Plays by Jelinek, Franzobel and Streeruwitz', in Janet Stewart and Simon Ward (eds), *Blueprints for No-Man's Land: Connections in Contemporary Austrian Culture* (Oxford: Peter Lang, 2005), 111–30.
——, 'Shifting Boundaries: Responses to Multiculturalism at the Turn of the Twenty-First Century', in Katrin Kohl and Ritchie Robertson (eds), *A History of Austrian Literature 1918–2000* (Rochester, NY: Camden House, 2006), 265–89.
——, 'A Political "Brief": Performativity and Politicians in Short Works of Austrian Satire', in Brigid Haines, Stephen Parker and Colin Riordan (eds), *Aesthetics and Politics in Modern German Culture: Festschrift in Honour of Rhys W. Williams* (Oxford: Peter Lang, 2010), 179–93.
——, 'Wie lange bleiben blaue Flecken? Erinnerungen und Gedanken aus Großbritannien zum 10. Jahrestag der schwarz-blauen Koalition', in Frederick Baker and Paula Herczeg (eds), *Die beschämte Republik: 10 Jahre nach Schwarz-Blau in Österreich* (Vienna: Czernin, 2010), 71–77.
——, 'Of Political Intentions and Trivial Conventions: Erika Pluhar's *Die Wahl* (2003) and Marlene Streeuwitz's *Jessica, 30.* (2004)', *German Life and Letters* 64(1) (2011), 133–44.
——, 'Fooling around with Film: Political Visions of Austria: Past, Present and Future', in Allyson Fiddler, John Hughes and Florian Krobb (eds), *The Austrian Noughties: Texts, Films, Debates*, special issue, *Austrian Studies* 19 (2011), 126–41.
——, 'Lights, Camera, ... Protest! Austrian Film-Makers and the Extreme Right', *Journal of European Popular Culture* 2(1) (2012), 5–18.
——, 'Performing Austria: Protesting the Musical Nation', *IASPM@Journal* 4(1) (2014), 10.5429/2079-3871(2014)v4i1.2en.
Fiddler, Allyson, Jon Hughes and Florian Krobb (eds), *The Austrian Noughties: Texts, Films, Debates*, special issue, *Austrian Studies* 19 (2011).

Fleischer, Ludwig Roman, 'Fremdenführung', in Awadalla and Korosa, *...Bis sie gehen*, 148–51.

Fliedl, Konstanze, 'Damenwahl', *Falter*, 21 March 2003.

——, 'A Field Guide to Names in Literature: Notes on Austrian Onomastics', *Austrian Studies*, 15(1) (2007), 155–68.

Flos, Birgit, 'Eintritt ins gestörte Bild: Paul Poet dokumentiert Schlingensiefs *Ausländer raus*', DVD notes, in Paul Poet, *Ausländer raus! Schlingensiefs Container*. DVD, Austria: Bonus Film, 2005.

Foltin, Robert. *Und wir bewegen uns doch: soziale Bewegungen in Österreich*. Vienna: Edition Grundrisse, 2004.

Forrest, Tara, 'A Realism of Protest: Christoph Schlingensief's Television Experiments', *Germanic Review: Literature, Culture, Theory* 87(4) (2012), 325–44.

Frahm, Ole, 'Too Much is Too Much: The Never Innocent Laughter of the Comics', *Image & Narrative* 3 (October 2003). Retrieved 6 May 2018 from http://www.imageandnarrative.be/inarchive/graphicnovel/olefrahm.htm.

Frank, Michael, 'Raureif: Die Konfrontation der EU mit Österreichs Regierung im Jahr 2000 war ein bis heute verleugneter Erfolg', in Strauß and Ströhle, *Sanktionen: 10 Jahre danach*, 25–30.

Franzobel, *Olympia: Eine Kärntner Zauberposse samt Striptease* in Franzobel, *Volksoper Olympia*. Weitra: Bibliothek der Provinz, 2000.

——, 'Chronologie der laufenden Scheiße', in Charim and Rabinovici, *Österreich: Berichte aus Quarantanien*, 59–71.

——, *Lusthaus oder die Schule der Gemeinheit*. Vienna: Paul Zsolnay Verlag, 2002.

——, with illustrations by Carla Degenhardt, *Mundial: Gebete an den Fußballgott*. Graz: Droschl, 2002.

French, Loreley, 'Prostitution and Sex Trafficking of Women in Austria: The Legalities and Illegalities of the Sex Trade Meet Marlene Streeruwitz's *Jessica*', in Rebecca S. Thomas (ed.), *Madness and Crime in Modern Austria* (Newcastle: Cambridge Scholars Publishing, 2008), 150–73.

Friedl, Harald, *Land ohne Eigenschaften*. Austria: Harald Friedl, 2000.

Frith, Simon, *Performing Rites: On the Value of Popular Music*. Cambridge, MA: Harvard University Press, 1996.

Fröhlich, Hannah, 'Hubsi Kramars Gratwanderungen', *Augustin*, 29 April 2000. Retrieved 6 May 2018 from http://www.augustin.or.at/zeitung/artistin/hubsi-kramars-gratwanderungen.html.

FURT, 'Volksmusik', *Defekt*. United Kingdom: Matchless Recordings, 2002.

Gerlich, Peter, 'National Consciousness and National Identity: A Contribution to the Political Culture of the Austrian Party System', in Anton Pelinka and Fritz Plasser (eds), *The Austrian Party System* (Boulder: Westview Press, 1989), 223–58.

Goldhill, Simon, 'The Influence of the *Oresteia*', in *Aeschylus: The Oresteia* (Cambridge: Cambridge University Press, 1992), 93–99.

Greif, Tatjana, 'Tödlicher Sport', *Dnevnik*, 7 February 2000.

Gross, Tom, 'Lou Reed's Stand for Israel and against Anti-Semitism', *National Review*, 28 October 2013. Retrieved 8 April 2018 from https://www.nationalreview.com/corner/lou-reeds-stand-israel-and-against-anti-semitism-tom-gross/.

Guenther, Christina, 'The Politics of Location in Ruth Beckermann's "Vienna Films"', *Modern Austrian Literature* 37(3/4) (2004), 33–46.

Haas, Franz, 'Die Komik und die Kürze in den Texten von Antonio Fian', in Wendelin Schmidt-Dengler, Johann Sonnleitner and Klaus Zeyringer (eds), *Komik in der österreichischen Literatur* (Berlin: Erich Schmidt, 1996), 300–8.

Haas, Georg Friedrich, 'In Vain', *In Vain* [CD]. Austria: Kairos, 2004.

Haderer, Gerhard and Leo Lukas, *Jörgi, der Drachentöter*. Vienna: Ueberreuter, 2000.

Hadolt, Bernhard, 'Shit and Politics: The Case of the Kolig Debate in Austria', *Iš: Medische Antropologie* 11(1) (1999), 179–98.

Haider, Hans, 'Anti-"Himmelblau": Wiener Volkstheater als parteipolitische Anstalt', *Die Presse*, 21 January 2002. Retrieved 6 May 2018 from http://diepresse.com/home/kultur/news/270638/AntiHimmelblau_Wiener-Volkstheater-als-parteipolitische-Anstalt?from=suche.intern.portal.

Haider, Jörg, 'Glücksgefühl nach bangen Stunden', *News*, 8 March 2000.

Hanisch, Ernst, 'Wien Heldenplatz', *Transit. Europäische Revue* 15 (1998), 122–40. Retrieved 6 May 2018 from http://www.demokratiezentrum.org/fileadmin/media/pdf/hanisch.pdf.

Hart, Marjolein t' and Dennis Bos, 'Humour and Social Protest: An Introduction', *International Review of Social History* 52(15) (2007), 1–20.

Hartwig, Ina, 'Jessicas Lauf gegen die Weiblichkeit', in Bong, Spahr and Vogel, *'Aber die Erinnerung davon'*, 136–48.

Haslinger, Josef, *Politik der Gefühle: ein Essay über Österreich*. Darmstadt: Luchterhand, 1987.

Hatab, Lawrence J., 'The Drama of Agonistic Embodiment: Nietzschean Reflections on the Meaning of Sports', *International Studies in Philosophy* 30 (1998), 97–107.

Heinisch, Reinhard, *Populism, Proporz, Pariah: Austria Turns Right*. New York: Nova Science, 2002.

Heinrich, Arthur, *Tooor! Toor! Tor! 40 Jahre 3:2*. Berlin: Rotbuch Verlag, 1994.

Hennenberg, Beate, 'Ich will auf Missstände im neuntreichsten Land der Welt aufmerksam machen', *Leipzig Allmanach*, 20 June 2001. Retrieved 6 May 2018 from http://www.leipzig-almanach.de/film_interview_mit_ruth_mader_deren_streifen_null_defizit_in_diesem_jahr_fuer_cannes_nominiert_wurde_beate_hennenberg.html.

Hermes, Manfred, 'Die Neue Wiener Schule: Der aktuelle österreichische Film und sein sozialer Realismus', *EPD Film* 4 (2004), 10–11.

Herzog, Andreas, 'Gespräch mit Franzobel', *Neue deutsche Literatur* 45 (1997), 11–21.

Hochgatterer, Paulus, 'Ready or Not, Here I Come', in Baker and Boyer, *Wiener Wandertage*, 91–98.

Hoffmann-Ostenhof, Georg, 'Das Holzpferd', in Dor, *Die Leiche im Keller*, 14.

Hofreither, Herbert, '"Kulturnation" Österreich: Anmerkungen zu Image, Identität, Sport, Film und Literatur', *Modern Austrian Literature* 32 (1999), 19–39.

Hois, Eva Maria, 'Wienerliedtexte der Jahrhundertwende als Spiegel sozio-ökonomischer, technischer und politischer Entwicklungen', *Newsletter Moderne*, special issue 1, 'Moderne – Modernisierung – Globalisierung' (March 2001). Retrieved 6 May 2018 from http://www-gewi.kfunigraz.ac.at/moderne/dok.htm.

Hollander, Jocelyn and Rachel Einwohner, 'Conceptualizing Resistance', *Sociological Forum* 19(4) (2004), 533–54.

Horak, Roman, 'Philharmoniker und Älpler. Wie Sport beim "inneren Staatsbildungsprozess" hilft', *Der Standard*, 9 February 2002.

Horvath, Thomas and Niki Griedl, *Grenze* (1 minutes), 2000, programme 1. Retrieved 6 May 2018 from http://www.medienwerkstatt-wien.at/files/titles/kunst-der-stunde.htm.

——, *Schaukel* (1 minute), 2000, programme 3. Retrieved 6 May 2018 from http://www.medienwerkstatt-wien.at/files/titles/kunst-der-stunde.htm.

——, *Tempelhüpfen* (1.5 minutes), 2000, programme 2. Retrieved 6 May 2018 from http://www.medienwerkstatt-wien.at/files/titles/kunst-der-stunde.htm.

Howes, Geoff, 'The Politics of Rhetoric in Some Recent Austrian Essays', *New German Critique* 93 (2004), 43–53.

Huber, Bernadette, *Wie böse ist Österreich?*, 1999, programme 3. Retrieved 6 May 2018 from http://www.medienwerkstatt-wien.at/files/titles/kunst-der-stunde.htm.

Hummer, Waldemar, 'The End of EU Sanctions against Austria: A Precedent for New Sanctions Procedures?', *European Legal Forum* (2000/2001), 77–83.

Hutchinson, Ben, and Susan Ranson (eds), *Rainer Maria Rilke's The Book of Hours: A New Translation with Commentary*. New York: Camden House, 2008.

Ingrao, Charles, 'Foreword', in Peter Thaler, *The Ambivalence of Identity: The Austrian Experience of Nation-Building in a Modern Society* (West Lafayette: Purdue University Press, 2000), vii–ix.

Jancak, Eva, 'Widerstand beim Zwiebelschneiden', in Milena Verlag, *Die Sprache des Widerstandes*, 78–80.

Janda, Alexander, and Mathias Vogl (eds), 'Islam in Österreich'. A report for the Österreichischer Integrationsfonds, 2010.

Janke, Pia, interview with Elfriede Jelinek, 'Tragödie und Farce in einem', *Der Standard*, 17 June 2000 (supplement magazine, 1).

Jelinek, Elfriede, 'In den Waldheimen und auf den Haidern'. *Der Streit* 32 (1987), 36.

——, 'Präsident Abendwind', in *Anthropophagen im Abendwind*, ed. by H. Wiesner (Berlin: Literaturhaus Berlin, 1988), 19–36.

——, 'Ich möchte seicht sein', in Christa Gürtler (ed.), *Gegen den schönen Schein: Texte zu Elfriede Jelinek* (Frankfurt am Main: Verlag Neue Kritik, 1990), 157–61.

——, *Stecken, Stab und Stangl*, in *Stecken, Stab und Stangl, Raststätte, Wolken. Heim. Neue Theaterstücke*. Reinbek: Rowohlt, 1997, 15–68.

——, 'Sinn egal. Körper zwecklos', in *Stecken, Stab und Stangl, Raststätte, Wolken. Heim. Neue Theaterstücke* (Reinbek: Rowohlt, 1997), 7–14.

——, *Ein Sportstück*. Reinbek bei Hamburg: Rowohlt, 1998.

——, *Macht nichts: Eine kleine Trilogie des Todes*. Reinbek: Rowohlt, 1999.

——, 'Meine Art des Protests', *Der Standard*, 7 February 2000.

——, 'Das Lebewohl (Les Adieux)', in *Das Lebewohl, 3 kl. Dramen* (Berlin: Berlin Verlag, 2000), 7–35.

——, 'Moment! Aufnahme! 5. 10. 99', in Isolde Charim and Doron Rabinovici, *Österreich: Berichte aus Quarantanien*, 100–9.

——, *Sports Play*, trans. Penny Black with translation assistance and a foreword by Karen Jürs-Munby. London: Oberon, 2012.

——, 'Mein Alterswerk, da geht es hin, da fliegt es rum', 17 November 2017. Retrieved 6 May 2018 from http://www.elfriedejelinek.com/.

Jocks, Heinz-Norbert, 'Über die Macht des Patriarchats', *TheaterFrauenTheater*, 146–55.

Kaputtnicks, 'Brief an den Kanzler'. Austria: Geco Tonwaren, 2000. Retrieved 6 May 2018 from https://www.youtube.com/watch?v=1tiZP5z99YI.

Karner, Christian, '"Austro-Pop" since the 1980s: Two Case Studies of Cultural Critique and Counter-Hegemonic Resistance', *Sociological Research Online* 6(4) (2002). Retrieved 6 May 2018 from http://dx.doi.org/10.5153/sro.654.

Karottnig, Hoppelmann, 'Wertedebatte mit einem noch zu zeugendem Kind: Zur Abwechslung ein vollkommen unpolitischer Text aus Wien im Jahre 2016', in Awadalla and Korosa, *...Bis sie gehen*, 89–90.

Kern, Peter, *1. April 2021: Haider lebt*. Austria: Hoanzl, 2007.

Kieninger, Ernst (ed.), *1. April 2000*. Vienna: Filmarchiv Austria, 2000.

Knaul, Susanne, 'Israel: "Der Haiderismus lebt auch ohne Haider weiter"', *Die Presse*, 12 October 2008. Retrieved 6 May 2018 from https://diepresse.com/home/politik/innenpolitik/421941/Israel_Der-Haiderismus-lebt-auch-ohne-Haider-weiter.

Koch, Wolfgang, 'Mytho-Wesen in Waldsaga', *Wiener Zeitung*, 19 October 2001.

Kogelfranz, Siegfried, 'Waldheim: die Schlinge zieht sich zu', *Der Spiegel*, 25 January 1988, retrieved 8 April 2018 from http://www.spiegel.de/spiegel/print/d-13528122.html.

Konzett, Matthias, *The Rhetoric of National Dissent in Thomas Bernhard, Peter Handke, and Elfriede Jelinek*. Rochester, NY: Camden House, 2000.

Kornberger, Silvia, 'Das Wiener Volkstheater als Teil politischer Widerstandskultur', dissertation, University of Vienna. Munich: GRIN, 2011. Retrieved 6 May 2018 from https://www.grin.com/document/121250.

Kosta, Barbara, 'Elfriede Jelinek's *Das Lebewohl [The Farewell]*: An Austrian Tragedy', in Matthias Konzett and Margarete Lamb-Faffelberger (eds), *Elfriede Jelinek: Writing Woman, Nation and Identity: A Critical Anthology* (Madison, NJ: Fairleigh Dickinson University Press, 2007), 157–73.

Kovacs, Teresa, 'Sanktion und Selbstzensur: Elfriede Jelineks Aufführungsverbote für Österreich'. Retrieved 6 May 2018 from https://jelinektabu.univie.ac.at/sanktion/zensur/teresa-kovacs/#_ednref58.

Kräuter, Luca Kilian, 'Luca, das Widerstands-Baby', in Baker and Boyer, *Wiener Wandertage*, 456–57.

Kriechbaumer, Robert, and Franz Schausberger, *Die umstrittene Wende: Österreich 2000–2006*. Vienna: Böhlau, 2012.

Krylova, Katya, 'Disturbing the Past: The Representation of the Waldheim Affair in Robert Schindel's *Der Kalte*', in Stephanie Bird et al. (eds), *Reverberations of Nazi Violence in Germany and Beyond: Disturbing Pasts* (London: Bloomsbury Academic, 2016), 107–24.

Kuhn, Rick, 'The Threat of Fascism in Austria', *Monthly Review* 52(2) (2000), 21–35.

Kupfer, Joseph K., 'Waiting for DiMaggio: Sport as Drama', in Judith Andre and David N. James (eds), *Rethinking College Athletics* (Philadelphia, PA: Temple University Press, 1991), 109–19.

Lajarrige, Jacques, 'Formation et appropriation d'un mythe: le cannibalisme et la littérature autrichienne de Nestroy à Jelinek', *Cahiers d'Etudes Germaniques* 26 (1994), 151–62.

——, 'Antonio Fian als Satiriker der österreichischen Literaturszene', in Jeanne Benay and Gerald Stieg (eds), *Österreich (1945–2000): Das Land der Satire* (Berne: Peter Lang, 2002), 241–67.

Larkey, Edward, 'Austropop: Popular Music and National Identity in Austria', *Popular Music* 11(2) (1992), 151–85.

——, 'Americanization, Cultural Change, and Austrian Identity', in David F. Good and Ruth Wodak (eds), *From World War to Waldheim: Culture and Politics in Austria and the United States* (New York: Berghahn Books, 1999), 210–235.

Lebrun, Barbara, *Protest Music in France: Production, Identity and Performance*. Farnham: Ashgate, 2009.

Le Rider, Jacques, 'The Austrian Crisis as Seen by a French Scholar of Germanic Culture', in Günter Bischof, Anton Pelinka and Michael Gehler (eds), *Austria in the European Union* (New Brunswick, NJ: Transaction, 2002), 56–66.

Leonhard, Ralf, '"Wie ein Kind": Ein unübertroffener Interpret seiner selbst: Zum Tod des "gesitteten Sprachkünstlers" Gert Jonke aus Österreich', *Die Tageszeitung*, 6 January 2009.

Lepuschitz, Rainer, '[bracket] #2: FURT', trans. Elfi Cagala, in Berno Odo Polzer (ed.), *Almanach Wien Modern*. Vienna, 2000. Retrieved 6 May 2018 from http://sammlung-essl.at/jart/prj3/essl/main.jart?content-id=1465039459955&rel=de&article_id=1399965034202&x=1&event_id=1399965034205&reserve-mode=active.

Lilienthal, Matthias and Claus Philipp, *Schlingensiefs Ausländer raus: Bitte Liebt Österreich. Dokumentation*. Frankfurt am Main: Suhrkamp, 2000.

Lockwood, Alan, 'Discordant Harmony: Ensemble Pi and Sarah Cahill Examine Political Activism in Music', *Time Out*, 2009. Retrieved 6 May 2018 from https://www.timeout.com/newyork/opera-classical/discordant-harmony.

Lorenz, Dagmar, 'The Struggle for a Civil Society and beyond: Austrian Writers and Intellectuals Confronting the Political Right', *New German Critique* 93 (2004), 19–41.

Marchart, Oliver. 'Was heißt Soundpolitisierung?', 2001. Retrieved 6 May 2018 from http://www.volkstanz.net/mind_nut/01.htm.

——, 'Austrifying Europe: Ultraright Populism and the New Culture of Resistance', *Cultural Studies* 16(6) (2002), 809–19.

Maschek, *Der graue Star 2: Die Wehrmacht* (8 minutes), 2001, programme 4. Retrieved 6 May 2018 from http://www.medienwerkstatt-wien.at/files/titles/kunst-der-stunde.htm.

——, *Unser schönes Kärnten* (6 minutes), 2001, programme 3. Retrieved 6 May 2018 from http://www.medienwerkstatt-wien.at/files/titles/kunst-der-stunde.htm.

Matuschka-Eisenstein, Uwe, 'Literatur und Politik: eine Analyse des politisch versierten Autors Robert Menasse und seines Schauspiels Das Paradies der Ungeliebten', unpublished dissertation. Vienna: University of Vienna, 2011.

Maurer, Thomas and Florian Scheuba, 'Widerstand', in Baker and Boyer, *Wiener Wandertage*, 247–49.

Mayer, Thomas, 'Haider: Kein James Dean', *Der Standard*, 13 October 2008.

Mayr, Elke, *Mad in Austria* (0.5 minutes), programme 3. Retrieved 6 May 2018 from http://www.medienwerkstatt-wien.at/files/titles/kunst-der-stunde.htm.

McMurtry, Áine, and Deborah Holmes (eds), *Austria in Transit: Displacement and the Nation State*, special issue, *Austrian Studies* 26 (forthcoming 2018).

Menasse, Robert, *Das Land ohne Eigenschaften: Essay zur österreichischen Identität*. Frankfurt am Main: Suhrkamp, 1992.

——, *Das Paradies der Ungeliebten: Ein Schauspiel*. Frankfurt am Main: Suhrkamp, 2006.

Messmer, Susanne, 'Stille Tage im Wienerwald', *Die Tageszeitung*, 22 January 2002. Retrieved 6 May 2018 from http://www.taz.de/index.php?id=archivseite&dig=2002/01/22/a0119.

Milena Verlag (ed.), *Die Sprache des Widerstandes ist alt wie die Welt und ihr Wunsch: Frauen in Österreich schreiben gegen Rechts*. Vienna: Milena, 2000.

Misik, Robert, and Doron Rabinovici, 'Vorwort: Aufbruch der Zivilgesellschaft', in Robert Misik and Doron Rabinovici (eds), *Republik der Courage Wider die Verhaiderung* (Berlin: Aufbau, 2000), 9–14.

Molden, Ernst, *Doktor Paranoiski*. Vienna: Deuticke, 2001.
Möller, Olaf, 'Undefeated', *Film Comment* (July/August 2007), 18–19.
Mölzer, Andreas, *Zur Identität Österreichs: Gedanken zum Millennium*. Vienna: Österreichische Landsmannschaft, 1996.
Müller, Gini, *Possen des Performativen: Theater, Aktivismus und queere Politiken*. Vienna: Verlag Turia und Kant, 2008.
Müllner, Romana, 'Wer sind die Demonstranten?', in Baker and Boyer, *Wiener Wandertage*, 266–69.
Murphy, Anthony, 'The Rise of the Austrian Freedom Party in the 1990s: A Culturalist Approach', *Zeitschrift für Politikwissenschaft* 33(3) (2004), 297–307.
Murray, Gilbert, 'Hamlet and Orestes: A Study in Traditional Types', in Robert A. Segal (ed.), *Ritual and Myth: Robertson Smith, Frazer, Hooke, and Harrison* (New York: Garland, 1996), 309–33.
Nikowitz, Rainer 'Lauter Sieger', *Profil* 6 (2001).
Nora, Pierre and Lawrence D. Kritzman, *Realms of Memory: Rethinking the French Past*. New York: Columbia University Press, 1996.
Norman, Beret, 'The Politics of Austrian Hip-Hop: HC Strache's Xenophobia Gets Dissed', *Colloquia Germanica* 39(2) (2006), 209–30.
Novotny, Franz, *Frühling in Wien*, (1.5 minutes), 2000, programme 1. Retrieved 6 May 2018 from http://www.medienwerkstatt-wien.at/files/titles/kunst-der-stunde.htm.
Oesterreich, Volker, 'Ironie unter der Straßenwalze', interview with Elfriede Jelinek, *Berliner Morgenpost*, 27 February 2000.
Omasta, Michael, 'Der österreichische Film: eine Momentaufnahme' *EPD Film*, 15(7) (2001), 28–33.
Oswald, John, 'Plunderphonics, or Audio Piracy as a Compositional Prerogative', *Musicworks* 34 (1986), 5–8.
Ottomeyer, Klaus, *Die Haider-Show: Zur Psychopolitik der FPÖ*. Klagenfurt: Drava, 2000.
Ötsch, Walter, *Haider Light: Handbuch für Demagogie*. Vienna: Czernin, 2002.
Panagl, Oswald, Peter Gerlich, Ewald Ehtreiber, Emil Brix and Österreichische Forschungsgemeinschaft (eds), *Wörterbuch der politischen Sprache in Österreich*. Vienna: Öbv, 2007.
Payne, Philip, 'Introduction: The Symbiosis of Robert Musil's Life and Works', in Philip Payne, Graham Bartram and Galin Tihanov (eds), *A Companion to the Works of Robert Musil* (Rochester, NY: Camden House: 2007), 1–52.
Pearton, Robert 'Violence in Sport and the Special Case of Soccer Hooliganism in the United Kingdom', in Roger Rees and Andrew W. Miracle (eds), *Sport and Social Theory* (Champaign, IL: Human Kinetics, 1986), 67–83.
Pelinka, Anton, 'Sport definiert "uns". Zum patriotischen Hochgefühl der Schination Österreich', *Profil* 6 (2001).
Petrey, Sandy, *Speech Acts and Literary Theory*. New York: Routledge, 1990.
Philipp, Claus, 'Retter der Erniedrigten und Beleidigten: Peter Kern', *Der Standard*, 19 April 2007. Retrieved 6 May 2018 from http://derstandard.at/2847809/Retter-der-Erniedrigten-und-Beleidigten-Peter-Kern.
Pick, Hella, *Guilty Victim: Austria from the Holocaust to Haider*. London: I.B. Tauris, 2000.
Pluhar, Erika, *Die Wahl*. Hamburg: Hoffmann und Campe, 2003.
Poet, Paul, *Ausländer raus! Schlingensiefs Container*. DVD. Austria: Bonus Film, 2005.

Porter, John R., 'Madness and Σύνεσις in *Orestes*', in *Studies in Euripides' Orestes* (Leiden: Brill, 1994), 298–313.
Price, Richard, *The Convict and the Colonel: A Story of Colonialism and Resistance in the Caribbean*. Durham, NC: Duke University Press, 2006.
Rabinovici, Doron, 'Nestbeschmutzer? Protest, Konfrontation und Institution: ein Blick zurück nach vorn', 1990. Retrieved 6 May 2018 from http://www.repclub.at/geschichte/.
——, *Der ewige Widerstand: über einen strittigen Begriff*. Vienna: Styria, 2008.
——, 'Vom Schutzreflex Europas', in Strauß and Ströhle, *Sanktionen: 10 Jahre danach*, 15–22.
Rancière, Jacques, Davide Panagia and Rachel Bowlby, 'Ten Theses on Politics', *Theory and Event* 5(3) (2001). Retrieved 6 May 2018 from http://muse.jhu.edu/article/32639.
Rassi, Barbara, 'Review of Haderer, Gerhard and Leo Lukas (2000) *Jörgi, der Drachentöter*, *Rethinking History: The Journal of Theory and Practice* 6(3) (2002), 365–67.
Ratzenböck, Veronika, Franz-Otto Hofecker and Anja Lungstraß, 'Austria', in *Compendium of Cultural Policies and Trends in Europe*, 9th edn (2008). Retrieved 6 May 2018 from http://www.culturalpolicies.net/web/austria.php?aid=%201.
Raudszus, Frank, 'Es ist etwas faul im Staate D…: Uraufführung von Robert Menasses "Paradies der Ungeliebten" im Staatstheater Darmstadt', *Egotrip*, 18 October 2006. Retrieved 6 May 2018 from http://www.egotrip.de/?p=11408.
Raunig, Gerald, *Wien Feber Null: eine Ästhetik des Widerstands*. Vienna: Turia und Kant, 2000.
Reddy, Srikanth, *Voyager*. Berkeley: University of California Press, 2011.
Reed, Brian M., 'In Other Words: Postmillennial Poetry and Redirected Language', *Contemporary Literature* 52(4) (2011), 756–90.
Reinhart, Martin, *Pinocchio* (1 minute), 2000, programme 2. Retrieved 6 May 2018 from http://www.medienwerkstatt-wien.at/files/titles/kunst-der-stunde.htm.
Reisigl, Martin and Ruth Wodak, *Discourse and Discrimination*. London: Routledge, 2001.
Riedl, Joachim, *Der Wende-Kanzler. Die unerschütterliche Beharrlichkeit des Wolfgang Schüssel*. Vienna: Czernin, 2000.
Robotka, Walter, 'Militanter Naturschutz: Ernst Molden, *Doktor Paranoiski*', *Evolver*, 3 January 2002. Retrieved 6 May 2018 from http://www.evolver.at/site/review.php?id=12139.
Rosa Antifa Wien, '"Er hat Euch nicht belogen"?'. 9 February 2000. Retrieved 6 May 2018 from https://raw.at/texte/gegenschwarzblau/er-hat-euch-nicht-belogen.
——, 'Newsletter boeses:oesterreich 1000', 6 October 2000. Retrieved 6 May 2018 from https://raw.at/texte/gegenschwarzblau/newsletter-boeses-oesterreich-1000.
Roscoe, Jane, and Craig Hight, *Faking it: Mock-Documentary and the Subversion of Factuality*. Manchester: Manchester University Press, 2001.
Rosellini, Jay, *Haider, Jelinek, and the Austrian Culture Wars*. Createspace Independent Publishing, 2009.
Rußegger, Arno, 'Walter Wippersberg: Ein nützlicher Idiot'. Retrieved 6 May 2018 from http://www.literaturhaus.at/index.php?id=3315&L=%2Fproc%2Fself%2Fenviron.
Scalla, Mario, 'Formvollendete Fragen. Über das Verhältnis von literarischer Form und gesellschaftlicher Aktualität in den Texten von Marlene Streeruwitz', in Bong, Spahr and Vogel, '*Aber die Erinnerung davon*', 149–63.
Scharang, Michael, 'Diesen Staat kann kein Skandal erschüttern, denn er ist selbst ein Skandal', *Der Streit* 32 (1987), 4–6.
Scharsach, Hans-Henning, *Stille Machtergreifung: Hofer, Strache und die Burschenschaften*. Vienna: Kreymayr and Scheriau, 2017.

Schiach, Morag, *Hélène Cixous: A Politics of Writing*. London: Routledge, 1991.
Schnittpunkt, *Opernball 2000: Chronik einer Amtshandlung* (26 minutes), 2000, programme 3. Retrieved 6 May 2018 from http://www.medienwerkstatt-wien.at/files/titles/kunst-der-stunde.htm.
Schlaffer, Hannelore, 'Habermas und Uschi Glas. Mein fremdbestimmter Körper: Marlene Streeruwitz führt Tagebuch', *Frankfurter allgemeine Zeitung*, 31 January 2003. Retrieved 6 May 2018 from http://www.faz.net/aktuell/feuilleton/buecher/rezensionen/belletristik/marlene-streeruwitz-tagebuch-der-gegenwart-habermas-und-uschi-glas-193438.html.
Schlipphacke, Heidi, *Nostalgia after Nazism: History, Home, and Affect in German and Austrian Literature and Film*. Lewisburg: Bucknell University Press, 2010.
Schrage, Dieter, 'Tomaten Widerstand', in Awadalla and Korosa, *...Bis sie gehen*, 42–46.
——, '"Zeugnis für Demo-Teilnahme": Anmerkungen zu meiner Vorlesung an der Uni Wien', in Baker and Boyer, *Wiener Wandertage*, 398–401.
Schuh, Franz, 'Unglückliches Österreich: eine Innenansicht', in Charim and Rabinovici, *Österreich: Berichte aus Quarantanien*, 19–32.
Schwärzler, Dietmar, 'Zukunftsvisionen. Ein Heimatfilm: Peter Kerns *1. April 2021: Haider lebt*', *Der Standard*, 3 October 2007.
Shahabi, Manocher, 'Der trojanische Esel', in Baker and Boyer, *Wiener Wandertage*, 311–13.
Skrinar, Hannah, 'Compositional Improvisation from the Electroacoustic Duo....', FURT *Defekt* review, 17 January 2003. Retrieved 6 May 2018 from http://www.bbc.co.uk/music/reviews/mpqv.
Solnit, Rebecca, *Wanderlust: A History of Walking*. London: Verso, 2001.
Sperl, Gerfried, *Die umgefärbte Republik: Anmerkungen zu Österreich*. Vienna: Paul Zsolnay Verlag, 2003.
Starsky, Julia, *Starsky: Gesamtkatalog*. Vienna: Starsky, 2014.
Stastna, Kazi, 'Jörgi, the Dragon Slayer', *Central Europe Review* 3(10) (2001). Retrieved 6 May 2018 from http://www.pecina.cz/files/www.ce-review.org/01/10/books10_stastna.html.
States, Bert, 'Performance as Metaphor', in Philip Auslander (ed.), *Performance: Critical Concepts in Literary and Cultural Studies*, 4 vols. London: Routledge, 2003, vol. 1, 108–37.
Steiner, Ulrike, 'Weltbilder verrücken – Die Doku-Fakes von Walter Wippersberg', *Porträt: Walter Wippersberg*, special issue, *Die Rampe* (2003), 99.
Stewart, Janet, '"Nicht die Kunst darf sich vereinnahmen lassen": Franzobel, Literature and Politics in the "New Austria"', *German Life and Letters* 55(2) (2002), 219–33.
Strauß, Martin and Karl-Heinz Ströhle (eds), *Sanktionen: 10 Jahre danach: Die Maßnahmen der Länder der Europäischen Union gegen die österreichische Regierung im Jahr 2000*. Innsbruck: Studienverlag, 2010.
Streeruwitz, Marlene, *Sapporo. Eine Revue*, in Barbara Engelhardt, Theres Hönigk and Bettina Masuch (eds), *TheaterFrauenTheater* (Berlin: Theater der Zeit, 2002), 156–81.
——, *Tagebuch der Gegenwart*. Vienna: Böhlau, 2002.
——, 'So ist das Leben. Wahlkampfroman'. Unpublished manuscript, 2006. Retrieved 6 May 2018 from https://www.freitag.de/autoren/der-freitag/so-ist-das-leben.
——, *Jessica, 30*. Frankfurt am Main: Fischer Taschenbuch, 2006.
——, 'Das Leben geht weiter'. Unpublished manuscript, 2008. Retrieved 6 May 2018 from http://www.marlenestreeruwitz.at.
Studio West, *Demo Stewardess*, (3 minutes), 2000, programme 3. Retrieved 6 May 2018 from http://www.medienwerkstatt-wien.at/files/titles/kunst-der-stunde.htm.

Sully, Melanie A., *The Haider Phenomenon*. New York: Columbia University Press, 1997.
Tagg, Philip, 'Caught on the Back Foot: Epistemic Inertia and Visible Music', *IASPM@ Journal*, 2(1/2) (2011) 12. Retrieved 6 May 2018 from http://dx.doi.org/10.5429/2079-3871(2011)v2i1-2.2en.
Tálos, Emmerich (ed.), *Schwarz-Blau: eine Bilanz des 'Neu-Regierens'*. Vienna, Lit Verlag, 2006.
Tauer, Brigitte, 'Rudi Riesenfuß muß flüchten', in Milena Verlag, *Die Sprache des Widerstandes*, 249–57.
Thompson, Marie, and Ian Biddle, 'Introduction: Somewhere between the Signifying and the Sublime', in Marie Thompson and Ian Biddle (eds), *Sound, Music, Affect: Theorizing Sonic Experience* (London: Bloomsbury, 2013), 1–24.
Thurnher, Armin, *Das Trauma, ein Leben: österreichische Einzelheiten*. Vienna: Paul Zsolnay Verlag, 1999.
———, *Heimniederlage: Nachrichten aus dem neuen Österreich*. Vienna: Paul Zsolnay Verlag, 2000.
———, 'Apartes Österreich: Notizen aus den paradoxen Tagen vor und nach der Wende in Österreich', in Charim and Rabinovici, *Österreich: Berichte aus Quarantanien*, 33–45.
T.K., 'Eine kollektive Degeneration', *Die Brücke*, 4 February 2000.
Treudl, Sylvia, 'Biedermensch erklärt einem Touristen, obwohl er Ausländer ist, die Welt', in Milena Verlag, *Die Sprache des Widerstandes*, 308–12.
Turino, Thomas, *Music as Social Life: The Politics of Participation*. Chicago: University of Chicago Press, 2008.
Turrini, Peter, 'Für Österreich', *Freitag*, 18 February 2000. Retrieved 6 May 2018 from https://www.freitag.de/autoren/der-freitag/fur-osterreich.
———, 'Ist Jörg Haider ein guter Schauspieler?', *Tagesspiegel*, 29 February 2000. Retrieved 6 May 2018 from http://www.tagesspiegel.de/kultur/ist-joerg-haider-ein-guter-schauspieler-herr-turrini/126264.html.
———, *Ich liebe dieses Land: Stück und Materialien*. Frankfurt am Main: Suhrkamp, 2001.
Turtledove, Harry, *In the Presence of Mine Enemies*. New York: ROC, 2003.
Uhl, Heidemarie, 'Das "erste Opfer": Der österreichische Opfermythos und seine Transformationen in der Zweiten Republik', *Österreichische Zeitschrift für Politikwissenschaft* 1 (2001), 19–34.
United Aliens, 'Blauer Planet', in Baker and Boyer, *Wiener Wandertage*, 246–47.
Valk, Üto 'Monogenesis', in *The Greenwood Encyclopedia of Folktales and Fairy Tales*, ed. Donald Haase, 3 vols (Westport, CT: Greenwood, 2008), vol. 2, 636.
Vasik, Monika, 'Allmächtiger Zeus! Lieber Papa!', in Milena Verlag, *Die Sprache des Widerstandes*, 63–69.
Volxtheater Favoriten/Videogruppe, Rosa Antifa and Martin Gössler, *Neubewertung* (12 minutes), 2000, programme 2. Retrieved 6 May 2018 from http://www.medienwerkstatt-wien.at/files/titles/kunst-der-stunde.htm.
'Warum Haider kneift', *Die Zeit*, 40, 28 September 2000. Retrieved 6 May 2018 from http://www.zeit.de/2000/40/Warum_Haider_kneift.
Wegenstein, Bernadette 'The Embodied Film: Austrian Contributions to Experimental Cinema', in Randall Halle and Reinhild Steingröver (eds), *After the Avant-Garde: Contemporary German and Austrian Experimental Film* (Rochester, NY: Camden House, 2009), 50–68.

Weidinger, Karl, 'Widerstand im Mehlspeisland', 2001. Retrieved 6 May 2018 from http://www.kawei.at/site_txt_2001.htm.
Weihs, Richard, 'Das Märchen von der Stadt Auswärts', in Awadalla and Korosa, ...*Bis sie gehen*, 41–42.
Wieland, Rayk, 'Die Welt als Wille zur Vorstellung', in Hermann L. Gremliza (ed.), *Braunbuch Österreich. Ein Nazi kommt selten allein* (Hamburg: Konkret, 2000), 151–58.
Wimmer, Michael, 'Staatliche Kulturpolitik in Österreich seit 2000: Zur Radikalisierung eines politischen Konzeptes', in Emmerich Tálos (ed.), *Schwarz-Blau: eine Bilanz des 'Neu-Regierens'.* (Vienna: Lit Verlag, 2006), 248–63.
Wippersberg, Walter, *Die Irren und die Mörder*. Salzburg: Otto Müller, 1998.
——, *Ein nützlicher Idiot*. Salzburg: Otto Müller, 1999.
——, *Die Geschichte eines lächerlichen Mannes*. Salzburg: Otto Müller, 2000.
——, *Die Wahrheit über Österreich: oder Wie man uns belogen hat*. Austria: ORF, 2001, no DVD release.
——, *Das Fest des Huhnes: das unberührte und rätselhafte Oberösterreich*. Austria: BMG Ariola, 2003.
——, ' "Mein Ehrgeiz ist es, gute Geschichten gut zu erzählen": Walter Wippersberg im Gespräch mit Christian Schacherreiter', *Porträt: Walter Wippersberg*, special issue, *Die Rampe* (2003), 7–18.
Wodak, Ruth, and Anton Pelinka, *The Haider Phenomenon in Austria*. New Brunswick, NJ: Transaction, 2002.
Wodak, Ruth et al., *The Discursive Construction of National Identity*. Edinburgh: Edinburgh University Press, 1999.
Zellhofer, M., 'Steckt's den Kopf nicht in den Sand, das Zauberwort heißt Widerstand!', *Unique*, University of Vienna, Student Union magazine, 6 (2006).
Zens, Franz, 'Fiktion und FPÖ: mögliche Anspielungen auf Darstellungen freiheitlicher Politik in drei Texten von Josef Haslinger, Milo Dor und Walter Wippersberg, unpublished Diplomarbeit. Vienna: University of Vienna, 2002.
Ziegler, Senta, 'Pluhar wird Bundespräsidentin', *News*, 20 February 2003, 132.
Zöchling, Christa, *Haider: Licht und Schatten einer Karriere*. Vienna: Molden, 1999.
Zöchling, Christa and Jakob Winter, 'Der Volksempfänger: Was uns bei Norbert Hofer Angst macht', 18 May 2016. Retrieved 6 May 2018 from https://www.profil.at/oesterreich/volksempfaenger-was-norbert-hofer-wahl-biographie-portrait-6368391.

Index

A

à clef (novel or play), 4, 20, 46, 73, 97, 145
Aeschylus, 149–52, 154, 175n36, 188
Ahtisaari, Martti, Jochen Frowein and Marcelino Oreja ('The Three Wise Men'), 13–14, 32, 73, 100n26
Albert, Barbara, 3, 8, 110, 120–122
Alliance for the Future of Austria. *See* Bündnis Zukunft Österreich
Ambros, Wolfgang. *See* Austria 3
Anderson, Benedict, 156
annexation of Austria. *See* Anschluss
Anschluss, 18, 37, 132, 142, 189
anti-fascism, 32, 49, 116, 185, 190
'O5', anti-fascist resistance, 118–19
anti-Semitism, 3, 16, 18, 20, 83, 87, 103n67, 125, 126, 130, 142, 145, 146, 148, 173n15, 190
Auracher, Dieter, 7, 112–13, 137n12
Austria 3, 44, 50
Austria First. *See* Österreich zuerst
Austrian national identity, 8, 13, 17, 109, 122, 126, 135, 155–58, 160, 165, 166
Austrian People's Party. *See* Österreichische Volkspartei
Austrofascism, 18, 111
Austropop, 43, 50. *See also* music
Awadalla, El, 3, 7, 66, 89–90, 105nn99–100

B

Bachler, Klaus, 167
Bachmann, Ingeborg, 84, 171
Baker, Frederick, 5, 8, 31, 35, 37–38, 52, 53, 105n106, 111, 118–20, 135, 136, 139n34, 139n39
Ballhausplatz, 38, 41, 92, 155, 185
banners and placards, 27n43, 32, 35, 36, 38, 39, 41, 52, 93, 95, 110, 112, 116, 132, 147, 171, 185, 187, 188
bank scandals, 15, 81, 103n65
Bärental, 53, 63n104
Barrett, Richard and Paul Obermayer. *See* FURT
BAWAG, Bank für Arbeit und Wirtschaft AG. *See* bank scandals
Beckermann, Ruth, 3, 5, 8, 16, 25n21, 123–25, 136, 139n46, 140n50, 188
Beethoven, Ludwig van, 114, 176n59
Beilein, Matthias, 25n19, 182n134
Beller, Steven, 17
Berlusconi, Silvio, 4, 170, 190
Bernhard, Thomas, 18, 135, 142, 156, 167, 171
Bethmann, Brenda, 76
Beuys, Joseph, 40
Beyes, Timon, 41
Bildungsroman, 84, 97
Binder, Ernst, 171
Bock, Ute, 189
Bohlman, Philip, 48
Böhmdorfer, Dieter, 72, 73, 152
Bondy, Luc, 39
Botschaft besorgter Bürger und Bürgerinnen, 35–36, 90–91
Bourriaud, Nicolas, 40
bow tie, 21, 53, 55, 121
Boyer, Elisabeth, 35, 93
Brambilla, 44–45
Brexit, 9, 184, 186, 189, 191n6, 192n14

Brus, Günter, 19, 26n31, 58n23. *See also* Wiener Gruppe
Bündnis Zukunft Österreich, 12, 14–15, 73, 78, 97, 131, 147
Burgenland, 90, 192n10
Burgtheater, 18, 22, 142, 155, 156, 167, 170–71, 188
Burschenschaften, 2, 186, 190
Busek, Erhard, 18, 146, 174n18
Bushell, Anthony, 6
BZÖ. *See* Bündnis Zukunft Österreich

C

Carinthia, region of Austria, 15, 19, 22, 42, 56, 63n104, 73, 97, 99n5, 116, 117, 121, 130, 131, 139n33, 148, 149, 162–63, 165, 171, 181n113
Ceiberweiber, 32
Charim, Isolde, 23
children
  bearing children, 46, 77, 121
  discrimination against or abuse of, 32, 77, 78
  perspectives of, 4, 7, 90, 91, 92, 93, 105n101, 112, 114, 115
Chmelar, Dieter, 132
Chumbawamba, 44, 49, 62n85
Cixous, Hélène, 98, 151
Communists, 31, 111, 157
Conny Chaos und die Retortenkinder, 3, 44, 46
Curtis, James, 159

D

dance, dancing, 1, 35, 48, 49, 51, 52, 53, 54, 63n99, 120, 126
Danzer, Georg. *See* Austria 3
demonstrations and demonstrators, 1, 2, 3, 5–8, 16, 18, 30–35, 41, 48, 51, 52, 55, 57n9, 58n20, 71, 78, 86, 88–90, 111, 119, 120, 124, 156, 170, 172n2, 185, 189, 190
dialect, 5, 38, 43, 47, 50, 55, 89, 117, 133, 146, 149
Die Ärzte, 44, 46
'Die drei Weisen'. *See* Ahtisaari, Martti, Jochen Frowein and Marcelino Oreja

'Die drei Weisinnen', 32, 66, 105n101
Die Grünen. *See* Green Party
Die Kaputtnicks, 44–46, 49
Donnerstagsdemonstrationen, 30, 33, 34, 41, 51, 52, 57n9, 58n19, 71, 124, 172n2, 185. *See also* demonstrations and demonstrators
Dor, Milo, 67, 99n5
Dorfer, Alfred, 32, 58n12, 172n1
Drahdiwaberl, 43, 46, 49, 117, 139n31
Duncombe, Stephen, 111
dystopia, 4, 5, 7, 67, 91, 130, 133, 134

E

Eberhartinger, Klaus. *See* Erste Allgemeine Verunsicherung
Einhorn, Ewa and Misha Stroj, 7, 113, 138n14
elderly, perspectives of the. *See* older age
elections
  local, 21–22, 116, 131–32
  national, 1995, 115–16, 138n23; 1999, 2, 8, 11–13, 23, 31, 45, 56, 71, 72, 98, 123, 156, 191; 2002, 12, 54, 70, 73, 119–20, 130; 2006, 2, 12, 15, 80, 82; 2008, 12, 15, 80, 97; 2013, 12; 2017, 12, 24n5, 79, 186–88
  presidential, 16, 17, 19, 21, 24n5, 71, 142, 158, 184–86, 189
Elias, Norbert, 159, 179n91
Embassy for Concerned Men and Women Citizens. *See* Botschaft besorgter Bürger und Bürgerinnen
Entwicklungsroman, 75, 97
Erste Allgemeine Verunsicherung, 20, 44, 47, 54
EU. *See* European Union
Euripides, 150, 175n43, 176n50
Europe, 33, 40, 52, 113, 121, 137n13, 169, 170
European Union, 7, 9, 13, 14, 43, 53, 73, 81, 114, 115, 121, 127, 129, 184–87, 190
  'Osterweiterung', European expansion to the east, 13
  sanctions against Austria, 14, 24n14, 30, 32, 33, 53, 126, 155, 158, 164, 169

F
Faccio, Luca, 57n9
fantasy, 7, 69, 92, 133, 134
fascism, fascist, 4, 18, 19, 21, 29, 31, 47, 49, 64n120, 72, 84, 121, 132, 151, 155, 159–63, 168, 175n33, 190. *See also* anti-fascism; Austrofascism
Faymann, Werner, 187
Femen, 55. *See also* Titten gegen Rassismus.
feminism, feminist, 5, 7, 67, 75–79, 81, 93, 97, 98, 106n118, 151, 188, 190
Fendrich, Rainer, 56. *See also* Austria 3
Ferrero-Waldner, Benita, 45, 49, 80, 126
Feschismus, 159, 161, 165
Fian, Antonio, 8, 46, 87, 95, 143–47, 159, 162, 170, 173n9, 174n21, 182n135
Fleischer, Ludwig Roman, 7, 92, 106n114
Fliedl, Konstanze, 145
Foltin, Robert, 18
Forrest, Tara, 40
Fortuyn, Pim, 168
FPÖ. *See* Freiheitliche Partei Österreichs
Frahm, Ole, 95
Franzobel, 3, 8, 66, 143, 156, 157, 159, 161–66, 170, 181n117
Fratelli Brothers, 119, 139n36
fraternities. *See Burschenschaften*
Freedom Party of Austria. *See* Freiheitliche Partei Österreichs
Freiheitliche Partei Österreichs, 1, 3, 6, 7, 8, 9, 11–14, 17, 21, 22–23, 24n6, 31, 32, 39, 42, 43, 45, 49–51, 53, 54–56, 63n104, 68, 70–73, 79, 84, 86–87, 89, 91, 93, 96, 99n5, 104n78, 110, 111, 113, 115–17, 119, 128, 130, 132, 134, 135, 144, 148, 149, 153–157, 163, 165, 167, 171–72, 184–87, 189, 190
  FPÖ-ÖVP coalition (*see* Österreichische Volkspartei, ÖVP-FPÖ coalition)
  politicians, 2, 8, 11, 14, 15, 24n5, 38, 42, 43, 46, 49, 50, 52, 70, 73, 89, 95, 105n100, 113, 129, 146–47, 152, 172, 185–86, 189
Ring Freiheitlicher Studenten, 89
Stop der Überfremdung (campaign slogan), 13, 45

Verband der Unabhängigen, VdU (predecessor party to FPÖ), 13, 166
French, Loreley, 77
Friedl, Harald, 124, 135
Frith, Simon, 50
Frowein, Jochen. *See* Ahtisaari, Martti, Jochen Frowein and Marcelino Oreja
FURT, 44, 47, 48

G
Gaugg, Reinhard, 51, 146
gay rights. *See* lesbian and gay rights
Gegenstimmen, 44, 47, 61nn72–73
Gehrer, Elisabeth, 46, 77
Gerlich, Peter, 164–65, 178n79
Gesswein, Anneliese, 32, 105n101. *See also* 'Die drei Weisinnen'
Glawogger, Michael, 3, 18, 120
Goisern, Hugo von, 43
Goldhill, Simon, 155
Gössler, Martin, 7, 112, 137n11
Graf, Martin, 89, 90, 105n100
Graff, Michael, 16
graffiti, 1, 7, 30, 31, 33, 36–38, 53, 95, 115, 118, 119, 138n21, 161
Grasser, Karl-Heinz, 45–46
Green Party (Austrian), 24n5, 31, 70, 71–72, 112, 132, 185
Griedl, Niki. *See* Horvath, Thomas and Niki Griedl
Gudenus, Johann, 147
Guenther, Christina, 124
Gusenbauer, Alfred, 125

H
Haas, Georg Friedrich, 44, 54
Habsburg Empire, 30, 36, 43, 121
Haderer, Gerhard, and Leo Lukas, 3, 7, 90, 93–97, 98, 108n140
Haider, Jörg
  anti-Haider, anti-Haiderization, 18, 19
  Ash Wednesday speech, 64n116, 145
  as FPÖ leader, 1, 3, 12, 13, 17, 45, 56, 72, 95–96, 121, 123, 131, 148, 149, 187
  as BZÖ leader, 14, 15, 39, 97

Haider, Jörg (*cont.*)
  controversial speeches by, and rhetoric of, 41, 42, 47, 51, 62n74, 64n116, 87, 116, 128–29, 138n27, 146, 153–55, 158, 174n28
  criticism of, by artists and intellectuals, 6, 15, 21, 64n120, 73
  death of, 15, 73, 78, 131–32, 140n60, 147–48
  as fictional character or as named in artistic work or product, 8, 46–49, 53, 55, 56, 66, 73, 78, 85, 87, 93–96, 99n5, 100n27, 105n102, 107n136, 114–115, 116, 125–26, 128–31, 133–34, 135, 143, 145–54, 160, 167, 172n1, 189
  legal action by Haider and FPÖ, 14, 49, 72–73, 99n5, 100n25, 104n85
  policies of, or associated with, 13, 22, 43, 50, 67, 77, 122, 167, 171
  personal life, 73, 78, 116, 131, 144, 148, 150, 158–59, 175n39
  sexuality, 15, 116, 131, 151–52
  as subject of graffiti, 7, 37, 53, 114–15
Haiderization. *See* Verhaiderung
Haneke, Michael, 109, 110, 122
Hartwig, Ina, 76
Haslinger, Josef, 21, 27n48, 73, 87
Häupl, Michael, 22, 27n50
Heldenplatz, 36–38, 41, 78, 129, 164
Heller, André, 72–73, 100n25
Hermes, Manfred, 122
Hight, Craig. *See* Roscoe, Jane and Craig Hight
Hitler, Adolf, 1, 7, 16, 17, 37, 48, 53, 91, 117, 121, 129, 157, 158, 162, 163, 168, 185, 191n3
Hochgatterer, Paulus, 7, 88, 104n88
Hofburg, Imperial Palace, 36–38, 112, 185
Hofecker, Franz-Otto. *See* Ratzenböck, Veronika
Hofer, Norbert, 24n5, 89, 185–86, 189, 192n18
'Holzpferd', 21, 27nn42–43, 27n45
homosexuality, 15, 116, 130–32, 151–52, 176n50
Höppner, Joachim, 128

Horak, Roman, 157
Horvath, Thomas and Niki Griedl, 7, 114
Howes, Geoff, 27n55
Hrdlicka, Alfred, 21
Huber, Bernadette, 7, 43, 116
Hummer, Waldemar, 14
Hurch, Hans, 116–17
Hypo Adria Bank. *See* bank scandals

I
Identitarian Movement, The, 188
immigration, 14, 139n41, 168, 189
  anti-immigrationist policies or views, 3, 13, 32, 33, 45, 79, 122, 132, 148, 149, 168, 185, 187, 188
  emigration, 18–19, 91
  migrants and migration in artistic work, 70, 75, 81, 91–92, 122, 132, 137n10, 147, 171
'island of the blessed', Austria as, 17, 30, 127

J
Jancak, Eva, 7, 88, 104n88
Jonke, Gerd, 171
Jelinek, Elfriede, 2, 3, 6, 8, 18–19, 21, 22, 23, 37, 46, 47, 51, 56, 60n46, 66, 87, 92, 99n4, 100n27, 110, 121, 131, 143, 145–56, 159–62, 166, 168, 170, 171, 172n2, 174n32, 175n33, 176n59, 177nn70–71, 188–89, 192n20
Jünger, Ernst, 71

K
Kabas, Hilmar, 50
Kampusch, Natascha, 81, 103n65
Karner, Christian, 43, 50
Kärnten. *See* Carinthia
Karottnig, Hoppelmann, 7, 91, 106n107
Kehlmann, Daniel, 67, 68
Kern, Christian, 187
Kern, Peter, 4, 5, 8, 91, 123, 125–26, 130–34, 136, 139n44
Khol, Andreas, 77, 145, 167, 182n137
Kickl, Herbert, 146, 173n1
Kirchschläger, Rudolf, 185
Klestil, Thomas, 52
Klima, Viktor, 22

Knittelfeldputsch, 70, 73
Kolig, Anton, 22
Kolig, Cornelia, 22
Konzett, Matthias, 160
Korosa, Traude, 66
Kosta, Barbara, 155
Kramar, Hubsi, 7, 38, 53, 93, 117, 138n29
Kräuter, Luca Killian, 7, 105n106
Kreidl, Maragaret, 47, 66
Kreisky, Bruno, 134, 147, 164
Krenn, Kurt, 95
Krüger, Michael, 152
Krylova, Katja, 20
Kuhn, Rick, 32–33
Kurz, Sebastian, 8, 12, 186–87

L
Lajarrige, Jacques, 146, 149
Larkey, Edward, 43
Le Pen, Jean-Marie, 4, 13
Le Pen, Marine, 190
lesbian and gay rights, 5, 32. *See also* homosexuality
  gay marriage, opposition to, 132, 185
Liberales Forum, 13, 95
'Lichtermeer', 13, 189
Liebeneiner, Wolfgang, 125–26, 133
literary resistance readings. *See Widerstandslesungen*
Löffler, Sigrid, 33
Lorenz, Dagmar, 124–25
Lukas, Leo. *See* Gerhard Haderer and Leo Lukas
Lungstraß, Anja. *See* Ratzenböck, Veronika

M
Macron, Emmanuel, 190
Marchart, Oliver, 33, 44, 45
marches. *See Donnerstagsdemonstrationen*; walking as protest
Martin, Wolf, 46–47, 91, 125
Maschek, 7, 117–18, 139n32
Mascherl. *See* bow tie
Matuschka-Eisenstein, Uwe, 169, 183n139
Maurer, Thomas and Florian Scheuba, 90, 172n1
Mayr, Elke, 124

Menasse, Robert, 2, 8, 23, 25n23, 135–36, 143–44, 156, 162, 166–70, 182n135
Messmer, Susanne, 67
migration. *See* immigration
Misik, Robert, 23
Molden, Ernst, 4, 7, 67–71, 72, 97, 99n7, 99n14, 100n17, 108n140
Mölzer, Andreas, 14, 22, 147, 165
Monochrom (activist group), 55, 64n118
Morak, Franz, 167, 183n139
Moscow Treaty or Declaration, 17, 25n25, 126, 158
Müller, Gini, 12, 63n99, 137n11, 171
Müllner, Romana, 32. *See also* 'Die drei Weisinnen'
Murphy, Anthony, 24n6
Murray, Gilbert, 151
music, 1, 5, 6, 19, 20, 22, 34, 36, 40, 42–52, 54–55, 71, 87, 114, 115, 117, 120, 125–26, 146, 164–65, 178n79
Mutombo, Kambowa, 71

N
National Socialist. *See* Nazism, Nazi era
Nazism, Nazi era, 1, 2, 3, 15, 16, 17, 18, 19, 21, 22, 47, 51, 53, 69, 83, 99n5, 104n85, 117, 121, 122, 124, 128, 129, 136, 142, 146, 148, 150, 156, 158, 185, 188, 189
  anti-Nazi resistance, 41, 57n9, 118, 127
  propaganda, 13, 21, 130, 149, 174n25
  SA (Sturmabteilung/Brownshirts), 19, 21
  Waffen SS, 16, 113, 165
  Wiederbetätigung (act of revival), 117
Novotny, Franz, 7, 117, 125

O
Obermayer, Paul and Richard Barrett. *See* FURT
older age, perspectives of, 32, 82, 88, 90, 105n101, 114, 115, 123, 130, 190
Omas gegen Rechts, 190
Omasta, Michael, 109–10, 122
Omofuma, Marcus, 70, 91–92
Opfermythos. *See* victimization myth
Oreja, Marcel. *See* Ahtisaari, Martti, Jochen Frowein and Marcelino Oreja

Österreich zuerst (referendum and campaign), 13, 53, 184
Österreichische Volkspartei, 1, 11, 12, 18, 39, 52, 70, 72, 79, 82–83, 86, 103n67, 115, 116, 120, 148, 185, 186, 187
  ÖVP-FPO coalition, 1, 8, 20, 23, 30, 33, 42, 43, 45, 73, 79, 130, 132, 133, 144, 155, 156, 158, 167, 170, 172, 173n16, 186, 188, 189, 192n10
  politicians, 16, 18, 45, 46, 49, 75, 77, 79, 95, 96, 121, 145, 148, 157, 167, 186
  ÖVP voters, 31
Oswald, John, 47–48
Oswald, Peter, 164
Ottomeyer, Klaus, 139n34, 148, 179n90
ÖVP. *See* Österreichische Volkspartei

P
Pallas Athene, statue of, 38, 92–93
Partik-Pablé, Helene, 38
Pasterk, Ursula, 22, 27n50
Pelinka, Anton, 13, 157
Performing Resistance (activist group), 38, 44, 51, 52, 93
Petzner, Stefan, 15, 78, 131
Peymann, Claus, 18, 22, 142, 167
Pfeiffer, Karl, 125
Pick, Hella, 16, 17
placards. *See* banners and placards
Plattform Demokratische Offensive, 25
Pluhar, Erika, 4, 7, 71–74, 87, 97
Poet, Paul, 39, 42, 59n40
Ponger, Lisl, 125
Price, Richard, 36
projectionism, 5, 8, 36–38, 40, 51–52, 119–20, 136
Proporz, 17

R
Rabinovici, Doron, 15, 23, 25n23, 31
racism, racist attitudes, 3, 7, 14, 15, 21, 33, 35, 45, 55, 60n46, 72, 94, 95, 121, 148, 165, 188, 190
Radio Orange, 44, 49
Rancière, Jacques, 41

Ratzenböck, Veronika, Franz-Otto Hofecker and Anja Lungstraß, 144
Raunig, Gerald, 110, 111, 137n6
Reinhart, Martin, 114–15, 138n18
Republikanischer Club – Neues Österreich, 18, 21, 23, 29
Riess-Passer, Susanne, 11, 73, 148, 151, 157
  as fictional character, 91, 95, 96, 130–34, 151–52
Rilke, Rainer Maria, 147, 174n22
Ringstraße, 36, 38
Robotka, Walter, 70
Roder, Gerhard, 77
Roma, minority community, 21, 32, 104n78, 146, 161. *See also* Sinti, minority community
Rosa Antifa Wien, also known as 'raw', 7, 32, 112
Roscoe, Jane and Craig Hight, 128
Rosellini, Jay, 21, 27n47, 64n120
Roth, Gerhard, 67, 99n5
Rühm, Gerhard, 19, 26n31. *See also* Wiener Gruppe
Rußegger, Arno, 87

S
sanctions. *See* European Union, sanctions against Austria
Schacherreiter, Christian, 84
Scharang, Michael, 18
Scheuba, Florian. *See* Maurer, Thomas and Florian Scheuba
Schindel, Robert, 17, 20, 23, 25n23, 26n37, 130, 188
Schlaffer, Hannelore, 66
Schlingensief, Christoph, 3, 6, 31, 33, 34, 36, 37, 39–42, 45, 59nn40–41, 60n46
Schlipphacke, Heidi, 168
Schmid, Michael, 113
Schmidt, Heide, 13, 95
Schnittpunkt, film co-operative, 7, 112, 137n10
Scholten, Rudolf, 22, 27n50
Schrage, Dieter, 88–89, 105n101
Schuh, Franz, 125, 153

Schüssel, Wolfgang, 7, 8, 11, 12, 15, 18, 21, 24n3, 32, 45–46, 54, 121, 148, 151, 157
   as fictional character or as named in artistic work or product, 47, 53, 54, 83, 95–96, 105n102, 107n133, 112–13, 119, 121, 125, 130, 134, 147, 167
Schwärzler, Dietmar, 134
Scrotum gegen Votum (protest group), 55, 64n118
Second Republic, 6, 16, 17, 29, 157, 185
Seidl, Ulrich, 3, 8, 110, 120–22, 140n50
Sinowatz, Fred, 21
Sinti, minority community, 21, 32, 146. See also Roma, minority community
Skrinar, Hannah, 48
Solnit, Rebecca, 35
SOS Mitmensch, 13, 23, 189
'Spitzelaffäre', 87, 93
Social Democratic Party of Austria. See Sozialdemokratische Partei Österreichs
Sozialdemokratische Partei Österreichs, 1, 11, 12, 22, 27n50, 31, 71–73, 75, 82, 85, 86, 115, 125, 130, 134, 148, 158, 166, 185, 187, 192n10
SPÖ. See Sozialdemokratische Partei Österreichs
sport, 8, 143–44, 151–52, 155–68, 172, 178n79, 181n116
   skiers, Hinterseer, Hansi, 164; Klammer, Franz, 157; Maier, Hermann, 157; Maier, Ulli, 161; Ortlieb, Patrick, 151; Sailer, Toni, 157; Schranz, Karl, 126, 158, 164, 181n122
Staberl (pseudonym). See Martin, Wolf
Starsky, 38, 59n35, 119
Starsky, Julia. See Starsky
Stastna, Kazi, 93
State Treaty, 125, 157, 170
States, Bert, 95
Staudacher, Gerd, 171
Steger, Norbert, 12, 17
Steiner, Ulrike, 129
Sternenhimml, Julius, 119
Stiedl, Peter, 34

Strache, H.C. (Heinz-Christian), 8, 14, 42, 60n54, 79, 132, 172, 185–87, 189
Strasser, Ernst, 70
Strauss, Johann, II, 36, 48
Streeruwitz, Marlene, 2, 3, 5, 7, 8, 35, 37, 66, 74–84, 97, 102n59, 108n140, 130, 143, 156, 158, 162, 164–66, 170, 188, 192n13
Stroj, Misha. See Einhorn, Ewa and Misha Stroj
Strutz, Martin, 130
Studio West, 7, 118
Sturminger, Michael, 3, 8, 120, 122
Sully, Melanie, 150

T

Tagg, Philip, 43
Tauer, Brigitte, 7, 91, 106n113
Third Reich, The, 16, 37, 47, 118, 129, 149, 150, 153, 158, 174n32
'Third Republic', 167
'Three Wise Men, The'. See Ahtisaari, Martti, Jochen Frowein and Marcelino Oreja
'Three Wise Women, The'. See 'Die drei Weisinnen'
Thurnher, Armin, 23, 158–59, 161, 162
Thursday demonstrations. See Donnerstagsdemonstrationen
Thuswaldner, Werner, 67, 99n5
Titten gegen Rassismus (action by Monochrom), 55
tourism, and theme of tourism, 7, 35, 36, 40, 42, 92, 93, 126, 144, 164
Treudl, Sylvia, 7, 92, 106n118
Trojan horse. See 'Holzpferd'
Trudgill, Peter, 49
Trump, Donald, 9, 184, 189
Turino, Thomas, 48, 51, 54
turn, political turn to the right 1999/2000. See Wende
Turrini, Peter, 130, 144, 145, 171

U

United Aliens, protest artists, 7, 91, 92
United Nations, 16, 19, 125

V

Van der Bellen, Alexander, 8, 24n5, 185, 186, 191n6
Vasik, Monika, 7, 92–93, 106n119
Verband der Unabhängigen, VdU. *See* Freiheitliche Partei Österreichs
Verhaiderung, 33, 73, 96
victimization myth or victimization thesis, 3, 16–17, 25n25, 126, 128, 129, 158, 163, 164
Volkstänzer, Volkstanz, 52, 63n99. *See also* dance, dancing
Volxtheater, theatre group, 7, 79, 112, 171
Vranitzky, Franz, 16, 21

W

Wague, Cheibane, 71
Waldheim, Kurt, 6, 17, 18–21, 142, 158
    as fictional character or as named in artistic work or product, 16, 19, 20, 21, 25n23, 26n39, 126, 149, 188, 189
    Waldheim affair, or Waldheim scandal, 3, 14–18, 29, 126, 188
Waldmüller, Ferdinand Georg, 36, 71
walking as protest, 6, 31–35, 39, 47, 52, 56, 58n23, 71, 189. *See also Donnerstagsdemonstrationen*
'Wiener Wandertage', 34–36, 90, 124
Weber, Stefan, 46, 50, 139n31
Wegenstein, Bernadette, 115, 138n19
Weihs, Richard, 7, 91, 106n111
Wende (political turn to the right of 1999–2000), 1, 2, 6, 11–15, 19, 20, 23, 23n1, 31, 39, 59n26, 71, 84, 97, 105n106, 122, 135, 136, 143, 155
'Wendekanzler', 12, 24n3
Werner, Emmy, 171
Wessely, Paula, 149, 174n32
Westenthaler, Peter, 14–15, 63n116, 73, 87, 134
Widerstandslesungen, 31, 35, 65, 66, 89, 92, 98
Wieland, Rayk, 144
Wiener Gruppe, or Wiener Aktionisten, 26n31, 29, 58n23
Wiener Wandertage. *See* walking as protest
Wiener, Oswald, 19, 26n31. *See also* Wiener Gruppe
Windholz, Ernest, 13
Wippersberg, Walter, 2, 3, 7, 46, 78, 84–88, 97, 103n73, 103n75, 123, 125–29, 136, 140n53
Wodak, Ruth, 13, 139n41, 156
wooden horse. *See* 'Holzpferd'

X

xenophobia, 3, 4, 13, 14, 17, 19, 33, 45, 92, 94, 97, 121, 122, 124, 128, 132, 156, 161. *See also* racism

Z

Zdarsky, Julia. *See* Starsky
Zens, Franz, 87, 103n75, 104n78

www.ingramcontent.com/pod-product-compliance
Lightning Source LLC
Chambersburg PA
CBHW072050110526
44590CB00018B/3109